Adventures in Paradox

PENN STATE STUDIES
in ROMANCE LITERATURES

Editors *Frederick A. de Armas* *Norris Lacy* *Allan Stoekl*

Adventures in Paradox

Don Quixote and the Western Tradition

CHARLES D. PRESBERG

The Pennsylvania State University Press
University Park, Pennsylvania

Publication of this book has been aided by a grant from the Program for Cultural Cooperation between Spain's Ministry of Education and Culture and United States Universities.

Library of Congress Cataloging-in-Publication Data

Presberg, Charles D.
    Adventures in paradox : Don Quixote and the western tradition / Charles D. Presberg.

        p.   cm.—(Penn State studies in Romance literatures)
    Includes bibliographical references and index.
    ISBN 0-271-02039-3 (alk. paper) ISBN 0-271-02364-3 (pbk)
    1. Cervantes Saavedra, Miguel de, 1547–1616. Don Quixote. 2. Paradox in literature.
I. Title. II. Series.

    PQ6353 .P72 2001
    863'.3—dc21
                                                                99-055297

For
Michael, Stephen, and Philip

CONTENTS

Acknowledgments ix

Introduction: Paradoxical Problems 1

PART I
Western Paradox and the Spanish Golden Age

1 Paradoxical Discourse from Antiquity to the Renaissance:
Plato, Nicolaus Cusanus, and Erasmus 11
2 Paradoxy and the Spanish Renaissance: Fernando de Rojas,
Antonio de Guevara, and Pero Mexía 37

PART II
Inventing a Tale, Inventing a Self

3 "This Is Not a Prologue": Paradoxy and the Prologue to
Don Quixote, Part I 75
4 Paradoxes of Imitation: The Quest for Origins and Originality 163
5 "I Know Who I Am": Don Quixote de la Mancha, Don Diego
de Miranda, and the Paradox of Self-Knowledge 193

Concluding Remarks 231
Works Cited 237
Index 247

ACKNOWLEDGMENTS

Mary Gaylord and James Iffland guided me in turning an earlier version of this project into a doctoral dissertation presented at Harvard University, heroically enduring drafts that resembled what Henry James would call "a loose and baggy monster." I am deeply grateful to both of them, not only for helping me tighten my argument and diction but also for their compelling blend of humanity and professionalism, which I have retained as a model for imitation in my own professional endeavors.

I also owe an enormous debt of gratitude to my friend and colleague Henry Sullivan, who read the entire manuscript, commenting insightfully on almost every page. With thankful enthusiasm, I have incorporated all his suggestions into my text.

I thank my colleagues Lucille Kerr, María Cristina Quintero, and Ramón Araluce for commenting on various chapters of the manuscript. I thank Carroll Johnson, Michael McGaha, Harry Sieber, and Luis Murillo for questions, conversations, and correspondence that have helped refine important parts of my critical argument. I express my thanks to Raúl Galoppe for his diligent assistance in proofreading, research, and editing; to Melinda Howard for her excellent research and proofreading, as well as for preparing a first draft of the index.

At Penn State University Press, I wish to thank Frederick de Armas, series editor, for his unflagging support; Romaine Perrin, for her expert copyediting; Peter Potter, Shannon Pennefeather, Cherene Holland, and Patty Mitchell, for their skill and patience in bringing this book to completion.

A section of Chapter 3 appeared in *MLN* (formerly *Modern Language Notes*) 110 (1995): 215–39; and an earlier version of Chapter 5 appeared in *Cervantes* 14 (1994): 41–69. I am thankful to the editors of both journals for permission to reproduce that material here. My thanks go, as well, to The Research Board at the University of Missouri for a summer research grant that permitted me to finish this project in a timely fashion; and to the Program for Cultural Cooperation for a generous grant.

I thank my ex-wife Elizabeth for her support at crucial stages of this book's preparation. And last, I thank my three children, Michael, Stephen, and Philip, for allowing me to rank happily among those persons who, in blessings and love, owe more than they can repay.

Introduction

Paradoxical Problems

More than twenty years ago, Francisco Márquez Villanueva wrote: "The study of *Don Quixote* as a masterwork in the genre of paradox has yet to be carried out and remains one of the sizeable gaps in Cervantes scholarship" (El estudio del *Quijote* en cuanto obra maestra del género paradójico no se ha realizado aún y constituye uno de los grandes huecos en la bibliografía cervantina) (Márquez Villanueva 1975, 214).[1] Since then, scholars have generally recognized the pervasiveness of paradox in *Don Quixote*, although no one has yet undertaken a systematic investigation of this trope in Cervantes' masterpiece.[2] My purpose in this study is to situate Cervantes' *Don Quixote* within the tradition of paradoxical discourse, or paradoxy, in the West. Hence, this book is a response, in part, to

1. Translations from Spanish to English are mine unless otherwise stated.
2. The subject of Cervantes' use of paradox is explicit in Russell 1969 and latent in an important study of semantic ambiguity and authorial ambivalence in *Don Quixote* by Durán (1960), both of which

the challenge set forth by Márquez Villanueva, though I recognize that the specific gap to which he refers will remain unfilled and, perhaps, unfillable.

In the first place, though I believe that Márquez Villanueva is right in pointing to *Don Quixote* as a work of literary paradoxy, my examination of that trope leads me to doubt whether one can properly speak of "paradox" as a "genre" (género paradójico) and, hence, to doubt whether Cervantes' fiction exemplifies such a genre.[3] The tradition of paradoxical writing encompasses works in disciplines as diverse as philosophy, rhetoric, and literature. And, among the literary works alone, a rhetoric of paradoxy informs a host of poems, dramas, prose narratives, anatomies, and miscellanies, all varying considerably in the selection—as well as the comic or serious treatment—of their subject matter. Paradoxy, in short, represents a particular if broad species of artful discourse. It is a trope of thought, a structuring principle, or a rhetorical strategy that moves freely and playfully across the boundaries that convention assigns to genres, modes, and intellectual disciplines.

In the second place, I am aware that my attempt to undertake a systematic investigation of a slippery trope in a slippery text must begin with what Rosalie Colie calls a "defense of the indefensible"; that is, a defense of this "attempt to treat systematically a subject [both the trope and the text] designed to deny and destroy systems" (Colie 1966, vii). Paradoxically enough, the defense and indefensibility coincide in that paradoxy both "denies" and "destroys" systems through a rhetorical gesture of self-reference. In other words, paradoxical discourse *systematically* uses the categories of language and logic to question and mock the very categories that undergird language and logic as discursive systems. As a consequence, paradoxist and public alike must reassess their formerly untested assumptions about logic and language, even as they realize that the measure of a writer or rhetor's *success* in using the system against itself is also a measure of his or her *failure* to undermine that system. In equal measure, what Colie would call destruction thus becomes a form of validation, denial a form of affirmation. In the present analysis of Cervantine paradoxy, it is therefore necessary to acknowledge, at once, the utility and futility of systematic treatment. The categorical limits set forth in these pages stand as only one possible means of arranging a

---

studies predate Márquez Villanueva's observation quoted above. Besides the study by Márquez Villanueva from which that quotation is taken (1975, 147–27), other discussions of paradox in *Don Quixote* include those by Eisenberg (1987, 188–93), Jones (1986), Martín (1991, 79–80) and Parr (1988, 103–19). Two studies by Forcione (1982, 1984) explore aspects of Cervantes' paradoxical discourse chiefly in relation to that author's *Exemplary Novellas* (*Novelas ejemplares*).

3. It seems that the "genre" that Márquez has in mind is the "paradoxical encomium," also called the "mock encomium," a burlesque species of declamation that I discuss in Chapter 1 of the present study.

subject that both implies the necessity and questions the fixity of all orderly arrangements in discourse.

In more specific terms, in this study I argue that *Don Quixote* exemplifies a species of literary discourse that is about, for, and against literary discourse, including its own. Cervantes' fiction represents a self-conscious text that is made from other texts, and a text that is about the reading and writing of texts. Indeed, one of the fiction's chief traits is that it dramatizes a systematic yet open method of paradoxy that simultaneously affirms, denies, and enlarges the categories by which we judge and speak about the mysteries of both art and nature. Further, in its development of both character and action, the fiction enlists a specifically *narrative* method that relates nothing less than the paradoxicality of both literature and life, and that prevents its readers from equating either "knowledge" or "truth" about those matters with a rationalist quest for closure or formulaic certainty.

What is more, as playfully dramatized in Cervantes' fictional work, the myriad manifestations of paradox emerge as variations on the problem of infinity—infinite regress, infinite series, the vicious circle, eternity—a problem that is insoluble solely within logical or linguistic *terms* (which invariably strive to *terminate* further discussion) and approachable only by way of negation. After the manner of Cervantes' text, I adopt in this study a method that relies heavily on what logicians call negative assertions, which are neither identical nor simply reducible to a denial of positive statements.[4] For logical and semantic contradiction need not be confined to a dogmatically skeptical *terminus* of "undecidability" and "canceling out."

A further consequence of their infinite and undefinable quality is that paradoxes are also "generative" (Colie 1966, 3–40). One paradoxical utterance about either literature or life necessarily gives rise to another, often its opposite, ad infinitum, thus militating against both the narrative and academic requirements of fitting one's discourse within a discernible beginning (thesis), middle (discussion) and end (conclusion). An examination of *Don Quixote* as a masterwork of paradoxy thus forces one to acknowledge the dual impossibility of identifying "all" the paradoxes that the text presumably "contains" or the infinite number of ways in which that text may be deemed paradoxical.

Moreover, in keeping with the tradition of paradoxical discourse—which resists the tidiness of logical, linguistic, or literary form—Cervantes' long tale about its mad protagonist and *about itself as tale* both begins and ends with startling abruptness. Rather than concluding, it simply comes to a halt. Put another way, the story (called a history) relates, at the start of its first chapter, how the

4. Barwise and Etchemendy (1987, 177) discuss the distinction, in both logic and semantics, between negations and negative assertions.

personality known as Don Quixote "comes to life" as the product of a nameless *hidalgo's* deranged imagination. In this "history," more than 120 chapters are then devoted to the "adventures" that the "knight" Don Quixote undertakes until, at end of the history, "amid the sadness and tears of the persons gathered there, [Don Quixote] gave up the ghost, by which I mean that he died (entre compasiones y lágrimas de los que allí se hallaron, dio su espíritu, quiero decir que se murió) (*DQ* II: 74, 591).[5] Likewise, what in this study takes the form of beginning, middle, and end amounts to little more than a series of somewhat arbitrary choices about where to start; what to include, expand upon, or hold in abeyance; and where, finally, to stop.

The title of the present study, *Adventures in Paradox: "Don Quixote" and the Western Tradition,* alludes to a twofold aim. First, as stated in the preceding paragraphs, I hope to open up further rather than fill a gap in the bibliography on *Don Quixote* and, more generally, on the tradition of paradoxy in the West. Next, the element of "adventures" in the title, besides suggesting the ideas of quest, surprise, and escape from the humdrum for all adventurers, signals my interest in examining paradoxical novelties that accrue for both characters and readers from the fictional and extrafictional aspects of Cervantes' narrative. I shall be concerned to examine how, at their respective levels of "being," characters and readers alike engage in a series of parallel adventures, as they negotiate the paradoxes within Cervantes' fictional world.

Designating the adventures of the characters and the reader as parallel implies that they are dissimilar and cannot simply be shared. To be sure, Cervantes' characters occupy their own world, or heterocosm. What for them, in their heterocosm, appears as history remains fiction for the reader of Cervantes' text. These commonplace observations become necessary, first, because I respectfully disagree with Américo Castro's sighting of "Pirandellism" within the Cervantine text (Castro 1967, 477–85). The characters in *Don Quixote* are never in search of an author and remain blithely unaware of either their imaginary status or a world outside their heterocosm. Second, I believe that Cervantes' careful preservation of the cleavage separating the fictional and extrafictional worlds increases the self-conscious quality of his work, expands the scope of his textual paradoxes, and enhances his examination of the literature/life and history/poetry boundaries.

That the narrative draws an analogy between the characters' adventures and those of the reader becomes clear from the prominence that readers, written

---

5. All references to Cervantes' *Don Quixote* are to the edition by Luis Murillo, by abbreviated title, part, chapter, and page number in instances of quotation. Hence, the above citation (*DQ* II: 74, 591) indicates *Don Quixote*, Part II, chapter 74, page 591.

texts, and stories enjoy in the narrative. For example, in Part I, if the madness of our anonymous hidalgo and his emergence as the protagonist Don Quixote are not simply the product of his reading the romances of chivalry, the identity of that protagonist and the shape of his pseudochivalric adventures remain defined by the stories he reads and by his interpretation of those stories as histories. The prominence of readers, texts, and stories is probably nowhere more evident within the heterocosm of Part I than at Juan Palomeque's inn (*DQ* I: 32–47), where characters exchange their life tales, listen to the priest's reading from a discovered manuscript titled "The Tale of Impertinent Curiosity" (*Novela del curioso impertinente*), and voice their opinions about the merits and demerits, truth and untruth, of chivalric romance. Further, the final version of the history concerning the exploits of Don Quixote is put forth, within the fiction we have before us, as the work of a narrator-editor, necessarily a *reader*, who is working primarily from the *manuscript* attributed to Cide Hamete.

In Part II of the fiction, the majority of the characters have either read or are informed about the contents of Cide Hamete's history, the fictional analogue of Miguel de Cervantes' own *Don Quixote*, Part I. What is important to stress here is that, in light of those allusions within the text, we can hardly avoid perceiving fictional analogues of ourselves in such readers and listeners of fictional and non-fictional tales, including a tale (for them a history, for us a fiction) about Don Quixote. And it seems that we can hardly avoid perceiving such parallels and analogies between the fictional and extrafictional planes of the work as the product of artistic design.

However, it is pertinent to add that parallels between the adventures of Cervantes' characters and those of his readers possess an ethical as well as aesthetic dimension. As a prime example of literary paradoxy, Don Quixote is a seriocomic book. Within Cervantes' heterocosm, all his characters' "lives" include interpretations regarding the deeds of other characters, material items (e.g., windmills, fulling mills, basins, "helmets," or "basin-helmets"), stories, manuscripts, and at least one "historical" narrative. About these matters, Cervantes' characters emit a host of judgments—which vary in their degree of wisdom and folly—and later act upon those judgments. Their spoken judgments and actions, including their actions as interpreters, are integral to their characterization, reflecting upon them for good or ill—usually ill. In their encounter with Cervantes' fictional text, readers may come to realize that their own conduct as interpreters of the tale and its protagonist likewise characterizes them, and that their reading and judging what occurs within the heterocosm amounts to their observing an analogue of their own extrafictional drama as readers and judges. The similarities between characters and readers—between the heterocosm and the historical world—point to the creating intelligence of a self-conscious author who makes each reader both accomplice and nemesis in a complex, metaliterary game. The boundary between cosmos and heterocosm, or literature and life, is alternately confirmed and undone, thanks in no small measure to the preservation of a fictional frame—a frame that allows the text to function as a mirror of its own readings.

In order to examine the analogous adventures in paradox that accrue for both readers and characters throughout *Don Quixote*, I have divided my study into two parts, which encompass five chapters. Part I, "Western Paradox and the Spanish Golden Age," encompasses Chapters 1 and 2. In Chapter 1, I explore the development of paradoxy in the West from Classical Antiquity to the Renaissance, paying special attention to three pivotal texts: Plato's *Parmenides*, Nicolaus Cusanus's *Of Learned Ignorance* and Erasmus's *The Praise of Folly*. After discussing how the term *paradox* was understood in Cervantes' time and how it is understood in our own, I focus in Chapter 2 on the slow rise of paradoxy in Spain's Renaissance, as exemplified, particularly, in popular works by Fernando de Rojas, Antonio de Guevara and Pero Mexía. For it was not until the beginning of the Baroque period that Spain underwent what Colie dubs an "epidemic" of paradoxy, already pandemic in the rest of Europe (Colie 1966). Poised between the Spanish Renaissance and the Baroque, Cervantes' thoroughgoing paradoxy in *Don Quixote* marks the infectious beginning of a literary epidemic that will persist until the advent of the eighteenth century.

Now it may seem, at first blush, that the historical reconstruction of Western paradoxical discourse in those first two chapters constitutes an overlong preamble to an exploration of Cervantes' rhetorical strategy in *Don Quixote*. In response, let me first point out that, as indicated in my title, the topic of this book-length study is not simply the rhetoric of Cervantes' masterwork, but the place of that rhetoric and that work within the formerly unreconstructed tradition of paradoxy in the West. Second, as I found in the process of composing this text, to have started my discussion with the practice of paradoxy in Cervantes' own age would have required me to keep explaining this rhetorical-poetic tradition in a piecemeal, desultory fashion. This would have blurred the outline of what is already a complex argument about a complex subject. Indeed, what I hope to contribute to the field of literary studies in general and Cervantes studies in particular is an increased understanding of how the Spanish Renaissance and, with Cervantes intervening, the Spanish Baroque remain indebted to and riddled with devices of paradoxical discourse inherited from a centuries-long praxis. More practically, for readers interested specifically in Don Quixote, the historical reconstruction constituting this book's Part I is an effort to provide a coherent, if selective, view of what Cervantes had at his literary disposition in crafting his great work.

In Part II of this study, "Inventing a Tale, Inventing a Self," I focus exclusively on *Don Quixote*, but without attempting a comprehensive reading of Cervantes' text. Adopting a method of *non multa sed multum*, I undertake a detailed analysis of selected episodes in that fictional work that illustrate a Cervantine vision of both artistic creation and the human subject. To this end, in Chapter 3 I examine a cluster of metaliterary issues against the backdrop of the Prologue to *Don Quixote*, Part I (1605). Those issues, which Cervantes both dramatizes and thematizes throughout his work, concern the complex and fluid relations between art and nature, literature and life, poetry and history, as well as author, reader and text. I argue in this chapter that, as both preface and epilogue to the subsequent narrative, the Prologue of 1605 represents a fictional work in nonfictional guise. That Prologue is also shown to form an integral part of the fiction *Don Quixote*.

Let me add at once, however, that in Chapter 3 I make no attempt either to extricate a Cervantine *theory* of fiction from the text or to contrast Cervantes' theoretical stance with the classical opinions that held sway among many of his contemporaries both in Spain and abroad. At best, such an attempt would merely duplicate the important work of E. C. Riley (1962) and Alban K. Forcione (1970).[6] Rather, my interest lies in discussing how the Prologue of 1605 broaches important metaliterary questions and how those questions are dramatized and played out more fully, as *questions*, and as instances of literary paradoxy, in other parts of the text.

Cervantes' dramatization of the overlap and interference between art and life yields what I discuss, in Chapter 4, as "Paradoxes of Imitation." In the Renaissance and Baroque alike, *art* was understood in both the Aristotelian sense as an "imitation of nature" and in a Ciceronian sense as an "imitation of models." Though seemingly at odds, both acceptations of the term were seen as complementary and inseparable. Moreover, it was only in a debased sense that artistic imitation (*imitatio*) was undertaken as, say, copying or aping. In its ideal form, *imitatio* was understood to involve *inventio*, from *invenire*, which means both "to invent" and "to discover." Artistic imitation was understood to be, at the same time, transformative and perfective. Hence, in Chapter 4, I shall examine three types of paradox that arise from how Cervantes dramatizes Renaissance *imitatio* in a seriocomic fashion: (1) the need somehow to combine what today we would call "originality" with a dependence on "the original"; (2) how each inventive imi-

6. Also in reference to Cervantes' aesthetics of fiction, see Martínez Bonati 1992; Avalle-Arce and Riley 1973, 293–322; and two other studies by Riley (1981, 69–85; 1986, 62–72).

tation strives somehow to be *truer* to "nature," "life," and the "source" than its predecessors, which may in turn be its "models"; (3) how art involves the power to embed imitations within imitations—stories within stories, plays within plays, pictures within pictures—whereby each successive act of embedding seems to create a level of imitation that is somehow less real or more imaginary.

Yet it is important to stress that, in *Don Quixote*, Cervantes' playful imitations are also in earnest. Indeed, Cervantes elaborates on a traditional link between artistic *imitation* and moral *exemplarity* in order to dramatize *imitatio* as both an ethical and aesthetic issue. In Chapter 5 I discuss paradoxes of self-knowledge and self-creation and the degree to which Cervantes shows that an individual life both is and is not a work of fiction, or of linguistic and literary art. There, in particular, we shall analyze the link that Cervantes establishes between self-awareness and "self-fashioning" in the episodes he devotes to Don Quixote's encounter with Don Diego de Miranda: a secondary character whose physical appearance, age, regional origin, and social status make him at once "mirror," "model," and "copy" of the protagonist.[7] In that encounter, we find that "knowledge" of "self" is dynamic rather than static. It arises as a quasi-poetic undertaking and a paradoxical *process* of *inventio* and *imitatio*: a creative dialogue between "self" and "other."

In the same vein, in the Concluding Remarks I discuss Cervantes' seriocomic system of paradoxy as a "committed rhetoric," with ethical implications. In affirming the necessity while questioning the fixity of our arrangements of thought and language, Cervantes' paradoxy allows us to forestall what we may dub a "hardening of the categories" in both our personal and collective lives. The paradoxy that informs *Don Quixote* at once parodies, celebrates, and invites reflection on the wisdom and folly of the fictions we live by. At the level of content and form alike, in *Don Quixote* Cervantes enlists human discourse in order to dramatize its agency in the continuing creation, or re-creation, of such artistic endeavors as history, knowledge, and the self.

---

7. Stephen Greenblatt (1980) provides a searching study of self-fashioning in the English Renaissance. Like Michel Foucault before him, Greenblatt derives this term from Montaigne.

PART 1

WESTERN PARADOX AND THE SPANISH GOLDEN AGE

Paradoxical Discourse from Antiquity
to the Renaissance

Plato, Nicolaus Cusanus, and Erasmus

In her groundbreaking study *Paradoxia Epidemica* (1966), Rosalie Colie provides a topical and historical overview of literary paradox from Classical Antiquity to the Renaissance. Neither her overview nor her studies of such Renaissance practitioners of literary paradox as Rabelais, Petrarch, Sidney, Donne, Shakespeare, and Burton need to be summarized or repeated here. Since the concern of this study is largely topical—paradox in *Don Quixote* and its Spanish antecedents—I shall invoke Colie only for background material. Moreover, the historical side of my discussion will draw from the rich tradition of paradoxy to spotlight three landmark texts: Plato's *Parmenides*, Nicolaus Cusanus's *Of Learned Ignorance*, and Erasmus's *Praise of Folly*. All three represent major advances in that tradition and illuminate important features of paradoxy in *Don Quixote*.[1]

1. It is not a question here of citing "sources" or influence in Cervantes' work. Rather, I claim only that these and other works form an integral part of a philosophical, rhetorical, and literary patrimony.

From Plato to Saint Francis of Assisi:
Paradoxy in Antiquity and the Middle Ages

As Colie points out, Plato's *Parmenides* represents one of the chief sources of paradox literature, and rhetorical paradoxy, in the West (1966, 7–8).[2] In a manner that typifies exchanges in paradoxical discourse, our dialogue elicits a response of wonder, bewilderment, and perplexity in the reader. This is so not only because of the dialogue's rhetorical mastery, its seemingly interminable litany of paradoxical utterances, and its inconclusive ending, but also because a young Socrates suffers defeat at the hands of the sage Parmenides in their dialectical contest. Besides dealing with the eminently philosophical questions of unity and diversity, likeness and unlikeness, and being and nonbeing, the dialogue provides a model of Plato's dialectical art, including a practical model for the training of novices. As Parmenides says to Socrates: "There is an art which is called by the vulgar 'idle talking,' and which is often imagined to be useless; in that art you must train yourself, now that you are young, or truth will elude your grasp" (Plato 1973, 379).

Parmenides goes on to demonstrate that in negative terms, this art consists of avoiding the "youthful" impulse to dogmatism. In positive terms, it consists of simultaneously arguing opposite sides of a question. Truth is thus shown to reside not so much between as beyond extremes, each of which is both enlightening and deficient, both partially true and partially false.

To be sure, the *Parmenides* is largely an abstract exercise, whose chief interest arises from the substance of its ideas, discussed by characterological types. Yet, for that very reason, a brief, anecdotal moment of human interest stands out in the text. After praising the young Socrates' desire to pursue the truth, and gently criticizing the youth's inclination to seek pat answers to complex problems, Parmenides balks at Socrates' request to demonstrate the dialectical method of a mature philosopher. For not only is the master advanced in years, but the demonstration would require a *physical* effort that is shown, as the dialogue progresses, to resemble a contest between two athletes, as in wrestling, boxing, or—anachronistically, yet more relevant to Cervantes' time and rhetorical practice—fencing.

Following its proliferation of paradoxes, stated and implied, the *Parmenides* reaches the disconcerting "conclusion" that, *in truth*, it is of little moment whether

---

This patrimony could have reached Cervantes and his contemporaries through a nearly countless number of sources, ranging from manuals in logic and rhetoric to works of philosophy and literature. As discussed in the following chapter, Spain underwent its own "epidemic" of paradox, of which Don Quixote is an extreme and unique case in point.

   2. Although I draw on Colie's insights, my discussion here of Plato's dialogue takes a different form from Colie's and highlights different elements of the philosophical text.

one affirms or negates the idea of the One: the radical unity of existence in the cosmos, encompassing all existents that merely "have" or receive their being. In any event, what one can "affirm" is that all existing beings both "are and are not." For, as observable and observed, they "seem to be" and "seem not to be" *at the same time*. The One, which is coterminous with everything as a whole, or as all in all, "appears" under the guises of both nothing and all things. As ultimate truth, the One therefore is and is not, does and does not exist. Indeed, the One lies beyond "being," understood here as temporal existence, which implies subjection to change, decay, and surcease. It also "resides" or has its (non)being in *no place*. Additionally, it is shown to lie beyond the reach of dialectical and linguistic categories that involve statements of *either* true *or* false, as set forth in the dialogue's final assertion of truth in strictly negative terms:

> [Parmenides]: Let this much be said; and further let us affirm what seems to be the truth, that, whether [the] one is or is not, one and the others [multiplicity of beings] in relation to themselves and one another, all of them, in every way, are and are not, appear to be and appear not to be.
> [Socrates]: Most true. (1973, 424)

In the *Parmenides*, one finds an example of paradoxical discourse in its barest and most abstract form. The dizzying array of paradoxes comprising the dialogue's content, together with the rhetorical command governing its form, serve to bring one to a state of reverence and awe in the face of mystery within the nontextual space, and to a pause of silence, which follow the dialogue's reading or recitation. What are in every sense the "apparent" contradictions of paradox find resolution outside the confines of time, space, and discourse, in the realm of mystery or of superrational and ineffable truth. Through discourse, the categories of logic and language succeed where they fail: appearing in order to vanish, signifying mystery through the nonsignifying method of pure negation, sometimes called the *via negativa*. As in the other Platonic dialogues, the *Parmenides'* dialectical contest between opponents and opposing views unfolds as a civilized debate—the playful, regulated conflict of competitive sport. If both contestants cannot strictly be victors, they can pursue, as friendly rivals, a mutually enriching sense of delight in the context of a serious game. Such "idle talking" is best suited to the treatment of ultimate questions, fulfilling a playful-sacred purpose.[3] Notably lacking in Plato's dialogue, however, are the self-reference and self-conscious attitude that

---

3. Classic studies on the centrality, even sacredness, of seemingly "idle" activity and "play" in culture are Huizinga 1970 and Pieper 1963.

will characterize works of Renaissance paradoxy, or Cervantes' *Don Quixote*. Even so, Plato's use of paradox is consonant with the height of Socratic wisdom, achieved by dint of painstaking study: namely, the self-awareness that entails knowing only that one (comprehensively) knows nothing.

It is hardly surprising that this work of Plato should have become one of the seminal texts of Western mysticism (Klibansky 1939, 281–330). Written in Plato's mature years, the dialogue is most often seen as a confident defense of his famous ideal philosophy, which understands earthly existence as a world of shadows, appearances, and mere imitations of eternal ideas, thus rendering all works of art imitations of imitations.[4] Neither is it surprising that, in such a defense, Plato should enlist the figure of Parmenides, whose own philosophy consists of critical reflections on the cosmology of both Empedocles and Heraclitus. With different emphases, these last two philosophers described the multiple, sensible manifestations of cosmic unity (the One) as the result of a continuing contest between contrary forces. Parmenides, for whom no middle ground was possible between the claims of being and nonbeing, judged becoming and plurality to be illusions. For him, both change and individual beings constituted visible, surface phenomena that both reveal and, to uncritical minds, conceal invisible "truth." For Parmenides, and so for Plato, the wakeful way of Truth opposes the way of Opinion that prevails among the "sleepwalking" masses (Swearingen 1991, 22–94).

The first justification for this excursus into the ideas of ancient philosophers is surely their preoccupation with "reality" beneath "appearance." Additionally, their assessment of the visible world as a composite of struggling contraries established both the thematics and the pattern that we find in all paradoxical discourse. Indeed, writing most of their philosophy in the form of either a literary dialogue or verse, Plato and his philosophical precursors represent the first Western figures to use such discourse in both a rhetorical and poetic fashion. More specifically, however, we are justified in discussing their doctrines and their rhetorical figuration because they represent the acknowledged sources of that Neoplatonist cosmology that formed part of Cervantes' intellectual climate, and that labeled nature as discordant concord (*discordia concors*).

In an article that is not specifically concerned with *Don Quixote*'s paradoxical rhetoric, Leland Chambers asserts that this Neoplatonist view of nature represents a governing "esthetic principle" in Cervantes' "novel of ideas" (as against a novel of character or action) (1981, 605–15). Leaving aside whether the *Quixote*

---

4. In his discussion of the chronology of Plato's dialogues, Copleston makes specific reference to the purpose of the *Parmenides* (1985, 135–41).

is such a "novel," or whether the "controlling idea" is the moral and salvific one that Chambers claims it is, one can certainly agree that, generally speaking, the Neoplatonist formulation accurately describes Cervantes' artistic simulacra of "nature" and "life." One may also claim, in agreement with Chambers, that a Neoplatonist view of nature as *discordia concors* and as a coincidence of opposites derives from such ancient sources as Plutarch and Plotinus and is transmitted to Renaissance writers through Marsilio Ficino and Pico della Mirandola (1981, 607).

To the ancient sources, however, one should add the negative theology found in Pseudo-Dionysius's *The Divine Names*. This work, which scholars have recently placed within the sixth century, presents its pseudonymous author's "harmonious" view of nature. It includes, as well, the first systematic formulation of the *via negativa* that greatly influenced the philosophy and mysticism of both the Middle Ages and the Renaissance.[5] Furthermore, the conception of nature according to musical metaphors (*harmonia, discordia, concordia*)—the image, that is, of a *musica mundana*, which continued to thrive in works by Renaissance and Baroque poets alike—originated in the philosophy of Pythagoras and Plato's *Timaeus*, reaching *both* the Middle Ages and the Renaissance through the *De Institutione Musica* of Boethius (Eco 1986, 30–33).[6]

In short, one can use this Neoplatonist formulation to describe an exceedingly disparate group of aesthetic *and* philosophical principles that inform the writings of nearly every artist, rhetorician, or philosopher from the early Renaissance to the late Baroque periods. To choose an extreme example, the presumed principle of unity in diversity, *discordia concors*, and the coincidence of opposites applies equally to the cosmological reflections of such an incongruous pair of writers as the Christian humanist Fray Luis de Granada and the pantheist philosopher Giordano Bruno.

It is therefore true, as Chambers claims, that Cervantes' literary cosmos portrays the world of human action as an instance of unity in diversity and a coincidence

5. Pseudo-Dionysius's threefold method for "naming" God consists of (1) predicating of him the perfections found in creatures (*via affirmativa*); (2) denying in him all creaturely limitations (*via negativa*); and (3) affirming of him these same perfections, but to an eminent, ineffable degree (*via eminentis*), which ultimately amounts to a negative assertion of the divine essence (a nameless name). Ironically enough, with this ancient, pseudonymous Christian author—confused in the Middle Ages with the disciple of Saint Paul who bore the same name—the problematic character of naming becomes an especially common feature of paradoxical writing. To be sure, the problematics of naming that spring from the tradition of paradoxical writing are fully exploited in Cervantes' works, most notably regarding his protagonist in *Don Quixote*. An excellent synopsis of Pseudo-Dionysus's thought is that of Copleston (1972, 50–54). Eco discusses Pseudo-Dionysus's equally paradoxical conception of nature and natural beauty (1986, 18).

6. Especially interesting in this regard is Eco's summary of John Scotus Eriugena's perception of natural beauty: "[T]he beauty of creation was due to a consonance of similars and dissimilars" (1986, 33).

of opposites. Yet such an assertion simply represents another way of saying that Cervantes shared the worldview of his age. Nonetheless, my purpose in relating the Platonist doctrine to *Don Quixote* is to underscore how Cervantes reworked what was already a philosophical and artistic commonplace, traceable to a literary-philosophical tradition that originated in ancient Greece.

Besides the Platonic dialogues, another important group of works within the rhetorical tradition of paradoxy in ancient Greece belong to the elusive category of Menippean satire. In recent times, the scholars who most extensively discuss Menippean satire as an expansive "genre" of considerable importance in the development of the modern novel are Northrop Frye (1973, 309–14) and Mikhail Bakhtin (1984, 112–21). Named after the Greek writer Menippus whose works are no longer extant, the satirical form was employed in ancient Rome by Varro, Petronius (*Satyricon*) and Apuleius (*The Golden Ass* or *The Metamorphoses*). A near contemporary of Apuleius who wrote within the same tradition was the Greek satirist Lucian, whom Erasmus openly acknowledges to be one of the sources of his own satirical writings. It was through Erasmus that Lucian's satirical methods were made known to Spain's Christian humanists and also to Cervantes.

As shown in the development of Menippean satire, paradoxy certainly flourished in ancient Rome, with varying degrees of artistry, but followed the tradition already established by the Greeks. Paradoxes concerning the enigmatic psychology of human love such as those found in Ovid and in Catullus's famous "odi et amo" are, of course, a constant in literature of virtually all ages and places and informed both the medieval and Renaissance traditions of courtly and chivalric love. As Colie observes, amorous paradoxes occurred to an unprecedented degree in the sonnets that Petrarch (1304–74) addressed to Laura. And it was primarily through these sonnets that Petrarch established the literary conventions for Renaissance writings on matters of the heart, in much the same way that he set the fundamental pattern for all Renaissance literature and scholarship.[7] The precedent for a paradox-oriented criticism of social ethics is established in Cicero's *Paradoxa stoicorum*—a clear favorite among Renaissance humanists. Though original in form, the work's content amounts to an elegant compendium of moral commonplaces, posed as rhetorical questions. Furthermore, these questions seem "paradoxical" only to the extent that Cicero contrasts them, satiri-

---

7. A detailed discussion of the paradoxes associated with literary treatments of love, either in poetry or in prose, is a virtually interminable one, clearly beyond the scope of this study. On Petrarch's psychological paradoxes of love and self-reference, see Colie 1966, 72–89. For a sound treatment of the literature of love in Spain, with particular reference to the Golden Age, see Parker 1985; for a specific discussion of Cervantes' "philosophy of love," see Parker 1985, 113–26. For a recent discussion of Petrarch's intellectual legacy in other fields, see Kelley 1991, 7–11.

cally, with the hypocrisy and immorality that he perceives in his Roman contemporaries (Colie 1966, 11–14).

Besides the perennial paradoxes of love poetry, including the special case of the Provençal troubadours, the most extreme forms of paradoxy—strongly influenced by Neoplatonism—occur in such writings of fourteenth-century mysticism as the works by Meister Eckhart.[8] In the secular sphere, the most conspicuously paradoxical statements appear in manuals of terminist logic belonging to both the thirteenth and fourteenth centuries. Under the rubric of dialectical problems called *impossibilia, insolubilia,* or *sophismata,* these manuals were used to train novice dialecticians in the art of disputation. The best-known precedents for the type of dialectical reasoning employed by medieval logicians in their efforts to dispute and to "solve" the *insolubilia* are found in such twelfth-century writings as Abelard's *Sic et Non,* Gratian's *Concordance of the Discordant Canons,* and Lombard's *Sentences or Book of Opinions* (Keen 1968, 99; Knowles 1962, 116–30; Copleston 1972, 82–85). As Joseph R. Jones has pointed out, variations of the same sophistical problems appeared in standard textbooks of logic that circulated in Spanish schools at the time of Cervantes, against the better judgment of such humanist scholars as Juan Luis Vives (Jones 1986, 183–93).[9]

Nonetheless, it is important to bear in mind that besides their familiarity with such logical paradoxes, and with the paradoxical doctrines of Pseudo-Dionysius and Boethius, medieval philosophers and artists were no less aware than were their Renaissance counterparts of the paradoxes inherent in the Christian faith: one God as a trinity of persons; Christ as both God and man; Christ, the King of Kings born in a stable as a child, later "enthroned" upon a donkey in Jerusalem, and then crucified in the manner of a slave; Mary as both virgin and mother; the need to die in order to live; the last shall be first; and so on. In short, Christianity inserted a fully paradoxical view of the world into Western consciousness—a view that prevailed until the rationalism and scientism of modern times. A fondness for paradox among the medievals derived chiefly from their expanding upon the doctrines of Saint Paul, and from such theologians of Christian Antiquity as Augustine and Tertullian. Indeed, it was Tertullian who coined this famous adage in reference to Christ's resurrection: "Certum est, quia impossibile" (It is certain, for it is impossible) (*Tertullian* 1954, 881; see Colie 1966, 23).

8. In two studies, Copleston gives excellent summaries of Eckhart's thought, with special reference to what his contemporaries perceived as his disconcerting use of paradoxical rhetoric (Copleston 1972, 279–85; 1985, 184–95).

9. The humanists' distaste for this species of paradox and for late scholasticism's attendant overemphasis on technical dialectic at the expense of rhetoric originates in Petrarch's *De sui ipsius et multorum ignorantia* (Barilli 1989, 52–53).

Probably the most paradoxical symbol of medieval Christianity was that of Christ's cross, traditionally called the "sign of contradiction," in paraphrase of the words that Simeon spoke to Mary at the time of Jesus' circumcision in the temple (Luke 2:35). The cross of Christ reconciled all the world's contradictions and strife (Pelikan 1987, 5–108). And yet the cross remained a sign of contradiction chiefly because Christ's execution defied the norms of reasonableness. Of course, Paul is clear about the "folly" of the cross in his famous disquisition about the difference between worldly and godly wisdom: "[H]ere are we preaching a crucified Christ; to the Jews an obstacle they cannot get over, to the pagans madness" (1 Cor. 1:22–23). Thus, as Jaroslav Pelikan remarks: "In seeking to celebrate the cross as wisdom, the Christian writers and artists of the Middle Ages often took pains to revel first in its 'foolishness'" (1987, 103). Indeed, paradoxical discourse in reference to Christ's cross abounded in the writings of such Church Fathers as Augustine, who asserts: "The deformity of Christ forms you. If he had not willed to be deformed, you would not have recovered the form which you had lost. Therefore he was deformed when he hung on the cross. But his deformity is our comeliness. In this life, therefore, let us hold fast to the deformed Christ" (Pelikan 1987, 104).

In a similar vein, Erich Auerbach argues that the paradoxes involved in the story of Christ's Passion and death—of God who consents to being killed by his creatures—brought about a Copernican revolution in rhetoric and literature: "That the King of Kings was treated as a low criminal, that he was mocked, spat upon, whipped, and nailed to the cross—that story no sooner comes to dominate the consciousness of the people than it completely destroys the aesthetics of separation of styles; it engenders a new elevated style, which does not scorn everyday life and which is ready to absorb the sensorily realistic, even the ugly, the undignified, the physically base" (1957, 63).

Next in importance to the symbol of the cross and the image of a crucified Christ, the Church herself was also described in paradoxical terms from Christian Antiquity onward. For instance, the second-century poem *Shepherd*, by Hermas, establishes the cliché of the Church as an elderly woman growing not only wiser but also ever younger over time (Curtius 1990, 103–4). Medieval philosophers, theologians and artists likewise inherited the paradoxical view of the Church, which Augustine set forth in *The City of God*. For Augustine, the Church remains both inside and outside of time, sometimes subject to periods of internal corruption yet ultimately incorruptible. The medievals also inherited Augustine's view of human history, and of every person's life on earth, as a continuing struggle between the rival "loves" of self and the Deity—loves that built two coexisting cities, Jerusalem and Babylon, the "city of God" and the "city of man."

While retaining its close ties with the paradoxes of faith, paradoxical discourse in the Middle Ages also extended to the secular sphere. Because of their inadequate knowledge of Greek and Roman texts, medieval writers lacked the wide range of rhetorical tools available to their Renaissance descendants. Hence, in the rhetorical field of paradoxy, secular subject matter in the Middle Ages was likewise confined to a reduced number of artistic topoi. For example, Ernst Robert Curtius has pointed out recurring instances among medieval writers of the "puer-senex" commonplace (1973, 98–101). As the same scholar also notes, owing mainly to their familiarity with Virgil's *adynata* (i.e., a string of impossibilities), medieval poets most frequently made use of the thoroughly paradoxical topos of "the world upside down"—also a favorite among Renaissance authors—especially evident in Curtius's illustration of the goliardic poem *Carmina Burana* (1990, 94–98; Colie 1966, 13).[10]

Furthermore, paradoxes relating to both secular and religious issues in the Middle Ages lie at the heart of what Mikhail Bakhtin broadly describes as the "folk" tradition of the medieval carnival (1968). Yet, as Auerbach observes, the cultural and social triumph of Christianity in the West tended to blur the distinction between "high" and "low" styles and occasioned an increasing overlap of "official" and "folk" culture.

If the *Carmina Burana* incorporates popular elements of the "carnival spirit," it is also a playful display of considerable learning, as are, to say the least, the best-known works of Bakhtin's main Renaissance heroes of "carnivalesque" laughter: Erasmus and Rabelais. We could make similar claims for the goliardic poems in general, the numerous religious parodies, the *blazons* (Bakhtin 1968, 426–30) and the fabliaux.[11] Such writers as Rabelais and Erasmus undertake their "rhypography" (their rhetorical exaltation of the lowly, the popular, and even the base) as a profoundly Christian exercise (Colie 1966, 25, 44–46, 63–65, 276–79). Equally important, that exercise is consciously philosophical, and learned, even bookish. It is inaccurate to claim, in the manner of Bakhtin, that such rhetoric—which Bakhtin never calls by the name of rhypography—derives from either the festival of carnival or the marketplace. The medieval carnival, including its most unofficial manifestation in the Feast of Fools, owes much to the paradoxes of Pauline *theology* concerning the crucified Christ. We

---

10. Grant examines the topos of the world upside down in relation to Spanish literature in two articles (1972, 119–37 and 1973, 103–6). Though included in studies devoted to Spain's Golden Age, her more recent article deals chiefly with nineteenth-century Catalan *aleluyas*, with occasional references to Golden Age texts.

11. Also in reference to such works as the Carmina Burana, Otis Green writes: "It would be an error to imagine that there existed a barrier between the religious and the profane lyric" (1960–63, 1:29).

can hardly exempt Lenten carnival from the influence of Christianity's "official" doctrines, transmitted to the common people through the pedagogy of the pulpit, the liturgy (including the liturgical calendar), and ecclesiastical art.[12] Hence, in reference to the Middle Ages, the contrast between high and low, official and folk, or lettered and unlettered seems to be less sharp than Bakhtin suggests. More to the point, it is a false dichotomy. In particular, Spain's tradition of Corpus Christi plays and its one-act religious dramas called *autos sacramentales* would prove unintelligible, except as a popularization of the doctrines of the incarnation and transubstantiation. Moreover, what Bakhtin calls the carnivalesque in literature is no different from the topos of "topsy-turvy" or the "world upside down"—a topos that celebrates the doing, undoing, reversal, and re-reversal of conventional norm and natural form. In literary texts, what the world upside down is to atmosphere or setting, grotesque is to imagery and paradoxy is to rhetorical figuration.

Hence, if the aesthetic theory informing what is generally recognized as the high culture of the Middle Ages stressed cosmic unity, harmony, and order and tended, ultimately, to understand the world in terms of symbol and allegory, it is because medieval thinkers and artists recognized—and strove to reconcile—the disparity they perceived between the visible and invisible worlds. In other words, they predicated their thinking and artistic activity upon the paradox of the supernatural hidden within the appearance of the natural, or the eternal within the temporal. Because of their belief in an incarnate, crucified, and resurrected Christ—who made all things new and who sanctified matter—they could never adopt the extreme spiritualism and intellectualism of the Platonic tradition in an uncritical fashion. If the spiritual constituted a superior plane of reality, it was hardly the only reality. Hence, as a result of the Christian story, the material and the spiritual remained distinct, but they no longer formed utterly separate spheres, as they did in Plato and his epigones. But nor did the carnival spirit of the Middle Ages exalt matter and the "lower stratum" in a manner approaching nature worship, as Bakhtin comes close to arguing.

Unlike their Renaissance descendants, the majority of medieval thinkers and artists in the West continued to place excessive stress on the supernatural and the eternal over the natural and the temporal. Like their Renaissance descendants, however, the carnivalesque or topsy-turvy spirit in both learned and less learned

12. Bakhtin puts forth his view on the "popular-festive" forms of carnival in *Rabelais and His World* (1968, 196–277). An excellent discussion of folly and the figure of the fool is *The Fool and His Scepter* (Willeford 1969). Grassi and Lorch (1986) explore the topsy-turvy logic of folly in Renaissance writers. Caro Baroja (1965) studies the popular manifestations of carnival in Spain.

medievals represented a playful, often irreverent, celebration of paradoxes resulting from the human being's mutable condition: a creature formed in the image and likeness of God, destined for eternity, yet immersed in the material and temporal order.

Hence the consciousness of medieval Christendom was continually torn between two extremes. On the one hand, there was a powerful strain of Hellenic intellectualism, which stressed the spiritual, the transcendent, and God's absolute being; on the other, the equally powerful influence of the doctrine concerning Christ's incarnation, passion, death, and resurrection, perceived as sanctifying the whole of the created order. Owing to this second strain of influence, orthodox Christianity consistently battled, using intellectual as well as military weaponry, against the absolute spiritualism of such religious sects as the Manicheans, the Gnostics, and the Albigensian Cathars.

It is in this conflicted historical context that one can best assess the most paradoxical figure of medieval Christendom, whose influence on both the official (high) and carnivalesque (folk) traditions of Christianity is equally powerful. That figure, Saint Francis of Assisi (1181 or 1182–1226), preferred to call himself "God's minstrel" and "God's fool." He strove, in a radical manner, to *model* his life after that of Christ, and to make Christian doctrines more a way of life than a way of thought, or a body of doctrines, precepts, and formulas.[13] Through his example in both word and deed, the latent paradoxes of Christianity reach their fullest, living embodiment—that is, they translate into something far more vital and palpable than a conflation of high and low "styles."

The son of a wealthy Italian linen merchant, Saint Francis combined a life of intense mortification and poverty with a playful, joyful spirituality (*laetitia spiritualis*). At the same time, he cultivated a genuine respect for the human body and a sense of kinship with all God's creatures. Furthermore, in his attempting to shape his own existence after the Gospels and to do away with the "separation between faith and life" (Dawson 1938, 178), Saint Francis is a forerunner of the practically oriented Christianity and rhetoric of Erasmian humanism—a set of teachings to which Erasmus gave the paradoxical name *philosophia Christi*, deliberately conflating religion, philosophy, and rhetoric, as well as action and contemplation.

---

13. An important collection of contemporary writings both by and about Saint Francis is *Francis of Assisi: Writings and Early Biographies* (Habig 1972). A biography by one of Edwardian England's most paradoxical writers is St. Francis of Assisi (Chesterton 1931). For Bakhtin's view on the role of Saint Francis in the carnivalesque culture of the Middle Ages, see *Rabelais and His World* (1968, 56, 57, 78). For a good synopsis of Saint Francis's historical role in medieval Christendom, see *Medieval Europe* (Keen 1968, 150–61).

Though Saint Francis had no artistic ambitions, his "Canticle of the Sun" is considered the first important literary work in the Italian vernacular (Pelikan 1987, 138; Curtius 1973, 33). His efforts to lead the life of a simple mendicant forced him into alternately amicable and hostile dealings with secular and ecclesiastical authorities. Though a contemporary of Innocent III and Honorius II, two popes who did more than virtually any other pontiffs to expand the influence of the Church, Francis was the one officially canonized a saint. By seeking worldly obscurity, he attained nothing short of legendary fame. The religious order founded in his name, for the purpose of emulating his spirit of poverty and simplicity, soon became one of the wealthiest and most powerful organizations in Christendom. It counted among its members such disparate *intellectual* luminaries as Saint Bonaventure, Duns Scotus, William of Ockham, and, indeed, François Rabelais. Later, among the best-known lay Franciscans, called members of the Third Order, figured Miguel de Cervantes. Throughout the Middle Ages and the Renaissance alike, extreme spiritualists and materialists, as well as defenders and enemies of the official Church, would continue to invoke Francis as the exemplar of their cause. Indeed, at no point in history did either the high or folk culture of Europe succeed in fully absorbing the *paradox* of Francis's life. Yet, as Dawson remarks: "The Franciscan attitude to nature and human life marks a turning point in the religious history of the West. It is the end of the long period during which human nature and the present world had been dwarfed and immobilized by the shadow of eternity, and the beginning of a new epoch of humanism and interest in nature" (1938, 179).

From Nicolaus Cusanus to Erasmus: Renaissance Paradoxes of God, Man, Art, and Nature

At the close of the Middle Ages, an unexpected and original example of paradoxical writing occurs in Nicolaus Cusanus's *Of Learned Ignorance* (*De Docta Ignorantia*), completed in 1440. With comparable philosophical depth, Cusanus returns to Plato's questions about being and nonbeing, likeness and unlikeness, plurality and unity, albeit within a Christian intellectual framework. A clear echo of Socrates' knowing only that he knows nothing, of the Pauline distinction between worldly and godly wisdom, and of Pseudo-Dionysius's via *negativa*, the "*ignorantia*" in the title of Cusanus's philosophical and quasi-mystical work refers to one's need to grow in the *knowledge* of God's transcendence. This knowledge would yield a growing awareness of one's ignorance of the supernatural and of God.[14] As the absolute "Maximum," God's infinite truth and essence utterly surpass the limits of human understanding and speech: "Sacred ignorance has taught us that God is ineffable, because He is infinitely greater than anything that words can express" (Cusanus 1986, 60). Fittingly enough, the title of his first chapter reads: "How Knowledge is Ignorance." Nonetheless, what renders such ignorance/knowledge "learned" is that it comes about only through a careful, reflective study of both revelation and the created order. Indeed, the more knowledge we acquire about God, the more aware we become of our infinite ignorance with respect to spiritual realities.

In both his theology and cosmology, Cusanus's central doctrine is the *coincidentia oppositorum*, the coincidence of opposites or convergence of contraries, inherited by the Renaissance Neoplatonists.[15] According to Cusanus, the temporal order comprises a host of diverse existents, composed of diverse parts. All creatures, both in themselves and with respect to one another, lack perfect unity and fail harmoniously to synthesize their internal and external oppositions, which exist in a state of greater or less tension and conflict. The harmonious convergence of contraries and the full resolution of all conflict among opposites, whether in individual creatures or in creation as a whole, occurs only in the providential mind of the Godhead (Cusanus 1986, 49–50). The created world therefore presents a perplexing admixture of unity and diversity, likeness and unlikeness, being and nonbeing—a progressively unfolding system of alternately converging and conflicting contraries. Hence the world's paradoxical nature, for, as an unfurling emblem of the divine essence—as what Cusanus calls an *explicatio dei*—it flows continuously from a compression or "contraction" of infinity into finitude, of absolute unity into a plurality of as yet, and forever, imperfect forms and of eternity into time (65–124). Within the *finite* frame of its limiting essence or nature, every creature paradoxically contains an *infinite* and inexhaustible store of divinely grounded truths. For every finite creature in the temporal order is a paradoxical emblem of the infinite Creator, the eternal God. In the domain of creation, the most notable *coincidentia oppositorum* is the "little world" of man, an often conflicted composite of matter (organic, animal, and sensible life) and spiritual intelligence. Thus, the only perfect convergence of

14. As a mystical writer, Cusanus acknowledges his debt to Pseudo-Dionysius and to negative theology (Cusanus 1986, 59–61).

15. It is worth noting that although Cusanus (1401–64) is usually considered a transitional figure between the Middle Ages and the Renaissance, barely a generation separates him from Marsilio Ficino (1433–99) and Pico della Mirandola (1463–94). On Cusanus's thought, see Copleston 1972, 314–24. For an excellent discussion of Renaissance Neoplatonism, including the place of Cusanus, see Kristeller 1961, 48–69.

contraries, and indeed the only perfectly resolved paradox, is found in (for human understanding) the insoluble *mystery* of the Incarnation. For only the person of Christ synthesizes and harmonizes both temporal and eternal existence as God and man, Creator and creature, spirit and matter (Cusanus 1986, 65–140). Not surprisingly, Cusanus's theoretical and atemporal reflections on the nature of Christ then give way to meditations on Jesus' role in human *history*, framed according to the spare narrative outline that structures the Apostles' Creed (141–56).

Despite the novelty of his rhetorical approach, Cusanus's chief interest clearly relates to traditional questions of theology and metaphysics. As Copleston remarks, Cusanus's work projects an attitude of nostalgia, an effort to salvage the legitimacy of these questions. Cusanus's rhetorical strategy of paradoxy may therefore represent his shrewd attempt to strike a conciliatory posture between the increasingly triumphant, skeptical strain of Ockham's nominalism—which seemed to leave the edifice of earlier theology and philosophy in ruins—and the excessive confidence of such earlier scholastics as Aquinas and Scotus to harmonize the rival claims of faith and reason, theology and philosophy, Church and State (Copleston 1972, 314–15).

Though a prolongation of medieval Platonism, Cusanus's Christian philosophy nowhere relegates the temporal order of sensible phenomena and "becoming" to the Platonic status of mere illusions. Creaturely "contractions" of the divine essence are here assumed to be real and "true" within their own sphere. And yet Cusanus is no Franciscan. When contrasted with the absolute, self-subsistent being, earthly realities are most aptly described as God's metaphors: "A creature is not a positively distinct [autonomous] reality that receives the image of the infinite form; it is merely the image and nothing more, and in different creatures we see accidentally different images of that [infinite] form" (Cusanus 1986, 74). Cusanus's innovation in the rhetoric of paradoxy, as a trope of both language and thought, refashions the typically medieval view of nature "in terms of symbol and allegory" (Eco 1986, 52–64), as it will continue to inform works in both the Renaissance and Baroque periods.

Cusanus's novel rhetoric also expands upon an earlier innovation in medieval dialectic—namely, the Thomistic concept of "analogy," aptly summarized, from the standpoint of that concept's theological and metaphysical implications, by David Knowles: "[Actual perfections found in creatures] are really present in the Godhead, but in a manner inconceivable and inexpressible by the human mind—beyond its limit, as one might say. Goodness, for example, is not predicated of God and ourselves univocally—men are not good as God is good—nor is it predicated merely equivocally—the same word with a different meaning—but analogically" (1962, 263).[16]

Last, Cusanus's resort to paradoxy marks a true epistemological turn in philosophy and logic. Through his use of paradoxy, Cusanus shows a budding self-awareness of the need simultaneously to affirm and deny the *univocal* veracity and the *equivocal* meaning of his doctrines about God, man and the world.[17] These doctrines, couched increasingly in terms of paradox, underlie later formulations of Renaissance cosmology and aesthetics. How else, but through the self-conscious rhetoric of paradoxy, does a more self-reflective philosopher than Aquinas write about a "uni-verse" that exists, and is the immediate human contact with truth, at the same time that it is only *analogically* real or true or one?

On the one hand, what Colie calls the Renaissance "epidemic" of paradoxy springs from a newly felt need among later writers of fiction and nonfiction—a need already evident in Cusanus—to affirm and deny the same things at once. These writers both tout and demote the "analogously" real, which lies somewhere on the frontier between being and nonbeing, made subject to a blend of change and sameness, or to the perfective and destructive powers of time. On the other hand, this epidemic of paradoxy springs from a new desire among a more select group of writers such as Cervantes to adopt a rhetorical posture of "learned ignorance" and Socratic wisdom. Their works exemplify a self-conscious

16. The doctrine of analogy was not limited in either Aquinas or his followers to theological questions. Rather, it extended across the whole field of dialectics, permeating myriad forms of "predication, " as is also evident in Cusanus. For a discussion of analogy's range, together with its influence and transformations in the works of Spanish philosophers of the sixteenth and seventeenth centuries (e.g., Suárez), see Klubertanz 1960. More recently, Ralph McInerny has written a fine study of analogy in Aquinas (1996), partly as a polemic against Cajetan. Furthermore, this doctrine plays a central part in a seldom cited treatise by Domingo Báñez, better known as a confessor of Saint Theresa of Avila and as the theological rival of Luis de Molina in the acrimonious *De auxiliis* controversy over the question of divine foreknowledge and man's free will (Báñez 1966). The original title of Báñez's work, published in Salamanca in 1584, is *Scholastica Commentaria in Primam Partem Angelici Doctoris ad Sexagesimam Quartem Quaestionem*. Of course, from a theological point of view, the promulgations at the three sessions of Council of Trent (1545–63) represent a triumph of Thomism. Concerning the role of Spanish theologians at the Council, Henry Kamen writes in *Spain 1467–1714*: "The last session (1561–63) benefitted from the collaboration of Philip and was heavily dominated by Spaniards in both number and quality" (1983, 181). *Españoles en Trento* (1951), by Constancio Gutiérrez, provides a comprehensive view of Spanish influence at the Council. Spanish religious and cultural life in Cervantes' time, in addition to its preexisting, and better studied, Erasmian and Neoplatonist strains, thus contained an equally strong element of Thomistic Neoscholasticism and presented a frequently conflicted blend of opposed philosophical, moral, and devotional traditions. On the confrontations between the Tridentine and humanist strains—comprising both Erasmianism and Neoplatonism—see J. H. Elliot (1990, 243–47).

17. Such was the thesis first put forth about Cusanus in *The Individual and the Cosmos in Renaissance Philosophy*, by Ernst Cassirer 1963).

awareness of the power and limitations, or of the permanence and transience of logical, linguistic, and literary categories. They dramatize how every *utterance* that strives to make sense and point toward "truth" must rely on *non*sense and duplicitous discourse.

In addition, a pandemic distaste among Renaissance humanists for metaphysical speculation and for the sophistries of decadent scholasticism combined with a new fascination for recently discovered texts from Classical Antiquity and the Church Fathers. This circumstance provided Renaissance writers with both an impetus and a rich stock of materials for their *practically* oriented emphasis on rhetoric, conflated into a rhetorically based poetics (Kahn 1985, 37).[18]

In broad outline, the method behind their own rhetoricoliterary "creations" relied on the Ciceronian principle, described in *De inventione* (2.2), of innovation (*inventio*) through the emulation of classical models (*imitatio*). That Ciceronian method itself represented an innovation with respect to the doctrine of Aristotle's *Poetics*, in which art is regarded as an imitation, not of models, but of nature. Significantly, Renaissance artists both "imitated" and refashioned the Ciceronian method of inventive *imitatio* in a highly original manner (Kinney 1989, 235–306). As Arthur F. Kinney writes:

> The understanding of imitatio in the Cinquecento, then, made striking progress, moving from a sense of imitating the classics through a sense of adding fiction to an increasing interest in the marvelous, in admiratio. We shall find the same progression in the development of humanist fiction, too, from the wordplay of Erasmus, which is always contained in its literary predecessors [from Castiglione and Marguerite de Navarre] to the admission of the marvelous in the fiction of Rabelais and Cervantes. (1989, 43)[19]

18. Alban Forcione addresses the conflation of rhetoric and poetics in his discussion of Don Quixote's dialogue with the Canon of Toledo, *Cervantes, Aristotle, and the Persiles* (1970, 97). In *Don Quixote*, the canon of Toledo assumes the conflation of the two sciences, as well as the conflation of genres, styles, and modes in his commentary on the ideal books of chivalry: "[T]he untrammeled writing of these books gives the writer the scope to show his epic, lyrical, tragic, and comical qualities, by means of all those parts encompassed within the most sweet and pleasing sciences of poetry and oratory; for one may write an epic in prose as well as in verse" ([L]a escritura desatada destos libros da lugar a que el autor pueda mostrarse épico, lírico, trágico, cómico, con todas aquellas partes que encierran en sí las dulcísimas y agradables ciencias de la poesía y de la oratoria; que la épica también puede escribirse en prosa como en verso) (*DQ* 1: 47, 567).

19. The first chapter in Kinney 1989, "*Poema rhetoricum et rhetor poeticus*," contains a penetrating discussion of the development of humanist poetics from classical rhetoric—and of the consequent conflation of rhetoric and poetics—as well as an excellent bibliography. Unfortunately, Kinney's essay on Cervantes contains some glaring misprints in its Spanish reproductions of *Don Quixote* and some errors concerning Cervantes' work. Also, for a recent, more socially oriented study along similar lines, but focusing on ethical "exemplarity" as opposed to literary *imitatio*, see Hampton 1990, 237–96. For other

Thus, in Renaissance texts, a literary method that is fraught with paradox deploys the rhetoric of paradoxy to portray both cosmos and microcosm as a convergence of contraries that conflict and converge over time. Not only does this method reflect the unstable and contradictory character of purportedly "truthful" affirmations. It also induces the reader, by resisting certainty or closure, to cooperate in refashioning commonplace truths and commonsense truisms about nature, art, society, and self.

A work much closer in both spirit and time to Cervantes' *Don Quixote* is Erasmus of Rotterdam's *Praise of Folly*, originally published in 1511 under the double and duplicitous title *Encomium Moriae* and *Stultitiae Laus*. *Both* titles can be taken to mean (1) Erasmus's praise of folly in general; (2) a discourse of self-praise pronounced by the allegorical figure of Folly, the work's only voice and character; (3) Erasmus's praise of his own main character, which would itself be an act of openly "foolish" pride; (4) a mock encomium of either folly in general or the main character, attributable to the author or the character or both. Such mockery of "folly" would thus amount to a denunciation of the subject matter, as well as a denunciation of both the character and the author. It would thus render the *seeming* self-praise an instance of self-censure that makes author, character, and subject matter, ipso facto, deserving of praise. Moreover, one of the duplicitous work's *two* titles, *Encomium Moriae*, can also be understood as a polysemous and punning allusion to the name, and to the folly, hence the wisdom, of Erasmus's friend Sir Thomas More, to whom the *Folly* is dedicated, and who is said to be its inspiration in the dedicatory letter prefacing the work.

Not to slight Petrarch, who is commonly considered the prototype of Renaissance humanism, it seems reasonable to claim that Erasmus inaugurates the efflorescence of Continental humanist poetics and hermeneutics (Kinney 1989, 46) as well as the Renaissance outburst of rhetorical and literary paradoxy. What is more, his best-known work seems a perfect encapsulation of his life achievements in rhetoric as well as religious and secular scholarship. With a mixture of irony and self-effacement, in his prefatory letter to Thomas More, Erasmus gives a helpful account of the classical models that he refashions in his masterpiece of inventive *imitatio*:

> Let any, however, who are offended by the lightness and foolery of my argument remember, I beg, that mine is not the first example, but that

recent discussions of literary imitation among Renaissance writers, see Lyons and Nichols 1982, Greene 1982, and Quint 1983.

the same thing was often practised by great authors. Homer, all those ages ago, made sport with a battle of frogs and mice; Virgil, with a gnat, and a salad; Ovid, with a nut. Polycrates eulogized Busiris; and Isocrates, though a castigator of Polycrates, did the same; Glaucon argued in praise of injustice; Favorinus, of Thersites and of the quartan fever; Synesius, of baldness; Lucian, of the fly and the parasite. Seneca sported with an Apotheosis of the Emperor Claudius; Plutarch, in a dialogue between Gryllus and Ulysses; Lucian and Apuleius, with an ass; and someone whom I do not know, with the last will and testament of Grunius Coro-cotta, a hog. Saint Jerome makes mention of this last. (1974, 2)

Clearly, Erasmus's *Folly* belongs to the same Christian understanding of "learned ignorance" and Socratic wisdom as Cusanus's *Learned Ignorance* and of the *Imitatio Christi* (1441) attributed to Thomas à Kempis. It is worth noting that, at different times, both Cusanus and Kempis boarded in their youth, as Erasmus did later, with the Brethren of Common Life at Deventer. This was pri-marily a lay brotherhood, devoted to a practical mode of piety and Christian simplicity called the *devotio moderna*, which clearly left its mark on all three writers.[20] More to our purpose, however, even a cursory reading of the *Folly* reveals thematic affinities with Cervantes' *Don Quixote*. To be sure, prominent Cervantes scholars have addressed similarities between these two writers since the publication of Américo Castro's highly influential *El pensamiento de Cervantes* (1974).[21] In light of such studies, only the most skeptical, source-hunting of Positivists would deny that Cervantes' writings are steeped in Erasmian ideas, or that the author of *Don Quixote* deftly employed them in his multiple imitations

20. In his illuminating study, Nauert discusses how the Brethren of the Common Life have been erroneously credited with originating the reforms of Renaissance humanism in northern Europe (1995, 97–100). A still reliable biography of Erasmus is Johan Huizinga's *Erasmus and the Age of Reformation* (1957). In *Erasmus* (1996), James Tracy provides a magisterial account of that famous Dutch scholar's program for social and educational reform.

21. On Cervantes' likely exposure to the ideas of Erasmus through López de Hoyos, the original Latin text or translations in either Italian or Spanish, see Castro 1967, 222–61; and 1972, 51, 114 n. 62, and 170. Also see the two groundbreaking studies by Forcione (1982 and 1984). The standard work on Erasmian influence in Spain is still *Erasmo y España*, by Marcel Bataillon (1966), including a now some-what outdated chapter titled "El erasmismo de Cervantes" (777–801). A study that all but definitively confirmed Erasmian influence in Cervantes, and thus the latter's clear familiarity with the writings of Erasmus, is Vilanova's *Erasmo y Cervantes* (1949), followed by a revised and augmented edition (1989). The same scholar related Erasmus' most famous work to *Don Quixote* in "La *Moria* de Erasmo y el pról-ogo del *Quijote*," in *Collected Studies in Honor of Américo Castro's Eightieth Year* (1965, 423–33). Marcel Bataillon, owing in large part to the studies by Vilanova, revised his formerly tentative position concern-ing Erasmian influence in Cervantes in "Un problème d'influence d'Erasme en Espagne: L'*Eloge de la Folie*," in *Actes du Congrès Erasme, 1969* (1971, 136–47).

and critical refashionings of previous literary texts.[22] Though it would be point-less to rehearse the many sound readings of Erasmus's *Folly* accessible elsewhere, a brief sketch of the structure and thematics of that work will prove helpful in assessing Cervantes' respectful subversion and enlargement of Erasmian paradoxy and, more generally, of humanist poetics.

Most scholars today accept the fundamental division of Folly's self-serving declamation into three parts of unequal length.[23] The work's comparatively loose structure is modeled after the classical type of "paradoxical encomium," many of whose classical precedents are cited in Erasmus's prefatory letter to More.[24] It was the purpose of such mock encomia to defend the indefensible and praise "things without honor" in a purely formal exercise that was aimed at showing off the rhetorician's oratorical prowess or, in the manner of the *Parmenides*, at honing the novice's skills for subsequent declamations on "serious" subjects (Colie 1966, 3). Of course, there is nothing "purely" formal about Erasmus's fictional pane-gyric; and the author of the *Folly* is hardly a novice. Every page of the work bears witness to its author's rhetorical prowess and his playfully serious message. Adding to the display of rhetorical mastery, Folly's use and misuse of many clas-sical allusions and quotations provide ample evidence that the author's memory was still bristling with the 4,500 learned and popular maxims contained in his recently completed *Adagia* (Miller 1979, ix).

In the first part of her declamation (1974, 1–67), Folly "reminds" her listeners that it is she, not wisdom, who brings happiness to human life. She asserts that those who are mad, provided they inflict no physical harm, are truly the happiest of mortals (Miller 1979, xxii). Thanks to her influence, both infants and the elderly elicit our affection. In fact, she keeps even the elderly emotionally and spiritually young. In her sweeping survey of the world, she portrays human activity as a veritable feast of fools, a carnival and a theatrical production whose

---

22. Cervantes as profoundly knowledgeable sympathizer and shrewd critic of the Erasmian tradition is a major thesis informing the learned essays in Marquéz Villanueva's *Fuentes literarias cervantinas* (1973) and *Personajes y temas del "Quijote"* (1975). Another study by Márquez Villanueva discusses folly, fools, Erasmian influence, and related forms of paradox in *Don Quixote* (1980, 87–112).

23. For many years, scholars claimed that the *Folly* adhered to the structure of a formal, Aphthonian encomium as laid down by Quintilian. The first scholars to put forth this view were Walter Kaiser (1963, 35–50) and Hopewell Hudson in his edition of the *Folly* (Erasmus 1974, 129–42). Arguments in favor of the more recent, tripartite division do not deny the loose resemblance between Erasmus's work and the formal encomium, but point out that Erasmus was following the freer model of the mock encomium (Miller 1979, xiv). For a discussion of this point and an excellent reading of Erasmus's work, see Miller 1979, ix–xxv. Other sound readings of the *Folly* to which I am indebted include Kinney 1989, 46–86; Olin 1979, 49–56; Colie 1966, 15–21; and Huizinga 1957, 69–78.

24. Standard studies on the paradoxical encomium are those by Pease (1926), Miller (1956), and Burgess (1902).

very existence depends on each character's continued willingness playfully to don a mask and to persevere in a foolish role. The happiness that Folly generates is evident in love, marriage, and friendship. The drives behind all military glory, every modicum of civility, and every advance in either the sciences or the arts are her "handmaidens," all of which are recognizable species of pride: vainglory, self-love (*philautia*), and flattery (*kolaika*). Besides her reflections on the foolish pageantry of mankind in toto, Folly also calls attention in this first part of her discourse to her indispensable role in the private manias of alchemists, hunters, gamblers, and superstitious worshippers of saints and relics (Miller 1979, xxiii). In sum, according to Folly's representation, the world amounts to a vast spectacle of what the humanists called *feritas*, or the brutish pursuit of physical and earthly delights.

By extreme contrast, the much briefer, third part of the declamation (1974, 103–24) centers on the few earthly followers of *divinitas*, or Saint Paul's "fools for Christ."[25] These holy children of Folly are never at home in this world because of their striving to *imitate* Jesus—the holiest and "wisest" of worldly "fools," as Folly herself paradoxically states—and to achieve the beatific vision. The union with God that such holy fools attain in this and the next life is their "Moriae pars," their portion of folly. This expression puns on the heavenly portion belonging to Mary (*Mariae pars*), the sister of Martha and Lazarus, who more wisely/foolishly than Martha chose conversation with Jesus over preoccupation with earthly affairs.

The second part of the discourse (1974, 67–103), "placed between two contradictory paradoxes" (Miller 1979, xxiii), shifts the focus from the gleeful pageantry of Folly's worldly devotees to the established order of human society, whose structures remain intact largely thanks to hypocrisy, yet another form of folly. To the degree that they reflect on the seriousness of their calling or the lofty symbols of their office, such members of the establishment as popes, kings, priests, theologians, rhetoricians, and grammarians confront their personal shortcomings and grow in the awareness that they are playing the role of hypocritical fool. Folly reserves her most stinging invective for the Stoics and members of religious orders who (foolishly? wisely?) insist on imposing their burdensome ethical doctrines on others—doctrines that they are themselves unable to honor.

Folly's devotees fail, in this second part, to come across as either the innocent children of Nature or the saintly fools of Christ. Rather, they are limned according to the predominant medieval conception of the fool as *sinner*, which permeates the monothematic *Ship of Fools* (1494) of Sebastian Brant. One also senses

---

25. To underscore the contrast between the first and last sections of the *Folly*, I follow Miller's lead here in discussing the third section before the second (Miller 1979, xxiii).

the influence here of Cicero's *Paradoxa stoicorum*. Are these fools, then, Folly's children or her enemies? Does the apparent breakdown of irony in this section suggest that Folly is now acting as a mouthpiece for the author's moral satire? Answer: an emphatic yes and no to all of the above.

From whatever worldly or heavenly vantage one observes the spectacle of human life, Folly reigns supreme and claims every "kingdom" as her own. Notably absent from her sovereignty, however, is the unnamed realm of *humanitas*, which comprises the cultivated members of Erasmus's famous "Republic of Letters" or followers of the educational and moral ideals of humanist reform, whose lives strike a mean between the extremes that Folly tendentiously describes as *feritas* and *divinitas*.[26] Nonetheless, before arriving at a conclusion about either the "moral" or the "meaning" of the declamation, the reader is obliged to consider the source. For it would seem very much in character that the speaker's pronouncements should endorse unethical animality and loose indecorous scorn upon the established order, coming as they do from Folly herself. In addition, Folly invites her audience to associate her paradoxical portrait of humankind with the image of the Silenus of Alcibiades, a figure that will appear either repulsive or attractive depending on one's angle of perception.[27]

In sum, simultaneous affirmation and negation, pronouncement and disclaimer—for both the protagonist and the author—are integral to the viciously circular structure of Erasmus's text. If the topsy-turvy *ethos* of the speech seems to endorse the conclusion that folly is at once good and bad, laudable and

26. The originally Ciceronian concept of *humanitas*, associated with Greek *paideia* in the second-century author Aulus Gellius, and passed on to Petrarch and the later humanists through Dante, expressed the hope, in all these ages, of a united humanity universally devoted to the achievement of its fully "human" (physical and spiritual) potential. Of course, interpretations of this ideal varied in each age and nation according to the different authors' religious and political preferences. On this subject, see Kelley 1991, 2–6. For a discussion of the humanist concepts of *feritas, humanitas* and *divinitas* and their relation to Cervantes, see Forcione 1982, 257–60; 1984, 15.

27. It would seem that in ancient Greece, a Silenus was a small statue or mask that when viewed from one angle revealed the figure of a portly, unprepossessing lute player. When viewed from a different angle, however, the statue or mask revealed the figure of a beautiful god. The most famous reference to Sileni occurs near the end of Plato's *Symposium*, where Socrates' scorned companion, Alcibiades, likens Socrates to "the masks of Silenus," described thus: "having pipes and flutes in their mouths, . . . they are made to open in the middle, and there are images of gods inside them" (Plato 1973, 358). The image of the Silenus is central to Erasmus's paradoxical view of Christianity and all human activity. He wrote a work that is much shorter but no less paradoxical than the *Folly*, titled *Sileni Alcibiadis*. Unlike the *Folly*, however, the *Sileni* is written in a serious vein, without parodic "mockery" or burlesque intent. In that work, Erasmus deploys the image of Sileni to underscore the idea of beauty in apparent ugliness, wisdom in apparent folly. Not surprisingly, the central Silenus in Erasmus's work is Christ himself. The beauty and wisdom contained in the figure of Christ, and in other wise men of the past, will show themselves, according to Erasmus, only to those who are capable of reading, judging, and probing beyond surface appearances. A good English rendering of the *Sileni* is found in *The "Adages" of Erasmus* (1964). On the influence of the *Sileni* in Cervantes, see two studies by Forcione on Cervantes' *Novelas ejemplares* (Forcione 1982, 251–53; 1984, 8).

despicable, the work resists univocal interpretation at any level, primarily owing to its status as an exaltation of folly pronounced by Folly herself. The subject speaking about and for (therefore against) herself lacks objectivity in every sense. In fact, the declamation presents an extreme case of self-praise, self-flattery, and self-love (*philautia*) that casts even its seemingly "truthful" utterances into doubt. Caught in a circular maze of self-referential paradox, and brought to a logical and semantic impasse, discerning readers alone must take responsibility for whatever closure or interpretation they freely impose on the text. What is more, it is readers who must give order and structure to the speech, since, thanks to her handmaid Forgetfulness (*lethe*), Folly is unable to provide her "listeners" with an epilogue. Of course, it is consonant with the paradoxical character of the text that, in both cases, and in many senses, the reader should freely choose to do otherwise.

After Erasmus, the texts corresponding to the Continental epidemic of paradoxical writing, as studied by Colie and others, show the same Janus-like double-mindedness in both their content and form, with varying degrees of sophistication. Indeed, the most inventive "imitators" of Erasmian poetics, including Cervantes, elaborate considerably on the lesson that Parmenides strove to teach the young Socrates and frame their writings as multilayered debates, in accord with the humanist dictum that urged one to argue both sides of a question: "*in utramque partem*" (Kinney 1989, 325). Such texts no longer seek to examine a single issue of great philosophical or moral import in the light of two contrary hypotheses. In such a text as Erasmus's *Folly*, the reader faces contradictions at every turn between what the protagonist says and what she seems to mean on a multiplicity of "issues"; between what she states either ironically or straight and what the author or the reader or both may take to be valid on the same subject. In addition, the original texts that she and, through her, the author, deploy in their inventive (and self-serving?) *imitatio* exert pressure on the declamation and on the "whole" text (including what is unstated). Thus, the "new" text both asserts and parodically disputes the validity of its original(s), thereby opening up countless other levels of inter- and extratextual debate. In what Terence Cave aptly calls the "cornucopian" texts of the Renaissance (Cave 1979), a true plurality of contrary "voices," opinions, and apparent truths engage in a struggle—now gamelike, now warlike—for simultaneous occupation of the same textual platform, somehow occupied by none and all.

At first, the paradoxy of such works enhances the festive, playful mood of implied, "discreet" readers, detaching those readers ironically from the surface conflict of contraries in the text, and converting them into accomplices of an equally discreet, implied author. In other words, readers of the text feel entertained because they "know" that, unlike the "vulgar" reader, and like the author, they can sort out the paradoxes and arrive at the "truth" (Lausberg 1975, 91–92, 166). Yet at some moment either during or after the reading, reflection and self-reflection may lead the reader of Erasmus's *Folly* and its descendants to equate "vulgarity" with attempts to find closure and to resolve the textual paradoxes. At that point, the erstwhile accomplice (implied author or reader) also becomes nemesis. Implied author and reader mutually frustrate and counter each other's presumptive intentions, vying for control over the meaning of what is "only" a work of literature. Should the reader then assume that the author "intended" this contest all along, the amicability between author and reader—an amicability based on deceit—is restored. That is, unless and until the reader comes to resent (then appreciate?) this deceit. For he or she then begins to doubt the author's "word," knowing that the author may well have intended that doubt, and so on indefinitely, in an interminably playful, *serio ludere* dialectic between an implied—and necessarily imaginary—author and reader in the imaginary spaces and silences outside the text. Indeed, it seems that a characteristic feature of paradoxical texts is that, acting as mirrors, they are able to entertain virtually all readers with the brilliance of their own readings and to keep those readers profoundly attached to their brilliant readings. Such readings may or may not involve the ability to recognize, or perhaps invent, an author of comparable brilliance.

Notwithstanding their shared thematics and a penchant for paradoxical discourse, the differences separating Erasmus's solitary work of fiction from *Don Quixote* are no less marked than those separating Erasmus from Cusanus. Furthermore, Cervantes' use of paradoxy in *Don Quixote* separates him just as markedly from other writers of Spain's Golden Age. Both the differences and similarities that obtain between Cervantes, his predecessors, and his contemporaries in their use of paradoxy become clearer if one bears in mind the major shifts in attitude that led Renaissance and Baroque authors to resort to paradoxical discourse.

Despite the strong objections of Johan Huizinga (1950), and important emendations by such later scholars as Paul Oskar Kristeller, the fundamental insight of Jakob Burckhardt's 1860 classic *The Civilization of the Renaissance in Italy* (1950) has withstood historical scrutiny; namely, that the Renaissance issued in a new "discovery of man," and a revival of ancient classical works in direct opposition to the perceived intellectual attitudes and the pedagogical ideals that prevailed in the previous age.[28] In the words of Christopher Dawson:

28. Charles Nauert (1995) provides an excellent discussion of Renaissance humanism, with ample bibliography.

The Renaissance has its beginning in the self-discovery, the self-realization and the self-exaltation of Man. Medieval man had attempted to base his life on the supernatural. His ideal of knowledge was not the adventurous quest of the human mind exploring its own kingdom; it was an intuition of the eternal verities which is itself an emanation from the Divine Intellect—*irradiatio et participatio primae lucis.* The men of the Renaissance, on the other hand, turned away from the eternal and the absolute to the world of nature and human experience. (1985, 7–8)[29]

It is perhaps an overstated claim that the Renaissance ideal of knowledge and education involved, in all cases, a "turning away" from the absolute and the eternal. Most Renaissance humanists, besides their interest in the "natural," shared the religious faith of their medieval forebears and owed more to the intellectual inheritance of the Middle Ages than they were in a position to acknowledge. For the most part, Renaissance and Baroque writers were no less interested than the medievals in discerning the invisible beneath the visible, the incorruptible beneath the corruptible, the abiding harmony of truth beneath the appearance of temporal strife and discord. Nonetheless, it seems clear that this period inaugurates a growing fascination among philosophers, writers, and artists with man and his world as a site of contingency and temporality.

As set forth in Pico della Mirandola's "Oration on the Dignity of Man" and Juan Luis Vives' "A Fable About Man," Renaissance writers—and their Baroque successors—showed a novel interest in probing the paradoxically *truthful* circumstance of man and the world as contingent entities. In such writings, fascination with both cosmos and microcosm arises from their blending such contraries as potentiality and actuality, presence and absence, and being and nonbeing in the fluid, protean condition of their becoming.[30] Unlike a medieval aesthetic of unadulterated "light and optimism" (Eco 1986, 18), which tended to purge temporal "imperfections" in its quest for a vision of "supernatural" truth in all its purity, Renaissance poetics often sought to reflect the "bright confusion" emerging from what Sir Philip Sidney called, in his *Apology for Poetry,* man's place in "the middest" (see Kermode 1967, 7, 181). It is hardly surprising, then, that many writers of the period should display a "mixed discourse," which embraces paradoxy, as studied by Walter Kaiser (1963).

29. A series of interesting, often neglected essays by Dawson on Renaissance and Baroque culture, based on lectures he delivered as occupant of the Stillman Chair at Harvard University, are found in *The Dividing of Christendom* (1965).

30. English translations of both Pico's and Vives' texts can be found in Cassirer, Kristeller, and Randall 1967.

Furthermore, such a vision of man and the world is bound up with what Ricardo Quinones aptly calls the "Renaissance discovery of time" (1972), which begins, characteristically, with Petrarch. This discovery often included a near obsession in some writers with time's destructiveness, as well as a hopeful recognition among Christian humanists of its perfective powers.[31] A novel determination to make time subject to human measurement and control contradicted attitudes that prevailed in the previous epoch: "The Middle Ages tended to value the ongoing rhythms in which man participated; the Renaissance, the continuities that he himself effected" (Quinones 1972, 17). Along the same lines, in a study that focuses primarily on Michelangelo, Cervantes, and Giordano Bruno, Giancarlo Maiorino traces a shift in artistic emphasis from being to becoming. He likewise discovers the basis for a "Baroque unity of the arts" in that period's mimesis of the world, the self, *and* artistic creation as "*process*" (1990).[32]

Written in a transitional period between the Renaissance and the Baroque, Cervantes' *Don Quixote* certainly deals with the pursuit of truth beneath appearance. But in doing so, it also portrays, and parodies, the unstable contingency inherent in man, the individual self, society and art—realities fraught with contradiction, subject to temporal processes of change, and continually undergoing construction and reconstruction in human discourse. We shall be in a better position to assess Cervantes' handling of such subjects and his unique use of paradoxy as a figure of both language and thought after briefly examining examples of paradoxical discourse in some of the major Renaissance writings of Spain.

31. Also, for a fascinating study of human measurement and perceptions of time from prehistory to the present, see Whitrow 1988.

32. Maiorino repeatedly points to the centrality of paradox in the rhetoric and artistic vision of this period. My thanks go to Paul Panadero for directing my attention to this work. Other excellent studies that have proved indispensable are those by Orozco Díaz (1970 and 1988).

Paradoxy and the Spanish Renaissance

Fernando de Rojas, Antonio de Guevara, and Pero Mexía

Three Definitions of Paradox

In this chapter and those that follow, I shall base my analysis of paradox in Spanish writers, especially Cervantes, on three acceptations of the term. First, in agreement with its etymology, paradox denotes any assertion that runs contrary to (para) conventional understanding or received opinion (doxa). It therefore elicits a response of shock or wonder, admiratio or "alienation" in the recipient, who is forced to observe and cooperate in the undoing of his or her common-sense assumptions. This understanding of the term prevailed in Cervantes' day, as shown in the following definition by Covarrubias:

> Paradox: Equivalent to something causing astonishment [*admirable*] and contrary to common opinion; as in maintaining that quartan fever is

good, that the sky does not move and that the globe of the earth is the [body] that turns, etc. *Graece dicitur "paradoxos," admirabilis, praeter opinionem, inauditus.*

(Paradoxa: Vale tanto como cosa admirable y fuera de la común opinión; como sustentar que la quarentena es buena, que el cielo no se mueve y que el globo de la tierra es el que anda a la redonda, etc. *Graece dicitur "paradoxos," admirabilis, praeter opinionem, inauditus.*) (Covarrubias 1984, 852)

Besides including the concept of *admiratio* and that of opposition to received opinion and common expectations, this definition encompasses the paradoxical encomium and the heliocentric theory of Copernicus, a paradox that was still— as paradoxes invariably are, for as long as they remain paradoxes—officially heterodox. Following the terminology of Rosalie Colie, many scholars have chosen to classify paradoxical encomia as "rhetorical paradoxes." Although the designation is certainly accurate, it may also prove misleading. Such encomia deserve the label "rhetorical" to the degree that an orator pronounces them in a purely formal exercise. More specifically, however, they belong to the third of Aristotle's three branches of rhetoric: the epideictic or panegyric. This branch constitutes a rhetoric of display that serves a nonutilitarian, commemorative, or even festive purpose, and consists in assigning praise or censure (*Rhetoric* 1.1358a).[1]

It is pertinent to remember, however, that the Ciceronian tradition of paradoxes, aimed at moral and social reform, and thus performing a deliberative and suasive function, are no less "rhetorical" than the paradoxical encomia. Moreover, as Erasmus's most famous work makes clear, paradoxical encomia in the Renaissance are seldom purely formal exercises. They likewise aim at persuading the reader to ponder what is often an important moral question. Indeed, Ciceronian paradoxes frequently take the form of paradoxical encomia and vice versa.

Second, the closely related acceptation that figures in most literary or rhetorical manuals defines paradox as an apparent contradiction that, upon examination, reveals a hidden, startling truth. Concerning this second acceptation, it is necessary to stress that contradiction occurs only in the surface meaning of the opposing statements, each of which is found to be true in some sense or some degree, and both of which resolve in some "higher" synthesis, beyond the *terms*

---

1. It will be remembered that the first branch (the deliberative or legislative) is undertaken in light of some *future* action and aims at either persuading or dissuading one's listeners. The second (judicial or forensic) consists in either accusing or defending someone in a legal setting and is based on a criminal action known or thought to have taken place in the past.

set by the contradictory statements. The natural "end" of paradoxical discourse is to "resolve" in the ineffable, extrarational domain of mystery—itself a paradoxical combination of what for human intelligence is excessive opacity and excessive light. Hence the need to resort to a language of apparent nonsense. Such an end, however, resists closure, constitutes a fresh beginning, and points toward a potential enlargement of linguistic and logical categories, which may in turn be pushed to an aporetic impasse that requires further reassessment, resolution, and enlargement of discursive categories. Increasingly, "learned ignorance" and generative openness are paradoxy's natural form of "closure." The rhetoric of paradoxy thus pursues truth in the form of a continuing, progressive, adventurous quest. It constitutes a rhetorical "way" that leads to the discovery that the infinite intelligibility of truth is what guarantees its incomprehensibility for the finite mind, but also what guarantees that mind the continued possibility of novel, truthful findings, infinite in number, from a potentially infinite number of perspectives within that mind's temporal sphere of existence.

From this standpoint, it is readily understandable that paradoxy should remain the preferred discourse of religion and human love. For especially in matters of faith and of the heart, an oxymoronic contradiction in "terms"—two bodies–one flesh, God-man, Virgin-mother, life-giving death, wise folly—need not denote a contradiction in fact. But each partial apprehension—not comprehension— of that mysterious fact obliges one to adopt the method of negative assertions, the *via negativa*. Paradoxy, then, is ultimately a discourse of *progressively* enlightening darkness. Thus it is also a discourse that reveals how, within the bounds of temporal existence, control and possession are the chief enemies of one's infinite desire for love, communion, and beauty, and how a quest for subjective certitude often precludes a quest for truth.

The third meaning of paradox is more properly called "antinomy": an insoluble contradiction in which asserting the truth of a particular proposition necessarily entails asserting that proposition's falsity or impossibility (Quine 1966, 3–20). Such, for example, are (or used to be) the paradoxes of Zeno (ultimately based on the problem of infinity) and the prototypical "Paradox of the Liar," reducible to the proposition "This statement is false." Yet, in the classical formulation of the liar's paradox, a native from the Isle of Crete named Epimenides is reported to claim: "All Cretans are liars." If we take the statement as true, we must deem Epimenides a liar, since he is himself a Cretan. So his statement is false if it is true, in the same sense and to the same degree. This paradox-antinomy lies at the origin of the medieval *insolubilia, impossibilia,* and *sophismata.* It is also the primitive source of the various "logical" and "semantic" puzzles that exercise many contemporary logicians and analytical philosophers, today's more sophisticated descendants of the medieval dialecticians.[2] From the "semantic paradox" of Epimenides come the more recent "logical paradoxes" of Bertrand Russell and Kurt Grelling, for example (Quine 1966).

It is worth noting that in a sense, all art, including fiction, presents a more or less self-conscious instance of the liar's paradox. For like every lie and error, fiction's "truth" resides in its untruth—in the "fact" that it is untrue. Its meaning likewise resides in its lack of empirical reference. When one views the existence of a work of art as a statement or metamessage, that work can be perceived as covertly or overtly stating: "This story, statement, image, book is fictitious."

Yet it is important to distinguish a work of fiction from, say, a fraudulent history. If a fictional work attempts to create some illusion of reality, as well as some illusion of truth, it does not aim at deceiving the reader into thinking that its characters and action refer to real persons or events.[3] Indeed, even if the enjoyment of a fictional tale requires its readers to "suspend disbelief," it does not require them to *believe* in the manner of Don Quixote. Hence fictional works may attempt to convey important "truths," including the truth of their own fictiveness, by "telling" what appear to be "lies." But those works require the reader to recognize the fact (truth) of their untruth, even though they may also aim at persuading that reader to believe the nonfactual, universal truths conveyed through their unreal characters and events, in other words, through their untruth.

As the case of overtly fictional works exemplifies, it is through such distinctions—which open up new levels of abstraction, and expand formerly rigid categories—that apparent antinomy becomes paradox. For a paradox is a contradiction whose opposing statements become both true and false, in some sense and to some degree, and resolve at some presumably higher level of abstraction or generalization. For the purposes of this study, it is important to note that what renders antinomies insoluble is their wholly internal reference and their self-contained quality. They can find no resolution on their own utterly fixed terms, beyond which there remains no logical or semantic space for an assertion, negative or otherwise, of even partial truth or falsity. Thus, if antinomy obviates

---

2. Among the more recent, important studies on the paradox of the liar, see Parson 1974, 381–412, two studies by Martin (1970 and 1984), and Barwise and Etchemendy 1987. On such other presumed antinomies, sometimes called paradoxes of cooperation, as the prisoner's dilemma," see Campbell and Sowden 1985 and Koons 1991. On the philosophical, logical problems associated with paradox, see Wolgast 1977, Champlin 1988, and Cargile 1979. Saintsbury (1988) discusses a host of well-known paradoxical puzzles and their logical solutions, including the paradox of the liar, the paradoxes of Zeno, and paradoxes of cooperation.

3. Riffaterre (1990) provides a rigorous semiotic study of the manner in which the discourse of fiction creates the effect of truth.

closure, its reliance on univocal terms also yields the effect of obviating both mystery and meaning altogether.

Literature and Life as Tragicomedy: The Pre-Erasmian Paradoxy of Fernando de Rojas

Unlike in the rest of Europe, paradoxy in Spain failed to reach what Rosalie Colie would call "epidemic" proportions until the Baroque period. Nonetheless, important precedents for Cervantes' paradoxical discourse—in many ways a subversive transformation of humanist rhetoric—occur early in writings of Spain's Renaissance. One such precedent, which would justify a separate study, is the pre-Erasmian work of Fernando de Rojas, now called *La Celestina*,[4] in which both the religious and secular influence of Petrarch looms especially large (Deyermond 1961). From the outset, however, it is necessary to underscore that the paradoxy in Rojas's work seems to concede very little space to "harmony" or "concord" in its dialogic representation of the contraries inflicting either the individual soul or the world.[5] Not unlike the second part of Erasmus' *Folly*, Rojas' work dramatizes a society and a self that are beset by sinful folly and held together in only *apparent* integrity and harmony by hypocrisy rather than virtue.

Beginning with her name, the worldly protagonist, Celest-ina, embodies and obversely reflects the drama's central paradox. As official outcast, she is in many ways the reverse emblem of a society that one may call Christ-haunted rather than Christ-centered, a city of man that pays lip service to the city of God. Despite her constant preaching in favor of worldly pleasures, her practice of witchcraft, her invoking Plutus (pagan god of riches and one of many names for Satan) for assistance in her endeavors as bawd, and her boasting about the control she exerts over all sectors of society, in the end she is responsible for setting in motion the chain of events that brings about her own demise and she dies pleading for sacramental "confession."

---

4. The original title of Rojas's work (1499) was *Comedia de Calisto y Melibea*, and its later version (circa 1502), consisting of twenty-one acts, bore the title *Tragicomedia de Calisto y Melibea*. I have used the edition of Dorothy Severin (Rojas 1974).

5. Castro (1965) perceives *La Celestina* as the *converso* Rojas's act of social protest by literary means. This view contrasts sharply with that in Green's study (1960–63, 2.52–63), in which Green argues that the work's handling of the topos of *discordia concors* favors a "harmonious" interpretation of nature and social life. Gilman (1953, 461–69 and 1956) studies the originality of Rojas's using conflicted dialogue as a means of psychological revelation and self-revelation. Other important studies on Rojas's artistic innovations include those by Lida de Malkiel (1962 and 1970).

As dramatized in Rojas's work, the exceedingly violent tensions coinciding in the human heart, the conflicts characterizing human interaction, and the contradictions inherent in the characters' mendacious bartering of language (Gaylord 1991, 43–58), all arise from a socially sanctioned discourse that shows only a surface commitment to the ideals of Christian belief and practice. In a fit of apparent rather than genuine honesty, Calisto equates his gazing upon Melibea with the beatific vision: "In this, Melibea, I see the greatness of God" (En esto veo, Melibea, la grandeza de Dios) (Rojas 1974, 46).[6] He later disavows his Christianity with the words "I am a Melibean" (Melibeo soy) (1974, 50), in a subversive echo of Petrarch's claim to be more properly a "Christian" than a *Ciceronianus*. But the real drives in Calisto, and in the other characters of Rojas's society, are shown to be not love of God or neighbor, but self-love, flattery, lust, envy, and greed (Clarke 1968).

In their frenetic pursuit of vice, disguised as either love or virtue, the characters are all shown to live in subservience to the pagan deities invoked and denounced in Pleberio's final plaint: World, Fortune, Love (Wardropper 1964, 140–52; Dunn 1976, 406–19). As exemplified in this character whom others take to be a staunch defender of official social values, the hypocrisy that seems to guarantee society's self-preservation is also shown to be the agency of that society's progressive self-destruction.[7]

The *potential* for an aesthetics of optimism, harmony, and light—for a hopeful *future in time*—appears only in the silences and gaps of the text, in contrast to the aesthetic and ethical darkness and discord of the dramatized events, wrought with exemplary, self-conscious artistry. Moreover, the "ugliness" of "sin" is dramatized for the reader in all its seductive charm, thus instancing the "human" element that Cervantes, as stated in his prefatory verses to *Don Quixote*, would have Rojas depict less explicitly: "[*La Celestina* is] a book in my opinion divine, / had it hidden more of the human" ([*La Celestina* es] libro, en mi opinión, divi[no], / si encubriera más lo huma[no]) (*DQ* I: *Preliminary Verses*, 65).

A dramatic exaltation and denunciation of human folly, specifically of sin, the work shows itself to be a masterful rendering of authorial purpose, and

    6. Compare Calisto's theological distinction, however, between his vision and that of the saints in glory: "But, woe is me, for we differ in this: they find pure glory without fear of falling out of beatitude, and I, a *composite* [creature], *delight with reservation* in the disdainful torment that your absence will make me suffer" (Mas ¡oh triste! que en esto diferimos: que ellos *puramente* se glorifican sin temor de caer de tal bienaventuranza, y yo, *mixto, me alegro con recelo* del esquivo tormento, que tu ausencia me ha de causar) (Rojas 1974, 46; emphasis added).

    7. As Peter Dunn astutely observes: "Pleberio is everyone's superego" (1976, 410).

therefore worthy of both praise and censure for the same reasons, and to the same degree. What is more, as dramatized in Rojas's work, ugliness and beauty, praise and censure, are made to coincide, even as the reality and intelligibility of both virtue and vice are shown to be complementary and mutually, if antagonistically, dependent.

Indeed, the paradoxical structure and purpose of Rojas's work are nowhere more clearly delineated than in his Prologue. Beginning with a one-sided misrepresentation of an ancient philosopher of paradox, Rojas states: "All things are created in the manner of struggle or battle, according to the words of the great sage Heraclitus: *Omnia secundum litem fiunt*" (Todas las cosas ser criadas a manera de contienda o batalla, dice aquel gran sabio Heráclito en este modo: *Omnia secundum litem fiunt*) (1974, 40). He likewise finds corroboration in Petrarch for his view of conflict and strife in the macrocosm:

> Truly it is thus, and so all things bear witness to this truth: the stars are found in the battered firmament of heaven, the inimical elements engage with one another in strife, the earth quakes, the seas stir, the air beats against itself, the fires rage, the winds are among themselves forever at war, age struggles and fights against age, one against the other, and all against us.

> (En verdad así es, y así todas las cosas de esto dan testimonio: las estrellas se encuentran en el arrebatado firmamento del cielo, los adversos elementos unos con otros rompen pelea, tremen las tierras, ondean los mares, el aire se sacude, suenan las llamas, los vientos entre sí traen perpetua guerra, los tiempos con tiempos contienden y litigian entre sí, uno a uno y todos contra nosotros.) (1974, 40–41)

The conflicted belligerence that afflicts the rest of animate and inanimate nature also afflicts the microcosm:

> And what shall we say of men, to whom all the foregoing realities are subject? Who will disclose the reason for their wars, their enmities, their envies, their excesses and passions and unhappinesses? Their change of raiment, their demolition and renovation of monuments, and many other attachments and waverings that issue from the frailty of our human nature?

(¿Pues qué diremos entre los hombres a quien todo lo sobredicho es sujeto?
¿Quién explanará sus guerras, sus enemistades, sus envidias, sus acele-
ramientos y movimientos y descontentamientos? ¿Aquel mudar de trajes,
aquel derribar y renovar edificios, y otros muchos afectos diversos y variedades que de esta nuestra flaca humanidad nos provienen?) (1974, 42)

The author hardly seems surprised that his work should also be the site of
contradictory criticisms, a *coincidentia oppositorum*: "Some said it [the play] was
prolix, others brief; others that it was pleasing, and others that it was dark"
(Unos decían que era prolija, otros breve, otros agradable, otros escura). He ironically restates the conventional truism that sorting out such contradictions "falls
only to God" (a solo Dios pertenece). No less paradoxical is the generic classification of the work itself. One author called it a comedy since its aim was to
give pleasure. Others claim that it deserves the label tragedy, since the characters
meet a sorry end. Rojas strikes a seemingly conciliatory posture—really a posture
that is hostile to both sides of the generic discussion—and enlists an oxymoron
deriving from Terence: "In light of such disputes, I cut a middle ground between
both extremes of the debate, calling it a *tragicomedy*" (Yo, viendo estas discor-
dias, entre estos extremos partí agora por medio la porfía, y lláméla *tragicomedia*)
(1974, 43).

Despite the considerable controversy surrounding the "meaning" of Rojas's
"tragicomedy," the work seems to resist final closure. Interpretations of the work
by major critics seem to revolve around the question of hope and despair, or the
work's ultimately optimistic or pessimistic view of human life and society. On the
one hand, it strikes me as untenable that, in the context of the drama, Pleberio
should deserve to be regarded as a spokesman for the author or that Rojas should
be considered a materialist or a nihilist, as argued by Stephen Gilman (1972) and,
less extremely, by other scholars (Casa 1968, 19–29; McPheeters 1954, 331–35).[8]
On the other hand, if one judges not only from the portrayal of his characters,
but also from Rojas's portrayal of his readers and critics, there seems to be little
hope for a cessation of conflict, hypocrisy, or self-importance in his view of human
society.

As noted by Peter Dunn, Pleberio's final words, *in hac lachrymarum valle*, do
indeed originate in the traditional prayer to Mary, the Salve Regina, rendered in
English as "Hail, Holy Queen" (Dunn 1976, 417). But this prayer depicts humankind as "poor banished children of Eve" (*exsules, filii Evae*), "mourning and weep-
ing in this valley of tears" (*gementes et flentes in hac lachrymarum valle*); it seeks

---

8. For very different views, see, for example, Bataillon 1961, and especially Dunn 1976 and 1975.

deliverance from the world "after this, *our exile*" (*post hoc exsilium*).[9] Its hope and optimism are "supernatural" rather than natural—that is, rooted in the promise for personal deliverance—with no promise at all for earthly progress or improvement. There is hope in this prayer without illusions.

G. K. Chesterton once claimed—not exactly as either a nihilist or a materialist —that the difference between the optimist and the pessimist is that the pessimist has more experience. In similar fashion, as set forth in Rojas's work, and in his Prologue, human experience on earth leaves little room for optimism. Moreover, as against the Salve Regina, one searches his text in vain for either an explicit or implicit reference to Christianity as the true source of hope or truth or harmony. A religious creed here seems relegated to the role of implying the professed ideal of corrupt human beings and of pointing up pandemic social hypocrisy. Hope for social improvement, and for personal deliverance, remains an open question and is incessantly deferred, in much the same manner as the way in which Celestina artfully defers and delays making good on her promises while keeping both her clients and her collaborators in a state of anticipation.

It is important to add, however, that each contrary reading of either the text or of life will continue to be haunted by its opposite. In a manner of speaking, the "temptation" to both hope and despair, optimism and pessimism, prove equally powerful the moment one chooses one position over the other. Does Rojas's fiction promise ultimately consoling resolutions for the paradoxes and contradictions it broaches? To quote again from the Prologue:

> Since it is an ancient problem, repeated over many years, I shouldn't wonder that this work has been a source of battle and strife for its readers, serving to point up their differences, with each reader's passing judgment on the work according to the fancy of his will.

> (Y pues es antigua querella y visitada de largos tiempos, no quiero maravillarme si esta presente obra ha sido instrumento de lid o contienda a sus lectores para ponerlos en diferencias, dando cada uno sentencia sobre ella a sabor de su voluntad.) (1974, 42)

In the end, it is the prerogative of the reader to invest the work—and perhaps society and his or her personal life—with hope or, indeed, with resignation. If the work suggests and even teases the reader with the *possibility* of either natural

---

9. For both the traditional Latin and English renderings of this prayer, which can be found in any number of collections and Catholic missals, I have relied on Albrecht 1975, 8–11.

or supernatural optimism, to the same degree it also leaves open the possibility of doubt, and thus of a contrary reading of the text and of life's meaning.

In Praise and Censure of Self and Society: Antonio de Guevara and the Homiletics of Paradox

A pair of Renaissance authors definitely known to Cervantes—contemporaries though by no means disciples of Erasmus—whose immensely popular writings provide important precedents for Cervantes' paradoxical discourse were Antonio de Guevara (1480?–1545) and Pero Mexía (1497–1551).[10] The reasons for these authors' success seem clear enough. In a word, they figure among Europe's first literary popularizers, shrewdly appealing to a new mass readership which arose thanks to the printing press.

Guevara tapped the vein of popular taste for what today we would call human interest, which related to such matters as the color of Mary Magdalene's eyes and the *private* lives of kings and emperors. In the main, his playful technique consists of falsely citing classical and medieval authorities to lend an air of credibility—or, better, verisimilitude—to his shamelessly spurious writings. Such writings include tracts of presumably confessional literature (about, say, his own life as a courtier or the invented love letters of none other than the stoic emperor Marcus Aurelius), as well as invented accounts of court gossip and private or pseudobio-graphical details about the rich and famous from biblical times to the present. Yet if it is true that most of his writings were written as pure invention, they were not exactly frauds. For only the most gullible readers would believe them to be factual or historical. Further, Guevara seemed utterly indifferent to whether his writings were believed, provided they were bought and read. Much of their uniqueness lies, not in their "fabulous" or "fraudulent" quality, but in their status as both transparent and deliberate acts of "pseudohistory" (Márquez Villanueva 1973, 197). Phrased another way, they constitute a Platonic contradiction in terms that we may call "icastic fantasy," very much akin to Cervantes' later his-torical *poesis*. In addition, however, a prominent feature of Guevara's Renaissance texts lies in his applying a host of topoi, culled from the ancient and medieval

10. In the Prologue to *Don Quixote*, Part I, Cervantes satirically refers to Guevara as an expert in prostitutes, calling the latter author by his ecclesiastical title: the bishop of Mondoñedo. Cervantes' insult to Guevara is therefore twofold. He not only makes Guevara a kind of prostitutologist, or an expert in a "scholarly field" that ill befits a cleric, bishop, and member of a religious order, but he also alludes to Guevara's having held an insignificant, backwater bishopric.

traditions, to a simulacrum of *private*, individual experience and particularly that of Guevara's literary self.

More scrupulous, or less inventive, in their imitative use of authorities, Mexía's *Diálogos* (*Dialogues*) or *Coloquios* (*Colloquies*) (1547) and his *Silva de varia lección* (*Chrestomathy of Assorted Reading*) (1540)—avidly read by no less a Renaissance personage than Montaigne—specialized in the dissemination of interesting trivia and "curiosities." These works by Mexía reveal his tireless effort to satisfy popular interest in such burning cosmological and social questions as the enmity between dogs and cats, how donkeys can safely eat plants that are poisonous to other animals, how a tarantula bite can be cured with music, or whether it is better to dine on the basis of "a solitary dish" (un solo manjar) than several. Through Mexía, authorities such as Pliny, Plutarch, Cicero, Diogenes Laertius, Plato, Aristotle, the Church Fathers, and others—authorities from Aristotle to Zeno, that is—work in concert to provide definitive and comforting answers to these otherwise unsettling enigmas. For, as shown in each of his "essays"—all of which are impersonal in character—Mexía was a firm believer in happy endings, in closure with a smile. Yet, as we shall examine, following our discussion of Guevara, Mexía was also the one Renaissance author in Spain who imitated the art of classical paradoxy in its barest, and most endearingly laughable, form.

Though its author makes no specific reference to Guevara's paradoxy, the most informative study concerning Guevara's influence on Cervantes is that of Francisco Márquez Villanueva (1973, 187–257).[11] Furthermore, the rhetorical devices of Guevara have already been thoroughly studied by María Rosa Lida de Malkiel, who notes important links between that Spanish author and the medieval rhetorical tradition (1945, 346–88; also see Gibbs 1960). Consequently, it is enough for my purposes here briefly to examine Guevara's most elaborate form of paradoxy, which concerns what Juan Marichal calls that author's use of rhetoric in an "organización personal": that is, in his act of public self-figuration and self-creation through writing.[12]

11. Although I share Márquez Villanueva's view that Guevara exerted influence on Cervantes, I do not subscribe to his thesis that Guevara is in some way a model for Cide Hamete, for reasons that I discuss below. Márquez Villanueva has also written a fascinating study on Guevara's "novelized asceticism" (ascética novelada) (1968, 17–66). The standard general work on Guevara in English is that of Ernest Grey (1973). For an introductory survey of Guevara's works, see Jones 1975.

12. This is one of the guiding concepts in Marichal's superb essay "La originalidad renacentista en el estilo de Guevara," *Teoría e historia del ensayismo hispánico* (a revised edition of his *La voluntad del estilo*) (1984, 36–52). Elaborating on the ideas of Lida de Malkiel, Marichal makes an interesting comparison between Guevara and Nicolaus Cusanus: "As Nicholas of Cusa achieves on a superior level, Guevara is able to play his part as a major innovator, since, spiritually, he both lives and acts within the matrix of

The self-consciously paradoxical character of this enterprise is nowhere more manifest than in one of Guevara's most popular works, *Censure of the Court and Praise of the Village* (*Menosprecio de corte y alabanza de aldea*) (1539), which presents an equivocal, nonclassical, and self-referential type of mock encomium.[13] At first glance, the title of this work seems to set the terms, and the outcome, of its internal "debate": *censure/praise; court/village.* And, to be sure, if one were to undertake a reading in search of the work's doctrinal "content," in the main one finds a hackneyed censure of the worldly life at court combined with an approving echo of Horace's *beatus ille.* But Guevara's work is far more sophisticated than its homiletic "doctrine," its content being inseparable from, even at one with, its form.

At bottom, the work takes shape as an internal debate or struggle within Guevara's own person, owing to his paradoxical circumstance as a courtly monk and as a worldling turned ascetic, turned worldling once again. Brought to the court at the tender age of twelve (at the same age at which Jesus taught in the *temple*), he grew up "more accompanied by vices if not by [worldly] cares" (más acompañado de vicios que no de cuidados) (1984, 106). God then chose to "remove me from the world's vices and make me a Franciscan" (sacarme de los vicios del mundo y ponerme en religioso franciscano), during which time he followed the example of "most observant men" (varones observantísimos) (1984, 106). Perhaps excessively complacent in his youthful piety, and thus ill prepared for his return to the world, Guevara answers a summons by Charles V to serve as chronicler and preacher, a post that he has held for the past eighteen years. In the last three chapters (18–20), Guevara voices his regrets about the time he has wasted in worldly affairs, trots out his professed vices and sins for public scrutiny, and bids a hopeful farewell to the world and its vain promises. The paradoxical statements that he writes at the start of chapter 18 are illustrative of both the rhetoric and structure of his work:

---

traditional ideas and beliefs" (Guevara, como en otro nivel muy superior Nicolás de Cusa . . . puede desempeñar tan bien su papel innovador porque vive y opera espiritualmente dentro del conjunto de las ideas y creencias tradicionales) (1984, 38).

13. See Asunción Rallo's critical introduction to Guevara's text, where she discusses the latter's entertainingly sermonic purpose, thereby explaining the Renaissance author's indifference toward the veracity of his citations, anecdotes, and rhetorical *narratio* of historical cases in point (Guevara 1984, 15–94). In my view, this understanding of Guevara is incomplete. As Rallo rightly claims, indifference toward, or mistrust of, the veracity of secular historiography for sermonic purposes would link Guevara with a Christian homiletic tradition beginning with Saint Jerome, whom Guevara invokes in order to "defend" himself against the censure of such humanists as Pedro de Rhúa. Nonetheless, one must still account for Guevara's very deliberate acts of falsification, not mere invention. Márquez Villanueva's assertions about Guevara's inveterate love of "spoof" (embuste)—which Rallo simply dismisses, but fails to refute—remains central to an understanding of that Renaissance author's writings.

My life has not been life but a drawn-out death; my living has not been living but a prolonged act of dying; my days have not been days but heavy shadows; my years have not been years but troublesome dreams; my pleasures have not been pleasures but thrills that embittered me and left me unmoved; my youth was not youth but a dream that I dreamed and an I-know-not-what that passed before me; finally, I saw that my prosperity was not prosperity but a decoy of feathers and alchemist's gold.

(Mi vida no ha sido vida sino una muerte prolija; mi vivir no ha sido vivir sino un largo morir; mis días no han sido días sino unas sombras muy pesadas; mis años no han sido años sino unos sueños enojosos; mis placeres no fueron placeres sino unos alegrones que me amargaron y no me tocaron; mi juventud no fue juventud sino un sueño que soñé y un no sé qué que me vi; finalmente, digo que mi prosperidad no fue prosperidad, sino un señuelo de pluma y un tesoro de alquimia.) (1984, 262–63)

On the one hand, then, Guevara's "censure of the court" and his "praise of the village" offer a variation, in which Guevara draws on Horace, of the Augustianian theme concerning the continuing strife between the city of God and the city of man. On the other hand, it will be remembered that Augustine himself views such cosmic strife as but an extension of the struggle that Saint Paul identified in every human heart between the yearnings of the spirit and those of the flesh, between heavenly and worldly cares, and between devotion to God and devotion to self. In typically Renaissance fashion, Guevara applies the moral and religious lessons of both Augustine and Saint Paul, not simply to the microcosm, man, but to himself. Despite the sources of Guevara's doctrinal inspiration, however, his protracted homily addressed to King John III of Portugal is less a piece of confessional literature along the lines of Saint Augustine—which would involve the story of the author's past conversion and rebirth as a new self—than an extended self-examination about his present state. In large measure, Guevara's work takes the form of what devotional literature would dub an *examination of conscience*, and often borders on public self-flagellation by other means. Indeed, Guevara is at pains to make his "censure of the court" appear as a *censure of the self.*

As he addresses the king in the Prologue, the author openly laments the Pharisaism that he, a sinful courtier, feels compelled to exercise as a result of his duties as both writer and preacher:

Would that I knew how to amend what I do as I know how to say what others ought to do! Woe is me, woe is me! For I am like the sheep that are shorn so that others might clothe themselves, like the bees that make the honeycomb that others eat, like the bells that call to Mass and that never enter the church; I mean by what I have said that with my preaching and writing I teach many the way and yet I remain wayward.

(¡Ojalá supiese yo tan bien enmendar lo que hago como sé decir lo que los otros han de hacer! ¡Ay de mí, ay de mí!, que soy como las ovejas que se despojan para que otros lo vistan, como las abejas que crían los panales que otros coman, como las campanas que llaman a misa y ellas nunca allá entran; quiero por lo dicho decir que con mi predicar y con mi escrebir enseño a muchos el camino y quédome yo descaminado.) (1984, 104–5)[14]

Nonetheless, besides being an act of self-denunciation, such "humble" admissions of his own shortcomings, together with his self-proclaimed status as a first-hand witness, aim at adding credibility to his narrated invective against courtly vices:

So that you will know that all that is said in this, your majesty's book, your humble servant has neither dreamed nor had to ask others about; rather he saw it with his eyes, walked it with his feet, touched it with his hands and even mourned it in his heart; thus all should believe him as a man who saw what he writes and endured what he speaks.

([P]ara que sepáis que todo lo que dijere en este vuestro libro este vuestro siervo no lo ha soñado ni aun preguntado, sino que lo vio con sus ojos, paseó con sus pies, tocó con sus manos y aun lloró en su corazón, por manera que le han de creer como a hombre que vio lo que escribe y experimentó lo que dice.) (1984, 107–8)

In keeping with the spirit of the Prologue, the main narrative nowhere claims to set forth the author as a paragon, though it does make him an emblem of the courtier's life, and of the interior struggles that every courtier should be prepared to face. Hence, in his first chapter, titled "Where the Author Proves that No Courtier Can Complain Except About Himself" (Do el autor prueba que ningún cortesano se puede quejar sino de sí mismo), Guevara argues that before one is

14. This passage also serves as a good example of Guevara's grandiloquent, Athenian rather than Attic, style, which grated on the ears of Spain's Christian humanists.

justified in denouncing worldliness in general, or worldliness at court, one must begin with a commitment to the delphic principle Know thyself.

If wisely pursued, detachment from worldliness, as well as self-examination and self-knowledge first yield detachment from vain desires that Guevara repeatedly calls "wanting" or "wishing" (el querer), as distinct from "having" (el tener), and yield finally a laudable form of self-denial:

> One ought to hold in high esteem the man whose heart is able to scorn a kingdom or an empire, but I esteem more highly the man who scorns himself and who is not ruled by his own opinion, for there is no man in the world who is not enamoured of what he *wishes for* rather than what he *has.*

> (En mucho se ha de tener el hombre que tiene corazón para menospreciar un reino o un imperio, mas yo en mucho más tengo el que *menosprescia a sí mismo* y que no se rige por el su parescer proprio, porque no hay hombre en el mundo que no esté enamorado de lo que *quiere* que no de lo que *tiene.*) (1984, 125–26; emphasis added)

Such an attitude provides the remedy for the state in which most persons find themselves—a state of the interior strife between flesh and spirit—which often leads to what Guevara describes in paradoxical fashion as a separation of self from self:

> Oh how many, many times do we find struggling and travailing in the center of our hearts both virtue, which obliges me to be good, and sensuality, which beckons me to be vain and frivolous; from which struggle my judgment remains darkened, my understanding disturbed, my heart altered and I, myself, remain estranged from myself.

> (¡Oh cuántas y cuántas veces en el centro de nuestros corazones se andan peleando y trebejando la virtud que me obliga a ser bueno y la sensualidad que me convida a ser vano y liviano, de la cual pelea se sigue quedar el mi juicio ofuscado, el entendimiento turbado, el corazón alterado y yo mismo de mí mismo enajenado.) (1984, 127)

Properly understood, "censure of oneself" leads to another paradox: to the discovery of one's true self and to what is indeed love (*aprecio*) of that self. Guevara asserts that "in this life no one can find so great a *treasure* as he who finds *himself*" (en esta vida ninguno puede hallar *tan gran tesoro* como el hombre que *halla a sí mismo*) (1984, 129–30; emphasis added).

Nonetheless, as described in Guevara's briefer second chapter, self-denial leading to self-discovery marks a lonely, individual quest. Hence, as he indicates in that chapter's cumbersome title, "That No One Should Advise Anyone Else Either to Seek or to Depart from Courtly Life, but Rather That Each Person Should Choose the State in Life That He Pleases" (Que nadie debe aconsejar a nadie se vaya a la corte o se salga de la corte sino que cada uno elija el estado que quisiere), Guevara's admonitions in the narrative against worldliness and the vanities of the court do not aim at discouraging readers from either pursuing or continuing the courtly life. Indeed, it would prove immoral—"rash and I think perhaps meretricious" (gran temeridad y aun no sé si liviandad) (1984, 134)—to advise other persons about what state they must choose in life. With respect to his choice of vocation, it is the responsibility of each person to "search after his [or her] own inclination" (mirar la inclinación que tiene) (1984, 135).

Akin to his use of "censure of the court" as "censure of oneself," Guevara's "praise of the village" is less an idealization of the country—indeed, he repeatedly warns against the tedium and pettiness that characterize rural life—than another example of preacherly advice about what the author is himself unable to practice. As a result, his praise for the country is, again, a *censure of oneself* in the form of *praise for other men*. In particular, Guevara seems to praise those courtiers who are spiritually nobler (and more fortunate) than he. Furthermore, he writes what amounts to a practical guide for his fellow courtiers about how *the individual* must effect his noble flight from the world, and about the difficulties such an individual can expect to face because of his own shortcomings (e.g., worldly ambition, habituation to vice) and those of the villagers. Of course, Guevara touts the advantages of country life: abundance of food, wholesome amusement, plenty of time for religious devotion, and so on. But he is also careful to stress the generally fallen, imperfect condition of both man and the world, and the possibility of each person's ability to live virtuously and responsibly no matter what the circumstances: "Vice and the vicious man are those who go about looking for the opportunity to do evil, whereas virtue and the virtuous man everywhere find the opportunity to do good" (El vicio y el vicioso son los que andan a buscar oportunidad para ser malos, que la virtud y el virtuoso a do quiera hallan lugar para ser buenos) (1984, 137).

On its face, the text would seem to represent the sincere admonitions and self-admonitions of a contrite author, a seasoned veteran of his homiletic art. Such a reading, however, misses much of the work's irony, and what Márquez Villanueva rightly points out as Guevara's incorrigible love of "spoof" (embuste). In the first place, Guevara claims no firsthand knowledge of country life. What is more, he admits that he knows of no one in his lifetime, including himself, who abandoned the court for the village. His examples of such noble souls are all taken from Classical Antiquity. In so undermining the credibility (if not the sincerity) of his praise for the country, he is also undermining the credibility of his invective against the court.

Next, the text invites the reader to become suspicious of Guevara's humility, contrition, and sincerity. For not only is the author still a courtier, despite his nearing the end of his life; he has also managed, as Castro, Marichal, and others have noted, to prove an underlying thesis of his work: namely, that he is rightfully an aristocrat, as shown even by the class of his vices. He is descended, after all, from the noble family of the Guevara, as he is careful to point out when explaining his being brought to court as a child. If every man must "know himself" and "search after his inclination" (mirar la inclinación que tiene), and know whether he is able to withstand a drastic flight from the court, as Guevara never ceases to repeat in his sermonic text, then it follows that the author knows himself to be far too aristocratic, far too talented, and thus "unfit," for life in a village or a monastery. Indeed, it seems that one would have to conclude that this is not God's will for him, providence having placed him where he is. His spiritual "weakness" can thus be read as proof of his worldly nobility, aristocratic lineage, and natural inclination; his verbal denunciation of worldly nobility, as proof of his genuine spirituality and repentance. Is it not the case that a man can be a true Christian anywhere (do quiera halla lugar para ser bueno)?

At the same time, his self-censure can also be taken as self-praise for the very trait of worldliness that he ostensibly set out to censure. Such censure therefore seems reserved for others (otros), the quasi-picaresque figures and court rakes whom he denounces with obvious relish throughout most of the book (especially chapters 8–17). In the end, the reader confronts an insoluble dilemma, a double-minded, contradictory reading about what is ultimately the target of either censure or praise: the court, the village, the author, his invented and literary self, others.

A final paradox of the text adds to this dilemma and bears directly on the relation between the implied reader and author. The headings of the Prologue's three parts forcefully call the reader's attention to the author: (1) "The Author Proposes" (Propone el autor), (2) "The Author Applies" (Aplica el autor), (3) "The Author Concludes" (Concluye el autor). Of particular interest, the first part narrates a series of classical and biblical stories to inveigh against the vice of curiosity and the temptation "to meddle in other persons' lives" (meterse en vidas ajenas). It is in the other two parts of the Prologue that the author acknowledges the special need to put his own soul in order, his desire to censure no one as much as himself, and his intention to try his humble best to play the faithful courtier by respectfully admonishing the king (the emblematic reader). Yet it is clear that

Guevara's self-examination yields easily, upon analysis, to a self-serving, sermonic invective against *other members* of the court. Further, the details that he includes in his truly satirical accounts betray more than a passing curiosity in the lives of his fellow courtiers. But, more important, the hook that he uses throughout the work to sustain his reader's interest is nothing other than voyeuristic curiosity about "other persons' lives," beginning with the *reportedly* depraved life of the author himself.

As framed in the Prologue, the very act of reading the text becomes a form of self-indictment—the reader's active yet inadvertent *censure of oneself*, as well as a tacit indictment from the author, who doubly and duplicitously indicts himself for analogous reasons. If Guevara's confessions seem verisimilar, or colored with the appearance of truth, the reader has every reason to doubt their authenticity. Again, readers can then come to resent or appreciate either their complicity or rivalry with the author, as well as their relationship based on initial seduction and deceit—on the complex interplay between *illusion* (*engaño*) and *disabuse* (*desengaño*) both inside and outside the textual (fictional?) frame, at the levels of both doctrinal content and form. In fact, the form presents the most fitting demonstration and articulation of the textual "message."

Guevara's text therefore provides an apt illustration of why paradoxes are often called "nothings." For they are nothing in themselves, at the semantic level. In particular, the *circulus vitiosus* structure of Guevara's text empties of stable, referential meaning the terms that define its own debate: "praise," "censure," "court," "village," "self," "others," "*curiositas*" (alabanza, menosprecio, corte, aldea, uno mismo, los demás, *curiositas*). At the level of signification, each instance of praise is an instance of self-praise, as well as an instance of censure and self-censure. Is the reader then left with the "nothing" of undecidability and with dialectical terms that elide any referent and simply cancel one another out? I think that Guevara's text resists such facile closure, including that of pure denial.

More plausibly, the function of Guevara's paradoxy is to point beyond the *terms* of his artificial debate, and beyond the limits of such logical binaries as either/or, neither/nor, all or nothing. In the manner of the author, readers are free to propose, apply, and conclude as they see fit. Simply put, court and village, real and perceived (and invented) self, real and perceived other, are thematized and dramatized in Guevara's text as less than *fully* real or realized. They finally emerge as *both* good *and* bad, worthy of both praise and censure, but in some sense and to some degree.

On the one hand, it may prove tempting to claim that the reader rather than the author must decide in what sense and to what degree both praise and censure prove appropriate to each hypothetical case. On the other hand, however, as an extreme example of Renaissance wit, the text dramatizes both the need for ethical categories and the futility of seeking categorical verdicts on the basis of moral casuistry. Guevara's work effectively instances and portrays both the reader's and the author's (the king's and the subject's, the courtier's and the villager's) shared moral and ontological locus "in the middest," a stage somewhere between being and nonbeing and, hence, between sanctity and depravity. The very act of reading and decoding the text provides a vivid demonstration of how the good in us (as moral agents and as readers) remains under construction, thanks to a continuing interplay between the contradictions of culturally sanctioned discourse and personal choice.

"Proposing," "applying," and tentatively "concluding" signal the choices that one is able to make in life. Final verdicts and self-pronouncements about the moral and definitive meaning of one's life-narrative must await the moment of death. Guevara's text, like its author, strives to avert the demise of closure. Indeed, the self-referential and other-oriented text dramatizes the resistance of an unfinished and *unconverted* self, not simply to physical death, but to the *worldly death* of definitive spiritual conversion. Indeed, the work's paradoxes seem to represent Guevara's extended paraphrase, not of Augustine's *Confessions* or of the latter's prayers for conversion, but of that ancient bishop's famous prayer of deferral: Lord, make me chaste (Guevara: make me a saintly villager). But not yet.

Humanism for Everybody: Classical Paradoxy in the Writings of Pero Mexía

Pero Mexía's *Chrestomathy of Assorted Reading* (*Silva de varia lección*) (1540) and his *Dialogues* (*Diálogos*) or *Colloquies* (*Coloquios*) (1547) clearly lack the degree of sophistication found in Guevara's works. The following discussion of Mexía makes no attempt to argue either for or against his being resurrected from what some important scholars think to be his well-earned place in literary obscurity. I am less interested in assessing his literary merits than acknowledging his role in shaping the paradoxical discourse of the Spanish Renaissance.

As suggested earlier, much of Mexía's historical importance lies in his staggering popularity both in Spain and abroad. Like virtually every literate Spaniard, Cervantes could not have remained unacquainted with Mexía's writings.[15] Additionally, however, the very ingenuousness of Mexía's works, at least partly a result

---

15. For a bolder statement concerning possible influence, see Castillo 1945, 94–106.

of their being written for mass consumption, allows one to observe the elemental features of paradoxy, shorn of both rhetorical sophistication and "higher" literary purpose.[16]

Mexía's most successful work, *Chrestomathy of Assorted Reading* (*Silva de varia lección*), referred to hereafter as *Silva*, belongs to a widespread tradition of Renaissance miscellanies.[17] The first such work in the Spanish vernacular, it consists of 148 brief essays or varied "readings," divided into four parts, not all of which deal with paradoxes. I shall make no attempt to summarize what Mexía himself punningly calls a "jungle" (selva) (1989, 161) of disparate pieces. But it is pertinent to bear in mind that, in the *Silva*, Mexía does have a twofold didactic purpose, analogous to that of Guevara (Concejo 1985, 39–41). First, in a more scrupulously historical manner than that of his clerical counterpart, Mexía intends to make the wisdom of the ancients accessible to the common man, who can then "apply" the moral lessons to his own life. More interesting, however, in an essay of paradoxical praise that sincerely, rather than mockingly, extols the moral exemplarity of the busy ant, he admits his desire to appeal to popular *curiosity*. "I did not wish to write about very common matters, but instead about curious things not easily accessible to others" ([N]o querría escrevir cosas muy comunes, sino que sean curiosas y que no fácilmente se alcançassen por todos) (4.5, 347).[18] Among the plethora of curiosities with which Mexía instructively entertains his readers are descriptions and exemplary accounts of paradoxes besetting both nature and man.

Subscribing to the common paradoxical conception of nature as a *discordia concors*, Mexía invokes Heraclitus in his litany about the persistence of love and strife among animals and the elements (3.4, 32). Regarding creaturely strife, Mexía observes:

> We see among many things a natural enmity; yet no one knows entirely the cause from which this comes or arises; and this enmity, certainly, is a wondrous thing, as that which the cat has for the dog, oil for the fish, the deer for the snake, and many other things that we shall discuss that bear malice toward each other as a natural and secret property.

> ([V]emos entre muchas de las cosas una enemistad natural . . . , sin saber nadie la causa enteramente donde nazca y venga esto, lo qual es,

---

16. Concerning the dissemination of Mexía's *Silva* both in Spain and abroad, see Antonio Castro (1989, 52–59). Regarding the precedents for this genre, from both antiquity and later times, see Castro (1989, 60–61, 162).

17. For recent studies of the miscellany, with good bibliography, see Rallo 1987.

18. References to Mexía's *Silva de varia lección* will be by book, section, and page number, in the edition by Antonio Castro. The above citation (4.5, 347) therefore indicates book 4, section 5, page 347.

cierto, cosa maravillosa; como la que tiene el gato con el perro, y el azeyte con la pez, el ciervo y la culebra, y otras muchas cosas que diremos, que se quieren mal por propiedad natural y secreta.) (3.4, 32)

In their animality, men, too, share in the high mystery of cosmic enmity: "Snakes bear malice and dare to offend man, when they see him fully clothed; yet when he is naked, they flee from him and fear him infinitely" (Las culebras quieren mal y osan offender al hombre, si lo veen vestido; y, desnudo, huyen dél y lo temen infinito) (3.4, 36). Vexingly, Mexía fails to inform the reader about how he came to acquire such intelligence. The author draws this essay to a cheerful close, reminding his reader of the equally pervasive force of cosmic love: "and in like manner we must speak of things that naturally love and bear good-will toward one another: like peacocks who delight in the company of doves; and as happens between lovebirds and parrots" (e, assí mesmo, de las cosas que naturalmente se aman y quieren bien: como son los pavones, que huelgan mucho con la compañía de las palomas; las tórtolas, con los papagayos) (3.4, 38). In his final paragraph, Mexía cites an impressive array of authors who have written more extensively about war and peace among such creatures as magpies and snakes and, most notably, among the fishes: "The authorities for what I have said thus far are Pliny . . . and Aristotle and Albert the Great and Elianus, in his *De pis[c]ibus*" (De lo que tengo dicho son auctores Plinio . . . y Aristóteles y Alberto Magno . . . y Eliano, en el *De pi[s]cibus*) (3.4, 39). It is in the next essay (3.5, 40–44) where Mexía marshals the same degree of "scholarship" to provide a full explanation of nature's continual oscillations between love and strife.

Mexía further observes the strangeness of nature's properties in an essay devoted to the following subject:

> Why is it that, when covered with straw, snow preserves its coldness and hot water remains hot, since these are contrary effects? And why does the air in summer refresh us when we fan it, since it is hot; and, on the contrary, when we stir hot water it burns us more?

> (Por qué, cubierta con paja, la nieve se conserva en su frior [y] el agua caliente se sostiene en su calor, siendo contrarios effectos. Y por qué el ayre en el verano, meneándolo, refresca, siendo caliente; y, al contrario, el agua caliente, meneándola, quema más.) (3.21, 142–45)

Two final examples of paradoxes that belong to the I've-always-wondered-about-that category are (1) Mexía's discussion about why it proves more tiring to walk the same distance over flat rather than hilly ground; why it can prove most tiring of all to walk an even shorter distance uphill; and why a person feels dizzy when walking in a small circular path (3.6, 45–47); and (2) his essay about why a dead body weighs more than a live one (1.16, 328–332).

In another type of essay devoted to paradox (3.15, 98–100), Mexía tells two versions of the same story, in which a man attempts to kill one of his enemies. In both cases, the protagonist wounds his enemy and leaves him for dead. Nonetheless, not only does the injury that he inflicts fail to bring about the enemy's death, but, in recovering from that injury, the enemy finds himself cured of a previous ailment. In other words, a seemingly lethal injury from an enemy proves to be a source of total healing, as well as a motive for gratitude and even friendship. Further on, Mexía likewise finds it a medical and moral oddity that some doctors should recommend drunkenness as a method for improving their patients' health (3.17, 113–19).

The foregoing examples from the *Silva* provide simple, not to say simplistic, illustrations of what Renaissance authors typically viewed as wondrous paradoxes of nature and the human condition, deriving in large part from their conception of the cosmos as *discordia concors* and of man as *mixtus*. Such paradoxes, however, were usually grouped under the more general name of "marvels" (cosa maravillosa) or, less emphatically, "curiosities," as shown in the passages already quoted from Mexía's text. In a far less sophisticated fashion than that of predecessors such as Plato or Erasmus, Mexía enlists the rhetoric of paradoxy to provoke a sense of wonder in the reader. But it is important to note that the type of wonder that Mexía attempts to call forth here is predicated not so much upon logical contradiction, wordplay, or aporia as upon marvelous strangeness. Moreover, what made such "marvelous" phenomena as the ones cited above inherently paradoxical is that they run contrary to (*para*) common perceptions or received opinion (the doxa) about the way things are or *ought to be*, or that they seem to be *impossibilia*, or, finally, that one would expect them to occur in a *contrary* manner. In its simplest form, then, Mexía's work represents a case of Renaissance *admiratio*. This central feature of paradox denotes both the marvelous content of a particular author's work and the response, ranging from surprise to awe, that it elicits in the reader (Riley 1963, 173–83). In line with his amusingly straightforward attempt at *admiratio*, the "curiosity" that Mexía often incites provides an inferior species of aporia, which the author of the *Silva* seldom sustains at any length.

Two subtler instances of paradox in the *Silva* deserve special attention. The first (1.18, 338–41) involves Mexía's version of what is probably a fictitious legal case, which is credited by the contemporary scholar James J. Murphy—though not by Mexía—with originating the tradition of Western rhetoric (circa 476 B.C.). The original problem involves a historical figure, Corax of Syracuse, who reportedly threatens to sue his student, Tisias, because the latter refuses to pay for lessons received in dialectic. Murphy gives a more succinct account of the case than Mexía:

> CORAX: You must pay me if you win the case, because that would prove the worth of my lessons. If you lose the case you must pay me also, for the court will force you to do so. In either case you pay.
>
> TISIAS: I will pay nothing, because if I lose the case it would prove that your instruction was worthless. If I win, however, the court will absolve me from paying. In either case I will not pay. (1983, 7)[19]

In a characteristically straightforward way, at the end of his essay, Mexía *un*characteristically resists the closure of a definitive solution: "These are the arguments. Now let the readers debate them" (Estos son los casos. Agora los lectores platiquen sobre ello) (1.8, 341).

The next, and last, example of paradox that I shall discuss from the *Silva* (4.18, 482–84) concerns Mexía's moral distinction between lying (*mentir*) and telling a lie (*dezir mentira*). The paradox that Mexía uses to spark his reader's curiosity, and to display his rhetorical cleverness, relies on a semantic ruse. In essence, the logic of this essay depends on the the strict definition of lying as one's telling an untruth with the *intent* to deceive. The morality of the action, which is the true subject of the essay, therefore arises from the agent's intent and not from the truth or falsity of the statement itself. One can be guilty of lying even though, inadvertently, the statement one makes is true. Failing such a deceitful intent, either because the speaker or writer believes his or her statement to be true, or because he or she implicitly disavows or makes no claim for the statement's veracity, what appears to be lying amounts simply to "telling lies" (falsehoods, errors) in a morally blameless fashion. Such a doctrine presumably absolves the fiction writer of guilt, provided that writer harbors no intent to offer fiction as history.

In addition, however, Mexía notes that culpable lying is not reserved for statements, but may also involve a person's behavior. He closes this essay with an anecdote about an elderly gentleman of considerable social importance who dyes his gray hair in order to appear younger than he is. When the gentleman pleads an unspecified case at court, he is rebuked in the following manner by the King of Sparta: "What truth or certainty could such a man say or bring forth when he

---

19. Mexía's characters, taken from Aulus Gellius's *Attican Nights* (book 5, chapter 10), are called simply Maestro and Evathlo. See the editor's notes to Mexía's text (1989, 338), which specify the classical sources for Mexía's essay, but do not include the data discovered by Murphy.

bears a public lie on his face and head?" ("[¿Q]ué verdad ni cosa cierta podría dezir ni traer el que traía la mentira pública en [el] rostro y en la cabeça [?]) (4.18, 484). Mexía concludes: "Thus, . . . they could say of anyone who behaved in like manner today, not that he tells a lie, but that he enacts it" (De manera que, . . . el que esto haze el día de oy, podrían dezir que no dize mentira, pero que la haze).

Mexía more explicitly imitated the art of classical paradoxy—again, in rudimentary form—in a smaller work consisting of ten short pieces, variously called *Diálogos* (*Dialogues*) or *Coloquios* (*Colloquies*) (1547) (Mexía n.d.), four of which are continuations of the one that precedes them.[20] The titles that Mexía gives these short pieces are as follows: (1) "Dialogue of the Physicians" (Diálogo de los médicos) (two parts); (2) "Colloquy of the Dinner Guest" (Coloquio del convite) (three parts); (3) "Colloquy of the Sun" (Coloquio del sol); (4) "Colloquy of the Disputant" (Coloquio del porfiado) (two parts); (5) "Dialogue of the Earth" (Diálogo de la tierra); and (6) "Dialogue of Nature" (Diálogo natural). Each is preceded by a "summary" (argumento) of its content. As Jesús Gómez points out in his very thorough study (1988), the direct sources varied considerably for the genre of the Renaissance dialogue in Spain, as elsewhere in Europe.[21] Renaissance writers were familiar with the ancient models of Plato, Cicero, Lucian, and Augustine; with the medieval debate poems, many of whose characters were allegorical figures; and with the scholastic method of disputed questions. Finally, they also knew the *Colloquies* of Erasmus. Mexía's collection belongs to the category of didactic dialogues. It faintly echoes the topics and the freer form characterizing Lucian, even as it seems to borrow little more than the term "colloquy" and a minimum of subject matter from Erasmus. Unlike either Lucian or Erasmus, however, Mexía seems constitutionally incapable of irony. And only the most aggressive misreading could invest Mexía's works with a self-consciously paradoxical structure. The disputes in his *Dialogues* emulate the Platonic and Ciceronian pattern of arguing both sides of a question, *in utramque partem*—often followed by appeal to an authoritative master—as well as the common understanding of the scholastic pattern: thesis-antithesis-synthesis.

Mexía's dialogues all take place in Seville, either in the home of one of the participants, or outside a church where the speakers have heard or are about to hear Mass. Furthermore, the speakers are all males from the petty-noble, or *hidalgo*, class, bearing conventional names, who express contrary opinions on a particular subject. In most of the dialogues, one figure endowed with special

20. I have used the edition titled *Diálogos del ilustre cavallero Pero* Mexía (n.d.). All page references are to this edition.

21. Other important studies on the dialogue in Spain include Savoye 1985; Murillo 1959, 55–66; and Morón Arroyo 1973, 275–84.

authority, either a "master" ("Physicians," 7–72; "Dinner Guest," 73–154) or a "graduate" ("Disputant," 183–230), resolves the point of dispute through an appeal to reason and, especially, to biblical and classical references. In the remaining dialogues, seemingly among social and intellectual equals, one speaker is entrusted with resolving the dispute by means of a "higher" synthesis that avoids the extremes of the other speakers' conflicting opinions. The tone of the dialectical disputations is one of unexampled courtesy and amicability.

In three of Mexía's dialogues ("Sun," "Earth," and "Nature") Mexía discusses nature as *discordia concors* in order to correct and contradict common misperceptions, or the *doxa* that Mexía specifically calls "common opinion" (común opinión) found in the "community of the weak-minded" (comunidad de los simples) ("Disputant," 193). Topics about which most persons remain unenlightened include the source of thunder and lightning ("Nature"), the roundness of the earth and its being smaller than the sun and larger than the moon ("Sun"), and the proximity of elemental fire to the moon "even though it [elemental fire] remains unseen" (aunque no se ve) ("Earth," 231). Again, such unconventional "truths" about the physical universe, which Renaissance authors less frequently called by the specific name of paradoxes than the more general one of marvels, lay beyond received opinion and mere appearances. They were therefore considered paradoxical in the same sense that the heliocentric theory of Copernicus was thought a paradox.[22]

Of particular relevance here are observations made by one of Mexía's more authoritative characters, Antonio, in "Dialogue of the Earth" concerning the nature of the physical universe and sense perception. In a conversation about how fitting it is that God should keep the oceans in their place and prevent them from covering the earth as they did at the time of creation, Antonio reminds his friends of what will happen at the end of time: "[W]hen the brute animals and *composite* things come to an end and are consumed, there being no need of a place for them, [God] will again command [the waters] to encircle the earth, as he did in the beginning" ([C]uando ya los animales brutos y las cosas *mixtas* se acaben y consuman, y no siendo menester lugar para ellos, [Dios] le torne a mandar que [el agua] vuelva a cercar la tierra, como hacía en su principio) (242–43; emphasis added).

---

22. Renaissance authors more frequently used the term paradox to denote mock encomia of such apparently unworthy subjects as the flea, the gnat, the ass, or baldness, in imitation of classical authors (especially Lucian), as mentioned by Erasmus at the beginning of *Folly*, in his prefatory letter to Thomas More. And most frequently of all, the specific term paradox referred to writings aimed at social criticism or moral reform, in the tradition of Cicero's *Paradoxa Stoicorum*. See the definition of *paradoxa* in Covarrubias's *Tesoro de la lengua* (1984 [1611]), cited at the start of this chapter.

In the same dialogue, Antonio must disabuse his friend Petronio of the following misconception concerning the nature and locus of elemental fire in the cosmos. Petronio asserts that "this whole affair is a hoax, about there being fire above the air, and I am ready to believe that everything is air, even the sky, because I do not doubt the air, because I can feel it" (que es burla este negocio, de decir que sobre el aire hay fuego, y estoy por creer que todo es aire, hasta el cielo, porque del aire no dudo, porque lo siento). Antonio replies: "Concerning your two doubts, Mister Petronio, the first one arises from your wanting to believe your senses over your reason and your holding as certain only what you see with your eyes; and the second, from your having neither heard nor understood the nature of fire as an element" (De vuestras dos dudas, señor Petronio, la primera nasce de querer vos antes creer al sentido que a la razón, y no tener por cierto sino lo que veis por los ojos; y la segunda, de no haber oído ni entendido la naturaleza del elemento del fuego) (244). The willingness of Petronio, a character cut from the same cloth as Sancho Panza, to divorce his powers of reason from his powers of sense perception and imagination, together with his failure properly to assimilate (oír y entender) what the wisdom of both secular and scriptural authority has stated about the character of elemental fire, have caused him to lapse into a "grave error" (engaño muy grande) (245).

As to Petronio's confusion between earthly and elemental fire, Antonio states: "There is a great difference between one and the other, because the one we use *is not true fire*, but rather an inflamed thing that is called fire, since it is dense and mixed and composite; the other, very much to the contrary, is *most rarefied and invisible*" (Hay grande diferencia del uno al otro, porque este de que usamos *no es verdadero fuego*, sino cosa encendida y calificada de fuego, porque es espeso y mezclado y compuesto; y el otro, muy al contrario, es *rarísimo e invisible*) (245; emphasis added). Moreover, in an assertion based on tacit, seemingly inadvertent oxymorons, Antonio describes earthly fire as a material admixture of light and darkness: "The density, and one might even say the *opacity*, of this material fire, is *clearly seen* . . . in that, should one place a lighted candle beside another, it casts a *shadow* of its own flame and *light*, which it should never do unless it had opacity and density" (La espesura, y podría decir *opacidad*, deste fuego material, *clara se ve* . . . en que si cerca de una vela encendida ponéis otra, hace *sombra* de la misma llama y *lumbre* della, que no hiciera si no tuviera opacidad y espesura" ("Nature," 245; emphasis added). The reasons for elemental fire's rarefied quality derive from its being "unmixed" (sin alguna mixtura) and from its residing "closer to heaven, with less occasion to become a composite" (más cercano al cielo y en menos ocasión de poderse mezclar) ("Earth," 245).

In this dialogue, Mexía popularizes the perfectly orthodox, epistemological stance of moderate realism—not to be confused with a naive correspondence theory—in line with the philosophy of both Aquinas and Cusanus. The individual's material powers of perception must work in harmony with the spiritual powers of understanding and right reason in order for the person to avoid being deceived (*engaño*). Indeed, all knowledge begins, but must not end, in the senses. In effect, as Antonio proves to his interlocutor, Petronio, in matters of actual "truth" (of which "true fire" is a case in point), human beings are limited to knowledge *by analogy*, since truth comes to us only in the form of glimpses and hints, through "composite creatures" (cosas mixtas) that are a blend of actuality and potentiality, presence and absence, darkness and light, "density and rarity" (espesura y rareza)—all earthly metaphors for unfathomable mysteries that are found "closer to heaven" (más cercano[s] al cielo). In probing such verities, Antonio calls upon the instrument of reason to adopt a rudimentary form of the *via negativa*, describing elemental fire as "*in*visible" and "*un*mixed" (*sin* alguna mixtura), showing that human minds know more what truth *is not* than what it is. In addition, what for human beings is the "opacity" of the mystery of invisible, elemental fire results from that mystery's luminosity, lying beyond the earthly sphere that circumscribes our faculties of sense and imagination, and finally exceeding our human powers of either sensible or rational apprehension. Hence the need for reason to check sense and imagination, the most common sources of confused impressions, mixed signals and *deception* (*engaño*).

Mexía supplements these doctrines in other dialogues, which do not deal directly with paradoxical wonders of the physical universe. Because of the constant tension in man between perception (matter) and reason (spirit), and because of the consequent tendency to err, Mexía has one of his spokesmen, the "graduate Narváez," extol the dialectical method (of Plato and Cicero, for instance) as the most effective means of discovering truth, albeit in secular matters alone: "If there were no disputation or altercation, no one would ever properly know or discover *the truth about* [*natural*] *things or about the arts*" (si no hubiese porfía y altercación, nunca se sabría ni descubriría bien *la verdad de las cosas ni de las artes*). He further clarifies that " to argue and dispute are the same thing" (disputar y porfiar es una misma cosa), and that "without which [argument and disputation] there could be no *practice of either letters or the sciences*" (sin lo cual no puede haber *ejercicio de letras ni de ciencias*) ("Disputant," 194; emphasis added). Only a foolish person would fail to acknowledge the utility and necessity of dialectical disputation, "which all the philosophers and saints used and which all schools and universities in the world use today" (que todos los filósofos y santos usaron y hoy día usan todas las escuelas y universidades del mundo) ("Disputant," 194).

Nonetheless, it is important to add that Mexía puts a practical, Renaissance spin on the dialectic of the Platonic dialogue, which seems to assume the sufficiency of purely *rational* thinking. For Mexía, as for other European writers in the Renaissance, just as sense must be checked by reason, so reason must be checked by practical experience, or *usus et experientia*, a catchprase that Mexía renders literally in the vernacular as "uso y experiencia" (e.g., "Physicians," 55). Man must strive to make sense and reason (and theory and practice) work in harmony, since, *in isolation*, neither is an adequate means of discovering truth or advancing human knowledge. As noted by Ernesto Grassi and Maristella Lorch, this doctrine finds its classical expression in Leon Battista Alberti's philosophical fable *Momus* (1420) (Grassi and Lorch 1986, 79–85). Mexía popularizes the same teaching in his two dialogues devoted to the relative necessity or nonnecessity of medical experts ("Physicians," 7–72).

As explained by Mexía's "Maestro," who bears no other name, the debate in the "Dialogue of the Physicians" involves the extreme positions of the "empiricals" (empíricos) who follow "experience alone" (la experiencia sola), and the "rationalists" (racionales) who desire to know "reasons and causes" (las razones y causas) (56). It hardly needs saying that the *maestro* advocates a middle position between the extremes. He acknowledges that experience (like sense) is the source of knowledge in the arts and sciences. Indeed, it seems that this truth holds equally for the "arts" of medicine and literature, as the *maestro* argues from authorities in poetry: "Thus sing both Marcus Manilius and Virgil; the first one saying: *experience created arts through a diversity of things*; and Virgil: in order that *custom and practice might reveal diverse arts*" (y Marco Manilio y Virgilio lo cantan; el primero diciendo: *por varias cosas hizo la experiencia el arte*; y Virgilio: *para que el uso y ejercicio descubriese diversas artes*) ("Physicians," 57; emphasis added). But he also observes that "unless [experiential knowledge] takes the form of rules and art [synonymous terms], all of life would be confusion and forgetting, and Nature's tendency to disorder would leave everything in disarray" (si esta cosa [la experiencia] no se redujera a reglas y arte, todo fuera confusión y olvido, y la discordia lo confundiera todo). And he adds: "[for] experience knows how to find but not how to store" ([que] la experiencia sabe hallar, pero no guardar) ("Physicians," 58–59). In short, art, or human artifice, which includes the acquisition of knowledge through the use of symbols and discourse, perfects nature and brings order to experience.

Furthermore, as the *maestro* insists, it is hardly surprising that experts in a particular field should often disagree. For disputes among the learned contribute to the advancement of knowledge: "it is well known that [acquiring] any art may prove taxing, but continued diligence and inventiveness can overcome all such obstacles . . . , and although one may discover a variety of opinions in ancient times, one also discovers more modern findings and solutions" (sabemos que el arte es luengo, pero todo lo vence el continuo trabajo y buen ingenio . . . , y aunque haya variedades de opinión, antiguas, también hay determinaciones y res-oluciones más modernas) ("Physicians," 61). Adding to the gallery of exemplary Renaissance figures, models for *continued* emulation that no individual was expected fully to embody in his or her own life, Mexía's spokesman asserts that "the perfect physician should be an expert and a man of letters . . . , possessing together mastery of his art, knowledge of rules and principles, in addition to his knowledge from experience" (el médico perfecto ha de ser experto y letrado . . . , y ha de tener arte y preceptos y fundamentos juntamente con la experiencia) ("Physicians," 62). From the civilized *conflict* of disputation and debate (porfiar) there emerges a harmonious convergence of opposites (*coincidentia oppositorum*): in the composite creature, man, between sense and reason; in the arts and sciences between the nonexclusive contraries, theory and practice; and in our increasingly knowledgeable ignorance of both nature and human culture, which are a neces-sarily mixed and wondrous blend of discord and concord, darkness and light.

Likewise, in typically Renaissance fashion, the two-part dialogue in which Mexía examines the virtues of dialectical disputation ("Disputant," 183–230) reveals that author's concern to demonstrate the utility of *rhetoric*. To illustrate this point, Mexía has the graduate Narváez engage in a paradoxical encomium of the ass ("Disputant," 214–29), which begins thus: "With your leave, I should like to assume the part of a *rhetorician*" (Pues que me dáis licencia, yo quiero esta vez hacer del *retórico*) ("Disputant," 214; emphasis added). Another character, Ludovico, recognizes the precedent for such a declamation in "Erasmus, who praises folly" (Erasmo, que alaba la locura) ("Disputant," 214). And among the sources for this exercise cited by the graduate himself are two classical authors of Menippean satire: "Marcus Varro . . . and Apuleius . . . , [who] composed that singular book, *which we all have read,* called the *Golden Ass*" (Marco Varron . . . y Apuleyo . . . , [quien] hizo aquel singular libro, *que todos habemos leído,* llamado *Asno de oro*) ("Disputant," 219; original italics in title, other emphasis added). The content of this encomium is utterly predictable. The Graduate's beloved animal eats little, works hard, remains docile, and requires no taming (unlike the horse). The ass was the animal of preference for many prominent fig-ures in the Old Testament and bore the person of Christ in Jerusalem.

More interesting, however, Mexía's two-part dialogue called "The Disputant" demonstrates the frequent overlap between paradoxical encomia, paradoxes of nature, and Ciceronian paradoxes of moral reform. For the declamation in praise of the ass contains at its core a panegyric of the virtue of humility and a pointed criticism of the "common" tendency to judge the essence and worth of both persons and things on the basis of first impressions and mere appearances. Moreover, Mexía's dialogue on logical and rhetorical disputation also demonstrates how all these species of paradoxy characterize the Renaissance practice of social satire, which encompasses works in *different genres* and derives from Erasmus, Lucian, Varro, Apuleius, and, ultimately, Menippus. For, although they all deserve the label Menippean satire, it seems untenable to argue that Erasmus's *Praise of Folly* or Burton's *Anatomy of Melancholy* belong to the same generic classification as the *Golden Ass* or Lucian's *True History*, or, for that matter, as Rabelais's *Gargantua* and Cervantes' *Don Quixote*. As shown forth in Mexía's dialogue, what those works share, in addition to their satirical purpose, is their reliance on a *rhetorical tradition*, and a *rhetorical method*, of paradoxy.

To recapitulate, the very ingenuousness of Mexía's *Silva de varia lección* and the *Diálogos* or *Coloquios* allows one to discern the fundamental mechanism and purpose behind his and other Renaissance writers' methodical contradiction of "received opinion"—in other words, behind their use of paradoxy. That mechanism and purpose consist in provoking aporetic crises (gentle crises, in the case of Mexía), *admiratio*, and the contemplative distance that rhetoric dubs alienation, in order to force a reexamination of untested assumptions.[23] Such assumptions include commonsense perceptions untested by reason, and purely rational or theoretical assumptions untested by experience.

Conspicuously exempt in Mexía's works, not only from dialectical disputation, but also from paradoxical treatment, are matters relating to the mysteries of religious faith. Indeed, in questions of religion, Mexía's "method" involves little more than a facile appeal to scriptural and ecclesiastical authority. He shows an uncanny ability to present Christian doctrines as unambiguous, unproblematic, and paradoxically, devoid of mystery altogether. In fact, anything contrary to the most formulaic understanding of established religious opinion is seen as a pernicious form of intellectual pride and dangerously inimical to Christian orthodoxy:

> [I]n matters of faith, most heretics have been men of imagination and learning, but also self-assured and proud. Thus, we must always pray for God to grant us humility of understanding, that we may follow *the com-*

---

23. Lausberg (1975) discusses the "alienating" effect of paradox (31, 37), as well as the rhetorical effect of alienation in general (57–59, 84–90).

mon and true path, rather than *false novelties and subtleties*, as many have done in our time.

([E]n las cosas de fe comúnmente los más de los herejes que ha habido, fueron hombres ingeniosos y letrados; pero confiados y soberbios. Por lo cual, siempre debemos rogar a Dios nos dé humildad en el entendimiento, porque sigamos *la común y verdadera carrera*, y no *novedades y agudezas falsas*, como han hecho muchos en nuestros tiempos.) ("Disputant," 187; emphasis added)

For Mexía, it seems that the unexamined Christian life is the only one worth living. But I submit that his attitude concerning religion is hardly at issue with the rest of his writing. His use of paradox is largely mechanical and resolves, not in mystery, but in formulaic answers that can masquerade as understanding. His species of the *via negativa* strikes this reader as altogether inadvertent. He gives the impression of having hit upon a definitive (rather than negative) reply to the particular question of elemental fire and, more generally, to questions concerning both natural and supernatural wonders. Similarly, his *imitatio* of either classical or contemporary writings barely rises above the level of aping their most obvious features. Despite his occasional correspondence with the aging Erasmus, Mexía seems to have absorbed little of that great humanist's teachings, which Spanish officialdom had since come to view as heretical novelties.

In all likelihood, Mexía represents the decadent and conformist brand of humanism, now tailored for popular consumption, which Cervantes parodies, in II, 24, through the figure of the "cousin" (*primo*, also denoting a gullible and uncritical dolt) who is busily preparing his *Spanish Ovid* (Ovidio español) and his *Supplement to Polydore Vergil, Concerning First Inventions in Ancient Times* (Suplemento de Virgilio Polidoro, en la invención de las antigüedades). Indeed, the *Silva* is replete with the same type of curiosities and ancient firsts (invenciones) that the humanist cousin expects to popularize and market in great numbers throughout the Spanish Empire. Besides many hours of genuine, if mindless, amusement (it is hardly far-fetched to say that the Silva appeals to the same type of curiosity as *The Guinness Book of World Records* or Ripley's "Believe It or Not") Mexía's best-known works provide a diminutive caricature and, indeed, a shorthand of the paradoxical discourse that Cervantes would both parody and exploit to the full in *Don Quixote*. Religious matters in Cervantes will hardly remain exempt from dialectical or paradoxical treatment. As I shall discuss later, part and parcel of the dialogue in *Don Quixote* between sanity and madness is a continuing dialogue between such apparent contraries as credulity and skepticism, and faith and knowledge, together with such nonapparent contraries as knowledge and certainty.

An Overview of Classical Paradoxy in the Spanish Renaissance

Although classical forms of paradoxy never approached the same degree of popularity in Spain as elsewhere in Renaissance Europe, it would be mistaken to view Mexía as the lone Spanish practitioner of the art. Examples belonging to the genre of the paradoxical encomium include the purely rhetorical, humoristic poems produced in the academy of the famous conquistador Hernán Cortés (1485–1547), titled *Paradox in Praise of Large Noses* (Paradoxa en alabanza de las narices grandes) and *Syphilis and Why It Is Fitting That All Men Should Seek and Esteem It* (Las Bubas y que es razón que todos las procuren y estimen) (Buceta 1935, xxvi–xxvii). Diego Hurtado de Mendoza (1503–75) produced such short works as *In Praise of Ugliness* (En loor de la fealdad), *Elegy of the Flea* (Elegía de la pulga), *Of the Carrot* (Sobre la zanahoria) (Buceta 1935, xxviii n. 2), and *In Praise of the Cuckoldry* (En loor del cuerno) (1935, xxvii n. 5). Gutierre de Cetina (1520–57?) also found cuckoldry worthy of mock praise in *Paradox: Treating of How It Is Neither Evil nor Shameful for a Man to Be a Cuckold, but Rather That Cuckoldry Is Good, Honorable, and Beneficial* (Paradoja: trata que no solamente no es cosa mala ni vergonzosa ser un hombre cornudo, mas que los cuernos son buenos, honrosos y provechosos) (Buceta 1935, xvii).

The tradition of Ciceronian paradoxes, "*admiribilia contraque opinionem omnium*" (Cicero 1953), aiming without humor or mockery at moral reform, found their most popular Renaissance expression in Ortensio Lando's *Paradossi cioè, sententie fuori del comun parere, novellamente venute in luce* (1543). A collection of paradoxical maxims, this "first book of paradoxy in a European vernacular" (Colie 1966, 461) inspired numerous works throughout Europe, including John Donne's *Paradoxes and Problems* (Peters 1980, xvi–xxvii; Colie 1966, 4, 11, 53, 461–63). It is impossible for me to say at what moment Lando's work may have exerted an influence upon Spanish authors. In any event, the start of a minor vogue of Ciceronian paradoxy in Spain predates Lando's writings, as shown by two texts written in Latin: Pedro Ciruelo's *Paradoxae Quaestiones Decem* (Salamanca, 1538) and *Paradoxorum, seu de Erratis Dialecticorum Libri Duo* (Salamanca, 1558) by Luis de Lemos (Buceta 1935, xxv). After the appearance of Lando's collection, Father Domingo Valtanás Mexía wrote a work of Ciceronian paradoxy in the Spanish vernacular entitled *Paradoxes and Maxims*

Chosen for the Increase of One's Understanding and the Reform of Manners
(Paradoxas y sentencias escogidas para la erudición del entendimiento y reformación de las costumbres) (Seville, 1558) (Buceta 1935, xxv). The champion of
Academic Skepticism, Francisco Sánchez, composed his Ciceronian exercise
Paradoxes (Paradoxa) in Latin (Antwerp, 1582) (Buceta 1935, xxv). In a religious
vein, Juan de Covarrubias Orozco (brother of Sebastián, author of the famous
Tesoro de la lengua, whose definition of "paradox" was quoted at the beginning of
this chapter) wrote a Spanish collection under the title *Christian Paradoxes
Against the False Opinions of the World* (Paradoxas Christianas contra las falsas
opiniones del mundo) (Segovia, 1592) (Buceta 1935, xxvi).[24] And the Spanish
vogue of Ciceronian paradoxy reaches its culmination, after Cervantes' death,
with the dialogues entitled *Paradoxes of Reason* (Paradoxas racionales) (1643) by
Antonio López de Vega.[25]

Broadly speaking, it is also within this Ciceronian tradition that one may situate the paradoxy found in many of the works of Erasmus's best-known Spanish
disciples, very thoroughly studied by Marcel Bataillon (1966). This is not the
place to discuss the extent to which paradoxical discourse characterizes such writings as *The Dialogue of Mercury and Charon* (El diálogo de Mercurio y Carón) by
Alfonso de Valdés, the *Satirical Colloquies* (Coloquios satíricos) by Antonio de
Torquemada, or such anonymous works as *El Crótalon* (*The Rattlesnake*) and the
Voyage to Turkey (Viaje de Turquía), to name only a few satires of the period,
clearly inspired by the *Colloquies* of Erasmus and the writings of Lucian. I have
chosen Rojas, Guevara, and Mexía as my primary examples of paradoxical discourse in Renaissance Spain in part because it is beyond scholarly dispute that
Cervantes knew these works—his knowledge of the Spanish Erasmians is far
more dubious—and especially because the writings of these three authors show
that paradoxy was by no means limited to avowed disciples of Erasmus. I simply
wish to suggest here that the specific phenomenon of paradoxical discourse in the
Spanish Erasmians (whether in works of spirituality, literary theory, or moral and
social satire) deserves scholarly attention.

It is true that none of Erasmus's Spanish followers in the sixteenth century produced a work of such thoroughgoing paradoxy as the *Praise of Folly*. Yet, as uniquely
Spanish reformers and satirists who wrote chiefly in dialogue, the followers of

24. Most of the paradoxical works cited by Buceta (1935) remain unpublished, and were made
known to contemporary scholars thanks to Gallardo (1863–69). Also see Eisenberg 1987, 191 n. 36 for
published versions of paradoxical works belonging to Spain's Renaissance. Eisenberg's citations of "paradoxa" in the Spanish Golden Age are limited to mock encomia.

25. López de Vega's work, which is typical of the genre, consists of six "Paradoxas," only the last five of
which are written in dialogue form. I have consulted the edition prepared by Erasmo Buceta (1935, v–xiii).

Erasmus dialectically disputed and contradicted the increasing solidification of common and official opinion. In doing so, they wrote what may be studied as extended encomia of such officially dishonorable subjects as the vernacular ("vulgar") language and literature over Latin and the classics (e.g., Juan de Valdés's *Dialogue on the Spanish Language* [Diálogo de la lengua]); interior devotion over religious formalism; the wisdom of the common person over that of the theologian, the philosopher, or the "grammarian" [scholar]; the lay state as a path to sanctity over that of monastic life; the superiority of marriage—as a means of living the virtue of chastity!—over celibacy; the *nobility* of work over aristocratic idleness; and the nobility of moral virtue over lineage. All such doctrines can be examined as instances of paradoxy.

Paradox as a Trope of Thought

At the risk of my laboring the obvious, it should be clear from the discussion thus far that paradoxy need not be confined to the content, subject matter, or doctrines of a particular work. On the one hand, it is plausible to claim that Renaissance (and Baroque) paradoxy, in Spain and elsewhere, focused on artificially separable subjects: (1) man and the natural world as a *discordia concors* and *coincidentia oppositorum* (i.e., an unfolding drama of wondrous contradictions), (2) praise of things thought to be "without honor," and (3) doctrines of moral and social reform that ran counter to received opinion.[26] The first category identifies paradoxes that derive from what we may consider to be the Renaissance *Weltanschauung*, while the two remaining categories identify, in turn, the type of paradoxy that derives from an imitation of classical models. A tripartite classification such as this would provide a helpful first step toward coming to grips with the undeniable slipperiness of Renaissance paradox.

26. Helen Peters, for example, puts forth a twofold classification of Renaissance paradoxy that includes only the mock encomium and the Ciceronian paradox in her General Introduction to John Donne's *Paradoxes and Problems* (1980, xvi–xxvii). This simple division is indeed helpful, up to a point. But a mere glance at the seemingly dishonorable things being praised in her quotations from Lando's officially Ciceronian paradoxes, not to mention Donne's paradoxes, points up that classification's limited utility and the overlap between the categories of paradox. Also, as already discussed, one should add the important category of paradoxy that judges both nature and man, cosmos and microcosm, to be a *discordia concors* or a *coincidentia oppositorum*. Indeed, this category can be seen as the *understanding* of both nature and man that, deriving from the paradoxes of Christianity, lies at the root of all Renaissance paradoxy, including the mock encomium and Ciceronian paradoxes.

On the other hand, despite this tripartite classification's utility, it is necessary to acknowledge that the considerable overlap between one presumed "subject" or type of paradoxy and the others leads such classifications ultimately to conceal more than they reveal about the nature and purpose of paradoxical discourse. For paradox not only represents a rhetorical device or a trope of language, but also a trope of thought. The art of paradoxy supplies a problematic method for assessing problematic and mysterious "truths" about man, the world, the worthiness of persons and things, and the proper boundaries of human behavior and action, including that of speaking, writing, and discursive, rational thinking.

Paradoxical discourse may come to permeate the whole of an author's text, depending on the degree of that author's self-conscious artistry, and depending on the degree to which paradoxy manifests itself there less as an isolated device than as a *mode of thought*. Such thoroughgoing paradoxy arises in Classical Antiquity with Plato, and it continues in a Christianized form to characterize the works of Cusanus, Erasmus, Rojas, and Guevara—though not, of course, the works of Mexía, whose ingenuously illustrative imitation of paradoxical discourse occurs almost exclusively at the level of content. The figure or trope of paradox ranges from the most condensed form of the oxymoron to the most expanded form, sometimes called synoeciosis.

A full commitment to paradoxical discourse, or synoeciosis, such as found in Cervantes' *Don Quixote*, will tend to inform a literary work's thematics, action, characters, setting, and diction with the internal (anti)logic of *coincidentia oppositorum*, often adopting a playfully serious (*serio ludere*) mode. Thus, paradoxical discourse may lead an author to invest individual words not simply with different, but with simultaneously *contrary*, meanings that blur logical and semantic distinctions (wisdom, folly), and to adopt seemingly oxymoronic terms or neologisms ("tragicomedy," "basin-helmet" [baciyelmo]). It will pattern and contextualize the "meaning" of individual statements, or of exchanges in dialogue, so as to leave them open to contrary readings, while denying the possibility of adopting either reading in isolation. Finally, extreme forms of Renaissance paradoxy both adopt and invite a self-conscious attitude toward the reading and writing of literature. They extend the dialectical disputation between contrary opinions and images to include a collaborative rivalry between author and reader, who vie for control and ownership of the "work." For paradox at its extreme drives home the wedge further between mind (of both author and reader) and artistic text (simulacrum of life). And this artistic text, like the life it inventively imitates, reaches increasing perfection and completion by continually beckoning toward integrity while remaining, forever, unfinished (Rajan 1985; Levao 1985).

PART 2

INVENTING A TALE, INVENTING A SELF

"This Is Not a Prologue"

Paradoxy and the Prologue to Don Quixote, *Part I*

A Typology of Renaissance Paradoxy

As suggested at the beginning of the previous chapter, despite the important precedents documented there, a true epidemic of paradoxical discourse occurs later in Spain than in the rest of Europe. Yet, when it does break out, near the beginning of the seventeenth century, that epidemic is no less extreme than elsewhere. Indeed, paradoxy lies at the heart of the poetic imagination, or *ingenio*, belonging to Spain's late Renaissance and Baroque period, during which periods it would prove difficult, if not impossible, to identify a major Spanish author for whom paradox was not a governing trope.

Critics have suggested a host of classifications for different "types" of paradoxical discourse which prevailed in the Renaissance. Colie provides the most comprehensive grouping, devoting the different parts of her study to paradoxes that she identifies as "rhetorical," "psychological," "ontological," and "epistemo-logical" (1966). Yet she does not seem to intend her designations as systematic categories of paradoxical types. For example, in her superb study, "rhetorical paradox" refers to the *genre* of the paradoxical encomium as well as the artistic practice of rhypography, regardless of genre. Her designations "ontological para-dox" and "psychological paradox" derive from the subject matter being discussed in a paradoxical fashion. Last, she uses "epistemological paradox" largely in con-nection with a particular effect of paradoxical discourse: namely, that of forcing the beholder to "question the process of human thought, as well as the categories thought out (by human thought) to express human thought" (1966, 7).

Without denying the utility of Colie's designations, and without denying that one may classify the subject in more than one way, I would suggest that the tra-dition of paradoxy inherited by Renaissance and Baroque authors reveals five topical strains that bear on the general subject matter that those authors discuss or dramatize in their works. First, what one may call an *ontological* or metaphys-ical strain of paradoxy treats of transcendental questions relating to the ultimate nature of being and, therefore, to the nature of truth, beauty, goodness, the One, and God. The resort to paradoxy in such matters results from the simulta-neous necessity and inability of time-bound *discourse* to express what are thought to be eternal, nondiscursive verities. A writer adopts a discourse of paradoxy because finite categories of language and logic fail to encompass, signify, or even approach the infinite, except through negative assertions or the ultimately non-sensical method of the *via negativa*. To the degree that such discourse bears on earthly phenomena, it does so through the prism of the transcendental ques-tions. Ontological paradoxy underscores the status of earthly matters as appear-ances ("images" in the language of Cusanus), or as imperfect manifestations of ultimate being and being's intangible, "transcendental" aspects: Truth, Beauty, Goodness, and Oneness. In the West, this strain of paradoxy originates in the questions that Plato discusses in the *Parmenides* concerning being and nonbeing, likeness and unlikeness, or the one and the many. And ontological paradoxy reaches Renaissance and Baroque authors after having been Christianized by such mystical writers as Pseudo-Dionysius and Nicolaus Cusanus.

Second, a *cosmological* strain of paradoxy treats specifically of the temporal rather than eternal order. To be sure, this strain of paradoxy among Renaissance and Baroque authors is predicated upon the assumption that the temporal order represents an imperfect manifestation of the transcendent (the One, God, Truth, Being). Further, as part of its imperfection, that temporal order remains unstable and in motion, resulting in a *discordia concors*, or a perennially unfolding admix-ture of contraries (*coincidentia oppositorum*). Nonetheless, this cosmological

strain of paradoxy arises when an author devotes direct attention to earthly phenomena, and only secondary attention to the relation between the temporal order
and transcendent "reality." And yet, because of its relation to transcendent reality,
together with its status as an unfolding of nonexclusive opposites in time, the cosmos remains a continuing source of wonderment (*admiratio*). To varying degrees,
mystical authors (Plato, Psuedo-Dionysius, Cusanus, et al.) tend to downplay
the importance of the ephemeral and the mutable world, often insisting that it is
wholly or chiefly a site of deceitful shimmer and vanity. This largely Platonist
tradition reaches an extreme in the Spanish, Baroque idea of the world as a
source of "*illusion*" (*engaño*). Yet, Renaissance writers generally show a more naturalist tendency (particularly the full-blown naturalist Giordano Bruno, but also
Pico della Mirandola, or even Pero Mexía) and are more apt to treat of the cosmos as a source of wonderment in its own right. Hence, this topical strain focuses
on startling, paradoxical phenomena that arise from the jointly subsisting and
changing condition of the world (nature) and of human activity (culture)—from
the temporal order's perplexing blend of actuality and potentiality, or being and
nonbeing. Furthermore, the cosmological strain of Renaissance and Baroque
paradoxy focuses especially on the paradoxical microcosm, or the protean human
subject, who not only joins actuality and potentiality such as found in other creatures, but who also joins the contraries of matter and spirit. Thus, for Renaissance and Baroque writers alike, "man" represents the most paradoxical of all
cosmological paradoxes: an ensouled body and an embodied soul.

Third, a *psychological* strain of paradoxy deals with the simultaneous necessity
and impossibility, not simply of knowledge, but specifically of *self*-knowledge.
The thematics of psychological paradoxy arise when one ponders not "man" in
general, but one's "self" as at once an abiding and evolving subject—a blend of
being and nonbeing, actuality and potentiality, stability and instability, which
pervades the conscious experience of one's identity and all one's physical and
spiritual operations. By far the richest source of psychological paradoxy is the
experience of love, fraught as it is with complementary and conflicting desires.
Regardless of whether the object of that love is human or divine, and regardless of
whether such love is requited or unrequited, the experience of love is shown to
involve the whole self: soul (mind and will), imagination, memory, passions, and
the body. Love brings the self a continuing admixture of joy and suffering. In the
Petrarchan tradition, the loving subject is ever the same (constant in love) and
ever changing (growing in, and being transformed by, love) (Colie 1966, 72–88).
Further, for virtually all authors writing on the subject, the experience of love is
itself a paradox that entails a necessary separation and fusion of self and other. If
mutual, the experience of love forges a bond between two individuals who, in

both their actions and their being, must remain distinct in order to become increasingly one. But they must also yearn to be one in order more fully to attain their individuality or their true "selves" (Colie 1966, 97–140).

Fourth, an *axiological* strain of paradoxy governs the paradoxical encomia and Ciceronian paradoxes, which often overlap in Renaissance and Baroque writings. Aimed at challenging popular "values" regarding the persons, natural objects, artifacts, physical traits, or actions that received opinion has deemed exalted or base, mock encomia and Ciceronian paradoxes (Erasmus's *Praise of Folly*, the *Paradossi* of Ortensio Lando, and Mexía's Christian imitation of Lucian and Apuleius in his praise of the ass) understandably represent the preferred genres and thematics of Renaissance and Baroque paradoxists. This preference seems especially understandable because of the emphasis among such writers on practical rather than speculative thought, as well as their attendant stress on ethics and rhetorical persuasion rather than metaphysics or dialectic. What is more, the paradoxical encomium lends itself, in particular, to parody and the serioludic mode, which Renaissance paradoxists found more persuasive than heavy-handed preaching.

Fifth, a *logical* strain of paradoxy deals directly with the categories of thought and language (*logoi*) themselves. And it does so by means of existing categories in thought and language. Hence one discerns this topical strain of logical paradoxy when the necessarily discursive exercises of human language and thought provide the principal subject matter of a work that explicitly shows how categories of language and thought become ensnared in the contradictory operation of self (identity)-reference (alterity) (Colie 1966, 355–95). Logical paradoxy therefore encompasses the various types of *insolubilia* and *sophismata* (e.g., paradoxes of rationality and cooperation, as well as Zeno's paradoxes), all of which represent variations on the Paradox of the Liar. Indeed, the logical strain of paradoxy deals directly in antinomy and serves to point up the ultimately tautological and self-referential quality of human thought and language.

It is important to reiterate that in Renaissance and Baroque writings, these five topical strains of paradoxy seldom occur in isolation. Indeed, most paradoxical works reveal two or more topical strains at once, although a particular author or work may emphasize one strain over the others. For instance, if Cusanus's *De docta ignorantia* devotes no attention to psychological paradoxes as such, his work explicitly combines the strains of ontological and cosmological paradoxy. Cusanus's work centers on eternal verities concerning the Godhead as these relate to eternal and historical verities concerning the incarnation of Christ: perfect God and perfect man. Yet from the title onward, Cusanus's work also constitutes a paradoxical encomium of human "ignorance," praised and "valued" as the most exalted form of "knowledge." Also from the title onward, the work deals in logical paradox, repeatedly stressing the inability of finite thought and language to encompass infinite Truth, "The Absolute Maximum," even insofar as that Truth is reflected in earthly phenomena. Furthermore, regarding psychological paradoxy, it would require but a short step (never explicitly taken in the work) for Cusanus to move from his reflections on ontology, cosmology, axiology, and logic toward self-conscious contemplation of his experience as a mystic, or as an author who knows that he succeeds and fails to signify the ineffable by means of the written word.

Thus, as even the work of a pre-Renaissance author such as Cusanus makes plain, each topical strain of paradoxy implies the others. If one begins, say, by reflecting on the "truth" about "beings" in the cosmos, one will likely sense the need to reflect on their relative worth or, more generally, on the very nature of Goodness, Beauty, and Truth. This may lead to reflections on the experience of one's own pursuit of Truth as manifest in other beings and the self, or more radically, on the categories of thought and language that govern such reflections. More important, paradox arises from human discourse itself, or from the twofold activity of rational thought and language. This relation is implied here by attaching the suffix -*logical* (from the Greek *logos*, signifying "word" and "reason" alike) to the name of each topical strain. Indeed, all paradoxes first appear as logical paradoxes, or as antinomies and contradictions *in terms*.[1] Moreover, they follow from the necessarily contradictory operation of attempting to match Being or Truth with the accepted categories of rational, propositional discourse. Or, perhaps more accurately, paradoxes follow from the attempt to impose existing categories of thought, language, or rational discourse on Being and Truth.

In a practical fashion, paradoxy leads one to acknowledge that even to approach the truth about Being, beings, actions, the cosmos, or the self, one must resort to a rhetoric of negatives, nonsense, and semantic contradiction. Put another way, paradoxy seeks to remedy the deficiencies of propositional discourse, which deals in truth-claims or univocal assertions, while bracketing or ignoring the limitations inseparable from the time-bound (discursive) quality of thought and language. Yet, as Colie points out, rather than denying Truth, paradoxy strives to illustrate "perhaps, really, only one simple truth, that Truth is One" (1966, 519). Moreover, paradoxy strives to illustrate that all transcendent aspects of Being—Truth, Beauty, or Goodness—are One. It illustrates, too, that Being, Truth, Beauty, Goodness, and Oneness are convertible terms. As a

---

1. It is no longer common to maintain the distinction between "logical" and "semantic" paradoxes. As Flew observes: "The work of Tarski and others in attempting to analyse or avoid these [semantic] paradoxes has resulted in making the semantic notions involved extremely precise logically, and has blurred the original distinction between the semantic and logical paradoxes" (1979, 323).

discursive strategy, however, paradox works against the common assumption that multiple "truths" (or multiple instances of beauty, goodness, and so forth) can exist in isolation from one another or from what Cusanus might call their "Maximum" in Being and Truth. Paradox questions whether any *proposition* can be fully expressive of Truth; or whether one can achieve a perfect fit between actuality and discourse, or being and telling.

Although paradox represents a shared feature among Spanish writers of the late Renaissance and Baroque periods, it is rare that a single author will exploit all of paradox's topical strains, or that an author will explicitly connect his or her preferred forms of paradox with the others. What is more, despite its being a shared feature, paradox occurs in poetic projects informed by vastly different ideologies.

On the strength of its paradox, *Don Quixote* demonstrates once again why Cervantes deserves a unique place among his contemporaries. In the first place, he exploits all of paradox's topical strains in virtually simultaneous fashion. In the second place, he alone among writers of that period exploits the connections obtaining between the various strains of paradox, allowing those strains to interpenetrate. But he does not favor one form of paradox over another, nor does he unduly favor one side of an apparent contradiction in an effort to put forth a definitive "answer," in the form of a proposition.

Specifically, Cervantes joins the various strains of paradox through his protagonist, the latter's adventures, and their narration. Don Quixote is the source of axiological paradox, in that he progressively develops as a perplexing embodiment of the paradoxical encomium and Ciceronian paradoxes. He represents a persistent challenge, as a unique refashioning of the "sane madman" (*cuerdo loco*), to what received opinion assumes to be either wisdom or folly in both intellectual and ethical matters. The protagonist likewise represents both an instance and a seriocomic parody of psychological paradox. He achieves this, first, in his unswerving yet developing love for Dulcinea, a simultaneously real and imaginary damsel, both "pure" and "impure" in her essence, conduct, and lineage. Second, he represents a psychological paradox in reference to his developing identity, through his simultaneously heroic and lunatic struggle to become and remain a knight-errant.

As a work of narrative fiction—rather than, say, a painting, an eclogue, or a work of natural philosophy—*Don Quixote* is not directly concerned, in its use of cosmological paradox, with paradoxes of the physical universe. Nonetheless, the narrative of the protagonist and his exploits do serve to point up the paradoxes and contradictions of "life," or of human action and interaction in society. These paradoxes follow, implicitly, from conceiving the protagonist, and every "person" or character within the heterocosm, as an ensouled body or an embodied soul who remains caught in a unique dialectic between the empirical and symbolic worlds. Last, the protagonist, his adventures, their narration, and their reading represent explicit instances of ontological and logical paradox. For the text leads its characters and readers alike to confront the nature of reality and truth, and to test the categories of thought and language through which they, or we, attempt this confrontation.

A Prefatory Epilogue

As I shall argue in the rest of this study, Cervantes' *Don Quixote* represents a synthesis and culmination of paradoxical rhetoric in Spain's Renaissance. And although that work also portends the epidemic of paradoxy that characterizes literature of the Spanish Baroque, none of Spain's later writers will display a greater commitment than Cervantes to fully paradoxical thinking, or to a fully paradoxical vision of "art" and "life." This vision is nowhere more evident, I believe, than in the Prologue to Part I (1605), where Cervantes examines the interplay and overlap between historical and poetic discourse.

Though studied less frequently than other sections of *Don Quixote*, the Prologue of 1605 has suffered no lack of critical attention.[2] Yet, among the studies dealing with these prefatory pages, few have engaged in a sustained analysis of the text itself. Hitherto, most critics have been concerned to draw from those pages the general direction of Cervantes' literary project,[3] to ascertain a definitive (if ironic) statement of authorial purpose concerning his most acclaimed work, or to comment, generally, on Cervantes' mastery of the prefatory genre.[4]

In his essay about both prologues of *Don Quixote*, Américo Castro was surely right to observe:

2. Important studies on Cervantes' prologues include Castro 1967, 262–301; Rivers 1974, 167–71; 1960, 214–21; Socrate 1974; Porqueras Mayo 1981, 29–38; Avalle-Arce 1976, 13–35, 36–59; Canavaggio 1977, 35–44; Allen 1969–79, 2:242–50; Parr 1984; Williamson 1984, 82–90; Weiger 1988, 15–45; Close 1993, 31–63; Martín 1993, 77–87; Saldívar 1980, 252–54; and Fajardo 1994. Also see Porqueras Mayo's studies on the art of the prologue in Renaissance and Baroque Spain (1957, 1968). Little work has been done on the theory of prefacing. An important exception to this traditional silence on the subject is the essay of Jacques Derrida, "Outwork," in *Dissemination* (1981, 3–59). Genette (1993) provides an interesting discussion of paratextual markers (79–81).

3. The most salient examples in this regard are Castro (1967); Socrate (1974); and Avalle-Arce (1976, 13–35, 36–59).

4. This is the chief focus of Porqueras Mayo's essay: "En torno a los prólogos de Cervantes" (1981).

More properly, they are epilogues, written after the work's conclusion; and not simply because prologues are customarily written *a posteriori,* but also because, in this case, their meaning comes to light only for the reader who possesses considerable knowledge of the work.

(En realidad se trata de epílogos, redactados después de conclusa la obra; y no precisamente porque los prólogos suelan escribirse "a posteriori," sino porque en este caso su sentido no se revela sino a quien posea noticia muy cabal del libro.) ([1957] 1967, 262)

My examination of the Prologue of 1605 in this chapter likewise follows from the conviction that it is inseparable from the rest of Cervantes' narrative. Indeed, I will argue in this chapter that although it was written some ten years before the publication of Part II, Cervantes' Prologue of 1605 constitutes a summation of his entire narrative's purpose, design, and rhetorical method. It functions, in Castro's phrase, as an a priori epilogue. In particular, the Prologue to Part I encapsulates literary issues that Cervantes both dramatizes and thematizes throughout the rest of the text, within the frame of his tale about the putative "history" of Don Quixote and Sancho.[5]

Nonetheless, I am also concerned to show here how the Prologue of 1605 is not only a fitting preface, but also an integral part of Cervantes' *fiction.* Indeed, that Prologue differs from conventional prologues, including even the Prologue to *Don Quixote,* Part II, in that it does not set forth an extrafictional, prefatory statement that the author addresses to his potential readership, but rather a wholly fictional work. As such, it remains inextricably linked to that aspect of Cervantes' fictional tale that concerns not so much the exploits of the knight and his squire, but the composition and compilation of their putative "history."

From the standpoint of content, the bulk of Cervantes' first Prologue to *Don Quixote* is devoted to a dramatization of specifically *aesthetic* issues, which today would travel under the rubric of literary theory. Yet it bears remembering that, no less *literary* in its subject matter, Cervantes' Prologue of 1615 encompasses such real-world concerns as a rival author, the business of publishing, and the commercial consumption of his work, all of which he incorporates into the fiction of Part II. Furthermore, in both prologues, but more conspicuously in the Prologue to Part I, Cervantes deploys the same rhetoric of thoroughgoing paradox in his handling of aesthetic and literary issues as he does in the principal narrative.

5. Other critical studies whose authors view the Prologue of 1605 as a key to the entire work are Socrate 1974; Saldívar 1980, 252–54; and Fajardo 1994.

As dramatized in the Prologue of 1605, the paradoxes that I shall analyze fall into two general, thematic categories. First, in what I take to be his fictional Prologue, Cervantes deploys a rhetoric of paradoxy to dramatize the apparent contradictions that follow from accepting the conventional Aristotelian and Ciceronian definitions of "art" as both an imitation of "nature" and an imitation of "models." Second, Cervantes' fictional Prologue deals with paradoxes related to the obligation of every author, and every writer of prologues, to establish the proper rhetorical posture with respect to his readership. In particular, Cervantes dramatizes how rhetorical convention demands, on the one hand, that an author set forth his credentials as a competent writer (*ethos*), whose work deserves the attention of his audience. On the other hand, that author is no less obliged by convention to elicit the proper mood (*pathos*) from his readers, which means that he must somehow combine proof of his own worth as a writer with proof of his modesty.

It bears stressing, however, that Cervantes' Prologue of 1605 is not an abstract discussion, but a fictional dramatization, of the foregoing aesthetic issues. As a dramatization, that Prologue broaches such *general* questions of poetics and rhetoric in circumstances involving a *particular* character, whose statements are directly linked to the composition of both the specific "Prologue" and "book" that we have before us. Further, as theoretical concerns, those same issues regarding poetics and rhetoric are shown to constitute one fictional author's (i.e., one character's) practical dilemma. Indeed, it is not only the theory, but also the practice, of art and rhetoric that are shown to generate their own series of paradoxes.

In addition, the Prologue of 1605 is emblematic of how the different topical strains of paradoxy interpenetrate and imply one another throughout the rest of *Don Quixote*. Let it suffice, for now, to note that interpenetration in general terms. Most explicitly, the Prologue cultivates a cosmological strain of paradoxy by dramatizing paradoxes about the nature (or definition) of "art," and about the mutual relation between "art " and "life" as nonexclusive opposites. It is in dramatizing such paradoxes of art and life that the Prologue also dramatizes logical paradoxes involving the apparently contrary discourses of "literature" and "history," employed in conveying what turn out to be ontological paradoxes regarding the nature and particular manifestations of Truth and Beauty. Equally an example of axiological paradox, the Prologue sets forth a *parody* (a playful, imitative counterstatement) of both the theory and practice of rhetoricoliterary convention—a convention that includes both the theory and practice of writing histories, fictions, and prologues. Last, the Prologue contains a fully self-referential form of psychological paradox, dramatizing a particular character's self-conscious reflections about the dilemmas he faces as the purported "author" of both the "Prologue" and

the "book" we are reading. Hence, the Prologue also constitutes a fictional analogue of Cervantes' own dilemmas as the actual (historical) author of the fictional
Prologue and the subsequent narrative, both of which form part of the actual
book, *Don Quixote*.

The Prologue of 1605 presents a threefold structure. Its first section includes a
monologue addressed to an implied reader ("leisurely/idle reader" [desocupado
lector]) (*DQ* I: *Prologue*, 50). In the opening paragraph, the narrator of the
Prologue briefly explains the travails he underwent in "giving birth" to his
beloved, if ungainly, "history" about a strange protagonist, thus seeming to apol-
ogize to his readers for the work's flawed artistry. In the second paragraph of that
monologue (also belonging to the Prologue's first section), the narrator tells us
how, assailed by a host of fears and doubts, he has hitherto found it all but
impossible to compose the very Prologue we are now reading. He closes that
paragraph by reporting the timely arrival of an anonymous friend, who receives
detailed reasons in the subsequent paragraph for the narrator's reluctance to
publish the story he has written about Don Quixote.

The second section (*DQ* I: 52–58), which constitutes the bulk of the Prologue, takes the form of a dialogue between the narrator and his friend. That
section is chiefly devoted to that friend's advice—largely a *monologue*—about
how to solve the spurious problems which narrator has seemingly created for
himself. The friend also provides the narrator with unsolicited advice about how
to make the history conform to authorial purpose and design, invest it with
proper aesthetic form, and attract a wide readership.

In the third section, which consists of only the final two paragraphs (*DQ* I:
Prologue, 58), the narrator again addresses his readers in the form of a monologue. Therein, he relates his awestruck acceptance of his friend's learned counsels. And he goes on to inform us that by transcribing his friend's statements,
presumably from memory, he has come to "compose" the Prologue we have
before us and, so, to remove the obstacles that might have prevented his publishing the subsequent "history."

A Fictional Prologue and a Fictional "Cervantes"

Before one can justly assess either the content or the form of the Prologue of
1605, it seems necessary to settle the question, Who is speaking? At first, the
question *seems* easy enough to answer: Miguel de Cervantes, in his capacity as

author of *Don Quixote*. Indeed, in reference to the Prologue, the answer strikes one as so obvious that the question seems hardly worth asking. Thus, it is hardly surprising that critics have generally identified the narrative voice in the Prologue with that of the author, Miguel de Cervantes. Aptly summarizing a view that has held sway among virtually all Cervantes' readers, Howard Mancing writes: "No one, to my knowledge, doubts that the *yo* of the prologue who relates himself to the character and text by claiming to be not the 'padre' ('father,' that is, the original author) but the 'padrastro' ('stepfather,' that is, the editor), and who tells the story of being visited by a friend while pondering the problem of writing a prologue for his book is anyone other than the person referred to on the title page where it says 'compuesto por . . . Miguel de Cervantes Saavedra'" (1982, 192–93).

To be sure, it runs contrary to convention, and to readers' expectations, that a prologue should be written as a fiction, and narrated by a fictional narrator. Furthermore, if an author intends his prologue to be taken as a fiction, we would expect some such indication at the start of the work—one that would lead us to infer that our imagination is being transported to an imaginary, fictional realm. Instead, the Prologue of 1605 begins with the voice of an implicit "I" (yo), which one would naturally assume, in the context of a prologue, is that of the author, addressing a "you" (tú), whom one would expect is the potential reader, in reference to what seems to be the book we now have in our possession:

> Idle/leisured reader: without my swearing an oath, *you* may believe me that *I* should wish that *this book*, as the child of my intellect, might have been the most beautiful, the most graceful and the wittiest book that one could imagine.

> (*Desocupado lector:* sin juramento *me podrás* [tú] creer que [yo] *quisiera* que *este libro*, como hijo del entendimiento, fuera el más hermoso, el más gallardo y más discreto que pudiera imaginarse.) (*DQ* I: *Prologue*, 50; emphasis added)

In fact, we receive no specific reason to doubt that the Prologue we are reading represents a statement issued to the reader in the voice of the historical author until we reach what seems a casual remark, at the start of the Prologue's second section. That pivotal remark, which I believe effectively discloses the narrator's fictional status, is found among the first words addressed to the narrator's "witty and learned friend" (amigo gracioso y bien entendido) (*DQ* I: *Prologue*, 52), and concerns the reasons for his (the narrator's) unwillingness to publish his "book":

And I have decided that the gentleman, Don Quixote, will remain entombed in the archives of La Mancha until heaven should provide someone who is able to adorn him with the many things he now lacks.

(Y yo determino que el señor don Quijote se quede sepultado en sus archivos en la Mancha, hasta que el cielo depare quien le adorne de tantas cosas como le faltan.) (*DQ* I: *Prologue*, 53)

Indeed, only at this point, from his reference to the "archives of La Mancha" (archivos en la Mancha), does it seem clear that the narrative voice who earlier claims to have written "this preface that you are now reading" (esta prefación que vas leyendo) (*DQ* I: *Prologue*, 51) is here claiming to have written a historical rather than fictional narrative about Don Quixote—a "historical" narrative that he mentioned in the Prologue's first sentence as "this book" (este libro) (*DQ* I: *Prologue*, 50), and for which "this preface" is clearly the prologue.[6]

As indicated in the above passage by Mancing, the narrator's clear, if tacit, claim to be a historian is complementary to his earlier assertion about his only *seeming* to be the "father" of Don Quixote. In any case, whatever his quasi-familial ties with the protagonist, or with the actual book we have in our hands, the narrator's tacit claim to be a historian rather than an author of fiction shows that he shares a kinship with the protagonist of another sort: both are fictional characters, created by the same author. For, in claiming to have written a history, the narrator clearly considers Don Quixote a historical (actual) person rather than a fictional character. For the narrator, Don Quixote is an empirical rather than imaginary referent. Moreover, since both the narrator and the protagonist belong to the same ontological plane and to the same (fictional) heterocosm, the "I," the "you," and the "book" of the opening sentence are necessarily fictions—

6. To my knowledge, John Weiger is only other critic to claim that the narrator in the Prologue of 1605 is a fictional character (1988, 22–45). Without linking his argument to a particular statement in the Prologue, Weiger also contends that the narrator presents himself as a historian rather than a writer of fiction. Unfortunately, Weiger grounds that argument on the claim that the narrator (whom Weiger calls the "prologuist") views Don Quixote as a knight, whereas the author, Cervantes, views him as an hidalgo. Thus (according to Weiger) the author's choosing to call his protagonist "the ingenious *hidalgo*" rather than the "ingenious *knight*" on the title page to Part I. Yet, surely, the fictional status of the narrator has nothing to do with his designating the protagonist as either an *hidalgo* or a knight, but with that narrator's referring, or his being made to refer, to the protagonist as a historical person rather than a fictional character. And it is relevant to note, first, that the original title page to Part II reads: "The Ingenious *Knight* Don Quixote of La Mancha" (El ingenioso *caballero* don Quijote de la Mancha) (emphasis added). Next, it is only in his capacity as a self-styled "knight," and not as a rural *hidalgo* who calls himself Alonso Quixano the Good on his deathbed (II, 74), that the protagonist bears the name "Don Quixote," such as found on *both* title pages.

also imaginary referents—which therefore cannot correspond to the author, the reader or the actual book written by the actual author, Miguel de Cervantes.

Furthermore, in light of the narrator's statement about the "archives of La Mancha," it would seem that the fictional status of both the narrator and his "Prologue" finds further confirmation in other parts of the text. If the narrator were indeed the author of what we know to be the fictional work we have before us, it is certainly odd that he should deny having "fathered" (i.e., invented through an act of writing) the protagonist of that fiction: "Yet I, though seeming to be the father, am the stepfather of Don Quixote" (Pero yo, que, aunque parezco padre, soy padrastro de don Quijote [i.e., the character]) (*DQ* I: *Prologue*, 50). Further, the timely arrival of the "witty and learned friend," whose comments perfectly suit the narrator's purposes, strikes me as transparently implausible. In addition, from even a cursory reading of the rest of the Prologue, it is plain that much of the friend's "advice" borders on the farcical. Indeed, the friend's comments also seem perfectly suited to the satirical purposes, not of the fictional narrator (the "historian"), but of the author, who is responsible for the fiction.

Moreover, the language of the "dialogue" between the narrator and the friend is bookish in the extreme, a form of written discourse rather than oral speech, and seems less than credible as a verbal exchange between friends. In paradoxical terms, their "conversation" is made to "sound" like pure print—a paradox involving the *written* version of what purports to be *oral* speech, which is more plausibly an *imitation* of *written* discourse. It also defies credibility that the narrator should so vividly remember his friend's words (occupying five full pages of the text) that he would be able to transcribe them verbatim. Indeed, what the friend is represented as "saying" has all the earmarks of an invention rather than a transcription. When combined with the narrator's pivotal remark about the archives of La Mancha, these added textual clues reinforce the conviction that the narrative voice, and the "world" in which that voice may be said to "speak," are not those of the historical author, Miguel de Cervantes Saavedra.[7] It is therefore only in a qualified sense that one can speak of this prefatory fiction as the author's "Prologue."

The entire prefatory utterance is thus the author's act of pretense, his fictional invention, which *simulates* an author in the act of addressing his readers, by means of a prologue, in order to tell them about the very Prologue and book they are now reading. Likewise, contrary to literary convention, and contrary to what we have been led to believe until this relatively late moment in the Prologue, the

---

7. It would seem untenable to object that, while "truly" writing the words about the story of Don Quixote remaining in the "archives of La Mancha" in his own "voice," the author, Cervantes, is only "pretending" to be a historian. That very act of pretense on the part of the author renders those words a fictional utterance, spoken by a fictional, imaginary voice.

presumed "Prologue," including the *story* of its "composition" by the narrator, must also be a work of fiction. Hence, the narrator's parenthetical remark not only obliges us to recast everything we have read up to that point as a fictional utterance, but also to realize that we have thus far been duped into thinking that the Prologue is not a fictional simulation, but an extrafictional utterance that the actual author addresses to his readers about the *actual* Prologue and book they are reading.

Now, although I have no intention of denying that both the narrator and the Prologue represent Cervantes' fictional creations, I believe that we would miss an engaging subtlety of the Prologue if we were to remain satisfied with identifying the narrator as a fictional character, whose voice and utterances must be kept *separate from* those of the author. Indeed, keeping the utterances of the author separate from those of the narrator proves to be a problematic task.

In speaking to his friend, the narrator makes two seemingly autobiographical references: (1) that he has been "idling for so many years in obscurity" (tantos años como ha que duermo en el silencio), and (2) that he now "carries all my [many] years on my back" (todos mis años a cuestas) (*DQ* I: *Prologue*, 52). These statements recall historical facts about the empirical author's life, which are as accessible to us as they were to Cervantes' contemporaries. Part I of *Don Quixote* was published in 1605. By that time, Cervantes was fifty-seven years old and had published nothing since *La Galatea* (1585). Thus, the narrator's self-referential remarks clearly echo, or parallel, historical facts concerning the life of Cervantes as *author*. What is more, even if they were unaware of such historical facts, it is extremely likely that Cervantes' contemporaries would take the narrator's remarks as *referring to* the actual Cervantes in his capacity as author of this text. Indeed, it is important to bear in mind that before we receive sufficient textual clues to identify the narrator as a fictional character—in other words, before his implicit claim to be a historian—we are faced with his deictic claims to be the "author" of both the prefatory remarks we are now reading and of *this* book. It is hardly a negligible fact that we read these seemingly autobiographical remarks and gestures of self-reference, uttered through the narrator's voice, in the conventionally nonfictional (and extrafictional) venue of a prologue. Thus, all these messages, conveyed by means of text and context, seem aimed at leading the reader to mistake the fictional narrator's voice for that of the actual author.

Yet another "historical" parallel between the narrator and the historical author is found, not in the Prologue, but on the title page of the book itself. On that page, one reads that *The Ingenious Hidalgo Don Quixote of La Mancha* (*El ingenioso hidalgo don Quixote de la Mancha*), published by Juan de la Cuesta, is "*composed by*" (*compuesto por*) Miguel de Cervantes Saavedra (emphasis added).

If anything, the title page of a book is traditionally thought to be even "more" nonfictional, extrafictional, and historical than its Prologue. Indeed, one of the chief purposes of a title page is to denote the existence of the text as a historical artifact. It will be remembered, however, that the narrator specifically claims to have *composed* the history we now have in our hands in the second paragraph of the Prologue (*DQ* I: 51): "it cost me no mean effort *to compose it* [i.e., the history]" (me costó algún trabajo *componerla*). That remark, then, is consistent with the "information" we read on the title page. Moreover, as Mauricio Molho observes, besides designating Cervantes as the "author" of the fiction, in conventional terms, the ambiguous verb form "compuesto" (composed) *literally* designates him as the book's "componedor" (composer/compositor/compiler) (Molho 1989, 275). In other words, if the term *compuesto* may be understood in an unproblematic sense, implying that the fictional work is "written by" a particular author, it may also be taken to mean "pieced together" or "compiled," in the manner of a *historical* work, which draws on various sources (Molho 1989, 275).

In case one is tempted to dismiss this coincidence as an excessive subtlety, I would suggest, in agreement with Molho, that the ambiguity of the word *composed* on the title page of Part I is all the more conspicuous in light of a clarification that, doubtless prompted by the publication of Avellaneda's "spurious" sequel, appears on the title page of Cervantes' *Second Part of the Ingenious Knight, Don Quixote of La Mancha* (*Segunda parte del ingenioso caballero don Quixote de la Mancha*), also published by Juan de la Cuesta. On that page, the book is proclaimed simply to be "by" (por [*not* "compuesto por"]) Miguel de Cervantes Saavedra, "*author* of *his own* First Part" ("*autor* de *su* primera parte") (Molho 1989, 274; emphasis added). In other words, on the title page of Part II, as in the Prologue of 1615, Cervantes seems very much at pains to assert his rights as the *author* of his *fictional* work. It is significant that he should do so by making the language of his second title page less ambiguous than that of his first.

Moreover, in the Prologue to Part II, Cervantes speaks in his own authorial voice, deftly making his rival, the pseudonymous Alonso Fernández de Avellaneda, an object of ridicule. There, too, Cervantes refers to both parts of *Don Quixote* as artistic creations: "[T]his second Part of *Don Quixote* is cut by the same maker and from the same cloth as the first" ([E]sta segunda parte de *Don Quijote* es cortada del mismo artífice y del mismo paño que la primera). What is more, he closes the Prologue of 1615 with a promise of his forthcoming literary productions: "I nearly forgot to tell you that you should expect the *Persiles* which I am now finishing, and the second part of *Galatea*." (Olvídaseme de decirte que esperes el *Persiles*, que voy acabando, y la segunda parte de *Galatea*) (*DQ* II: Prologue, 37). Needless to say, the "I" of this voice does not claim to be a "stepfather" rather than a "father" to Don Quixote, to be a historian, to have written a historical work, or to have drawn any of his material from such sources as "archives in La Mancha." Hence, both the title page and the Prologue of 1615, unlike those of 1605, are offered as purely extrafictional utterances, written in the voice of the actual author.

From the title page of Part I onward, then, Cervantes engages the reader in a subtle, semantic puzzle concerning the relation between history and poetry (or fiction). Or, more specifically, he involves the reader in a paradox concerning the relation between the *shared language* of historical and poetic discourse, or empirical and imaginary reference. Thanks to a parenthetical remark about the archives of La Mancha, it seems untenable for the reader to identify the narrator as "author" of the *fiction*. Yet it also seems untenable, on the basis of the *linguistic* evidence alone—that is, on the basis of what we are "told" in the Prologue and on the title page—simply to dismiss the narrator's deictic claim to be the author of both the "Prologue" and the "book" we are *now* reading.

In a sense, the *language* of those pages does belong to the narrator, forming part of his (imaginary) utterance. For that language is written in his "voice," or his fictional "I," and belongs to his fictional world. Within that fictional world, the "actions" of the narrator consist of writing a "Prologue" and a "book," whose language is indeed that of the text we have before us. We read that language as his (the narrator's) by transporting our imaginations, as actual readers, to the heterocosm that that narrator inhabits, and by adopting the role of *his readers*. We form part of his (imaginary) linguistic present. Through his deixis, the narrator seems to reciprocate our efforts, meeting us, as it were, on the *linguistic frontier* between fictional and historical existence, between an imaginary and empirical here and now. Not only does the implied "you" of the Prologue come close to making each of us sense that we are the character's narratee, or implied, fictional reader. The narrator's (imaginary) prefatory utterance also reinforces the illusion that he is referring to the "here" and "now" of our present experience as readers of the text we have before us, through his reference to both "this book" and "the preface you are now reading."

Furthermore, it is by no means incidental to Cervantes' game involving the shared language of historical and poetic discourse that we infer the narrator's fictional status, and the *pretense* of the Prologue, from that character's tacit claim to be the *actual* author of a "*history*" titled *The Ingenious Hidalgo Don Quixote of La Mancha* (*El ingenioso hidalgo don Quijote de la Mancha*). That feigned "history" does not parallel just any work of fiction, which belongs to our extrafictional (historical) world, but the one we are *now* reading. What is more, the reader is all but compelled to identify that narrator and his autobiographical references with the *name* Miguel de Cervantes Saavedra, as it appears on the book's title page after the words "composed by" (compuesto por).

At first glance, then, it seems that the author's interrelated fictions (title page, Prologue, and subsequent narrative) constitute the same "text" and bear the same title and the same chapter headings—and thus even contain the same legitimating elements of publishing permit (*aprobación*), price (*tasa*), and "corrector's statement" (*fe de erratas*)—as the homonymous narrator's (imaginary) "history." For, as deployed in the book's front matter, signifiers, and media (i.e., language and context) that are conventionally used to denote and individualize empirical realities—the author's name, the book's title, as well as printed documentation of that book's legal approval and its date and place of publication—afford us no help in distinguishing the author from his character. Of themselves, this language and context provide no help in our efforts to distinguish a fictional from a historical work. And more generally, it is neither the language nor the context that will aid us in discriminating (historical) fact from (poetic) fiction.

More specifically, within the linguistic *terms* of the author's semantic game, we are unable to *name* or to cite either the historical author or the historical book without thereby *naming* and citing their fictional counterparts. In each case— the actual title page, Prologue, author, book—the fictional analogue not only shares the same title or name, but is also *said to have* the same identifying traits and a parallel "history." Indeed, at the heart of the author's game in these prefatory pages is his ability to create fictional referents analogous to both his book and himself—purely fictional referents, that is, that are identified by the same signifiers and occupy the same signifying space as historical referents that are the presumed "originals."

When we say or write the names "Miguel de Cervantes," "Prologue," or "book," for example, we may be denoting either actual or imaginary referents, or both sets of referents at once. The empirical author, Prologue, and book have fictional analogues to which we may refer, and to which we most accurately refer, by using the same designations. Further, should we *cite* any segment *from* the title page, we may be citing the factually oriented utterance by the actual author and publisher, the fictional utterance of the narrator and *his* imaginary publisher, or both "utterances" at once. When we cite any passage from the "Prologue" or the "book," we are citing the imaginary utterance (including the imaginary transcriptions of other characters' words) of a *character* whose name, we may infer from *his* title page, is "Miguel de Cervantes": the imaginary author of an imaginary book titled *The Ingenious Hidalgo Don Quixote of La Mancha*. Last, when we *cite* the title page, the "Prologue" or the "book," we may be referring to the *text and context* of an actual author's poetic utterance, to the imaginary text and context of a character's pseudohistorical utterance, or, again, to both at once. Briefly stated, in each of these instances, the same denotative language operates simultaneously at two levels of reference: one actual (or historical); the other imaginary (or fictional).

One consequence of the author's semantic game of double reference is that the mutual interplay between the language of the title page and that of the Prologue allows the *fictional* heterocosm of the narrator's "history" simultaneously to appropriate, undermine, and reassert the historical factuality of the book, through the linguistic equivalent of a trompe l'oeil. For, as an object that depends on its language for its empirical existence, the book is made, through the language of its title page and Prologue, alternately to *proclaim itself* as historical reality and *mock itself* as fictional illusion.

It would be difficult to find a more apposite dramatization of how—thanks to the *artifice* of language, and its ability to create impressions, images, or illusions in the mind—the reach of poetry (or fiction) is made *to seem* equal to that of historical experience. To be sure, as dramatized in the front matter of *Don Quixote,* whatever an actual person can be said to do (or think or speak or write) in the actual world, a fictional voice or character *can be said* to do likewise in his or her fictional heterocosm. In particular, the narrator's "book" seems to operate in the reader's imagination as a parodic *mirror* with respect to the actual book (and the actual world) of which it forms part.

Through the artifice of language, the "frame" of the author's fiction (*Don Quixote*) is made to seem not identical to, but certainly coextensive with, the temporal and spatial boundaries of historical reality. For any historical act or event that relates to the actual book is made to seem as though it creates a fictional analogue (reflection) of itself within the heterocosm. What is more, any such event seems to reproduce a mirror image of itself within the heterocosm in the very moment of that event's historical, actual occurrence in the empirical world, outside the fictional frame. For example, in the very act of reading the text, each reader *can be said* to become the historical (actual) analogue of the narrator's *imaginary* idle/leisured reader. Likewise, attempts, by means of language, to instantiate or denote the book's empirical rather than intentional existence—title page, publishing permit, and so on—become *historical* analogues of implied, verbal "actions" within the *fictional* heterocosm. In a sense, the narrator's fictional "history" is made *to seem as though* it absorbs the form of the actual author's book and the actual world to which that book belongs. In short, Cervantes' semantic game dramatizes an unsettling variation of the prototypical, *logical* antinomy: "This statement is false." It is unsettling because just as the author *seems* to adopt, so he *seemingly* obliges his reader to adopt, a role like that of a Cretan liar, whose linguistic references to historical fact operate as references to fictional illusion at the same time and to the same degree. In other words, every time a reader chooses to make a statement such as "The author is named Miguel de Cervantes," "This is his book," or "This is its title page," that reader is also "saying," "This is not Cervantes, his book, or its title page." By referring simultaneously to the real and imaginary author, book, or title page, that reader is referring, through language, to both and neither.

Nonetheless, it would surely be overstated to claim that the author's semantic game of simultaneously actual and imaginary reference, directly involving both the title page and the Prologue, precludes our ability to discriminate in our own minds between the fictional and extrafictional planes of the work. It is likewise within the competence of virtually every sane reader to discriminate between the historical author (of the fiction) and the author's fictional character, who claims to be "author" of both "this preface" and a subsequent "history." Moreover, despite the cleverness of the empirical author's semantic game involving the front matter of *Don Quixote*, we hardly feel moved to share the assumption of his mad protagonist that there is no pertinent distinction to be made between historical reality and artistic mimesis, between cosmos and heterocosm, or between stories and histories.

Indeed, the chief difference between the utterance of the actual author and the pseudoutterance of the narrator, on both the title page and the Prologue, lies in this: the narrator *himself* is the creation of the actual author and exists only as *part of* the author's *utterance*, rather than vice versa. An actual person named Miguel de Cervantes, acting in a certain capacity within the world of empirical experience, became the author of *Don Quixote*, Part I, and of the discourse on the title page and in the fictional, prefatory utterance. As *part of* that written utterance, an imaginary "author" (the Prologue's narrator) makes an equally imaginary claim to have written (imaginary) prefatory and narrative utterances.

Hence, in order to make sense of how we intuitively discriminate between the fictional and extrafictional, and to appreciate how Cervantes' semantic game leads us both to question and refine that intuition, it is necessary to distinguish between the two seemingly opposite *modes of discourse* that, in the Prologue and the rest of *Don Quixote*, come to function in a complementary fashion. For, in distinguishing those modes of discourse and making them function as complements, Cervantes' fiction transforms logical antinomy into logical paradox.

To extrapolate from Barbara Herrnstein Smith's insightful contrast between "natural" and "fictive" discourse (1978, 1–75), we do well to discriminate between

Cervantes' complementary use of what I have called, in Aristotelian terms, "historical" and "poetic" discourse.[8] Such a discrimination seems relevant not only to the Prologue, but also the entire fiction. As Bruce Wardropper states in an important study: "We have to deal, then, with a story masquerading as history, with a work claiming to be historically true within its external framework of fiction. The study of *Don Quixote*, it seems to me, must begin with this paradox" (1986, 80). Yet it is also important to bear in mind that in Cervantes' work, the paradox involving historical and poetic *discourse* includes, without being limited to, the poetic and historical *narratives* we call "stories" and "histories." Indeed, in the manner of the subsequent narrative, the very meaningful *form* of the Prologue of 1605 represents the paradox of a poetic utterance masquerading as an instance of historical discourse.

The term "discourse" is here taken to mean any exchange of ideas *through language* by actual persons, with the terms "historical" and "poetic" denoting two uses, or modes, of discourse.[9] Thus, according to this distinction, actual persons (and only actual persons) engage in discourse, whether in a historical or a poetic mode. Without attempting to discern whether it is more or less "natural," we may say that "historical discourse" occurs whenever actual persons (individually or collectively) produce an utterance in which they intend and are rightly known to present *themselves*—in whatever social role or capacity (e.g., author, king, censor, publisher)—as the speaking or writing subject (the "I" or "we") who produces that utterance.[10] By contrast, "poetic discourse" occurs whenever *actual persons* produce an utterance *within which* they intend and are rightly

    8. As will become evident, Herrnstein Smith's categories of "natural" and "fictive" discourse differ significantly from what I call "historical" and "poetic" discourse. In other words, I do not intend my categories as equivalents for those of Herrnstein Smith.

    9. Hence, "discourse" is not to be understood as coterminous with "language"—i.e., with the whole range of spoken and written signs available to speakers and writers. My distinction between "language" and "discourse" is, furthermore, similar though not identical to the common structuralist distinction between *langue* and *parole*. Specifically, as used here, discourse is *language in use* by actual persons.

    10. As Barbara Herrnstein Smith writes: "By 'natural discourse' I mean here all utterances—trivial or sublime, ill-wrought or eloquent, true or false, scientific or passionate—that can be taken as someone's saying something, somewhere, sometime, that is, as the verbal acts of real persons on particular occasions in response to particular sets of circumstances" (1978, 15).

    Of course, Herrnstein Smith's insistence here on actuality and particularity leads her definition of "natural discourse" strongly to resemble what, in his *Poetics*, Aristotle calls history, as distinct from poetry. Nonetheless, since Herrnstein Smith is attempting in her study to encompass all discourse, her "natural discourse" is meant to cover more ground than Aristotle's "history," just as her "fictive discourse" is meant to cover more ground than Aristotle's "poetry." Indeed, within the category of fictive discourse, she includes such discourse as the exemplary statements of logicians, greeting-card messages, and commercials. For her interesting discussion of the latter, see the chapter titled "On the Margins of Discourse" (1978, 41–75). Likewise, my distinction between the historical and poetic modes is meant to encompass discourse generally.

known to present an imaginary, feigned entity (an imaginary "voice," character, or characters) *as though that entity were* the speaking or writing subject who produces that utterance.[11] Though necessarily consisting of verbal acts produced by actual persons, poetic discourse thus involves what those actual persons *intend their recipients to recognize as an act of pretense.* At a minimum, that pretense entails the feigning of an imaginary speaking or writing subject, whose "verbal acts" are *consequently* imaginary.[12]

---

11. In an important moment of her discussion of fictive discourse, Barbara Herrnstein Smith states: "For the essential fictiveness of literary artworks is not to be discovered in the unreality of the characters, objects, and events alluded to, but in the unreality of the *alludings* themselves" (1978, 11; original emphasis). Without disputing Herrnstein Smith's main point in this statement, I would stress, however, that the unreality of such "alludings" *follows from* the unreality of the (imaginary) speaking or writing subject—the alluding "I" or "we." This simulated subject need not be a character. It may be nothing but what narratologists call a "voice" to which no name is attached. Indeed, as simulations, what Smith calls "alludings" are unreal precisely *because* it is both intended and understood that they are "done" by no one and can therefore "allude" (more properly, refer) to nothing in the real world. The "speaking or writing subject," as well that subject's "verbal acts" and "world" are all intended and rightly understood to be, not simply unreal, but invented and feigned. They form part of an utterance effected by an empirical person or empirical persons who act in a particular capacity (e.g., author, storyteller, or group of authors and storytellers) and who employ discourse in the poetic mode. What is more, an invented speaking or writing subject's "voice," "verbal acts," and "world" constitute hypothetical, supposititious realities, endowed with only intentional or imaginary rather than empirical existence. The empirical existence belongs only to the empirical person or persons who invented those hypothetical realities and to the verbal acts, or poetic utterance, that those persons thus performed in their empirical world. Besides the compelling study by Herrnstein Smith, some important contemporary discussions of the distinction between historical and poetic discourse—a question that has concerned thinkers and writers since Plato and Aristotle—are those by Genette (1993, 1–84), Todorov (1990), Barthes (1989, 127–40), Searle (1979) and Hamburger (1973). Dijk (1974) studies the more specific distinction between what some narratologists call "natural" and "artificial" narratives. Along similar lines, in two related studies, Umberto Eco brilliantly explores the difference and interplay between the "small worlds" of fiction and the larger world of actuality or empirical experience (1994, 64–82; 1995, 75–96).

12. It is worth recalling here that the term "character" is a transliteration of the Greek word for mask. As already discussed in connection with Erasmus, it was, of course, a commonplace for Renaissance authors to speak metaphorically of the world, or society, as a stage in which we are repeatedly obliged to don different "masks." Nonetheless, the fictional "I" or "we" (voice, character, or characters) that *forms part* of an author's poetic utterance can hardly be construed as a person acting in a particular social "role" (or capacity). Rather, that fictional "I" or "we" is *nothing but* a role (mask)—a supposititious "reality"—hypothetically instantiated through the artifice of language and thus made to *simulate* an actual human agent. To be sure, acts that one intends to be understood as instances of pretense need not be limited to discourse. An interesting and particularly clear example of poetic discourse combined with other forms of what we may call poetic (artistic) rather than historical "activity" is found in theater. The dialogue of a play clearly stands as a record of the playwright's poetic utterance and is thus an example of his or her poetic discourse. Furthermore, in the dialogue, a feigned "I" (e.g., Oedipus) or "we" (e.g., Chorus) is clearly marked at the outset of each poetic utterance by the playwright, signaling that *what follows thereafter* is that character's supposititious utterance. But when, say, an actor (an actual person) invests his whole person in *playing a part* (a feigned agent), his pretense is, of course, not limited to speaking or reciting that part. It is relevant to note, as well, that the stage directions of a theatrical work are an instance of the playwright's *historical* discourse, though deployed in creating a *spectacle* of *pretense.*

In view of these distinctions, one can readily identify the Prologue of 1605 and the subsequent narrative about the protagonist, Don Quixote, as an instance of poetic discourse: that is, a poetic utterance that the empirical Miguel de Cervantes, only in his capacity as author of *Don Quixote*, addresses to his readers. This amounts to the same thing, I believe, as claiming that the Prologue and subsequent narrative belonging to *Don Quixote* represent the work of an "implied author." For the author which the text implies is an empirical person acting in a very specific capacity: namely, as author of *this* fiction.

By contrast, the language of the title page to Part I belongs at once to that actual author's historical and poetic discourse. More concretely, on the title page, the *same language* is made to serve two *apparently antithetical* functions at the same time, and in the same signifying space. For that language is there put to both historical and poetic *use*, in the simultaneous production of two different utterances in two contrary modes of discourse. On the one hand, that language instantiates the historical utterance of an actual author. On the other hand, it instantiates the same author's poetic utterance: a verbal act of pretense that *contains* the pseudohistorical utterance of a fictional "author," whom we may identify as the Prologue's narrator or *narrative voice*. Likewise, thanks to the interplay between the language of the title page and that of the Prologue, other instances of historical (and extrafictional) discourse by persons *other than the author*—for example, the publishing permit, price, corrector's statement, the publisher's cover, and so on—may *also* function as instances of the implied author's poetic discourse. This is so because, if readers agree to suspend disbelief in the "existence" of the narrator and the heterocosm, they may assume that the narrator's history includes imaginary analogues, or mirror reflections, of the fiction's publishing permit, price, corrector's statement, and the like.

In dramatizing how both historical and poetic discourse can speak, as it were, in the same idiom, the author of *Don Quixote* also dramatizes what Mary Gaylord calls, in reference to *La Galatea*, "the limits of language and the language of limits" (1982, 254–71). In other words, that author employs discourse self-consciously, in both the historical and poetic mode, to dramatize the limits, as well as the strengths, of discourse itself.

Although their referents are not equally "fictional," both historical and poetic discourse are shown to be equally fictive and insubstantial.[13] Hence the author's ability to have us take the same language that forms part of a historical utterance as forming part of a distinct, poetic utterance. Cervantes' semantic game in the

---

13. And it seems appropriate to add that historical and poetic discourse are equally "natural" modes of *representing* and translating the "truth" or actuality of historical experience. In complementary fashion, both modes of discourse render such experience intelligible, if far from wholly "present," to the mind.

Prologue therefore dramatizes rather than formulates an elementary feature of language and reference, or perhaps better, language and its relation to the referent. In particular this semantic game dramatizes that, as a type of *artifice*, what even the most "historical" and "nonpoetic" discourse is able to "tell" is but a *simulation* or, indeed, a translation of historical "truth" in linguistic terms. This game invites readers, as they play, to ponder how "reality"—including historical fact—becomes intelligible through categories of thought and language. It thus invites them playfully to confront the paradox of how "truth" represents a partial *discovery* and a partial *invention* (i.e., *inventio*), but not simply one or the other.

Whether we utter the name of the author, the title of the book, or pronouncements about its legal approval and historical existence, "what is said" through language conveys, but can never fully convey, the "truth" (actuality, being, presence) of those entities or events. The text shows further that, as a result, neither can "what is said" through language fully convey "what is meant" by the uttering subject, or what significance or effects that subject's utterance might have now, at some later moment, or in a different context. As deployed in both the title page and the Prologue of 1605, poetic and historical discourse are shown to represent two *contrary and complementary modes* of revealing, concealing, and framing "truth" through language. Its "fictiveness" and insubstantiality are shown to endow discourse with the wondrous yet limited power to reveal "truth," together with the wondrous yet limited power to shape one's understanding of the actuality ("truth") of what is or what occurs in either the inner world of the self or the outer world of sensible phenomena.[14] Further, especially regarding the inner world of self, the "truthfulness" of discourse is likewise shown not only, or primarily, to be a function of "*what* is said" (i.e., its referential meaning, or the language it uses), but of the spirit in which that discourse is both uttered and understood.[15] This spirit may be playful, serious, honest, or deceitful. For it is possible to lie and, inadvertently, tell a factual truth. And, of course, it is possible to take either a playful or serious statement the wrong way.

To be sure, nothing in the linguistic (or extralinguistic) features of the author's prefatory utterance—in other words, nothing in its diction or context—*obliges us* to take it as an instance of *either* historical *or* poetic discourse. For our

---

14. For a splendid examination of Cervantes' ambivalent attitude toward the insubstantial nature of language and its capacity for creating illusion, especially in relation to the ideas set forth in Erasmus's *Lingua*, see the chapter titled "Language: Divine or Diabolical Gift?" (Forcione 1984, 186–236).

15. Azar (1988) provides a compelling study that relates Cervantes' view of language to Wittgenstein's ideas about language games, and that investigates Cervantes' dramatization of how the "truth" and "reality" of "*self, thoughts, feelings* come neither before nor after language, but *in* it" (117; original emphasis).

ability to discern historical from poetic discourse ultimately depends not on the linguistic form of the utterance, but on our recognizing that the person who produces the utterance *intends for us to take it* as an act of pretense. In the front matter of his book, then, the author of *Don Quixote* dramatizes that a fundamental assumption of discourse is that it operates on the basis of convention and on a principle of mutual trust. It is assumed that speakers or writers will indicate, though not necessarily *state*, the historical or poetic intention of their utterance in a recognizable fashion. And it is further assumed that their recipients will take those utterances in accord with such intentions, thus distinguishing between a historical and poetic utterance. In this way, a *poetic* utterance exemplifies an instance of what Mexía calls "telling lies" (*dezir mentiras*) rather than "lying" (*mentir*), since it does not involve the *intent* to deceive the listener or reader.[16] Similarly, in the strict sense of the term, "lying" is an act of pretense (and intentional deception) that would therefore belong solely to the province of historical discourse. The act of lying bears only on the deceptive intention of the one producing the utterance, who thus transgresses the conventional and fiduciary basis of discourse.

However, the author's axiological paradox in the Prologue and on the title page clearly challenges the tidiness of such distinctions as "truth-telling" and "lie-telling" without thereby negating them. By "telling lies," the poetic discourse of the fictional Prologue proves more effective than historical discourse in representing the "truth" of historical reality and the complexity of historical *experience*. *Because* its *referents* are wholly imaginary, the Prologue's poetic discourse creates the illusion of aesthetic distance, the better to simulate the *particular circumstance* of an "author" named Miguel de Cervantes, in the act of writing a Prologue for his book, *Don Quixote*. Additionally, however, the same imaginary reference (or "lie-telling") of that poetic discourse creates the illusion of aesthetic distance in order to dramatize *general* "truths" about nothing other than historical and poetic discourse: their strengths and limits; their differences and similarities; their opposition and complementarity.

Nonetheless, perhaps a more intriguing observation that the author of *Don Quixote* dramatizes through his *poetic utterances* is the shadowy border between one verbal act of pretense and another—that is, between a poetic utterance and a lie. When the author, Cervantes, has the narrative voice of the Prologue implicitly claim to have written a *historical* work about Don Quixote, whom we know to be a fictional character, it would seem that the only plausible inference

---

16. Because of their purely imaginary existence, of course, neither fictional voices nor fictional characters are capable of "lying." Rather, a real speaker or writer may use either a fictional voice or a character to *simulate* an act of lying.

we can draw is that the author intends for us to understand the narrator as a fictional "I," and the Prologue as a poetic utterance. Yet here again, the author of *Don Quixote* seems to engage in a discourse of "limits," enlisting our collaboration in his testing of the logical and linguistic regions where opposites seem to coincide and converge. For we are also led to infer that the veiled manner in which the actual author "reveals" the fictional status of his narrator in the Prologue is done by design, and therefore *borders on* an act of deception. Indeed, that author would seem to have had every *intention* of temporarily misleading, if not ultimately deceiving, his readers about the poetic quality of his prefatory utterance and the fictional quality of his narrator. He thereby illustrates the frail bonds of convention and mutual trust that hold together the discursive system *within which* "truth" is able, in part, both to appear and to occur. Indeed, whether he is writing in either a historical or poetic mode, the author, Cervantes, sets forth this problematic view of discourse by exploiting the concept of *componer* or "to compose" in yet another sense of the term, as defined by the lexicographer Covarrubias in his dictionary of 1611: "[To] compose: *to lie*, because *the liar both composes and feigns his lie, making it verisimilar* [i.e., truthlike]" (componer: *mentir*, porque *el mentiroso compone y finge la mentira, haziéndola verisímil* [*sic*]) (1984, 344; emphasis added) (Molho 1989, 275).

At bottom, then, the poetic-masquerading-as-historical *form* of the Prologue dramatizes the impossibility of our acting in a manner other than as *componedores* or composers, compositors, and compilers when we use language or engage in *either* mode of discourse. What is more, *awareness* of the fictive and insubstantial nature of language—the instrument that we enlist in our historical and poetic modes of "telling"—therefore makes our every utterance an instance of *intentional* truth-telling and lie-telling at once. A lack of such awareness would entail the belief that one can "tell it like it is" or "state" the whole truth about what is or occurs. Consequently, it is in dramatizing human discourse as a "tissue of fictions" that, in my view, the Prologue of 1605 both anticipates and encapsulates the subsequent narrative.

Moreover, both the Prologue and the subsequent narrative form part of an imitative parody, and a paradoxical encomium, that aim an equal measure of praise and censure at historical and poetic uses of language. In its duplicitous discourse, the Prologue prefigures a narrative that engages in the mockery and praise of both "stories" and "histories" as bearers of truth. As part of the same poetic utterance, however, both Prologue and narrative are likewise concerned with the mutual interplay between the fictive categories of both thought and language that organize and constitute human discourse in either the historical or poetic mode. As dramatized in the Prologue and narrative alike, it is these *fictive categories* that give rise to the *fictions* we call "knowledge" and "history," and that ensure, in Cusanus's phrase, that our "learning" is increasingly "ignorance" of the truth. In short, both the Prologue and subsequent narrative invite reflection upon the fictive categories and conventions through which we and other persons interpret, fashion, and refashion the world of empirical experience. But it is particularly the Prologue, I believe, that invites reflection upon the fictive categories and conventions through which we judge either poetic or historical intention—the same categories, in other words, that presumably keep us from losing our "wits" (*juicio*) in the manner of Don Quixote.

To be sure, the form of the Prologue, like the form of the narrative, both exemplifies and dramatizes discourse as a blend of truth, falsehood, discovery, and invention. But Cervantes' fictional work seems far less concerned with such abstract formulations than with dramatizing, through discourse, the place of discourse and its "fictions" in either achieving or preventing an increase of communication and communion among persons; in our pursuing knowledge and self-knowledge; and in our carrying out various acts of truthful revelation, or of deception and self-deception. As an instance of overt logical and axiological paradoxy, the quasi-historical yet poetic *form* of the Prologue therefore manages both to parody and praise historical and poetic discourse; to have each mode of discourse both parody and praise the other; and so to enlist discourse in the subversion and transcendence of its own limited, fictive categories.

In light of the entire fiction's paradoxical form, it would surely prove misguided to read the *poetic* discourse, not only of the narrative about Don Quixote, but also of the Prologue, as a series of straightforward propositions (or statements) about the historical "facts" (or "truth") concerning the book's ontological status and composition. More specifically, I think it misguided to read any part of the Prologue of 1605 as a univocal "statement" of the author's purpose or intentions. Yet I also believe that it would prove misguided to dismiss the author's poetic utterances in the Prologue as though they had nothing to "say" about the "truth" of the actual book and the motivations behind its production. If the narrator is a fictional character, he is also unlike any other character of the fiction. No doubt he simulates and parodies the situation of any author who is obliged to write a Prologue for his book. But in addition, he both imitates and parodies the actions and circumstances of his creator. Hence, as *both* a fictional and prefatory epilogue, the Prologue of 1605 can be said to hint or *allude*, though not directly to *refer*, to the actual author and his actual book. In examining the rest of the Prologue, then, we shall aim to respect both its self-allusive and poetic quality by reading its discourse in a twofold manner: first, *as though it were* the utterance of the narrator; and next, as the poetic utterance of the author.

In the first place, it hardly needs saying that the author characterizes his narrator through the latter's pseudohistorical discourse. For this reason alone, it is surely worth analyzing what the narrator is simulated as "meaning" by his prefatory "statements." More important, however, the author uses those imaginary "statements" both to broach and to parody important issues of the prevailing rhetorical and literary convention—issues that bear directly on the composition of both his Prologue and his book. In particular, the actual author uses his narrator's "statements" to dramatize the theoretical contradictions (antinomies) that inform the prevailing aesthetic convention (*doxa*), as well as the practical contradictions that result from the implicit demand to take one side or another in "disputed questions" about the theory and practice of prologues, poetry, or history.

In the second place, however, we do violence to the author's poetic utterance if we attempt to purge its fictional and parodic qualities, seeking to identify *which* of the narrator's "statements" are meant by the author as *either* "true" *or* "false," "ironic" or "straight"; searching out what we hope to be the kernel of a coherent doctrinal treatise; and finally discarding what we assume to be but a "poetic" and "rhetorical" husk. Since the Prologue is indeed a poetic utterance, its author neither "denies" nor "says" what his narrator is *represented as* saying. By simulating the circumstance of an (imaginary) author named "Miguel de Cervantes," the actual author ingeniously achieves a measure of both self-reference, or better, self-allusion, and distance.

The author does not *mean* what his character "says," because the total message of the author includes not only his character's "statements," but also the character himself, as well as all the other characters, "objects," "actions," and "circumstances" that form part of the fictional heterocosm. In his Prologue, the author can be rightly said to *dramatize and thematize* the rhetoricoliterary issues that his narrator *seems to discuss*. Moreover, they are the same "theoretical" issues that the author will dramatize and thematize throughout the rest of his fictional work.

In a qualified sense, then, it seems possible to read the actual author's fictional Prologue in accord with his implicit *intentions*. For whether the author, Cervantes, can be said to "intend" or hold a coherent aesthetic theory, it would seem that his primary intention in offering a poetic dramatization rather than a discussion of such issues consists of inviting us to reflect on the multiple, perhaps countless, meanings that *emerge from* the simulated circumstance: that is, from the theoretical and practical dilemmas that his fictional "author," "Miguel de Cervantes," claims to confront in composing his "Prologue" and his "book." Indeed, because those issues arise in the context of the narrator's contradictory "statements," and in the context of the author's poetic rather than historical discourse, they come to the fore as open questions, whose examination and possible "solution" become the sole responsibility of the reader.

A final point to be made here about the innovative quality of the actual Cervantes' prefatory fiction is that in parodically dramatizing issues of aesthetic theory, that author both subverts and enlarges upon a specific rhetorical tradition. As a critical disciple of Erasmian poetics, the author, Cervantes, clearly rejects the artificial separation of what contemporary parlance would call "theory"—and what the humanists would have called *philosophia*—from poetry (or fiction) and rhetoric. Cervantes' fiction in the form of a Prologue, or his Prologue in the form of a fiction, is no less a fiction, no less theoretical or philosophical, and no less serious and comic, than Erasmus's *Praise of Folly*. Yet, unlike the *Folly*, Cervantes' Prologue is a fictional *dialogue* that traces its pedigree to Erasmus's *Colloquies* and to the equally fictional writings of Plato, who was but one of the Greek philosophers to cultivate the genre of Socratic dialogues.

Indeed, the Prologue of 1605 both imitates and transforms the serioludic rhetoric, theory, and poesy of Plato and Erasmus to produce a fictional and parodic dialogue on *poetic philosophy*. But more important, that Prologue includes a serioludic philosophy of *prologues*; and it is written within the proximate tradition of the *Ancient Philosophy of Poesis* (*Philosophía antigua poética*) (1596), by Cervantes' contemporary Alonso López Pinciano (Canavaggio 1958, 13–107; Gaylord Randel 1986, 65–67; Weiger 1988, 35–36). In a revealing passage, López Pinciano underscores the fictional (poetic) status of Plato's Socratic dialogues, thereby signaling the rhetorical tradition to which those works belong, as well as the self-consciously *fictional*, hypothetical status of his own "theoretical" dialogue:

> Did the dialogues and colloquies in which Plato wrote his teachings occur in the same way as they are written? Yes or no? It is clear that they could have occurred, but did not occur. Hence, he imitated what could have been but was not.

> (¿Los Diálogos y Coloquios en que Platón escriuió su doctrina passaron assí como él los dexó escritos? [¿]Sí o no[?] Claro está que pudiera acontescer, mas no acontescieron, de manera que imitó a lo que pudiera ser y no fué.) (1969, 200–201; qtd. in Weiger 1988, 230 n. 40)

Besides its overt conflation of fiction and "philosophy," López Pinciano's work shows other structural affinities with Cervantes' Prologue of 1605. For instance, the bulk of López Pinciano's fictional-theoretical work consists of what purports to be a transcribed dialogue, in which the author's fictional surrogate discusses matters of poetic theory with two companions, Fadrique and Hugo. What is more, this (imaginary) dialogue *is said to be transcribed* within a letter that the author's fictional surrogate addresses to a *friend* (Weiger 1988, 35–36). Significantly, too, the name of the author's fictional surrogate, El Pinciano, is almost, but not quite, identical to that of his creator, thereby achieving both authorial self-allusion (if not self-reference) and distance. No doubt, this character fails to represent the same degree of self-parody as that of the actual Cervantes' narrator. But in the dialogue, the character, El Pinciano, never assumes the role of an authoritative master, such as found in most of the dialogues by Mexía. Rather, that character's revelatory function in every sense is limited to *posing* provocative questions. His friends, Fadrique and Hugo, then provide replies, whose validity is left to the judgment of the proverbial "discreet reader." As we shall now examine, the narrator and the friend of the actual Cervantes' Prologue both serve a similar function, by "posing" problems, issues and dilemmas that are relevant not only to general questions of literary aesthetics, but also to their author's fictional creation, which includes the Prologue itself.

The Naturalness of Art and the Artifice of "Nature"

In the opening paragraph of the Prologue's first section, before the arrival of the narrator's friend, that narrator touches upon two issues that are central to the thematics of *Don Quixote*: (1) the relation between human artifice and nature and (2) the rhetorical relation between author and reader. And at the level of propositional statement or surface meaning alone, in the Prologue the treatment of both issues would seem to be highly conventional.

The narrator broaches the first issue, not in an abstract manner, but chiefly within the context of a commonplace analogy between the *process of artistic creation* and the *natural process* of conception, gestation, and birth. Indeed, the narrator identifies the book as his spiritual progeny: "like a child of my intellect" (como hijo del entendimiento) (*DQ* I: *Prologue*, 50).[17] Just as the son is said to

---

17. This was, of course, a commonplace analogy in Cervantes' day, as shown by Porqueras Mayo (1968, 13–14). In his *Ancient Poetic Philosophy* (*Filosofía antigua poética:*) (1596), Cervantes' Spanish contemporary Alonso López Pinciano writes that "poets love their poems as parents love their children" (los poetas aman a sus poemas como los padres a los hijos) (López Pinciano 1969, 187–88, qtd. in Weiger

resemble the father, and not the other way round, so, too, the story of Don Quixote can be said to resemble the narrator who purports to be its author: "every thing begets its like" (cada cosa engendra su semejante). Furthermore, the narrator implies that any other type of relation between authors and their creations would "contradict the laws of *nature*" (contravenir al orden de natu-raleza) (*DQ* I: *Prologue*, 50). From the outset, then, the narrator of the Pro-logue seems to confirm the perfectly orthodox belief that a relation of hierarchy obtains between an author who is the source of a work that resem-bles and reflects that author's mind, and between art (the copy) and nature (the original).

In a manner that is no less orthodox, the narrator seems to acknowledge the defective quality of his literary offspring and of the latter's intellectual origin:

> [W]hat could my sterile, uncultivated intellect beget but a history about a native son who is dry, wrinkled, whimsical and steeped in a host of thoughts never imagined by anyone else—much in the manner of a child begotten in a prison, where every misery has its home and where every mournful noise has its dwelling?

> (¿[Q]ué podrá engendrar el estéril y mal cultivado ingenio mío sino la historia de un hijo seco, avellanado, antojadizo y lleno de pensamientos varios y nunca imaginados de otro alguno, bien como quien se engendró

1988, 230 n. 41). Cervantes uses an interesting variation of this analogy concerning the gestation, birth, and growth of his artistic work in his Prologue to the *Exemplary Novellas* (*Novelas ejemplares*) (1613): "[M]y genius conceived them [the novellas], my pen gave them birth, and they continue to grow in the arms of the printing press" ([M]i ingenio las engendró [las novelas], y las parió mi pluma, y van creciendo en los brazos de la estampa) (1985, 52). It is likewise in this Prologue where the author, Cervantes, writes that he would prefer to avoid writing another prologue, since "the one I attached to *Don Quixote* did not go so well for me that I should now feel inclined to follow with this second one" (no me fue tan bien con el que puse en mi *Don Quijote*, que quedase con gana de segundar con éste). And he adds: "And for this the blame lies with a certain friend" (Desto tiene la culpa algún amigo) (1985, 50). Indeed, the Prologue to the *Exemplary Novellas* provides another interesting example of the author's disguising himself through an act of apparent self-revelation and self-portraiture. Further, that Prologue contains numerous fictional elements, including what an imaginary "friend" *might say* about a painting that is *said to be* a portrait of the author (Miguel de Cervantes), by "the famous Juan de Jáuregui." Yet, despite those elements and the reference to "a certain friend"—presumably an illusion to the fictional "friend" in the Prologue to Part I of *Don Quixote*—the Prologue to the *Exemplary Novellas* remains a historical (and extrafictional) rather than poetic utterance. For, instead of putting forth an imaginary "I" who belongs to a fictional hetero-cosm, Cervantes there presents himself, chiefly in his capacity as author of both prologues, the novellas, and his other fictional works, as the subject producing the written utterance we have before us. It is telling, in this regard, that Cervantes should avoid referring to that "certain friend," whom the author treats in an unfriendly manner, as "my friend."

en una cárcel,[18] donde toda incomodidad tiene su asiento y donde todo triste ruido tiene su habitación?) (*DQ* I: *Prologue*, 50).

Nonetheless, despite this admission, cast in the form of a rhetorical question, the seemingly modest narrator again draws on the "natural" image of a doting parent, in order to imply that he may still remain blind to the shortcomings of his beloved "child": "It sometimes happens that a father will have an ugly son, utterly lacking in social graces, and yet the love he bears that son will place a blindfold over his eyes so that he fails to see the son's flaws" (Acontece tener un padre un hijo feo y sin gracia alguna, y el amor que le tiene le pone una venda en los ojos para que no vea sus faltas"). Also in keeping with his paternal sentiments and his posture of modesty, the narrator employs a counterfactual subjunctive in order to inform his reader at the start of the Prologue about the type of book/child that he longed, but was unable, to produce: "*I should wish* that this book, as the child of my intellect, might have been the most beautiful, the most graceful and the wittiest book that one could imagine" (*quisiera* que este libro, como hijo del entendimiento, *fuera* el más hermoso, el más gallardo y más discreto que pudiera imaginarse) (*DQ* I: *Prologue*, 50; emphasis added).

The deficiencies of the story and its origins notwithstanding, the narrator again follows established convention by implying that the work, as an *imitation of nature*, is still worth reading. For he seems to remind the reader of the general principle that if an uncultivated mind portends literary barrenness, moments of quiet meditation in communion with the nurturing powers of *nature* will lead even the poorest writer to yield aesthetic fruit:

> Quiet, the peaceful hideaway, the charms of the country, the stillness of the skies, the rippling of the brooks, the repose of the spirit, all play a large part in rendering fertile even the most barren muses, who will bear offspring which fill the earth with wonder and delight.

> (El sosiego, el lugar apacible, la amenidad de los campos, la serenidad de los cielos, el murmurar de las fuentes, la quietud del espíritu son grande parte para que las musas más estériles se muestren fecundas y ofrezcan partos al mundo que le colmen de maravilla y de contento.) (*DQ* I: *Prologue*, 50)

18. In the context of the Prologue, the word *prison* (cárcel) seems to refer figuratively to the confining, prison-like quality of the narrator's mind, or imagination (*ingenio*). Whether the term also refers literally to one of Cervantes' imprisonments—to my mind, a dubious assumption—has no direct bearing on my argument. On this phrase in the Prologue of 1605, see Murillo 1988, 50 n. 2.

As to the rhetorical stance that the narrator adopts in this section of the Prologue, he not only appears to show modesty, but also to show his reader both confidence and respect. As suggested in the Prologue's first words, the narrator may be thought to consider the "reader" a dignified person of "leisure" (desocupado lector) now enjoying a moment of quiet repose. Later in the same paragraph, the narrator seems to address that reader affectionately as "dearest reader" (lector carísimo) (*DQ* I: *Prologue*, 51), and in the Prologue's final paragraph as "gentle reader" (lector suave) (*DQ* I: *Prologue*, 58).

Moreover, acknowledging that all readers are endowed with sovereignty over their persons and their homes, and in no way bound to the book by quasi-familial ties, the narrator apparently chooses to avoid burdening those readers with the customary pleas for sympathy: "I do not want to follow the pull of custom, imploring with tears in my eyes, as other authors do, dearest reader, that you forgive or pass over the defects you come to see in this child of mine" (No quiero irme con la corriente del uso, ni suplicarte casi con lágrimas en los ojos, como otros hacen, lector carísimo, que perdones o disimules las faltas que en este mi hijo vieres) (*DQ* I: *Prologue*, 50–51).

In sum, while echoing a commonplace about the process of artistic creation, as well as the most common understanding of Aristotle's doctrine concerning art as an imitation of nature, the narrator seems to issue a standard *captatio benevolentiae*, in an effort to ensure amicable reception of his work. Hence, were we to focus solely on these messages, and solely on the surface level of their meaning, we may well conclude that the first section introduces us to a highly conventional prologue, produced by a "writer" of mediocre intelligence. Nonetheless, even what seem to be that narrator's most conventional and straightforward remarks prove, upon analysis, to be rife with ambivalence and contradiction.

Let us first consider how, in this opening section of his fictional Prologue, the author deploys his narrator's contradictory statements to dramatize general, "theoretical" issues about poetics and poetic creation. Set in bold relief, the narrator's statement in the first paragraph of the Prologue about the salutary effects of "quiet, the peaceful hideaway, the charms of the country, the stillness of the skies" follows from what seems to be the narrator's fully accepting the core principle of Aristotle's *Poetics*: namely, that art is the imitation of nature.[19] Here, to be sure, "art" and "nature" appear as contraries.

19. As Aristotle asserts near the beginning of his *Poetics*: "Epic poetry and Tragedy, also Comedy, the Dithyramb, and most of the music performed on the flute and lyre are all, in a collective sense, Imitations" (1982, 45).

Directly related to this principle is Aristotle's equally famous assertion that both history and poetry imitate "life" or human action, with the difference that history imitates events that are real (actual), whereas poetry imitates those that are fictitious (possible): "Thus the difference between the historian and the poet is not that the historian employs prose and the poet verse . . . ; rather the difference is that the one tells of things that have been and the other of such things as might be" (1982, 54). It is, of course, the distinction between the "actuality" (*ser*) of history, as against the "possibility" (*poder ser*) of fiction that inspires López Pinciano's remarks about the fictionality of Plato's (and, by extension, his own) dialogical work: "[H]e imitated what could have been, but was not" ([I]mitó lo que pudiera ser, mas no fué). In Aristotle, this distinction renders poetry more "philosophical" than history, in that the latter is confined to truths that derive from particular facts or events, whereas poetry is free to deal with truths that are universal in scope.[20] As early as the Prologue, then, and especially in the narrator's above mentioned statement, Cervantes gives evidence of what scholars have long recognized as his active engagement not only with López Pinciano, but also with Aristotle, and particularly with the two central distinctions of that philosopher's literary theory: (1) the distinction between art and nature, or literature and life, and (2) the distinction between poetry and history, or more generally, between what we earlier discussed as poetic and historical discourse.

As a "story," *Don Quixote* is, of course, less about examining the enigmas involved in artistic representations of the physical universe (a special use of the term "nature") than representations of human action ("life")—action being understood as deeds joined to their motivation in personality or "character" (Aristotle's ethos), to various types of emotional or mental "activity" (*dianoia*), or to any combination thereof (Aristotle 1982, 60–61, 65–66). But it is significant that, in the passage just quoted, Cervantes should have his narrator broach the question of "art" and "nature," as Aristotle does, at its highest level of generalization. Cervantes' engagement with Aristotle therefore begins, in the Prologue, with the central principles of Aristotle's poetic doctrine.

However, one striking feature of the narrator's solitary "image" of "nature" in the Prologue is that this image exemplifies little more than a hackneyed rendering of a *locus amoenus*. By far one of the most stylized (i.e., "unnatural") passages

---

20. Aristotle states: "Poetry, therefore, is a more philosophical and a higher thing than history, in that poetry tends rather to express the universal, history rather the particular fact" (Aristotle 1982, 54). See Castro's famous, and highly personal, discussion of "poetic universals and historical particulars" (lo universal poético y lo particular histórico) in reference to Cervantes' writings, particularly *Don Quixote* (1972, 27–35).

of the Prologue, the narrator's statement thus seems an apt demonstration of how the very intelligibility of nature depends on the *artificial* categories of language, which here take the form of nonreferential, artistic topoi. Indeed, the passage seems to undercut its informing principle—"art as imitation of nature"—since that quasi-lyrical statement amounts to a parodic imitation of literary commonplaces and, indeed, an imitation of the *mechanism* of artistic imitation. Here, art imitates not only art, but also its own imitative process. An added paradox of self-reference arises from the fact that it is a character, a parodic imitation of the author, who is here represented as imitating the imitative process of art.

Nonetheless, it is necessary to add that the narrator seems blithely unaware of how that passage undercuts its informing principle that art is an imitation of "nature," or that art and nature denote utterly separate categories. In fact, I would contend that throughout the Prologue, the narrator's statements are fraught with unwitting contradictions, and that his voice is consistently naive and unselfconscious. It seems reasonable to read the narrator's statements that way, once we realize that his voice does not belong to the actual author of the fiction, but to a character who claims to have written a "history" about Don Quixote. Indeed, the narrator's statements throughout the Prologue are as naive and overstated as his reasons for wanting to keep the history of Don Quixote buried in the archives of La Mancha: "until heaven should provide someone who is able to adorn him with many things he now lacks" (hasta que el cielo depare quien le adorne de tantas cosas como le faltan) (*DQ* I: *Prologue*, 53). One detects the same combination of ingenuousness and overstatement when, apparently dissatisfied with the paradox of barren muses who turn fertile, the first-person narrator utters the absurdity of "the *most barren* muses [who become] fertile and who will bear offspring that fill the earth with wonder and delight" (las musas *más* estériles [que] se muestren fecundas y ofrezcan partos al mundo que le *colmen* de maravilla y contento) (*DQ* I: *Prologue*, 50; emphasis added), as though sterility were a condition that not only admits of degrees, but that also occasionally results in a type of overpopulation.

To be sure, such overstated comments are markers of irony. But, if one may draw on the classical acceptation of irony feigning ignorance, the feigning here belongs wholly to the author, and is achieved through the unselfconscious "ignorance" of his narrator. In my view, there are no textual markers and no contextual clues in the Prologue that would lead us to infer that in the narrator's contradictory, naive, and hyperbolic statements, there is any distinction between *that narrator's* intended and ostensible meaning. He is demonstrating rather than feigning his ignorance. Indeed, I believe that ascribing self-conscious irony to the narrator amounts to confusing the perspective of the character, the "historian," with that of the author responsible for the fiction. It is the same author who is responsible for creating a narrator who, as self-proclaimed "author" of the "Prologue" and of the "history" we are reading, repeatedly becomes entangled in a host of theoretical and practical contradictions. And it is the author, moreover, who uses that unselfconscious narrator in an ingenious self-parody, the better to underscore that actual author's awareness of the theoretical and practical contradictions attending his own circumstance as creator of the fiction's Prologue and subsequent narrative.

Thus, if the narrator's rendering of "nature" can ultimately be read as his unwitting affirmation and negation of a central Aristotelian principle, it is pertinent to ask about the implicit purpose behind what seems to be the author's parody of that principle. Instead of denying the validity of the Aristotelian principle and its corollaries, the author, Cervantes, seems to be using this parodic passage in order to foreground that Aristotelian doctrine's central paradoxes, which run not only through the rest of his Prologue but also the rest of *Don Quixote*. Such paradoxes emerge from the author's continually dramatizing the complex *interplay* between what we intuitively perceive, and what Aristotle's principle assumes, to be the distinct spheres of "art" and "nature," "literature" (or "poetry") and "life." In particular, through the statement of the narrator, the author tests Aristotle's abstract formulation in a practical fashion, at the level of "experience" (*usus et experientia*). By pushing the principle and its underlying distinction to their logical and practical limits, Cervantes' text draws our attention to the point at which the presumed opposites of art and nature, literature and life, overlap and converge. If these contraries are distinct, they are not therefore separate. They remain complementary, rather than exclusive, oppositions. Hence, the author of *Don Quixote* enlarges upon, rather than negates, Aristotle's chief aesthetic doctrine—both imitating and perfecting his "model."

In fact, both the content and form of the narrator's statement about the salutary effects of "nature" body forth the author's first dramatization of the problem that, *at some point*, such contraries as art/nature, literature/life, and real/imaginary become convertible. And, as illustrated in that stylized rendering of "nature," the point at which such opposites become convertible is precisely when human beings strive to render their experience intelligible through some form of *imitation*. For an idea implicit in the *Poetics* is that imitation is, indeed, the very activity that makes knowledge possible and which makes "life" self-aware and specifically human. As we read in the *Poetics*:

> Thus from childhood it is instinctive in human beings to imitate, and
> man differs from the other animals as the most imitative of all and *getting*

his first lessons by imitation, and by instinct also all human beings take pleasure in imitations. For this again the reason is that the experience of learning is highly enjoyable, not only for philosophers but for other people as well, only their share in it is limited; when they enjoy seeing images, therefore, it is because as they look at them they have the experience of *learning and reasoning out what each thing represents.* (1982, 47–48; emphasis added)

Through the narrator's statement about "nature," Cervantes seems to elaborate on Aristotle's insights in a practical fashion, showing that not only what we make from nature, but also what we know about "nature" and what we know *as* "nature" are the result of imitative artifice, or "art" in the broadest sense. Further, since the process and products of imitation are among the most conspicuous "facts" and "events" of "life," Cervantes here demonstrates that they are themselves among the most fitting objects for artistic imitation.

Another corollary of Aristotle's core principles that Cervantes develops in a way that the Greek philosopher does not is that knowledge is invariably the result of artifice and imitation. The author of the fictional Prologue to *Don Quixote* seems interested in showing, not only that "art" constantly interferes with "nature," and that "poetry" interferes with "life." It seems, further, that he goes so far as to dramatize that "life," understood as specifically human and conscious life, is chiefly a continuing process of imitation. Imitation is therefore among the most conspicuous "facts" of life. What is more, our imitations of "life" and "nature" are ineluctably based on previous imitations, which act as models and establish the terms and categories which make our imitations possible. For it is shown that nature cannot appear without art. And there can be no imitation of "nature" that is divorced from the imitation of artistic, fictive "models."

Like Aristotle, the author of *Don Quixote* seems primarily interested in the *linguistic* form of imitation known as "poetry," contrasted with what both authors recognize as but another form of linguistic imitation known as "history." In using linguistic imitation to dramatize the process of linguistic imitation, the author of *Don Quixote* seems to be self-consciously dramatizing the process—here a creative, constructive process—of human knowledge. For "nature" is shown to be transformed into "art," and translated into the terms of human artifice, the moment that nature (or experience) becomes an object of human knowledge, and thus of human discourse. Hence, as part of the author's poetic utterance, the passage about "nature" at the beginning of the Prologue represents the author's first parodic enlargement of Aristotle's *Poetics*. As such, it reinforces the idea that knowledge as imitation constitutes a paradox: part discovery and part invention; original and derivative; free and yet limited by both the "natural" constraints of matter, time, and space and the "fictive" or "cultural" constraints of our "models" and discursive categories. Moreover, the passage quoted above underscores how knowledge as imitation represents a dialectic between the givenness of experience unfolding in time and the potentially expansive categories of thought and language. But perhaps more important, that passage is also the first in a series of continuing parodies throughout the fiction of how—in various ways, and to varying degrees—human beings either grow or fail to grow in knowledge and self-knowledge, owing to their commitment to that dialectic, and to the size and suppleness of fictive categories that govern their discourse.

In sum, the reason for dwelling on this passage is that it seems emblematic of the entire fiction's content and form. As to content, that fiction delivers a parodic narrative about a protagonist who confuses a particular type of poetry with history, or imaginary with empirical reference. Acting on that confusion, he seeks to impose categories deriving from the poetic utterances of chivalric romance upon his historical world. Further, as to form, we encounter this narrative within the paradox of poetry masquerading as history. The Prologue offers the analogous paradox of poetic discourse masquerading as its historical counterpart. And the title page of the fiction, as linked to the Prologue, presents each contrary mode of discourse alternately masquerading as the other. Thus, that passage in the Prologue where "art" overtly masquerades as "nature" serves to dramatize a view of knowledge, culture, and history that underlies the entire work.

The fiction repeatedly shows that knowledge and culture, or "life"—as a continuing blend of discovery and invention—follow from our allowing the fictive categories of our "telling" or discourse to masquerade temporarily as categories of "being." The paradox of form and content in *Don Quixote* therefore seems to represent a self-conscious use of discourse that parodies discourse itself, dramatizing and thematizing the "being" of "telling." Such paradoxy yields, in other words, a dramatization which reminds us of, or alerts us to, every such "masquerade." It points, not to a dichotomous conflict between the Ideal and the Real, but to a cooperative tension and mutually creative dialectic between being and telling. Cervantes' paradoxy therefore points, as well, to our status as *componedores*, or as editors, compositors, fabulators, and *fabricators* whenever we employ or produce discourse.

In this light, the paradoxical discourse that pervades the fiction from the start of its Prologue seems hardly to represent a simplistic act of the author's debunking or defending "official values." Rather, Cervantes' logical and axiological paradoxy seems aimed at dramatizing how the evolving quality of knowledge and culture issues from the fictive, evolving categories of thought and discourse. As a parody of discursive practices, and especially of practices that conflate "being" and "telling," the paradoxy of Cervantes' *Don Quixote* therefore enlarges upon a philosophical and literary tradition that portrays knowledge as learned ignorance and portrays history, or biography, as a mingling of wisdom and folly alike.

Fathers, Stepfathers, and Sons

Besides Aristotle's definition of "art," an allied question of aesthetic import that Cervantes puts to a practical test from the first paragraph of his Prologue to Part I concerns the relation obtaining between artists and their "creations." Once again, his dramatization of this question and its attendant paradoxes anticipates what occurs in the subsequent narrative. Is a literary work an author's intellectual progeny? Does the process of *artistic* creation resemble the *natural* process of conception, gestation, and birth? Should the attitude of an author toward his or her work therefore resemble that of a doting parent? If conventional wisdom tends to answer such queries in the affirmative, Cervantes makes that conventional wisdom an object of complex parody, or reflective presentation, though not of straightforward acceptance, rejection, praise, or censure. More specifically, in having his narrator state, "Yet I, though seeming to be the father, am the stepfather of Don Quixote" (Pero yo, que, aunque parezco padre, soy padrastro de don Quijote) (*DQ* I: *Prologue*, 51) Cervantes seems to enlist the voice and perspective of that narrator to convey his own characteristic attitude of radical ambivalence, not only toward his book, but also toward his protagonist—an attitude that finds apt expression in the self-allusive terms "father" and "stepfather."

It is important to emphasize that, as Allen points out, the narrator's remark about his being a stepfather instead of a father refers to the protagonist and not to the "history" (Allen 1969–79, 2:43). After all, that narrator refers to "this book" (este libro) in the very first sentence of his Prologue as "the child of my intellect" (hijo de mi entendimiento). In a statement that would seem to link him directly with the protagonist, the narrator still claims that his uncultivated wit engendered but the "*history* of a native son who is dried, wrinkled, and whimsical" ("*historia* de un hijo seco, avellanado, antojadizo") (*DQ* I: *Prologue*, 50; emphasis added). Furthermore, in the same sentence where that narrator disavows paternity over the character of Don Quixote he also informs his readers that he will avoid begging them either to forgive or conceal the flaws "that you might come to see in this child of mine" (que en este mi hijo vieres), that is, in the "book." The narrator therefore remains consistent in his attempt to uphold a distinction between his relation as father to the book and stepfather to the protagonist.

And yet, the narrator's remark about his only appearing to be "father" of the protagonist seems nonsensical, particularly since it occurs at the start of the Prologue and, thus, before the reader has reason to believe that the narrator's voice differs from that of the author. As one begins reading the Prologue, it would therefore seem reasonable to assume that the narrative voice—taken to be that of the actual author—is trying to make a proverbial distinction without a difference. For if both the protagonist and tale are fictional entities—the "children" of the actual author—the protagonist has no existence outside of his tale and the tale has no existence without its protagonist. To "beget" (engendrar) the tale is to beget its protagonist.

Yet within what one may now recognize as the fictional frame of the Prologue, it seems appropriate that the narrator should disown the title of creator or father of Don Quixote, whom the former must thus deem a *historical* figure. On the one hand, then, the narrator's denying that he is the *father* of the protagonist is, from the narrator's perspective, a matter of simple fact. On the other hand, of course, when viewed as the utterance of the historical author, the narrator's disclaimer has the effect ("unintended" by the narrator) of reserving "paternity" for the author himself. Yet it also is important to bear in mind that there are other, self-serving reasons for the fictional narrator simultaneously to distance himself from the main character and to maintain some sense of kinship with him, as evinced in his claim: "I am the stepfather of Don Quixote."

Even in the Prologue, the "history's" schizoid, paradoxical protagonist becomes the recipient of both praise and censure. On the one hand, it seems plausible to infer that the hidalgo (coming from *hijo d'algo*, "son of someone [i.e., someone important]")—who claims to be Alonso Quijano on his deathbed, who is called "señor Quijana" by his neighbor Pedro Alonso (*DQ* I: 5, 104), but who remains effectively anonymous throughout Part I—is the *personality* to whom the narrator refers to as "a native *son* who is dried, wrinkled [and] whimsical" (un *hijo* seco, avellanado [y] antojadizo) (emphasis added). It is significant, I believe, that when he seems either to criticize or distance himself from the hidalgo who fancies himself a knight, the narrator fails to use the *name* "Don Quixote." Besides playing off *hidalgo*, the polyvalent lexeme, *hijo*, or "son," can here refer to that individual simply as a man, as the now elderly "son" of his natural parents, as the "son of his deeds" (*hijo de sus obras*) or as the "native son" of his geographic region. What is more, the modifiers following that lexeme ("dried, wrinkled, whimsical") correspond to the portrait we read of the hidalgo in the first chapter of the narrative, before that hidalgo becomes the full-blown *protagonist* of the "history" in the character and personality of Don Quixote.

Indeed, by describing the hidalgo as "steeped in a host of thoughts never before imagined" (lleno de pensamientos varios y nunca imaginados), the narrator anticipates information which we receive in the first chapter of the narrative. There, as on the title page itself, this particular "son of man" (hidalgo) is described as *ingenioso* or "imaginative" to a fault. He consistently confuses a particular species of imaginary referents with historical referents. Furthermore, the qualifiers "dried" and "wrinkled" not only allude to the character's advanced age and dried-up flesh, but also to his choleric (hot and dry) distemper. As we read in the first chapter, before this "idle" (ocioso) and lunatic character, called simply "the aforesaid hidalgo" (este sobredicho hidalgo) (*DQ* I: 1, 71), becomes Don Quixote: "his brain *dried up*, thus leading him to lose his wits" (*se le secó* el celebro, de manera que vino a perder el juicio) (*DQ* I: 1, 73; emphasis added). Despite the loose diction of his opening paragraph, or his confusing use of the term "son" (hijo) in reference to both his "book" and the hidalgo, our narrator seems to maintain a clear distinction between the hidalgo and the protagonist of the "history." Further, the narrator seems at pains to emphasize that this anonymous "son" is not his child, and that the hidalgo does not "resemble" that narrator in the way that a son resembles his father. Despite the reader's first impressions, then, the similarity between the narrator's uncultivated wit and the "dried-up son"—the hidalgo—is made to seem pure coincidence.

On the other hand, the narrator does claim to be the "stepfather" of the personality who is really the story's protagonist, mentioned *by name* as "Don Quixote." The narrator praises this personality or figure, calling him "such a noble *knight*" (tan noble *caballero*) (*DQ* I: *Prologue*, 52; emphasis added). In this, the narrator echoes the opinion of "all the inhabitants in the district of the Montiel Plains" (todos los habitadores del distrito del campo de Montiel), who reportedly consider our hero "the most chaste lover and the bravest knight to be seen for many years in those regions" (el más casto enamorado y el más valiente caballero que de muchos años a esta parte se vio en aquellos contornos). Furthermore, just as the narrator chose not to plead "with tears in my eyes" (con lágrimas en los ojos) for us to look kindly upon his historical narrative, "my son" (mi hijo), he will avoid begging our gratitude for his having introduced us to such a laudable stepson, who is not an hidalgo: "I do not wish to make you beholden to me for the service I render you in acquainting you with such a noble and honorable *knight*" (Yo no quiero encarecerte el servicio que te hago en darte a conocer tan noble y tan honrado *caballero*) (*DQ* I, 58; emphasis added). For the narrator, then, it would seem that the "ingenious hidalgo" and the "noble knight" represent two distinct personalities, though embodied in the same historical "person."

As "stepfather," the narrator claims what amounts to the legal, social, and familial role of father over the protagonist, Don Quixote. He therefore assumes or usurps someone else's role as "father," but without claiming responsibility, or credit, for the generation of that protagonist. So the question remains: Who does the narrator, self-proclaimed father of the "history," understand to be the father of his stepson, the knight? A related question: Why does the narrator assume the role of stepfather over Don Quixote?

In response, it is necessary to insist that, from the narrator's perspective, Don Quixote's "father" cannot be another historian. As the narrator implies throughout the text of the Prologue, historical writers (editors, compilers) are the fathers of their histories, but not of the subjects about whom they write. For this reason, the narrator never states or implies that Don Quixote is the creation of a rival author's *mind*, or even that the conception of Don Quixote issues from an act of writing. Thus, the narrator would not be tempted to attribute the paternity of Don Quixote to Cide Hamete, for instance, or to any other "author" or historian. Additionally, since he does not consider Don Quixote the character of a fictional narrative, the narrator cannot be deferring to the paternal status of the fictional narrative's historical author, Miguel de Cervantes Saavedra, who, in any case, inhabits a world that remains inaccessible from the heterocosm inhabited by the narrator and the protagonist. Furthermore, within the narrative itself, the protagonist qua protagonist, namely, Don Quixote, is not represented as the product of natural human conception and birth.

In the opening chapters of the narrative, we confront the simulacrum of a human being, presumably the product of human parents ("a son," like any other son of man), in the character of an anonymous hidalgo, whom the narrator of the Prologue describes in a manner consistent with the "history's" first chapter. From the narrator's point of view, and as described in the "history," it is this *ingenious hidalgo* whose imagination acts as both father and mother of Don Quixote, or the narrator's "noble knight." In other words, within the "history" that the narrator of the Prologue claims to have written or compiled, the agent known as Don Quixote is the historically verifiable offspring of one hidalgo's literary species of *ingenio*: that is, his severe humoral imbalance, imagination, wit, madness or inventive "genius." The hidalgo—neither the son nor stepson of the narrator—is the one who "begets" the knight. And, despite the literary origins and quality of his *ingenio*—a clearly ambivalent term denoting both his madness and hyper-poetic "genius"—the protagonist is not a writer, having finally chosen the profession of arms over that of letters.[21] What is more, unlike the hidalgo, Don Quixote is anything but "idle." He is shown to incarnate and to will (rather than write) a literary surrogate of himself into historical existence. The narrator of the Prologue therefore assumes what is tantamount to the role of stepfather through the act of writing his "book," that narrator's "son," which is also the protagonist's "history."

By continuing to adopt the narrator's perspective, and borrowing his dizzying array of generative, familial, and filial imagery, one can assert that the (pro)creative *imagination* (*ingenio*) of the hidalgo ("a dried-up son") is the "father" of the narrator's stepson. The history of that stepson is, in turn, the "son" of the narrator's "sterile" *intellect*. Thus, according to the internal logic of the "history"—a logic that the narrator respects by claiming in his Prologue to be father of the book and stepfather of Don Quixote—the subsequent narrative presents a paradoxical character who is at once the *fiction* of a historical self (the hidalgo) and, as that fiction, a *historical* personage. Moreover, for the narrator, Don Quixote incarnates the oxymoron of a historical fiction—the *other*, contrary personality or "self"—of an anonymous hidalgo, with whom the "history's" *protagonist* shares a body. But, despite their common body, the knight and the hidalgo have different names, the second of which remains unknown. Thus, the hidalgo–Don Quixote union that the "history" sets forth, in a manner consistent with what the narrator asserts in the Prologue, represents a perplexing *coincidentia oppositorum*: a unique convergence and *embodiment* of history and poetry, literature and life, or art and nature.

Yet it bears stressing that in Don Quixote's "mind," such distinctions fail to apply. For him, there are no contraries to reconcile, which means that such oppositions do not simply converge, but collapse. As protagonist of the "history," then, his quest goes to the extreme of attempting to obliterate such paradoxes and to embody what Juan Bautista Avalle-Arce calls "life as a work of art" (1976, 144–72). For the knight, some poetry remains coterminous with history; literature and discourse with life; and art with nature. To add to Avalle-Arce's insight, the hidalgo–Don Quixote union underscores yet another paradox, which the protagonist also attempts to embody in the most extreme fashion, and

---

21. On the specifically literary quality of the protagonist's insanity, see Murillo 1988, 28–34. For a classic study on Don Quixote's distemper in relation to the humoral psychology of Cervantes' time, see Green 1957. Riley refines Green's findings in light of more recent scholarship (1986, 48–49). In addition to providing a compelling analysis of the genesis and development of the protagonist's madness in *Don Quixote*, Johnson (1983) offers a masterful survey of important psychological treatises in Renaissance Spain and their relation to that protagonist of Cervantes' best-known fiction (13–25). In his fine study of *Don Quixote*, Part II, Sullivan (1996) recasts and builds upon Johnson's insights from both a theological and Lacanian perspective.

which he thus fails to see as a paradox at all: the reader as a species of author. Don Quixote attempts to imitate his chivalric models, not only at the level of discourse, but also and especially at the level of deeds. But the "work of art" that he strives to complete, in imitation of his models, involves not only his own life, but his entire age. He strives to "restore" the chivalresque "age of gold" (edad de oro) to a decadent "age of iron" (edad de hierro). For this "decadent" age effaces rather than imitates what for the protagonist are that age's true nature and its "true" historical and ethical models.[22]

To be sure, as represented in both the Prologue and the narrative—and as embodied in the unique character of Don Quixote—the conventional opinion that holds that books and characters are an author's intellectual progeny becomes the object of the author's playful and illustrative parody. But the playful features of such parody are not confined to the narrator's bewildering array of familial and filial terms. Nor, I believe, does that parody aim chiefly at criticizing authors' parental attachment to their creations, or their consequent blindness to the flaws in these creations. Indeed, a more important question of aesthetic, rhetorical, and humanist *philosophia* is at stake.

As Antonio Vilanova has observed with considerable erudition, Cervantes' terminology and imagery relating to authorial "paternity" in the Prologue, and especially the phrase about the narrator's being the stepfather instead of the father of Don Quixote, evoke several passages in Erasmus's *Folly* (Vilanova 1965, 425–26). Unlike Vilanova, however, I do not read the relevant segments of Cervantes' Prologue as a mere echo of Erasmus's humanist doctrines, which Vilanova seems to equate with ethical and aesthetic topoi in the writings of both authors.[23] Furthermore, as is evident from the genesis and characterization of Don Quixote in the narrative, the issue of authorial and artistic "paternity" is not limited to the Prologue, but permeates the entire work.

In the relevant passage of Erasmus's paradoxical and parodic masterpiece, the character of Folly speaks about Nature as truly a *mother* who, in but one particular, *resembles* or *acts like a stepmother*. In the translation of Hoyt Hopewell Hudson, Folly proclaims: "[N]ature, in many respects a stepmother rather than a mother, has sowed some seed of evil in the breasts of mortal men, and particularly of

22. The restoration of chivalry's Golden Age as the crux of Don Quixote's quest is argued with cogency and erudition in Williamson 1984.

23. Vilanova suggests that Cervantes' twofold purpose in borrowing his phrase from Erasmus is to illustrate that "paternal love does not blind him to such an extent that he ignores his work's defects or that he expects others to forgive or conceal the defects it possesses" (que no le ciega el amor paternal hasta el punto de ignorar los defectos de su obra y de pretender que los demás perdonen o disimulen los defectos que posee) (1965, 426).

men somewhat judicious, which makes them dissatisfied with what is their own, while admiring what belongs to another" (Erasmus 1974, 28–29).

In keeping with both her character and her "philosophy," Folly goes on to note that the best remedy against despising what is one's own and envying what belongs to others is found, paradoxically, in unbridled self-love (*philautia*). Lacking this quality (one of Folly's handmaids), a person is incapable of doing anything "pleasing or graceful or seemly." As Folly further states: "Take this ingredient from life, and at once the orator, like his style, will be flat and cold, the musician will be as sour as his notes, the actor, with all his mimicry, will be hissed from the stage." Significantly, however, Folly later observes that the mother who implanted the defect also supplies the remedy: "Oh, the singular foresight of nature, who, in spite of such differences of condition, equalizes all things! Where she has withheld some of her bounties, there she is wont to add a little more self-love" (1974, 29). In other words, if in some respects nature *resembles* a stepmother, in others she reveals herself *to be* a mother.

Broadly speaking, Cervantes' Prologue and Erasmus's most renowned fiction show similarities of both imagery and theme. Both writings employ filial, generative, and familial analogies, and both writings treat of artists' or rhetoricians' regard for their handiwork. But Cervantes subjects Erasmus's image of *mother* nature's occasionally resembling a stepmother—an image that Erasmus derives from both Pliny and Quintilian—to a double reversal.[24] In the first place, Cervantes transforms the contrast between mother and stepmother (*madre/madrastra*) into one between father and stepfather (*padre/padrastro*). In the second place, besides this change of "sex" and gender, Cervantes has his narrator claim that he, the narrator, *seems to be* (parezco) the *parent* (padre), though he *is truly* the stepparent (soy padrastro). Furthermore, as against his creator, the ingenuous narrator of the Prologue seems to mean his words unambiguously. The allusion to Erasmus, to be sure, most plausibly represents an instance of dramatic irony that belongs not to the narrator's, but to the author's, utterance. For the narrator praises rather than censures his stepson, the knight called Don Quixote. And that narrator claims no responsibility at all for having "sowed" a defective "seed" in the hidalgo.

In light of his allusion to Erasmus through the propositional "statements" and voice of his narrator, Cervantes seems to call our attention to his having made his protagonist/son an object of ridicule for readers and characters alike. He also calls our attention to his having endowed his "ingenious hidalgo" with a glaring defect—a seemingly contradictory species of humoral imbalance (choleric

---

24. As Miller notes in his translation of Erasmus's *Folly*, the phrase derives from Quintilian, *Institutiones oratoriae*, 12.1.2, and from Pliny, *Historia naturalis*, 7.1 (Erasmus 1979, 34 n. 2).

melancholy), disposing him to an equally paradoxical type of madness (life as literature). Interestingly, too, an important element contributing to Don Quixote's losing his "wits" (juicio) finds expression in the protagonist's continual attempts to *resolve* such contrived paradoxes (antinomies) and equivocations as found in the works by the popular Spanish author Feliciano de Silva: "With these words [literally: "reasons" or the seventeenth-century Spanish equivalent of *logoi*] the poor knight lost his wits and spent long evenings trying to understand them and draw out their meaning" (Con estas razones perdía el pobre caballero el juicio, y desvelábase por entenderlas y desentrañarles el sentido) (*DQ* I: 1, 72).

In creating this less than ideal reader afflicted with a less than ideal insomnia, the author, Cervantes, seems to act more like his protagonist's stepfather than his "father." Furthermore, in a way that seems far more extreme than the narrator's apparently detached attitude toward his "historical" book (his "son"), the author builds his fictional narrative upon his protagonist's flaws, and never resorts to pleading "tearfully" that we overlook them. But does the author, like Folly's assessment of "mother nature," finally reveal himself a "parent," and supply his main character with some remedy for the latter's flaws? Or does the author consistently show his protagonist to be *nothing but* a madman, a fool, and thus an object of ridicule?

Let me suggest that an important insight into this question, which has divided many critics of the *Quixote* for the past hundred years, may also found in the Prologue of 1605. At bottom, I think it hasty to claim that Cervantes acts simply as *either* a "father" *or* a "stepfather," or that he makes his protagonist a consistent object of *either* praise *or* censure. An inventive and critical contribution to the humanist tradition, Cervantes' work represents a highly complex variation on the mock encomium, though his subject is not the allegorical character of Folly, but a particular, paradoxical "fool." To return to the first section of the Prologue, it is already implicit in the words of the narrator that one's judgment of the protagonist will vary according to whether one perceives him as a crazed hidalgo or a noble knight or, finally, somewhere between or even beyond those categorical extremes.

To be sure, the so-called hard or negative view of the protagonist is not reserved for literary critics alone. The vast majority of characters in the work, ranging from those who show genuine concern for the protagonist to those who aim only to divert themselves at his expense, would clearly agree that Don Quixote is *nothing but* a lunatic hidalgo. Such is the view, for instance, of the hidalgo's niece, his housekeeper, the curate Pero Pérez, and the barber *maese* Nicolás. This is also the view of, say, the duke and duchess, their servants at the palace, and Sansón Carrasco. Though oblivious to the narrator's self-serving distinction between the hidalgo and the knight, the factually oriented history

attributed to Cide Hamete contains, in the main, a host of unflattering judgments and descriptions of what are portrayed as the protagonist's follies. Hence
Don Quixote's rejection of that history's ultimate "truth." For very different
reasons, of course, Sancho is shown to be equally uninterested in determining
whether his master is truly a knight-errant (whatever that term means for Sancho)
or a crazed hidalgo. Yet, very briefly put, the squire's complex relationship with
Don Quixote includes that illiterate peasant's admiration for the knight's presumed learning and wisdom, combined with impatience and mockery regarding
Don Quixote's lunacy. In short, according to all the foregoing perspectives, Don
Quixote is either nothing but, or little more than, a crazed hidalgo.

By contrast, aside from Don Quixote himself, the only character (or, perhaps,
the only perspective) in the narrative explicitly adhering to what we may call a soft
view of the protagonist and his chivalric ethos is the "second author" (segundo
autor), a narrative voice emerging at the start of I, 8. As I explore more fully in
the following chapter of this study, that "second author" seems to consider Don
Quixote *nothing but* a noble, heroic knight. Finally, however, a minority view prevails among those characters who seem willing to engage in a respectful dialogue
with Don Quixote, and who are apt to find a truly startling measure (provoking
admiratio) of cogency in his words, if less often in his deeds. Most notably, such
characters include the Canon of Toledo, Don Diego de Miranda, the latter's son,
Don Lorenzo, and the inhabitants of the "feigned Arcadia"—all of whom are
reported as either judging or explicitly calling the protagonist a puzzling type of
sane madman (*cuerdo loco*).[25] Which, if any, of these assessments does the author
finally represent to be the "true" portrait of his protagonist?

On the one hand, I would contend that none of the ideologies represented in
characters or perspectives casting judgment on Don Quixote is shown to be
"exemplary," or beyond criticism. To varying degrees, most characters become
ensnared in the fictive categories of their own discourse. Indeed, in the manner
of a "stepfather," Cervantes seems to have implanted some defect of judgment in

---

25. As we read in the "history": "The canon was *astonished* at the *cogent nonsense* that Don Quixote
had spoken (*Admirado* quedó el canónigo de los *concertados disparates* que don Quijote había dicho) (*DQ*
I: 50, 588; emphasis added). In similar fashion: "Once again father and son [Don Diego and Don
Lorenzo] were *astonished* at the *blend of sense and nonsense of Don Quixote's words*" (De nuevo *se admi-
raron* padre y hijo [don Diego y don Lorenzo] de *las entremetidas razones de don Quijote, ya discretas y ya
disparatadas*) (*DQ* II: 18, 177; emphasis added). And, concerning the reaction of the "shepherds and
shepherdesses" in the "Feigned Arcadia," the protagonist is shown "leaving his listeners in *a state of astonishment, leading them to doubt whether they should take him to be sane or mad*" (dejando *admirados* a los
circunstantes, *haciéndoles dudar si le podían tener por loco o por cuerdo*) (*DQ* II: 58, 480; emphasis added).
Interestingly, these characters all react to Don Quixote with astonishment, wonder, or "alienation" (*admiratio*) rather than laughter.

almost every character and perspective that appears in his work. On the other hand, not all judgments are shown to be defective in the same manner and to the same extent. Hence it seems that no character can be labeled simply as the author's spokesperson or his foil.

Nonetheless, those characters who dub the protagonist a "sane madman" (cuerdo loco) are shown to be capable of attentive dialogue and, in Erasmian fashion, to be capable of discerning wisdom in folly, and nobility in apparent lowliness. As to the other characters, a lack of critical intelligence utterly discredits the judgments of Pero Pérez, *maese* Nicolás, the housekeeper, the niece, and the "second author" on matters of wisdom, learning, or perhaps even simple logic. Likewise, idleness and self-indulgence—sometimes resulting in cruel mockery and injustice—discredits the judgments of characters such as the duke and duchess or Sansón Carrasco on matters of moral wisdom or ethical "nobility."

In each case, the manner in which a character treats the protagonist (or his "history") reflects that character's worth as a judge, reader, and moral agent. Don Quixote is, indeed, the paradoxical agency—some sort of madman by any estimation—whereby Cervantes forces his other characters to prove, and perhaps to face, the shortcomings of their own "philosophical" and moral judgments. Significantly, the "hard" characters, like the "soft" "second author," are shown to be incapable of self-reflection. By extension, through the agency of a fiction about a protagonist and his history, the author invites his readers to examine, or leads them to reveal, the underpinnings of their own aesthetic and ethical categories.

So to speak, the author's artistic paternity seemingly obliges him, at the same time, to act in the manner of what Folly would call a stepfather. For if Don Quixote represents a fool whose laughable and often harmful exploits parody a facile understanding of virtue and "heroism," the innocent nobility and wisdom informing his lunacy remind attentive listeners (readers) of ideals that their society is striving to forget, placing a mirror before myriad ideologies, discourses, and fictions that enjoy the official status of "sanity." Furthermore, in Cervantes' Prologue, as in Erasmus's *Folly*, the issue of an artist's acceptance or rejection of his own handiwork occurs in the context of a discussion about *self*-hate and *self*-love, which can lead to extreme utterances of either self-censure or self-praise.

For both Erasmus and Cervantes, it seems that Folly's assessment of the "defect" and its remedy is not so much false as partial and simplistic. An unstated defect afflicting Folly, Don Quixote, and Cervantes' other characters, including the narrator of the Prologue, is a paradoxical excess of *both* self-love *and* self-hate that issues from a lack of self-knowledge and self-reflection. Such characters become the object of their author's complex parody. As *both* "father" and "stepfather," the author portrays how—regarding his book, his characters, and especially his protagonist—their virtues remain bound up with their vices, their flaws with their strengths. In particular, despite the narrator's spurious distinctions, and despite the disclaimer of the character claiming to be *nothing but* "Alonso Quijano *the Good*" on his deathbed, the crazed hidalgo is inseparable from the "noble knight." As broached through the one-sided and hackneyed discourse of his narrator in the Prologue, what the author sets forth for his readers' reflection, in both the "history" and character of Don Quixote, is an aesthetic and ethical paradox that calls for continual self-examination and continual reassessment of accepted commonplaces and received opinion (*doxa*).

Predictably enough, Cervantes can hardly avoid relating such an ethical and aesthetic "lesson" to his own circumstance as "creator" of the paradoxical Prologue, book, and protagonist that we confront in the pages of *Don Quixote*. As "stepfather," Cervantes seems purposely to implant defects within his protagonist and so his entire fiction. As "father," however, he shows those defects to be the source of his protagonist's, and his fiction's, strength and *admiratio*. Likewise, from the standpoint of historical "truth," Cervantes is the literal "author" and metaphorical "father" of a specific tale and a specific protagonist: *Don Quixote* and Don Quixote. Yet, as he indicates through his narrator in the Prologue, the empirical Cervantes, in a sense, remains as much an editor/"stepfather" as any other "author." For even the most *inventive* imitator or "composer" (componedor) must adopt and transform existing models, or existing forms of historical and poetic discourse, in order to "beget" or "bear" textual offspring.

Idle Readers as Active Authors

Cervantes' handling of general aesthetic issues in the first section of the Prologue points to the self-conscious and parodic dramatization of his own dilemma as an author compelled to write a Prologue for his book, and as *the* author compelled to write *this* Prologue for *this* book. From the first words of his Prologue, the author seems to strike an ambivalent rhetorical posture toward his Prologue and book's potential readership. Yet, once again, the author communicates his attitude of ambivalence, and the paradoxes informing the reader-author relation, by means of his narrator's theoretical and practical contradictions, or antinomies.

In light of the author's ruse concerning his own identity, it seems both fitting and odd that the Prologue should begin with an assertion of the narrator's reliability: "Idle/leisured reader, *without my swearing an oath you may believe me*" ("Desocupado lector, *sin juramento me podrás creer*") (*DQ* I: *Prologue*, 50; emphasis added). Indirectly, this narrator tries to guarantee his credibility through the solemnity of an oath. He does so by using the trope of paralipsis, whereby the addresser manages to emphasize an idea by seeming to pass over it (e.g., "without my swearing an oath" [sin juramento]). If viewed as part of the author's *utterance*, the narrator's opening "statement" both dramatizes and parodies the traditional need of any writer or rhetorician to establish his or her credentials of reliability and competence (ethos), thus eliciting the "proper" emotional response (pathos) of sympathy, confidence, and trust from the audience. In short, beginning with these words, it seems plausible to read the two paragraphs belonging to the first section of the Prologue, addressed to the "idle/leisured reader," as the author's parody of a standard *captatio benevolentiae*.

In large measure, Cervantes' parody of that tradition serves to dramatize what is perhaps the latent desire of all authors to produce the perfect book and their apparent obligation, in essence, to denounce what they consider to be their good, if imperfect, attempts. No doubt, an author's decision to write and publish a book at all proves that he or she thinks it worthy of the reader's attention and, thus, worthy of praise. As the author strives to fulfill contradictory obligations of ethos—denouncing one's work, while calling attention to its value—convention and decorum require that he or she also avoid the twin evils of arrogance and affected modesty. Thus, in his parody, Cervantes has his narrator strive yet fail on all counts. That character's attempt and failure in this regard begins when he naively expresses two *impossible* wishes and the reasons for their remaining unfulfilled.

First, after asking his reader to believe him "without my swearing an oath," the narrator states that he "would wish" (quisiera) that his book might prove to be "the most beautiful, the most graceful and the wittiest book *that one could ever imagine*" (el más hermoso, el más gallardo y más discreto *que pudiera imaginarse*) (*DQ* I: *Prologue*, 50; emphasis added). Stating more "truth" about that impossibility than he seems to realize, the narrator lapses into affected modesty when he points to the cause of his presumed "failure": "But I have been unable to thwart the laws of Nature" (Pero no he podido yo contravenir al orden de naturaleza). It is in his equally affected corollary—significantly, a rhetorical question—where he makes only token mention of his barren, uncultivated wit: " And so, what could my sterile, uncultivated intellect beget but a history about a shriveled son?" (Y así, ¿qué podrá engendrar el estéril y mal cultivado ingenio mío sino la historia de un hijo seco?) (*DQ* I: *Prologue*, 50). Moreover, here he seems to blame the story's defects on the hidalgo or "shriveled son" (hijo seco) who, it turns out, is not the narrator's creation, or "son of his intellect." The narrator concludes his failed attempt at expressing modesty with a hackneyed image of how an author's love for his intellectual progeny will blind him to its defects:

"It sometimes happens that a father will have an ugly son, utterly lacking in social graces, and yet the love he bears toward that son will place a blindfold over his eyes so that he fails to see his son's flaws" (Acontece tener un padre un hijo feo y sin gracia alguna, y el amor que le tiene le pone una venda en los ojos para que no vea sus faltas) (*DQ* I: *Prologue*, 50).

It is noteworthy, however, that the narrator should speak about an undetermined father, thus failing to say that this image of *a* doting father (*un* padre) reflects his own bias in favor of his book. Indeed, despite his willingness to utter a series of conventional phrases favoring authorial modesty *in general*, it seems that the narrator cannot bring himself to acknowledge that either he or this particular book suffer from any shortcomings. In other words, he seems unable to acknowledge that he has failed to produce not the perfect protagonist, but the perfect book. Following his expression of the most ingenuous of authorial desires, the narrator's first paragraph therefore fails either to argue effectively for the value of his book or to acknowledge that book's possible defects. Additionally, the narrator's failed attempts at modesty are shown to arise from his resistance to self-criticism and his naive belief that what is *desirable* (the perfect book) must therefore be *possible*. It hardly needs saying that the author makes his narrator's facile equation between the desirable and the possible an object of parodic censure.

The affected quality of the narrator's modesty is further confirmed at the start of his transcribed dialogue. To his friend, he utters fawning, hyperbolic remarks concerning his own age ("bearing all my years on my back" [con todos mis años a cuestas] [*DQ* I: *Prologue*, 52]), his lack of publications and the presumed shortcomings of his book: "with a story dry as hemp, bereft of invention, paltry in style, poor in conceits and utterly devoid of learning and doctrine" (con una leyenda seca como un esparto, ajena de invención, menguada de estilo, pobre de concetos y falta de toda erudición y doctrina) (*DQ* I: *Prologue*, 52). He therefore seems to be fishing for compliments from a *known reader* and *friend*, bound to show sympathy. Moreover, those remarks come on the heels of the narrator's comment about his potential readership as "that ancient lawgiver they call the masses" (el antiguo legislador que llaman vulgo) (*DQ* I: *Prologue*, 52), implicitly attributing intellectual inferiority to any reader who would fault that narrator for the "defects" cited by the narrator himself. Thus, both his self-deprecation and modesty seem token and insincere.

Second, the narrator conveys an equally impossible desire, not only concerning the "book," but specifically the "Prologue": "I should *wish* only to present it [the history] to you in its purest and barest form, without the frill of a Prologue" (Sólo *quisiera* dártela [la historia] monda y desnuda, sin el ornato de prólogo) (*DQ* I:

Prologue, 51; emphasis added). Here the reader faces the paradox of a prologuist who states, in "this" very prologue, that what prologuists state in their prologues is a superfluous "frill" (ornato). The author makes his narrator seem unaware that, owing to its self-reference and self-contained quality, that character's assertion seems true to the degree it is false, useful to the degree that it is superfluous. Moreover, it would seem that the narrator must disbelieve what he claims, in "this prologue," to believe about the futility of composing "this prologue" for "this book." For only thus can he produce, and only thus was he presumably able to produce, "this prologue" that asserts the "important" message concerning its own futility. From his reader's standpoint, the message that would make the narrator's Prologue worth reading would be that the Prologue "you are now reading" is not worth reading. To accept that message as worthwhile is to accept it as worthless, thus worthwhile, and so on. Regarding ethos, such lack of self-awareness argues against the narrator's competence and reliability.

The narrator's failure of ethos—his failure to show modesty, competence, and reliability—is thus seen to result specifically from his capitulation to the conventional demands of the *captatio benevolentiae:* the seemingly contradictory need to tout and denounce one's talents and one's work.[26] His failure stems as well from his related desires to emulate some ineffable archetype of beauty, and to present the bare truth of his "history"—shorn of rhetorical "frills"—together with his inability to recognize those commonplace desires as a practical impossibility. Thus, too, many of his rhetorical failures in the Prologue's first two paragraphs both dramatize and parody what amounts to a prototype of an author's "ethical" dilemma. In particular, however, the narrator's rhetorical failures allude to the specific dilemma of the author responsible for the actual Prologue and book—the actual fiction—we have before us.

In matters relating more directly to pathos, which is nonetheless inseparable from ethos, the narrator's situation reflects that of an author who must elicit trust and sympathy from an *unknown* readership. Hoping for his readers' acceptance, yet fearing their rejection, an author is prone to affirm or deny their critical acumen according to how they judge both his talents and his work. Addressing an audience of potential friends and enemies, that author will want to show confidence and respect toward the first group, thereby eliciting sympathy, even as he will harbor feelings of hostility or indifference toward the second, convincing himself that their opinions (and their sympathy) are unworthy of his attention. In Cervantes' time, one famous method of dealing with the constant authorial

26. In his *Prologhi al 'Don Chisciotte,'* Socrate argues that throughout the Prologue of 1605, the author ironically portrays himself as caught between the contrary demands of the *exordium* and the *captatio benevolentiae* (1974, 88–111).

dilemma of how to address an audience of potential friends and foes, and how to sift critical wheat from chaff, is found in the two separate prologues of Mateo Alemán's *Guzmán de Alfarache*: one addressed as "To the Masses" (Al vulgo), the other "From the Selfsame [Author] to the Discreet Reader" (Del mismo al lector discreto) (Alemán [1599, 1602] 1983, 91–92, 93–94). The unwittingly ambivalent statements of Cervantes' narrator in the Prologue serve to parody both that authorial dilemma and Alemán's authorial method for striking the "correct" posture with the "proper" readership.

Faced with an audience of potential sympathizers and critics, the narrator clearly chooses to perceive the first group as "discreet," the second as part of the "masses." He is therefore made to seem incapable, despite his best efforts, of sustaining a tone of cordiality in the words he addresses to the implied reader of the Prologue. Hence his unwitting ambiguity in his various modes of address. As Porqueras Mayo points out, the opening words "idle/leisured reader" (desocupado lector) constitute an unprecedented mode of address in Spain's prefatory tradition (1981, 77). If those words can be understood in a favorable light, they can also be taken to imply the reader's idleness or lack of involvement in his or her reading. Similarly, the narrator's words, "gentle [literally: soft] reader" (lector suave), in the final paragraph of the Prologue may refer to either the implied reader's benevolence or his or her uncritical, soft-headed gullibility. We know not which. In both cases, the narrator's diction resembles the ingenuous laxity of such a statement as "I cannot recommend this candidate [reader] too highly." Furthermore, the narrator addresses the reader as "dearest reader" (lector carísimo) only when stating that the latter need not forgive or conceal the flaws he or she may perceive in the narrator's intellectual "child." But, while seeming respectfully to exonerate and endear his reader, the narrator appears to strike an accusatory, hostile tone: "You are neither its relative nor its friend" (ni eres su pariente ni su amigo) (*DQ* I: *Prologue*, 51). Indeed, the reader may well take this to suggest that his critical assessment of the book is, in the narrator's opinion, of little import.

In addition, the narrator proves ambiguous in his acknowledgment of the reader's inherent dignity and freedom. For if the reader's gift of freedom is acknowledged in theological language, "you have your soul in your body as well as your free will" (tienes tu alma en tu cuerpo y tu libre albedrío) the reader is said to possess those qualities "as much as the most perfectly *wrought* man" (como el más *pintado*) (*DQ* I: *Prologue*, 51; emphasis added), in idiomatic terms that implicitly equate that reader with such soulless, unfree entities as a literary character or "painted image." Further, the narrator calls the reader "Lord [of your house], as the king is lord of his revenues" (señor della, como el rey de sus alcabalas). And yet the narrator no sooner likens the reader to a "king" than, in the next clause, he seemingly negates the compliment, again by means of an ambiguous idiom: "[A]nd you know the commonplace saying, that beneath my own cloak I can kill the king." ([Y] sabes lo que comúnmente se dice, que debajo de mi manto, al rey mato) (*DQ* I: *Prologue*, 51). As Williamson succinctly observes: "The 'king' here refers to the reader who has just been invited by Cervantes to view himself as the sovereign judge of the text" (1984, 82–83). Far from putting the reader at ease, the statement can thus be construed to mean: "Reader/king, beware." Of course, this latter message is also at issue with the apparently respectful meaning of the first paragraph's concluding words, which can likewise be read as potentially dismissive and hostile: "[Y]ou may say of the history whatever you please, without fearing that anyone will slander you for the bad things, or reward you for the good things, which you may say about it" ([P]uedes decir de la historia todo aquello que te pareciere, sin temor que te calunien por el mal ni te premien por el bien que dijeres della) (*DQ* I: *Prologue*, 51). Indeed, the narrator's words of praise for his readers can also be understood as conveying his indifference about whether his readers enjoy the work, or about whether anyone reads the book at all. What is more, after the narrator tells his reader that the latter may judge the work with impunity, that reader learns at the start of the dialogue between the narrator and his friend that criticism of either the narrator or his work will equate such a reader with "that ancient lawgiver they call the masses" (el antiguo legislador que llaman vulgo) (*DQ* I: *Prologue*, 52). The narrator tries, in other words, to write a Prologue to a person whom he would like to consider the *discreet reader* (sympathizer), while remaining haunted by the implied presence of the *vulgar reader* (critic).

Caught within the contrary demands of literary convention—and couching several of his "ideas" in the conventional language of popular sayings (*refranes*)—the narrator seems unable to elicit a fitting emotional response (pathos) of sympathy, confidence, or trust. Thus, if perceived as an utterance of the narrator, the Prologue's *captatio benevolentiae* represents nothing less than a prototypical failure to establish a proper rhetorical posture.

In a sense, of course, it is necessary to view the narrator's failure of rhetorical posture as a measure of the author's success. The narrator's incompetent statements of "authorial" purpose both signal and constitute the implied author's competent parody. Indeed, through the author's combined use of fiction and parody, the narrator's failures and contradictions (matter and substance of the author's parodic fiction) *generate* that author's rhetorical success.

In particular, the mediation of a fictional narrator and a fictional prologue allows the author not only to *state* the prototypical desire of an author to create a perfect book, but also to parody that desire as an impossibility. On this point, the same statement that signifies the narrator's naïveté also signifies, from a different perspective, the author's shrewdness and self-knowledge, specifically in his capacity as author of "this" Prologue and "this" book.

By implying, through his parody, that no book is perfect, the author *seems* to acknowledge that his own book is therefore defective. But if it is folly to expect (rather than desire) a perfect book, then failure to produce such a book can hardly be considered a defect that makes the author deserving of censure. As a result, the narrator's apology for being unable to "thwart the laws of Nature" (contravenir al orden de naturaleza) (*DQ* I: *Prologue*, 50) not only represents an instance of his affected modesty and, as such, an object of parody. That statement also calls attention, in a way that the narrator seemingly fails to realize, to an immutable state of affairs that requires no apology. Indeed, the narrator's opening statements about his yearnings and his presumed failures call our attention to the mysterious fact that art arises out of a *legitimate desire* to strive after ideal beauty, which is also a practical impossibility, or a species of wise folly. Both utopian desire and imperfection are shown to lie at the heart of human artifice.

Thus, if the author both states and acknowledges through his narrator that his book is less than perfect, he falls short of taking blame for such "imperfection," implying that it is simply "natural." Using a method akin to Mexía's distinction between "telling lies" and "lying," the author issues a statement of "apology" through the narrator, but without therefore apologizing. The author's utterance thus represents a nonapology in the form of an apology. Here, as throughout the rest of the Prologue, the author avoids having to engage in *either* self-praise *or* self-censure. As a consequence, he avoids striking a rhetorical posture of either arrogance or affected modesty.

A similar strategy is at work in the author's enumeration of what appear to be his *personal* defects through the voice of the narrator. To be sure, the pseudobiographical data concerning the narrator's age and lack of publications allude to the historical author. Yet it is pertinent to recall that this enumeration of presumed defects forms the substance of the *narrator's* affected modesty. The author manages to absolve himself of *that* defect by making it the object of censure, in that the narrator's affected modesty is the author's *parody* of affected modesty. It is also far from clear that the narrator's advanced age and lack of publications, for instance, are meant to be taken as defects. In any case, the author's utterance conveys no other "truth" through these statements than his own dramatization and parody of the narrator's insincerity. There would seem to be no justification for reading such a parody of the narrator's statements as the author's attempt either to affirm or deny those statements' self-deprecating content in relation to the author himself.

Thus, regarding authorial ethos, the technique of fictional self-parody is again made to yield a paradox. The author is able to issue a series of self-deprecating "statements" that nonetheless fail to make him the object of censure. His self-deprecating *words* (*logoi*) fail to signify an *act* of self-deprecation. Yet neither do they, of themselves, make him an object of praise. Nor do they constitute an act of self-praise or *philautia*. Furthermore, as part of the author's utterance, the narrator's statements neither deny nor attempt to conceal the possible deficiencies of the author or the work. Indeed, the affected modesty of his fictional analogue is, paradoxically, the means whereby the author avoids his character's dual folly of both *philautia* and affected modesty.

Also regarding authorial ethos, it is relevant to note that the narrator's defect of affected modesty follows from *the convention* of having somehow to praise and denounce one's own work. Indeed, within the context of a work that an author has chosen to write and publish, statements of self-censure seem inexorably to lead to affected modesty. Likewise, statements of self-praise invariably betoken arrogance. The author's parody of the narrator's defect, affected modesty, therefore includes and *dramatizes* the conventional discursive arrangement that brings that defect about. Furthermore, as the author's fictional surrogate, parodically representing the writer responsible for the Prologue we are now reading, the narrator faces the same conventional demands as his creator. So it is through his parody of the narrator's false modesty that the author also parodies the narrator's *having accepted* the demands of *rhetorical convention* on their own impossible terms: self-praise *or* self-censure; arrogance *or* affected modesty. But the parodic representation of the narrator's acceptance does not so much signal the author's simple rejection of the same terms as his rejection of their apparent fixity. Moreover, as set forth in the narrator's statements, those categorical terms are also the *medium* whereby the author averts, dramatizes, and moves beyond them—in other words, he moves beyond having to choose either one or the other course of writerly action.

In creating a story and a parody about a character who fails to resolve his "ethical" dilemma as "author of this book," the empirical Cervantes, in his capacity as author of *Don Quixote*, elides that dilemma himself. He therefore fulfills the demands of ethos in the act of subverting them, just as he simultaneously upholds and undoes the terms of those demands. The author's parody of his own authorial dilemma dramatizes how he both is and is not bound by those terms (self-praise/self-censure, arrogance/affected modesty). Fictional self-parody likewise distances him from the contradictoriness of his "ethical" demands as author of the book: how to effect self-praise without arrogance; or self-censure without affected modesty. Yet the "resolution" of his dilemma is intelligible only in light of those contradictory demands.

It may prove tempting to read the narrator's statements of affected modesty concerning his own shortcomings as an enumeration of the author's *possible* defects or motives for criticism. As such, the author's willingness to present them at all, even in the form of fictional parody, would seem to indicate his humility. Nonetheless, the issue of whether these potential defects are either true or false in reference to the author, his Prologue, or his book—or whether those potential defects are truly defects—remains unaddressed, much less answered. The upshot of the author's "ethical" posture is, characteristically, to defer all decisions to the reader about which traits of that author, his Prologue, or his book are finally deserving of praise or censure.

Along the same lines, the author reveals self-awareness and competence concerning his particular dilemma as author of "this" Prologue in the highly self-referential second paragraph, which begins with the narrator's express desire to deliver his story "in its purest and barest form" (monda y desnuda) and to avoid writing a necessarily useless prologue. Thanks to his method of fictional self-parody, the author of the fiction is thus able to suggest a prototypical desire to sidestep literary convention (i.e., to avoid writing prologues); to uphold its legitimacy as a desire; and, last, to acknowledge that desire's impossibility. Again, through parody, the author transforms the narrator's rhetorical failure and lack of self-awareness into his own rhetorical success. Similarly, in an act of self-allusion and self-parody, that same author dramatizes the narrator's dilemma to be an obverse reflection of his own.

More important, however, is the Prologue's second paragraph, where the unself-critical narrator calls attention to himself as "author" of the Prologue, to the futility of all prologues, and to the arduous labor involved in composing "the preface you are now reading." These statements show the *author's* Prologue, or his prefatory fiction, to be a competent, inventive paradox of self-reference. When perceived as part of the author's utterance, these statements by the narrator reveal that the author chooses to fulfill his own obligation to write a prologue by writing a *fictional parody* about (1) the convention that demands that authors write prologues to their books, (2) the conventions governing the writing of prologues, and (3) his writing/not writing, and having to write, this specific, prefatory utterance for his *Don Quixote*. Yet an example of Cervantes' tendency to reverse reversals, or in a Spanish phrase, *rizar el rizo* (to curl the curl), his Prologue also represents a parody of its own self-parody. For, as a parody of prologues, the author's Prologue is also a *parody of an author* who, within the context of his own prologue, would denounce the value of all prologues and the need to write them. Deftly avoiding the contradictions of his narrator, whose circumstances parallel his own, Cervantes produces a prologue that parodies the theory and practice of prologues. Yet, in doing so, he writes what is generally recognized as a masterful prologue, which also has the effect of a metaprologue and an antiprologue, but is not simply one or the other.[27] Without owning or disowning *the desire* to avoid writing a prologue, Cervantes writes his prologue, *acting* on both the assumption and the awareness that it is impossible to avoid writing prologues.

Yet a question remains that applies to both the narrator and the author: Do they succeed or fail in their obligation to write a prologue? On the one hand, it seems plausible to assert that the author fulfills his obligation to write a prologue, even as he achieves his purpose (desire?) to write a fully parodic prologue, or a prologue that parodies all prologues. This achievement means that the author both fulfills and avoids his obligation in equal measure. It means, too, that one is justified in construing his antiprologue as a defense of prologues. In fact, regarding the author's obligation, his fulfillment is made coterminous with avoidance. The method he employs in fulfilling the demands of convention remains identical to the method employed in subverting those demands. It therefore remains unclear whether "fulfillment" or "avoidance" of his obligation to write a prologue best describes the *purpose* behind the author's utterance. In what sense, then, are we to judge the author's prefatory utterance a success or a failure? And in what sense are we to consider this fictional, prefatory utterance the author's prologue to his book?

In a manner that parallels the evasive "achievement" of the author, the narrator's means of both fulfilling and skirting the obligation to write his own prologue consists of transcribing, or claiming to transcribe, a conversation with a garrulous friend. According to its own internal "logic," the narrator's utterance originates from his presumed inability to write a prologue and his express desire to avoid writing a prologue. What is more, the prologue that presumably cost the narrator so much work to "compose" or make—"I found no [task] more laborious than that of making the preface you are now reading" (ninguno [i.e., ningún trabajo] tuve por mayor que hacer esta prefación que vas leyendo) (*DQ* I: *Prologue*, 51)—coincides with a prologue that we never see and that the narrator

27. Canavaggio, in "Cervantes en primera persona," rightly observes that the Prologue of 1605 concerns the art and science of writing prologues—that it is, in other words, a meta-prologue (1977, 38). Rivers deems the Prologue of 1605 an "anti-prologue" in "Cervantes' Art of the Prologue" (1974, 169). Alberto Porqueras Mayo uses the term "counterprologue" (contra-prólogo) in reference to the same text, in "En torno a los prólogos de Cervantes" (1981, 80). Rivers (1960) provides a brief discussion of the prefatory matter in Part II, arguing that Cervantes himself is probably the author of the Letter of Approval that was supposed to be by Márquez Torres, whose name appears at its close (*DQ* II: *Approbation*, 29–31).

never "writes." For the "prologue" whose "writing" led him to sit "pensively" at his desk, pen behind his ear, cannot correspond to the prologue that results from his effortlessly transcribing, and perhaps doctoring, a conversation with his friend. Yet he also identifies that "preface" as the one we are "now reading." Indeed, if we assume the narrator's perspective, what we have before us represents neither his "original" transcription nor the "original" Prologue. Yet neither does it represent an "antiprologue." Instead, we encounter the narrator's prelude to a prologue, or even his *non*prologue, which bears the name "Prologue."

Furthermore, the reader reaches the end of the narrator's prologue only to hear about, not what the narrator did, but what he "tried" and "decided" to do: "From those very [words of my friend] I tried / *decided to make* this Prologue" (de ellas mismas [i.e., las razones del amigo] *quise hacer* este prólogo). In the very next clause, the narrator refers to his prologue in the future tense: "in which [prologue] *you will see*, gentle reader, the sound judgment of my friend" (en el cual *verás*, lector suave, la discreción de mi amigo) (*DQ* I: *Prologue*, 58; emphasis added). Hence we are left to await the appearance of the narrator's "real" prologue as the one we are now reading draws to a close. Indeed, the *conclusion* of the narrator's prologue seems to *preface* its own beginning, or "birth." More accurately, though, this "conclusion" suggests the possible "beginning" of a nonexistent prologue, "to be seen" (*verás*) at some moment that remains forever in a state of deferral. Accordingly, for reasons both parallel and opposed, the Prologue of the narrator and that of the author could justifiably bear such paradoxical titles as: "This Is Not a Prologue," "This Prologue Is Not a Prologue," "This Prologue Is Not 'This Prologue,'" "This Prologue Has Not Been 'This Prologue,'" "This Prologue Will Not Have Been This Prologue," or even "This Prologue Will Not Be 'This Prologue.'"[28]

Hence the most elementary questions about authorial ethos—that is, about the author's establishing his credentials as a competent writer of prologues—seem unanswerable in such simple terms as yes or no, true or false. Indeed, we would have to affirm and negate both sides of such questions as the following. Did the author fail or succeed in his obligation to write a prologue? Did he mean to fulfill or avoid his obligation to write a prologue? Does he present the conven-

---

28. In *Dissemination*, Derrida engages in a similar logical or semantic paradox by means of the opening/anti-opening, prefatory/antiprefatory negative assertion of the first chapter/antichapter titled (or translated as) "Outwork" that remains inside/outside of his book/antibook: "This (therefore) will not have been a book" (1981, 3). Similar, yes, but not identical. In Cervantes' text such antinomies remain implicit and draw attention to *both* opposing sides of a question. As evinced in the apodictic quality of the above quotation, Derrida's writings show a penchant for antinomy, which relies on rigid dichotomies and univocal terms (e.g., "presence/absence"). This penchant remains consistent with a radically skeptical position that seeks and laments the inability to obviate meaning and mind.

tion of writing prologues, as well as his own "prologue," as worthy of praise or censure? Does the author's utterance reveal a serious or comic purpose? Is "this," or is this not, the author's complete Prologue, or does "the preface you are now reading" remain to be written?

It would seem that in the end, readers alone must ascertain whether it is folly or wisdom that engenders the obligation to write prologues. With no assistance from the implied author, they must decide for themselves whether the fictional parody of prologues they are "now reading" truly puts forth a prologue and in what sense that parodic prologue proves either a success or a failure. But, more important, the reader alone must decide whether it seems necessary to make such either/or judgments, or to favor one extreme position over the other in aesthetic and rhetorical matters. Indeed, I would suggest that Cervantes' handling of his own, and of the typical author's, "ethical" dilemma is more an invitation to ponder and play with the paradoxes, *impossibilia*, or *sophismata* that that dilemma brings forth than to provide "solutions" to a series of logical and semantic "problems."

Just as parody and an ambivalent, reflective openness to contrary positions characterize the author's ethos, established in the *captatio benevolentiae* of the Prologue's first section, so an ambivalent, reflective laughter characterizes his pathos. For that implied author establishes his credentials, or his ethos, through a parody of ethos, and of his own "ethical" dilemma. In similar fashion, it seems especially apt that he should elicit a response of laughter from his readers as he induces them to observe the admixture of wisdom and folly, truth and falsity, or necessity and impossibility involved in reducing the theory and practice of literature to a series of rigid tenets or formulations. Thus, by parodically dramatizing the art and science of literature as a *discordia concors*—a mysterious reality that ultimately defies ratiocinative logic and finds apt expression only in the nonsensical language of paradox—Cervantes elicits a *mixed* response of *admiratio* and laughter. Indeed, this response remains consistent with what Cide Hamete reportedly asserts in reference to the protagonist: "Don Quixote's exploits should be celebrated either with wonder or with laughter" (los sucesos de don Quijote, o se han de celebrar con admiración o con risa) (*DQ* II: 44, 368). Regarding this passage, Williamson observes: "Cervantes himself points out that laughter should not be the sole response to the knight's lunacies. *Admiratio*, just as much as mirth, forms part of his intention in the *Quixote*" (1984, 90). Williamson also astutely observes that Cervantes is able to elicit such a novel response from his readers owing to the knight's paradoxical lunacy: "Cervantes effectively redefines the nature of the marvelous by seeking it, not in the supernatural, but in the madness of his protagonist; although the madness is consistently mocked, it is used all the same to turn the tables on the reader, whose common sense is never actually confounded but neither is it ever decisively triumphant over the knight's inspired lunacy" (1984, 90–91).

Elaborating on Williamson's remarks, I would add that in Cervantes' fiction—both its Prologue and subsequent narrative—the discourse of common sense (*doxa*) is never decisively triumphant over the inspired nonsense of paradoxical discourse. Indeed, Cervantes deploys the rhetoric of paradoxy, and his protagonist's lunacy, not simply to confound, but to enlarge and "open up" the fixity of conventional assumptions about truth, falsity, sanity, or madness. If the lunacy of the protagonist, like the apparent nonsense of paradoxy, leads us to laugh at *transparent* "folly," the *hidden* cogency of such lunacy and nonsense provokes *admiratio*, which aims at shocking us into a critical, self-reflective response.

The first section of the Prologue of 1605 invites us to wonder (*admiratio*) and laugh at the interplay between necessity and impossibility that frames the narrator's failures of rhetoric, logic, and semantics. As a result, we may laughingly marvel in that section of the Prologue at the slyness of the author's corresponding achievements. Thanks to the author's fictional self-parody, we are able, with special awareness, to observe and laugh at a central paradox of artistic creation: the necessary yet impossible desire to produce the most beautiful work imaginable. We also observe and laugh at a central paradox of rhetorical convention: the relative necessity and impossibility, within the context of one's own writings, of touting one's own talents without arrogance, and of decrying them without affected modesty. We are led to admire and laugh at Cervantes' ability seemingly to achieve the impossible, or to "solve" by transforming, these *impossibilia*. For he reveals his ability to fulfill and avoid his obligation to write a prologue in accord with the demands of convention, together with his ability to create an innovative prologue through a fictional parody of conventional categories.

And yet the laughter that Cervantes elicits from us in his Prologue does not allow us to remain complacent, or satisfied with our superiority over the objects of his parody. For the parody is not limited to the writers of books and prologues, but also extends to the paradoxical circumstance of the reading public. Indeed, that parody extends to the paradoxical relations between both the implied author and the prospective reader. In particular, we are doubtless able to laugh, but we laugh uneasily, at the irresolution of the narrator as he tries proffer words of endearment to his addressee, while his impulse toward hostility often gains the upper hand. With respect to his potential, unknown readership, the narrator wavers between hope and obsequiousness on the one hand and fear and insult on the other. He is therefore moved, in the manner of Mateo Alemán, to divide his potential friends and foes into the facile categories of "discreet readers" and "the masses." We can hardly avoid feeling implicated by the narrator's modes of direct address, or by the statements he aims directly at his prospective readers. We are thus left to ask where the author might stand regarding his narrator's failed overtures of pathos. We remain unsure of the emotional response the author is trying to elicit through his parody, which means that our chief response is a mixture of laughter, uneasiness, and uncertainty. Is the author pandering to our vanity or is he criticizing us? On what grounds would he do one or the other?

Rather than choosing one *answer* or the other, we do well to recall that, in the context of the author's fictional self-parody, the unwitting ambivalence of the narrator's statements implies his creator's conscious ambivalence. The narrator's waverings between contrary impulses, and the implicit parody of those waverings, originate from his acting on the assumption that he must address the reader as *either* friend *or* foe and thus defensively as either a "discreet" or "vulgar" reader. In a sense, the reader is both and neither. Furthermore, in exactly what sense, or to what degree the reader is friend or foe, "vulgar" or "discreet," will not only vary in each case, but also vary from one moment to the next. In a manner of speaking, the author uses the binary logic of his narrator to expose two extreme positions and to avoid making a definitive choice between them. Unlike Alemán and the narrator in the Prologue of 1605, the author of *Don Quixote* seems to respect the *uncertainty* attaching to the response of a *prospective* readership. Through the parody of his narrator, the author reveals an openness to the *possibility* of confidence in his unknown readership, but without affecting naive optimism. He is therefore able to show an attitude of skeptical caution, but without giving offense.

More to the point, the author's parody dramatizes the internal conflict of every author who must address an unknown readership, and it dramatizes, too, the relation between implied author and prospective reader as an unfolding *coincidentia oppositorum*. Without affirming or denying either *possibility*, the author, Cervantes, deploys his narrator's statements of failed pathos in order to address a *potential* friend or foe, a *potential* member of either the discriminating elite or the "vulgar" masses. He addresses prospective readers, whose actuality is permeated with the possibility of their continually showing varying degrees of friendliness or competence. Appropriately enough, the author's parody raises the possibility of the reader's friendliness or competence, which yet remains an open question. And no less open are the very criteria by which one numbers some readers among the "vulgar" and others among the "discreet." Moreover, it is discernible from the parody that the author, unlike his narrator, resists yoking the concept of the reader's friendliness to that reader's competence.

In this ambivalent, fluctuating light, we may judge the message that the author conveys about his readership, through a parody of his narrator's statements and tactics. For the author's Prologue dramatizes and parodies the circumstance of the reader no less effectively than it does the circumstance of the author himself. The reader, like the author, must also establish his or her credentials. It is doubt-less true, as the narrator claims, that readers need not fear or expect to receive either praise or blame for how they judge the work: "without fearing that anyone will slander you for the bad things, or reward you for the good things, which you may say about it" (sin temor que te calunien por el mal ni te premien por el bien que dijeres della) (*DQ* I: *Prologue*, 51). Yet this rather limited exemption from "fear" does not mean that the manner in which one reads either the story or the Prologue remains devoid of consequences, or even certain perils.

Again, if we regard the narrator's unwitting ambivalence as the conscious ambivalence of the author, it seems that the latter portrays the circumstance of the reader as a paradoxical blend of "free will" (libre albedrío) and constraint ("as the best-wrought person" [como el más pintado]) with respect to both the author and the text. As set forth in the author's fictional Prologue, author, reader, and text are involved in a paradoxical relation of mutual antagonism, dependence, and cooperation. In fact, concerning the text, the reader appears both enthroned and dethroned, both allowed and made to share in the author's presumed "sover-eignty," which is therefore far from absolute in either case. As a person, citizen, and child of God, "with your soul in your body" (con tu alma en tu cuerpo), or what have you, the reader is dutifully acknowledged as lord and king over his actions and his estate: "you are in your house, where you are lord, as the king is lord of his revenues" (estás en tu casa, donde eres señor della, como el rey de sus alcabalas). And yet, "kingly" readers, specifically in their capacity as readers of this text, may encounter the equivalent of grave danger, since "beneath my own cloak, I can kill the king" (debajo de mi manto, al rey mato) (*DQ* I: *Prologue*, 51). Each reader's personal method of reading and judging will reflect on that reader for good or ill. Each reader is therefore responsible for his or her own exercise of "free will" In fact, readers may find themselves already inscribed in the text as targets of what is, beginning with the Prologue, the author's elaborate parody of how literature is both written and read. Thus readers may find them-selves, at some point in either the Prologue or the story, laughing at their own assumptions and habits as readers.

Depending on their *involvement* with the work—and depending on how they employ their *leisure*—readers will invest the ambivalent address "idle/leisured reader," in each case, with a specific, active meaning, thereby inscribing them-selves into the text in a particular fashion. Similarly, we may read the openness and ambivalence contained in the words "dearest reader" and "gentle reader" as neither a gratuitous compliment nor a veiled insult from the author, but as another unanswered question. Implicitly, these modes of address pose *open* questions that challenge readers truly to *make sense* of the text in a personal manner. Simply put, the author compels the reader to determine in what sense(s) the latter will be "idle/leisured," "dear," or "gentle." Yet in none of those senses does the status or competence of readers depend on their making Cervantes' text an object of praise or censure. For unlike his narrator, Cervantes does not seem to seek uncritical adulation, which would just as likely secure our membership in the "ancient lawgiver, the masses," as our denouncing work for unsound reasons.

Beginning with the ambiguity and ambivalence informing his narrator's statements and modes of address, the author leads his readers to recognize that, now and hereafter, they will be continually revealing and reading themselves according to how they invest ambiguities, ambivalences, and paradoxes in the text with meaning; according to what they choose to praise or censure in the work; and their reasons for doing so. Beginning with the Prologue that "we are now reading," each act (and moment) of reading becomes integral to the self-conscious text, which serves as a fictional mirror of its own writing (encoding) and reading (decoding), in turn another form of "authoring" or encoding.

The fiction (of both the Prologue and "the book") therefore presents a blend of potentiality and actuality. Though already written, its meaning depends on how it is read, which will differ in each case, with each reader, from one moment to the next. If the *prospective* reader will invest the text with a particular meaning—similar to, yet different from, other readings of the same work—the jointly open and constraining text will also give meaning to that reader's activity. We are led, then, not only to contemplate the paradoxes of reading and writing in general, but also to focus on the "uniqueness" of "this," our reading, of "this" Prologue and also "this" book, for which each of us shares responsibility with the author as co-creator and co-sovereign. Regardless of whether we receive reward or calumny for how we negotiate the apparent contradictions, or *impossibilia* and *sophismata*, inherent in the text, we shall continually earn or forfeit our credentials as either "discreet" or "vulgar" readers, in some, still open, sense of those terms.

Cervantes' ambivalent, open method for addressing potentially competent or incompetent readers thus underscores the failure of pathos besetting the prefatory rhetoric of Mateo Alemán, which "inspires" the rhetorical "method" of Cervantes' narrator. In the end, Alemán's prefatory utterance, like that of the fictional narrator, fails to produce any meaningful effect on its audience. First, as Cervantes' prefatory parody throws into relief, a rhetorical method like the one found in Alemán's prologues simply equates "vulgarity" and "discretion" with friendly or hostile reception of the writer and his work. Such an equation renders both categories virtually meaningless as designations of readerly competence. Second, few readers can be expected to volunteer for membership in the "vulgar" sect. We readers all know ourselves to be "discreet," thank you very much. The narrator's hostile remarks, like Alemán's invective, thus fall on deaf ears, at the same time that his laudatory statements and expressions of modesty are made to seem insincere.

By contrast, Cervantes' parodic utterance manages to pose a challenge to those who would either accept or reject his work. The challenge is latent in the author's parody of the self-serving impetus of both Alemán and the narrator to set up a logical mechanism, based on dichotomous categories, whereby every potential reader receives automatic designation as either "vulgar" or "discreet." As is his custom, Cervantes opens rather than rejects these categories.

From the Prologue's first, ambivalent words, "idle/leisured reader," each reader is very much *involved* in the challenge of investing the textual ambiguities with intelligibility, identifying the narrative voice, sorting out wisdom from folly, truth from falsity, and deciding what is meant in jest or in earnest (as *burlas* or *veras*), or both. Readers may choose to reject the author and his work. Or perhaps those readers may choose, at some moment, to forego reading the rest of the Prologue and the narrative. In either case, these hypothetical readers can hardly fail to realize that they are rejecting a challenge and hence showing themselves either unwilling or unable to undertake the hermeneutic task that the text sets before them. Such readers can hardly avoid doubting that by shunting the work aside, they are proving themselves unequal to their role as that work's co-sovereigns and co-creators. Moreover, failure to realize such a challenge, or to feel such a doubt, would only argue more effectively against their "discretion" as readers. In addition, as an instance of Cervantes' dramatic irony, the narrator's seemingly perfunctory remarks about his "reader's" freedom and lack of obligation to praise, or even read, the text increase rather than mitigate Cervantes' reader's sense of challenge and responsibility.

Yet the Prologue proves no less challenging, or threatening, to readers who choose to persevere in their reading. On the one hand, as a result of the Prologue's paradoxes that invite and prevent resolution, accepting the challenge to involve themselves with the text will inexorably lead readers to consider themselves accomplices (friends) of the author. From their perspective, they form the ranks of those readers who understand the author's ironies and the subtlety of his clues. It is in this regard that Cervantes elicits a pathos akin to sympathy. Indeed, we may well come to believe, at least at first, that we are able to grasp what the author says, parodies, and dramatizes about the relation between art and nature; about the analogy between artistic creation and natural conception, gestation, and birth; about the theory and practice of writing prologues and narratives; or even about the art and science of establishing a proper rhetorical posture (ethos and pathos) between author and audience. To the degree that we think ourselves accomplices of the author, we shall believe, further, that we are able to discern what is being praised or censured, and what the author intends in jest or earnest.

On the other hand, because of the openness of the text, and the absence of an authoritative voice in either the Prologue or the narrative, we are unable to number ourselves definitively among the elect on the basis of how we interpret Cervantes' work. Accordingly, for each reader, Cervantes in his capacity as *author* of *Don Quixote* remains an author *implied* by the text and *invented* by the reader. The open structure of the Prologue, emblematic of the entire fiction, all but requires us as readers to acknowledge that the *meaning* of the utterance we are now reading as well as the implicit authorial position are in large part our own responsibility. The parodic text implicitly requires us to acknowledge, in other words, that we are therein reading a reflection of ourselves in our capacity as negotiators of contradictory statements and circumstances. But we receive no assurance that our judgments are "correct," and no assurance that we are able to avoid inscribing ourselves as objects of parody within the text.

The ambiguities and paradoxes that *open* the text therefore *constrain* us to construct through our reading a fluid allegory of our own acts of reading, urging us continually to reassess what constitutes a critical or "discreet" understanding of the text. For such an "understanding," the text and implied author provide no explicit mechanism, no technique, and no rules, except those of general linguistic competence and, especially, those that readers must continually improvise and invent for themselves. Hence there is nothing automatic or permanent about one's membership among the readerly elite. Indeed, what emerges from the Prologue is that critical *involvement* with the text, rather than some set of fixed norms, or gratuitous praise or censure of the work, remains the chief criterion for readerly "discretion."

Furthermore, involvement with the Prologue itself calls attention to our remaining very much alone with the text, in the loneliness of our "souls within our bodies," and thus engaged in a *process* of textual examination and self-examination. At every step in the Prologue, we may hear the echo of our own laughter, and that of the implied author whom we partially or wholly invent, as we confront now one, now another, image of ourselves as readers—an image both like and different from our abiding, yet evolving, selves. Cervantes' text dramatizes how, starting with the Prologue, the complementary and contrary activities of reader and author become (con)fused. In particular, his text dramatizes how reader and author jointly "beget" the fiction of each other and their shared, textual circumstance mingling rivalry with collaboration, and solitude with communion.

Bookish Buffoonery: The "Amusing and Well-Informed Friend" (El amigo gracioso y bien entendido)

If, in the opening and closing sections of the Prologue, the narrator's discourse represents a caricature of the generic "author" and "historian," that simulated discourse also represents a self-parody by the empirical author. Likewise, if the friend's discourse in the second, middle section of the Prologue represents a parodic caricature of the generic "reader" and "critic," it also implicates the actual reader or critic of the author's text. The embedded dialogue in this middle section purports to be a transcribed "conversation" between the self-proclaimed "author" of the "book" and one of his first readers, though we are unsure how much of the "history" this friend actually read. Yet, more important, the dialogue also represents the overlap between the roles of reader and author. First, like other "authors" offered in the narrative, the narrator of the Prologue represents, before all else, a reader of "sources" and previous versions of Don Quixote's "history." Second, for his part, the friend represents both a reader and critic who attempts to exercise nothing short of authorial control over the content, form, and purpose of his interlocutor's narrative.

At the start of the dialogue, the narrator overstates his own personal shortcomings and tells his friend of six technical defects that presumably render the work "utterly devoid of learning and doctrine" (falta de toda erudición y doctrina) (*DQ* I: *Prologue*, 52). These defects, the narrator claims, dispose him toward keeping the history of Don Quixote buried in the archives of La Mancha. What is more, those defects coincide with important, laudatory features to be found in other contemporary works. These features are

1. "*marginal citations*" (acotaciones en las márgenes) (*DQ* I: *Prologue*, 52);
2. "*explanatory annotations at the end of the book*" (anotaciones en el fin del libro) (*DQ* I: *Prologue*, 52);
3. *sententious maxims* "from the whole horde of philosophers, which strike awe [*admiratio*] in the reader and which make their authors seem men of wide reading, learning and eloquence" ([sentencias] de toda la caterva de filósofos, que admiran a los leyentes y tienen a sus autores por hombres leídos, eruditos y elocuentes) (*DQ* I: *Prologue*, 52);
4. *pious sermonizing*, or "little Christian sermons" (sermoncico[s] cristiano[s]) and quotations from Sacred Scripture ("And when they quote Sacred Scripture!") (¡Pues qué cuando citan la Divina Escritura!) (*DQ* I: *Prologue*, 52);

5. *a list of classical authorities* "beginning with Aristotle and ending with Xenophon and Zoilus or Zeuxis" (comenzando en Aristóteles y acabando en Xenofonte y en Zoilo o Zeuxis) (*DQ* I: *Prologue*, 53);

6. *prefatory* "*sonnets* whose authors are dukes, marquises, counts, bishops, ladies or poets of great renown" (sonetos cuyos autores sean duques, marqueses, condes, obispos, damas o poetas celebérrimos) (*DQ* I: *Prologue*, 52).

In sum, doctrinal and learned references ought to appear, according to the narrator, in *three places within the text:* in the *prefatory pages,* at the e*nd of the narrative,* and *in the margins of the "history."* Furthermore, the content of such references ought to include edifying religious and philosophical maxims and ought to derive from Sacred Scripture, classical authorities, or writers of historical or literary renown.

Once again, in enumerating his book's presumed defects, the narrator uses diction fraught with ambiguity and contradiction. In attempting to express praise, he betrays his suppressed hostility toward the works of his contemporaries. In particular, the narrator observes that the seemingly praiseworthy features of marginal notes, explanatory annotations, and philosophical maxims form part of "other books," even though these latter "are fabulous and profane" (sean fabulosos y profanos) (*DQ* I: *Prologue*, 52). Those adjectives, possibly disparaging in themselves, also suggest those books' lack of decorum. The narrator overstates, and thus seems unwittingly to undermine, his praise for authors of profane and fictional works who quote from Scripture: "People will surely say that they are a bunch of Saint Thomases and other doctors of the Church" (No dirán sino que son unos santos Tomases y otros doctores de la Iglesia). Less than fitting praise, it would seem, for either a secular historian or an artist. These authors' quotations from sacred writings also reveal what is oxymoronically described as their inventive or imaginative (i.e., their disregard of) decorum: "maintaining in all this such *ingenious decorum*" (guardando en esto un *decoro tan ingenioso*") (*DQ* I: *Prologue*, 52; emphasis added). The narrator praises a kindred type of indecorous decorum in reference to their sermonizing: "in one line of print they have portrayed an abstracted lover and in the next they give a little Christian sermon" (en un renglón han pintado un enamorado destraído y en otro hacen un sermoncico cristiano). Indeed, if the narrator "intends" the diminutive "little sermon" (sermoncico) to convey a sense of endearment and praise— "a delight to hear and read" (que es un regalo oílle y leelle) (*DQ* I: *Prologue*, 52)—the reader can scarcely disregard that lexeme's disparaging overtones. The narrator further implies that the same aesthetic rationale informs the citation of authorities in contemporary books, beginning with Aristotle and ending with Xenophon and Zoilus or Zeuxis, "though the first [of these last two] was a scandalmonger and the second a painter" (aunque fue maldiciente el uno y pintor el otro) (*DQ* I: *Prologue*, 53). This assertion likewise prevents the reader from deeming, or fully believing that the narrator deems, such citation either praiseworthy or necessary.

At this stage of the Prologue, however, it is important to remember that the enumeration of our narrator's technical problems constitutes the *fictional* utterance of a historical author. In his narrator, Cervantes invents a character who, trapped by the categories of conventional wisdom, is made to issue foolish praise of what we can readily identify as literary folly. Here, as elsewhere, the fictional narrator's seemingly careless diction—unwittingly censuring what it praises—follows from a hidden or implied author's contrivance and artistic design. Specifically, we may read the narrator's incompetent praise for the "scholarly" apparatus in "other books" as an uncharacteristically *straightforward satire* by Cervantes of the sophomoric pedantry found in the prefaces, endnotes, and marginal citations of many contemporary works. As scholars have generally recognized, Cervantes' mordant satire is aimed chiefly, though not exclusively, at Spain's most famous playwright of the period: Lope de Vega.[29]

The author of *Don Quixote* elaborates on his satire of the same literary practices, albeit from a contrary perspective, in what is made simultaneously to appear as the friend's "advice" and the latter's dialectical refutation of the narrator's remarks. But before we examine the "substance" of the friend's counsels, it is important to note that the latter is portrayed, through the voice of the narrator, in a parodic fashion. From the narrator's ingenuous perspective, the dubbing of his friend as "amusing and well-informed" (gracioso y bien entendido) (*DQ* I: *Prologue*, 52) is doubtless meant as a flattering description. Yet our justifiable assumption that a subtler "writer" than the narrator is ultimately responsible for the latter's ambiguous remarks most likely leads us not only to detect a possible irony in the words "well informed" (bien entendido), but also to ponder the appropriateness of the seemingly irrelevant adjective amusing ("gracioso"). Surely, this represents an unusual designation, which links traits of cynicism and undue levity with one who is said to be, and who implicitly claims to be, versed in the *serious* disciplines of rhetoric and poetics. It also calls to mind a stock character of the Spanish theater: the *gracioso, bobo, bufón donaire,* or *loco*—the clown, booby, buffoon, jester, or fool.

---

29. As Close bluntly states: "[T]he way in which he [Cervantes] lashes out at literary rivals" makes the "brilliantly stylish and witty" Prologue of 1605 "the bitchiest piece that Cervantes ever wrote" (1993, 40).

Indeed, the two adjectives used to describe the narrator's friend can be read as the implied author's ironic or parodic means of calling our attention to two elements of that friend's advice. The counsels that the friend sets forth as a "well-informed" consultant are hardly the shrewd, learned comments that both characters take them to be. Rather, the reader recognizes that in this caricature the "theory" or aesthetic "philosophy" informing those counsels emanates from an uncritical understanding of conventional opinion. Furthermore, the *practical* element in the friend's advice shows him to be a rather typical "booby." Indeed, the revisions he suggests for *improving* the "history" seem both frivolous and dishonest. They emerge, I believe, as an object of ridicule and as a sign of that friend's middling intellect. Adding to the portrait of the friend as part buffoon, the text relates that friend's overstated reaction to the narrator's enumeration of the latter's technical difficulties: "After hearing this, my friend slapped his forehead and burst out laughing, and told me . . ." (Oyendo lo cual mi amigo, dándose una palmada en la frente y disparando en una carga de risa, me dijo . . .) (*DQ* I: *Prologue,* 53).

As quoted by the narrator, the friend's first words likewise reveal a combination of arrogance, pedantry, and hackneyed thinking:

> Good Lord, brother, I have now come to be undeceived of a deception in which I have believed all these many years I have known you, according to which I have always judged you to be discreet and prudent in all your actions. But I now see that you are as far from that as the heavens from the earth.
>
> (Por Dios, hermano, que agora me acabo de desengañar de un engaño en que he estado todo el mucho tiempo que ha que os conozco, en el cual siempre os he tenido por discreto y prudente en todas vuestras aciones. Pero agora veo que estáis tan lejos de serlo como lo está el cielo de la tierra.) (*DQ* I: *Prologue,* 53)

Providing another early sign of his arrogance, frivolity, and fustian discourse, the friend considers the problem of investing the "history" with erudition of so little moment that he promises the narrator the following: "So pay close attention to me and you will see that in the blink of an eye, I shall remove all your difficulties and mend the flaws that you say are making you indecisive and fearful" (Pues estadme atento y veréis cómo en un abrir y cerrar de ojos confundo todas vuestras dificultades y remedio todas las faltas que decís que os suspenden y acobardan) (*DQ* I: *Prologue,* 54).

Regarding additions that the narrator should make to the "history" in order to remedy its lack of erudition, the friend's advice is fourfold. His first counsel concerns "the sonnets, epigrams or verses of praise that you are lacking at the beginning" (los sonetos, epigramas o elogios que os faltan para el principio). According to the friend, the narrator should write those prefatory verses himself and attribute them to such legendary characters as "Prester John of the Indies" or the "emperor of Trebizond." Should some pedant wish to point out this blatant falsification, the narrator need not worry, since "even if they discover the lie, they are not about to cut off the hand with which you wrote it" (ya que os averigüen la mentira, no os han de cortar la mano con que lo escribistes) (*DQ* I: *Prologue*, 54).

Next, the friend addresses the issue of the narrator's having to "cite in the margins the books and authors from which you drew sentences and sayings that you put into your history" (citar en las márgenes los libros y autores de donde sacárades las sentencias y dichos que pusiéredes en vuestra historia) (*DQ* I: *Prologue*, 54). The friend assures the narrator that "they may even take you for a grammarian [i.e., scholar]" (os tendrán siquiera por gramático), provided that narrator checkers his work with pithy Latin sayings, to be drawn from Scripture and classical authorities. Obligingly, in the examples he cites, the "well-informed" friend displays his deficient scholarship by attributing to Cato a well-known maxim of Ovid (*DQ* I: *Prologue*, 55).

The friend recommends a similar approach to the narrator's obligation to write "annotations at the end of the book" (*DQ* I: *Prologue*, 55). The narrator should seize virtually any name, story, or circumstance in his narrative as an opportunity to refer to Scripture, classical authors, or the work of a respected contemporary. One benefit that the narrator will derive from heeding this advice is that of proving himself "a man learned in humane letters and a cosmographer" (hombre erudito en letras humanas y cosmógrafo) (*DQ* I: *Prologue*, 56). It is also in the context of the friend's counsel about notes at the book's close that the author satirizes both the credibility and propriety of the populist prelate, Antonio de Guevara: "[I]f [you should deal with] harlots, you may call upon the bishop of Mondoñedo, who will *lend you* Lamia, Laida and Flora, the citing of whom will *bring you great credit*" ([S]i [tratárades] de *mujeres rameras*, ahí está el obispo de Mondoñedo, que *os prestará* a Lamia, Laida y Flora, cuya anotación *os dará gran crédito*) (*DQ* I: *Prologue*, 56; emphasis added). Before giving his final bit of practical advice about what to add to the text, the friend makes a startling suggestion, offering his services as *critical editor* of the narrator's "history": "In sum, all you need is to make every effort to name those names, or to touch on those histories in your own, as I have told you here, and *leave to me the task of writing the notes and marginal citations.*" (En resolución no hay más sino que vos procuréis nombrar estos nombres, o tocar estas historias en la vuestra, que aquí he dicho, y *dejadme a mí el cargo de poner las anotaciones y acotaciones*) (*DQ* I: *Prologue*, 57; emphasis added). Indeed, it would seem that, thanks to the pseudoauthor's or the narrator's "well-informed friend," not even those who prepare critical editions of *Don Quixote* can avoid inscribing themselves into Cervantes' parodic text. In a manner of speaking, the words of the friend here allow the *fictional* narrative to encompass, and parody, both its "actual" and "possible" marginalia.

Concluding his practical, fourfold advice about what the narrator should append to his narrative, the friend states: "Let us now turn to the citing of authors that other books contain and that yours is lacking." (Vengamos ahora a la citación de los autores que los otros libros tienen, que en el vuestro faltan). To remedy this presumed defect, the friend encourages the narrator to engage in outright plagiarism: "[L]ook for a book that lists them all, from A to Z, as you say. You will then put the same ABCs in your book" ([B]uscar un libro que los acote todos, desde la A hasta la Z, como vos decís. Pues ese mismo abecedario pondréis vos en vuestro libro). Again, such a practice cannot but redound to the narrator's benefit: "[A]t the least, that long catalog of authors will lend the book instant authority" ([P]or lo menos servirá aquel largo catálogo de autores a dar de improviso autoridad al libro) (*DQ* I: *Prologue*, 57).

It seems untenable to read the friend's fourfold advice as anything other than a straightforward, unambiguous satire aimed at the common literary practices of Cervantes' contemporaries. But here, too, I believe that the intended satire and irony belong to the author rather than the character, portrayed as a half-educated pedant. The friend is humorous and comical, but not witty. It is the author who, after the fashion of a classical *eiron*, feigns ignorance behind the "mask" of his character. In part, then, it seems fitting that the author should have the friend finally dismiss as irrelevant *all* his own counsels about textual revisions, which occupy most of the textual space in the Prologue: "[T]his book of yours needs *none of those things that you say it lacks*" ([E]ste vuestro libro no tiene necesidad de ninguna cosa *de aquellas que vos decís que le falta*) (*DQ* I: *Prologue*, 57; emphasis added). The bulk of the narrator's "Prologue" therefore becomes a transcription of counsels by a consultant whose final counsel about what to affix to the narrator's book is to disregard all those previous counsels.

In addition, as yet another instance of dramatic irony, the friend is made to seem unaware that the literary practices he endorses before this piece of advice are not simply unnecessary, but also unhelpful, in the particular case of the narrator-editor's "history." In fact, such practices are themselves defects, which yield the *opposite* of their desired effect. Through the friend's advice, the author dramatizes how pedantic annotations and references do nothing to enlighten the reader. Instead, they reveal their author's lack of learning and detract from the "authority" of that author's work. What is more, a pedant such as the friend—or, perhaps, such as Lope de Vega—is shown to confuse learning with the appearance of learning. Further, only the most gullible reader would believe that a book's prefatory sonnets, often written plainly in the style of the book's author, represent the handiwork of the illustrious persons whose names they bear. Such a practice does little more to enhance one's credibility than it would, for example, to attribute those sonnets to the "emperor of Trebizond." Appropriately enough, it seems that the author has his narrator heed this bit of advice from the friend, thus failing to heed the friend's later advice to ignore it. Likewise, far from making it "a delight to hear and read," grafting a "little Christian sermon" or a philosophical maxim on to a narrative makes their "doctrine" all the more unpalatable.

The chief object of the author's satire here is therefore neither "erudition" nor "doctrine," but pedantry and preachment. For, in contradiction to the now discredited view of Cervantes as an "untutored wit" (ingenio lego), his text suffers from no lack of "erudition," drawn from classical, biblical and contemporary sources of fictional and nonfictional kinds. Furthermore, as occurs in this section of the Prologue, the author's textual references in the narrative often take explicitly parodic form. His subsequent allusions to *both learned and popular sources,* however, are deftly woven into the narrative proper, without their taking the form of an appendage at the beginning, at the end, or in the margins of the work. The covert quality of such allusions renders them effective, parodies what one may call the "vulgar" equation between erudition and bombast, and defers the work of discovery and judgment to the potentially discerning reader.

Although the author of the fiction never resorts to heavy-handed preaching in either the Prologue or the narrative, I would suggest that his work shows no aversion to "doctrine," and even contains what the friend disparagingly calls an admixture of "the human with the divine" (lo humano con lo divino). Indeed, it hardly seems coincidental that the friend himself should mingle the human with the divine when he decries such an admixture in *secular works* as "a species of admixture in which no *Christian mind* should clothe itself" (un género de mezcla de quien no se ha de vestir ningún *cristiano entendimiento*) (*DQ* I: *Prologue,* 57; emphasis added). In other words, the friend seems unaware of the practical contradiction, or antinomy, involved in claiming that this "admixture" vitiates the *secular* quality of such works by making them *un-Christian.*

The rest of the friend's counsels in the second section of the Prologue, which come after his counsel to add no marginalia to the narrator's "history," do not therefore concern specific textual additions. Rather, they bear on more general questions of authorial purpose and literary principle. Indeed, as the friend concludes—and finally dismisses—his fourfold advice about textual revisions, the author, in essence, concludes the straightforward satire aimed at his contemporaries. Thereafter, the author uses the commonplaces and antinomies of the friend's discourse to draw our attention, once again, to his ambivalent authorial posture as well as to the paradoxical quality of his rhetorical and literary endeavor.

Rather than being a spokesman for the author, the friend remains very much in character as he delivers his final counsels. What is more, he speaks as though his counsels should guide the narrator in the latter's writing of the "history." In other words, those counsels are relevant only if the "history," which the narrator has already stated is ready for publication, *has yet to be written*. It would seem that, apposite or no, the friend is unable to resist displaying his "erudition," in the form of "well-informed" advice. Similarly, the narrator seems prepared to accept almost any bit of advice, provided that advice is sufficiently conventional, and provided he can use it to write his "Prologue." The narrator nowhere suggests that his friend's advice is untimely.

By representing a near prototype of pedantic discourse and reductive, dichotomous thinking, the narrator's "well-informed friend" clearly perceives both the purpose and genre of the narrator-editor's "history" in the narrowest terms: "[T]*he whole of it* is an *invective against the books of chivalry*" ("[T]*odo él* es una *invectiva contra los libros de caballerías*"). In equally reductive fashion, he all but restates the same idea, though adding a social dimension to the "history's" purpose, which would please even the most traditionally minded defenders of public morals: "this written work of yours *aims at nothing more than* undoing the authority and sway that books of chivalry hold in the world and among the masses" ("esta vuestra escritura *no mira a más que* a deshacer la autoridad y cabida que en el mundo y en el vulgo tienen los libros de caballerías") (*DQ* I: *Prologue*, 57; emphasis added). No less reductively, the friend's final recommendations state the same purpose for a third time, and implicitly criticize chivalric romances on aesthetic, as against social or moral, grounds: "Indeed, *keep your aim fixed* on demolishing the *ill-founded construction* of those knight books" (En efecto, *llevad la mira puesta* a derribar *la máquina mal fundada* destos caballerescos libros) (*DQ* I: *Prologue*, 58; emphasis added).

In the friend's opinion, such a straightforward purpose doubtless requires a straightforward method. Clearly unafraid of preaching, he recommends just such a method in an altogether conventional manner: "You need *only* have recourse to *imitation* in whatever you write; for the *more perfect* it [imitation] is, the better your writing will be" ("*Sólo* tiene que aprovecharse de *la imitación* en lo que fuere escribiendo; que cuanto ella fuere *más perfecta, tanto mejor* será lo que se escribiere") (*DQ* I: *Prologue*, 57; emphasis added).

Like the narrator, the friend remains happily unaware of the contradictions involved in his aesthetic "philosophy." For instance, the "history" constitutes *nothing but* an "invective" against the romances of chivalry only if its protagonist remains *nothing but* a crazed hidalgo, whose lunacy consists of imagining himself a knight-errant. Yet without a trace of irony or "invective" on the part of the friend, that character also refers approvingly to both the protagonist and his fantastic profession. In his customarily overstated and commonplace way, the "well-informed" friend calls Don Quixote "light and mirror of *all* knight-errantry" (luz y espejo de *toda* la caballería andante) (*DQ* I: *Prologue*, 54; emphasis added). Indeed, both the narrator and his friend implicitly link the invective elements of the "history" with the reading of chivalric romances, which led an hidalgo to consider himself a knight. On this view, those romances caused at least one man to lose his wits and to commit a serious breach of social decorum. Yet neither the narrator nor his friend seems to find anything fanciful, or even anachronistic, about the profession of knight-errantry or the existence of knights-errant. Rather, the two characters of the Prologue remain consistent in their comments about "Don Quixote"—though not about the hidalgo—as a "noble knight."

The form of "imitation" that the friend implies seems to be superficial, perfectly aligned with his perception of the narrator's "history" and "invective." No doubt the friend bases his specific conception of "perfect imitation" on both an Aristotelian "imitation of nature" and a Ciceronian "imitation of models." But for the friend to believe that a work of history could be such a "perfect" imitation requires him to assume that historical discourse, and thus historical writing, are capable of revealing the "truth" of events ("nature") in a transparent manner. It requires, as well, that at least some of the historian's sources or "models" prove reliable and likewise transparent in their discourse. Hence, they are worthy of being transcribed, in much the same way that the narrator-historian claims to have transcribed the conversation between himself and his friend in order to produce "this" Prologue. Adopting that line of reasoning, it would certainly follow that, to the degree it is a perfectly imitative history, the narrator's work will prove a truly *exemplary* invective. For in presenting the particular, factual "truth" about what happened to an hidalgo who read chivalric romances, that work will set forth a negative "model," which readers will feel moved to avoid in their own behavior.

In short, the overstated phrase "perfect imitation" denotes a faith in the transparency of language, the objectivity of history, and the reliability of sources that one can hardly ascribe to the author of *Don Quixote*. As discussed earlier, what the content and form of both the Prologue and the narrative call to our attention is that "nature" or "experience" reach us as "knowledge" through conventional models and conventional categories of imitation, particularly through that form of linguistic imitation we call discourse. Yet there is a character in the subsequent narrative who seems to share the friend's view of what history, as "perfect imitation," both can and should be. Indeed, a character to be discussed more fully in the following chapter of the present study whom the "history" identifies only as "second author" at the close of I, 8 shows a similar penchant for hyperbole and pedantic preaching. Further, this "second author" clearly assumes that one can transparently reveal "truth" (perfectly imitate the facts) through discourse; discover utterly reliable sources; and thereby fulfill the exemplary purpose of historical writing. Hence his assertion that historians should guard against all emotional bias, lest they "stray from the path of truth, whose mother is history, portrait of the times, repository of deeds, witness to the past, example and warning in the present, and portent of the future" (torcer del camino de la verdad, cuya madre es la historia, émula del tiempo, depósito de las acciones, testigo de lo pasado, ejemplo y aviso de lo presente, advertencia de lo porvenir) (*DQ* I: 9, 144–45). It hardly seems a coincidence that as part of the author's fiction, this "second author," a consistent admirer of the protagonist as a "good knight" (buen caballero) (*DQ* I: 9, 145), should himself prove a negative exemplum of emotional bias. In addition, the friend's idea of "invective" makes no room for a parody such as that of the author, which is not devoted simply to "demolishing" (derrumbar) but to enlarging its model. And while the "chivalric romances" remain a chief object, they are hardly the sole object, of the author's complex parody or mock encomium of literary discourse.

Furthermore, although the friend is never shown to confuse historical with poetic models, it is worth noting here that his simplistic understanding of *imitatio,* in both the Aristotelian and Ciceronian sense, resembles that of the protagonist. This similarity comes to the fore especially in I, 26, where Don Quixote finally decides, after some vacillation, to shape his penance in Sierra Morena as perfectly as possible after what he considers the *historical model* of Amadís: "[A]nd let [Amadís] be imitated by Don Quixote *in every way possible*" ([S]ea

---

30. Riley rightly notes that a particular understanding of the Renaissance doctrine of *imitatio* provides the direct inspiration for the protagonist's mock penance: "It is Don Quixote who states the precept of the imitation of models in I. 25. . . . His [Don Quixote's] efforts might not have been very significant in relation to artistic imitation if Cervantes had not made him consciously aware of the doctrine. But Cervantes does, and the Knight recalls it with direct reference to his intended penance" (1962, 64). Riley also observes that the protagonist not only vacillates over whether to imitate the literary models of Amadís or Orlando, but also that the protagonist's "new exploit could very plausibly have been suggested to him by the real example of Cardenio (life)" (1962, 64). Similarly, Hampton argues that it is the fren-

imitado [Amadís] de don Quijote de la Mancha *en todo lo que pudiere*) (DQ I: 26, 319; emphasis added).[30] Indeed, it would prove difficult to find a greater champion of "perfect imitation" than the protagonist himself. And it would prove even more difficult, not to say impossible, to divorce the features of Don Quixote's perfectly imitative method, as portrayed in the narrative, from his lunacy. Through the protagonist, the "second author," and the friend, the author demonstrates that narrowness of mind, and in extreme cases even lunatic fanaticism, go hand in hand with the conviction that discourse and art can perfectly imitate life, or that life must perfectly imitate fictive categories and exemplary models of art and discourse. Indeed, these characters represent what one may consider historical and poetic fundamentalists of "perfect imitation." Thus, too, one's approach toward a historical and aesthetic method (i.e., *imitatio*) is shown to go hand in hand with *ethical* practice.[31] As a second-rate reader and critic, the friend thus resembles the second-rate aesthetician and social ethicist Don Quixote. For both characters understand the Renaissance doctrine of aesthetic *imitatio* and moral exemplarity as an uncritical and *noninventive aping*, not simply of models, but of either stories or histories about models.

Referring to the purely aesthetic domain, E. C. Riley points out that in Cervantes' time, such slavish and unimaginative imitation of models was considered to be a typical practice of mediocre artists and was often criticized as a reprehensible form of plagiarism, or even as "stealing" (1962, 61–63). In his *Epilogue to the Parnassus* (*Adjunta al Parnaso*), Cervantes himself criticizes what the friend would doubtless consider "perfect imitation" as a type of theft that is worthy of the legendary Cacus:

> Item, it is declared that one ought not to deem a thief the poet who steals a verse from someone else and fits it into his own [verses], so long as it not the whole concept and the entire poem, for in such a case he would be as great a thief as Cacus.

> (Item, se advierte que no ha de ser tenido por ladrón el poeta que hurtare algún verso ajeno, y le encajare entre los suyos, como no sea todo el con-

---

zied madness of Cardenio that reminds the protagonist of Orlando, thereby deflecting Don Quixote momentarily from the most perfect model for action—in this case, Amadís: "[W]hy should Don Quixote suddenly add the imitation of Orlando to his project when he has just spent several paragraphs instructing Sancho that the imitation of Amadís is sufficient to make one a perfect knight? The answer lies in the figure of Cardenio, whose 'furia' was described only a few pages earlier, and whose appearance recalls that of the mad Orlando in canto 23 of Ariosto's text" (Hampton 1990, 261).

31. Riley points out, "There is nothing notably unusual in his [Don Quixote's] seeking to imitate some exemplary hero in life, or, like a courtier, to emulate the best in previous models. But what is noteworthy is that he is also behaving very like an artist" (1962, 64).

cepto y toda la copla entera, que en tal caso tan ladrón es como Caco.) (1973, 190)[32]

It is no mere coincidence, I think, that the friend who encourages a superficial form of *imitatio* is the same character who flippantly encourages other forms of plagiarism, together with the false attribution of sonnets. Nor does it seem mere coincidence that Cervantes should show him to be conversant with the classical literature of theft: "'If you deal with thieves, I can tell you the *story of Cacus,* since *I know it by heart.*'" ("Si tratáredes de ladrones, yo os diré *la historia de Caco*, que *la sé de coro*") (*DQ* I: *Prologue*, 56; emphasis added).

The type of *imitatio* that the friend counsels, moreover, is shown to be the narrator's method of choice as a writer of prologues and a historian. In a thoroughly uncritical fashion, that narrator chooses to compose his prologue chiefly by *transcribing* his friend's pronouncements, paradoxically called *razones*, or "words," but also denoting "reasons," thus akin to the Greek *logoi*: "[W]*ithout questioning them* [the friend's words and reasonings] I judged them to be fitting and *from them verbatim I attempted to make this prologue*" ([S]*in ponerlas* [las razones del amigo] *en disputa* las aprobé por buenas y *de ellas mismas quise hacer este prólogo*) (*DQ* I: *Prologue*, 58; emphasis added). I shall discuss in the following chapter how, as editor as well as narrator of the "history"—for us the fictional narrative about Don Quixote—the narrator does everything within his power to make his narrative appear a sequential ordering and transcription of sources and models; that is, to make his "work" appear as patchwork. Imitation, understood as unquestioning transcription, is assumed to be a sign of historical credibility. Hence, as it is for the friend, and for Don Quixote, a slavish imitation of models— "perfect imitation"—is the guiding ideal behind the narrator's endeavors.

The upshot of the foregoing observations about the narrator's friend is not that the author simply affirms or denies the "truth" of that character's statements, or that he offers those statements simply for the reader's praise, censure, approval, or disapproval. As the parody of a particular kind of reader and critic, the friend plainly describes the purpose, genre, and method of the "history" to the *narrator's* satisfaction. Indeed, both characters in the Prologue—both *friends*—are cut from the same "philosophical" cloth. For them, it seems that the "historical" work represents nothing but an "invective," since the folly in the narrative springs solely from the hidalgo and the romances of chivalry. According to their own remarks, the friend and the narrator seem to perceive nothing but *nobility* in the *knight's* profession and his "philosophy." Because they nowhere imply that knights-errant

---

32. Without referring to the friend in the Prologue to *Don Quixote*, Part I, Riley also quotes this passage from the *Epilogue to the Parnassus* in connection with Cervantes' equation between unimaginative imitation, plagiarism and "theft" (1962, 62–63).

or knight-errantry as described in the romances constitute an *impossibility*—something that either does not, or cannot, exist—they are shown *to share* the protagonist's "philosophy" in much the same way as the "second author." Their invective is therefore limited to aping a conventional denunciation or "invective" of chivalresque books that led an hidalgo to lose his wits. Yet with no sense of irony or contradiction, these characters extol the protagonist's lunatic project as the endeavor of a cavalier and, implicitly, accept the veracity of chivalric romance.

On the one hand, then, the friend and narrator would seem to represent the author's parody of those persons who, while denouncing the romances in conventional terms, still hold to simplistic, quixotic *doxa* concerning the "Christian hero"—the conceptual *foundation* of the "*ill-founded construction of those knight books*" (emphasis added). On the other hand, those two characters in the Prologue also represent an aspect of the *parody* that Cervantes seems to aim at those persons who would censor the romances of chivalry on the grounds that they will be read as true histories. As a proponent of such "reasoning," one would have to assert that a chief purpose behind Cervantes' creation of his protagonist would be to show how the romances of chivalry might well lead to a proliferation of Don Quixotes throughout the Spanish Empire and, perhaps, the whole of Christendom. Is it at all plausible to think that in creating his protagonist, the author of *Don Quixote* shares, rather than ridicules, such a social and moral "concern"? Is it really plausible to hold that Cervantes thinks that some readers of *Don Quixote*, like the protagonist and, perhaps, the "second author," the narrator and his friend need to be thoroughly disabused of the opinion that the romances are historically true? Finally, is it plausible to believe that Cervantes' fiction would change the minds of such "readers"?[33]

What emerges from the text, then, is that the author uses the friend in much the same way that he uses the narrator of the Prologue. In particular, that author deploys the statements of the friend, as he does the statements of the narrator, to broach conventional categories and issues that call our attention to the unconven-

---

33. The critic to argue most forcefully in favor of Cervantes' sharing this "concern" is Daniel Eisenberg (1982, 119–29). As Eisenberg later claims: "Certainly one lesson Cervantes wanted the reader to take from *Don Quixote* was not to read such works [the romances of chivalry], or at the very least to use them properly, recognizing them as entertainment, not as true history or guides for behavior" (1987, 58). Eisenberg also asserts that in Cervantes' narrative, characters who "read" the romances of chivalry "have serious problems." Although he immediately mentions Maritornes and her approving attitude toward "sexual liasons between unmarried people," it is clear that she is unable to read, and far from clear that the romances are the "cause" of her attitude. She does not seem to require the romances to believe as she does. Like so many other characters in Cervantes' narrative, her *interpretation of what she knows* about the romances of chivalry is a function of who she is, or perhaps who she is compelled to be. Eisenberg also makes the same equation between the romances (cause) and folly (effect) with respect to the protagonist: "It is the unmarried country *hidalgo* who devours them passionately, loses his reason, his teeth, which are

tional genre, purpose, and poetic method of his work. Yet the friend also resembles the narrator in that his conventional categories, and his conventional understanding of the pertinent aesthetic issues, become the object of parody and bog down in antinomy. If, for instance, the friend is right to claim, and exemplify, that the romances of chivalry are "abhorred by many and praised by many more" (aborrecidos de tantos y alabados de muchos más) (*DQ* I: *Prologue*, 58), *uncritical* abhorrence of those works, in perfect imitation of received opinion, seems no less an object of the author's parodic craftsmanship than uncritical praise.

Moreover, as in the case of the narrator—and as in the case of Erasmus's Folly—the "learning" of the friend comprises a random collection of maxims (*adagia*), commonplaces and *misquotations* that he is eager to trot out at the slightest provocation. So in their use of "learning" and "doctrine," both the friend and the narrator seem to bear no small resemblance to Sancho in his parroting of "popular maxims" and proverbial "wisdom." In this light, it seems entirely appropriate that the already discredited narrator should react to his friend's conventional remarks with speechless awe: "I remained *in great silence* as I listened to what my friend was telling me" (*Con silencio grande* estuve escuchando lo que mi amigo me decía) (*DQ* I: *Prologue*, 58; emphasis added). In addition, one can hardly avoid noting the *author's* irony behind the *narrator's* laudatory remarks:

> [I]n which [prologue] you will see, gentle reader, my friend's sound judgment, my good fortune in coming upon such a counselor in a moment of

---

worth more than diamonds, and, ultimately and tragically, his life" (1987, 58). Again, on such a view, Cervantes puts forth his protagonist as a verisimilar character (and I believe he does), whose madness stems *solely* from his reading the romances, in order to issue two warnings to his readers. First: "Stop doing this"; and Second: "This could happen to you." My resistance to such a view follows from the conviction that it is at best unlikely that Cervantes thought the romances of chivalry to have such magically transformative powers on their readership. I also think it unlikely that Cervantes wrote with the hope of reaching such a gullible audience whom he would cure of their perverse reading habits—that is, if they can read in the first place. Moreover, in contemporary parlance, the cause of the protagonist's madness seems overdetermined. In the opening chapter of Cervantes' fiction, a petty, unmarried, and conspicuously nameless hidalgo is given to a life of frustration, idleness, and routine. He is, in short, a "nobody" bereft of heroic accomplishments such as those of his ancestors. Unmarried, he is also loveless, or deficient in both heroics and erotics. He also suffers from a severe humoral imbalance that predisposes him toward madness and deranged fantasies. He is, additionally, the type of *reader* who looks upon the sophistical phrases of Feliciano de Silva as philosophical problems clamoring for a logical solution. The role of the romances is to provide Don Quixote with "artistic" raw material for him to *enact* his madness and give that madness its peculiar form. Our hidalgo suffers from severe problems no matter what he reads. Banish the romances of chivalry from the Spanish Empire and, instead of a Don Quixote, the same country hidalgo might well become the lovelorn shepherd Quijotiz, as he thinks of becoming as he approaches his village for the last time, at the close of Part II. Banish all romance or secular literature from the Spanish Empire, and that kind of reader might well fancy himself a Joshua, a Samson, or one of the Machabees.

great need, and your relief in coming upon *such a sincere and straightfor-ward history* of the famous Don Quixote of La Mancha.

([E]n el cual [el prólogo] verás, lector suave, la discreción de mi amigo, la buena ventura mía en hallar en tiempo tan necesitado tal consejero, y el alivio tuyo en hallar *tan sincera y tan sin revueltas la historia* del famoso don Quijote de la Mancha.) (*DQ* I: *Prologue*, 58; emphasis added)

As implied here, it seems that one would have to be a "gentle" reader indeed to accept the statements of the friend in an uncritical fashion, without considering the moral and intellectual authority of the source. And as implied in this passage, it would seem that only an "idle" reader would understand either the narrator's or the author's *historia* [story or history] about Don Quixote to be "sincere and straightforward." In fact, it would seem that to accept the friend's statements as the author's own *voice* or the author's own declaration of authorial purpose is to inscribe oneself in the text as the kind of "amusing and well-informed" reader and critic which the author parodies through that very character, or "reader."

Just as the narrator's "Prologue" is distinct from that of the author, so the pur-pose and genre of the "history," as described by the friend, differ from those of the author's *fiction*. As the friend both accurately and reductively suggests, the "book" of the *narrator* strives at once to be a narrow "invective" against the romances of chivalry as well as an equally narrow, and antithetical, "history" about a "noble" protagonist. It is a "history," in other words, that strives, *per impossibile*, to be "hard" on the chivalric romances and the hidalgo, while remaining "soft" on the project of the "noble knight." As the author subtly suggests amid the conven-tional opinions and contradictions of the friend, *the fiction* will use the "history" and its paradoxical hero in a complex parody of chivalric romances, which not only exploits both the strengths ("nobilities") and weaknesses of the genre, but also parodies the facile "philosophies" according to which those works are com-monly made the object of praise or censure.

In characteristically paradoxical fashion, the author enumerates the strengths of the "romances of chivalry" through the canon of Toledo—the character who also provides the most sustained criticism of the genre on both aesthetic and ethical grounds.[34] Briefly stated, the Canon is said to claim that the primary strength of those works lies in the scope they provide for the author's imagination. He

34. For a sustained analysis of this passage, in the light of literary theory that prevailed in Cervantes' time, particularly that of Cervantes' Italian contemporary Torquato Tasso, see Forcione 1970, 91–130.

speaks, specifically, of "the opportunity they [offer] for a good mind to reveal itself through them, since they [provide] a broad and spacious field in which the pen may flow, free from all hindrance" (el sujeto que [ofrecen] para que un buen entendimiento pudiese mostrarse en ellos, porque [dan] largo y espacioso campo por donde sin empacho alguno pudiese correr la pluma) (*DQ* I: 47, 566). This strength relates to what the canon calls the "untrammeled writing of these books" (escritura desatada destos libros), which permits the author to exploit a virtually infinite range of generic, poetic, and rhetorical registers: "to display his skill in the epic, lyric, tragedy, and comedy, with all the parts contained in the sweet and pleasant sciences of poetry and oratory" (mostrarse épico, lírico, trágico, cómico, con todas aquellas partes que encierran en sí las dulcísimas y agradables ciencias de la poesía y de la oratoria) (*DQ* I: 47, 567). He even repeats the idea of those *prose* works' *epic* potential: "for one can write epic in prose as well as verse" (que la épica también puede escrebirse en prosa como en verso). Oddly, too, those same works allow the author to achieve nothing less than "the worthiest purpose that writing can seek, which is to join instruction and delight" (el fin mejor que se pretende en los escritos, que es enseñar y deleitar juntamente) (*DQ* I: 47, 567). Presumably the author of such a work would be capable of delighting his readership without lapsing into the absurdities that the canon roundly denounces (*DQ* I: 47, 564–66), and to instruct his readership, in both ethical and intellectual matters, without preachment. Indeed, unlike the friend, though seeming to echo his words, the canon also perceives in the chivalric romances the possibility for an author's deft use of erudition: "He can display his powers now as an astrologer, now as an excellent cosmographer, now as a musician, now as learned in affairs of state, and he may even have occasion to display his powers as a conjurer if he so pleases" (Ya puede mostrarse astrólogo, ya cosmógrafo excelente, ya músico, ya inteligente en las materias de estado, y tal vez le vendrá la ocasión de mostrarse nigromante, si quisiere) (*DQ* I: 47, 566).

It is important to keep in mind, however, that the canon's laudatory remarks are limited to the *potential* strengths that *actual* romances of chivalry fail to realize, thereby making those works, in the character's view, deserving of censure. It also bears stressing that the canon's remarks represent an oblique rather than direct allusion to *Don Quixote*, the fictional work in which they occur. Hardly a mere "invective," Cervantes' work exploits the aforementioned strengths, but in a different manner from what is expressed through the words of the canon. For that character clearly does not discourse about a work of literary parody, whose protagonist is in any way a fool or a madman. Rather, the canon discusses and claims to have begun, without finishing, a wholly *serious* epic centering on an

exemplary hero. He thus points to a work that (unlike *Don Quixote*) contains no
trace of "mockery" in relation to the protagonist, paradoxical or otherwise.[35]

Though accurate, it would reveal little of the author's own inventiveness simply to
state that he advocates a type of *imitatio* combining a keen observation of "life"
with the transformative and inventive use of models. Indeed, Cervantes' conception of *imitatio* seems more complex than can be expressed by way of simple formulation. The friend's statements on the subject of *imitatio* in the Prologue to Part
I both broach and dramatize the paradoxes of the problem. For, through that character, the author inventively illustrates his own understanding of the "doctrine" of
inventive *imitatio* by *perfectly imitating* the most conventional pronouncements in
favor of slavish imitation. It is thus left to the reader to weigh the distinction
between artless and inventive *imitatio,* now that some form of perfect imitation
and invention *are shown to be* inseparable. Put another way, a conventional type of
perfect imitation is shown to preclude invention. Yet the best type of invention is
shown to require some enlarged type of perfect imitation, a "more perfect" form of
"perfect imitation." In short, the author uses the friend's statements concerning
imitatio not so much to discuss, as to demonstrate, his *paradoxical method of imitating models*: that is, to demonstrate his own, mixed brand of *parody.*
    Cervantes alerts his readers to the parodic context of the friend's solemn pro-
nouncements by consistently portraying that character, through implicit mockery, as a *semi*literate (*bien entendido*) fool (*gracioso*). Hence, the friend anticipates
such half-educated characters in the fiction as the curate mentioned as one of
the protagonist's only two friends at the start of the narrative, the humanist *primo*
(a word meaning both "cousin" and "dolt") who accompanies Don Quixote and
Sancho to the Cave of Montesinos (II, 22–23) and the "university graduate"
Sansón Carrasco who informs the knight and squire about Cide Hamete's history, Part I (II, 2–3) and who twice dons the garb of a knight in a first unsuccessful (II, 15) and later a successful effort (II, 54) to defeat Don Quixote in
combat and thus force the crazed hidalgo to return home. Besides serving their
other functions, these characters in the narrative, like the friend of the Prologue
to Part I, provide "models" of conventional opinion and superficial learning.
But, when seen as "models" for the *author's* parodic utterance, the friend's hackneyed, or *perfectly imitative*, statements about the "history's" genre, purpose, and
method take on an *innovative* meaning. In reference to the author's work, the

---

35. Eisenberg argues that Cervantes began to write, and may have completed, a serious epic about
the legendary Spanish hero Bernardo del Carpio along the lines described by the canon, in "El 'Bernardo'
de Cervantes fue su libro de caballerías" (1983, 103–17). Eisenberg convincingly elaborates on this claim
in *A Study of "Don Quixote"* (1987, 45–77).

friend's statements represent *partial* "truths." Thus for reader and implied author alike, those statements also become the object of discriminating (rather than simply dismissive) laughter.[36] Similarly, this character's reductive orthodoxies, and consequent antinomies, represent the conventional material (model?) from which both author and reader may inventively piece together (*componer*) the mixed purpose of the fiction.

In what amounts to a recapitulation of his previous remarks, the friend admonishes the narrator to respect the univocal genre, purpose, and method of the "history," by telling that narrator to write thus: "portraying [literally: painting] *your intention* to the best of your ability and by all possible means" (pintando, en todo lo que alcanzáredes y fuere posible, *vuestra intención*) (*DQ* I: *Prologue*, 58; emphasis added). Through this statement, as well, the author seems to give figuration (*pinta*) to the three elements composing his own "intention" and artistic design. To be sure, those three elements of the fiction's intent—its genre, purpose, and poetic method—can be broadly described as "parody," which may display a varying measure of praise and censure for the model on which it depends. In particular, however, each of these three elements that seem to make up the fiction's intent finds its expression in a paradox. *Generically* a poetic "history," in which each of those two modes of discourse mocks and elevates the other to an extreme degree, the fiction pursues an implicit, dramatized *purpose* of enlarging categories of thought and expression through a playful strategy of mock praise. Within this generic or antigeneric framework, the fiction, beginning with its fictional Prologue, pursues its shocking, "alienating" purpose through an artistic method of inventive imitation, or textual and intertextual refashioning. Indeed, this mixed, parodic intent of Cervantes seems reflected, first of all, in his use of the friend's statements to effect nothing other than a *parody of authorial intent*. And, as exemplified here through the friend's citational and recitational pronouncement of "half-truths," the author's parody in both the Prologue and the narrative dramatizes a partial affirmation and partial denial of his models' content and form. But the author's work also yields a complex parody that *transforms* its models and their meaning, not excepting the "model" of the friend's conventional remarks. It thereby transforms and enlarges the rhetorical and literary tradition, or "construct" (*máquina*), to which those models belong.

As discussed earlier, the author's models in *Don Quixote* are by no means limited to chivalric romance, though these latter form a primary object of his parodic

---

36. For an interesting discussion of Renaissance laughter, see Bakhtin 1984, 59–155. Therein, Bakhtin observes: "[F]or the Renaissance . . . the characteristic trait of laughter was precisely the recognition of its positive, regenerating, creative meaning. This clearly distinguishes it from the later theories of the philosophy of laughter, including Bergson's, which bring out mostly its negative function" (1984, 71).

imitation, in that they form a primary object of the protagonist's unique species of "perfect imitation." But as Luis Murillo has argued, even the protagonist's "code" of chivalry echoes such other literary models as chivalric verse and balladry (1988, 7–16). More important, both the Prologue and the narrative represent transformative parodies of fictional and nonfictional genres. As a whole, the fiction masquerading as *epic* history, a forerunner of both the modern and postmodern novel, derives its generic form from a parodic conflation of historical and poetic (romance) narratives. Further, Cervantes' unprecedented act of historical *poesis* in *Don Quixote* inventively derives its rhetorical strategy of paradoxy primarily from the Renaissance merger "mock encomium/Ciceronian paradox" and the multiple genres, including the mock encomium, which belong to the "mixed," Renaissance tradition of Menippean or Varronian satire.[37]

Encapsulating the paradoxes that constitute the fictional "history's" generic form, its mock-encomiastic purpose and its inventively imitative method, the author's Prologue would thus represent a fictional parody of nonfictional prologues, as well as a complex parody, or mock encomium, of what Cervantes' contemporary Alonso López Pinciano would deem *fictional dialogues* about aesthetic theory or "poetic philosophy." Similarly, besides the author's fictional targets, the narrator's invective "history" forms part of the author's "poetic" (fictional) parody, functioning as a mock encomium, of historical narratives. For the poetic utterance titled *Don Quixote* parodies, or mockingly praises, the futile/necessary attempt of

---

37. Admittedly, these instances of literary overstretch that I perceive in Cervantes' *Don Quixote* evoke identifying traits of what Frye (1973, 309–14) and Bakhtin (1984, 112–21) designate as Menippean satire or, in Frye's term, the "anatomy." Drawing on both those renowned critics, the scholar to argue most insistently in favor of categorizing *Don Quixote* within the "genre" of Menippean satire or the "anatomy" is James Parr, as indicated in his title, *Anatomy of Subversive Discourse* (1988, 123–51). With less insistence, Forcione's earlier study discussed the similarities between that "satirical" tradition and some of Cervantes' writings, including *Don Quixote* (1984, 22 and passim). Eisenberg puts forth the persuasive thesis that if pressed, Cervantes himself would have probably classified his most acclaimed fiction as a "burlesque [or perhaps mock] book of chivalry" (libro de caballerías burlesco) (1987, 79–107). Urbina (1990, 5–78) shows that "irony," though less of a satirical than a parodic kind, pervaded medieval romances of chivalry as far back as the works of Chrètien de Troyes. He judges Cervantes as an innovator within that tradition and therefore prefers to designate the genre of Cervantes' masterpiece with the English term "romance" (35). Riley (1981; 1986, 11–13) argues for a flexible understanding of genre and against expecting either too much or too little from genre as a classificatory concept. Without claiming that Cervantes himself would have categorized his work thus, Riley prefers to call *Don Quixote* a novel rather than a romance, since that work is clearly concerned to maintain literary verisimilitude in a way that chivalric or pastoral romance is not. Murillo (1980, 51–70) is likewise less in favor of labeling and suggests understanding *Don Quixote* as a secularized, "festive" (referring to the popular feast of carnival rather than solemn "feast days") affirmation and reversal of the "Renaissance epic" in the Italian tradition of Ariosto.

Combining these views, I would contend that Murillo's idea of a reverse (mock) epic signals, so to speak, the height and depth of Cervantes' generic reach in *Don Quixote*. Furthermore, one can plausibly argue that, if pressed on the matter by, say, a suspicious inquisitor, Cervantes would have probably labeled

such narratives to conceal their *dependence* on various forms of "poetic" truth and discourse, which are shown to constitute the only traceable "sources" of a history's partial imitation and partial invention of "life."

In a similar fashion, through his parody of the friend's limitations as reader and critic, the author enlarges, transforms, and opens up the category of "discreet reader." He points toward a *method of reading* of which the friend is shown to be incapable, bound as he is by dichotomous thinking and a narrow understanding of conventional orthodoxies. That character seems blind even to the possibility of a book that mingles praise with censure for the "chivalric romances" and their ideals. He would fail to understand how such an admixture of praise and censure, rather than a simple invective, better serves the *purpose* of enlarging aesthetic and ethical categories, while retaining their strengths, *moving beyond* their limitations and so undoing their fixity.

The friend, Cervantes' caricature of bookish folly, is shown incapable, I believe, of providing a critical and discriminating reading of any work that belongs to the same rhetorical tradition as Erasmus's mock encomium, much less a *generic innovation* within that tradition. Probably nothing would prove more bewildering, or more unintelligible, for either the friend or the narrator, than a paradoxical work whose jests (*burlas*) are in earnest (*veras*); a work that further breaks with convention by freely mingling varying degrees of truth and falsity, or praise and censure; that places "wise" words in the mouths of such transparently "foolish" characters as Folly or Don Quixote; that portrays the folly in accepted forms of wisdom; that reveals the wisdom in what the world, or received opinion, judges

---

his work as Eisenberg suggests: "burlesque book of chivalry" (libro de caballerías burlesco). Under less threatening circumstances, however, I think it more in consonance with the rhetorical strategy evinced in *Don Quixote* that he would have responded with some polysemous equivalent of "basin-helmet in prose" (baciyelmo en prosa), a gesture that would expand rather than negate a designation such as the one suggested by Eisenberg. In light of Cervantes' text and its classification by excellent readers, it seems that what Cervantes achieves in *Don Quixote* represents a remarkably comprehensive synthesis and double-minded, parodic refashioning of, for him, the known tradition of fictional and nonfictional discourse, both oral and written. In a spirit of inventive imitation, he enlists his masterwork to transform that tradition from within, affirming, denying, and enlarging the prevailing systems of discursive form and norm. It is my view, then, that Cervantes *invents*, in *Don Quixote*, a seminal, transitional work of fiction that respectfully validates, irreverently undoes, and successfully refashions the literary tradition of his time. His work integrates and moves beyond what are thought to be contradictory categories of genre, stylistic register, and rhetorical persuasiveness (e.g., epic/farce, high/low, history/poetry) into a work that remains paradoxical at all levels of content and form. Fittingly enough, Cervantes chose to perceive himself as a "great inventor" (gran inventor): an artist who discovers, ponders, and playfully re-creates his textual models. In view of such self-awareness and such ambition, it seems likely that he would recognize, and aim at, the groundbreaking quality of his achievement in *Don Quixote*. He would recognize that he had succeeded in creating a new genre, anti-genre and counter-genre which ultimately remains unclassifiable, except in anachronistic, protean reference to its continuing generation of modern, postmodern, or later literary "offspring."

to be nothing but folly; that "renders" (*pinta*) a "world" that is neither wholly upside down nor right-side up, but always and everywhere moving in the middest. Respectively, the friend and the narrator are not only shown to be incapable of reading or writing such a paradoxical praise of "base things" as Erasmus' mock encomium. They are especially incapable of reading or writing such a *mock epic*, and satirical romance "history," as the author's *Don Quixote*—namely, Cervantes' doubly paradoxical encomium of chivalric romance, or of the epic in its "base" form. They are incapable, in short, of realizing that, when viewed from a different perspective, the narrator's "history" represents that very work.

In sum, both the narrator and his friend are shown to suffer from what we may call a hardening of the categories. Thus the friend's statements regarding authorial intent provide a model of orthodox categories that invite enlargement and transformation. In self-allusive fashion, those "model" statements of the friend are also the *means* whereby the author first brings such a transformation about. Conversely, the friend's discourse also represents a model of what readers of the author's fiction are called upon not simply to negate, but to enlarge and move beyond in their critical engagement with the text. The author's narrative thus beckons to be read as an extreme instance of paradoxy, which invites its readers to expand and, unlike the narrator, "to dispute" (poner en disputa) the many forms of aesthetic and ethical *philosophia* that appear in the fiction, without simply dismissing them, and without aping or uncritically "approving them as good" (tenerlas por buenas). But, more important, the narrative first startles readers into self-awareness; into acknowledging that, as such, all imitations and all statements in discourse—including "this statement"—are both true and false in some sense and to some degree.

Next, that narrative challenges readers to exert their inherently mysterious "freedom" (libre albedrío). Up to a point, our lack of familial ties to the narrator's "history" makes us exempt and "free from all respect and obligation." We are free to "say of the history whatever you please" (*DQ* I: *Prologue*, 51). By extension, we are only partially bound to the poetic discourse of the author's fiction. We can say and even *make* what we please of the text. Yet, as the Prologue of 1605 implies, how we exercise our readerly prerogative upon Cervantes' text reflects not only our status as some type of "discreet" or "vulgar" readers, but also the wise/foolish manner in which we remain idle or involved with "this" or other texts. As set forth in the fiction, and specifically in the competing ideologies of its characters, the exercise or failure to exercise the inherently mysterious power of one's freedom determines one's growth in knowledge and self-knowledge over time. Beginning with the Prologue, Cervantes' fiction dramatizes, rather than preaches, that it is also freedom that allows us continually to exercise and expand our complementary powers of *inventio* and *imitatio*, to grow in our capacity as "inventors" (*ingeniosos*) and *componedores*, or compositors, of discourse; and thus to enlarge our categories of judgment, speech, and action.

A final contrast in the Prologue between the character's statements and the text's dramatized message emerges from a concluding bit of advice from the friend to the narrator:

> Strive as well that, reading your history, the melancholic will feel moved to laughter, the merry will be more so, the simpleminded will not feel annoyed, the discreet will admire its inventiveness, the grave will not scorn it, nor the prudent cease to praise it.

> (Procurad también que, leyendo vuestra historia, el melancólico se mueva a risa, el risueño la acreciente, el simple no se enfade, el discreto se admire de la invención, el grave no la desprecie, ni el prudente deje de alabarla.)
> (*DQ* I: *Prologue*, 58)

Of course, it is reasonable to assume that the author intended his fiction to appeal to the tastes of a variegated readership, in full agreement with his character's rather conventional remarks. Owing to the range of its rhetorical and thematic registers, the text has the power to appeal to "serious" readers, full of ethical and aesthetic purpose ("grave," "prudent"); the most diverse temperaments ("melancholic," "merry," or sanguine) and the most diverse intellectual gifts ("discreet" or "simpleminded"). And yet, one detects another dimension beneath those remarks: namely, the author's allusion to the fact that each reading of his fiction remains as much a function of the reader as it is of the text. Cervantes' fiction self-consciously suggests that we will read and judge the narrative, the author, the protagonist, or other characters according to who we are and whom we are willing to laugh at, or see, in the textual mirror.[38]

---

38. From the discussion above, Cervantes' text seems to imply an understanding of its readers that closely resembles that of a contemporary critical tradition called Reader-Response Theory. Important writings within this tradition can be found in the collections by Tompkins (1980) and Suleiman and Crosman (1980). Furthermore, Cervantes' *Don Quixote* would also seem to offer a prime example of what Barthes calls a "writerly" work, in which the aim is "to make the reader no longer a consumer, but a producer [rewriter] of the text" (1986,4). Like Iser's "implied reader" of modern and contemporary fiction (1987), Cervantes' "consumers" are invited to make incremental sense of paradoxes and ambiguities that they encounter in the fiction. Nonetheless, it is important to recall that today's "reader-response" was "rhetoric" or rhetorical posture for writers and productive readers in the Renaissance. Besides Colie's book on Renaissance paradox (1966), in more recent studies by Kahn (1985), Levao (1985), and Rajan (1985), it is argued throughout that Renaissance practitioners of humanist, Erasmian poetics strove to create perplexing, self-conscious works and held a sophisticated view of the reader's role in negotiating and inventively refashioning textual paradoxes and puzzles.

Paradoxes of Imitation

The Quest for Origins and Originality

One unsettling consequence of identifying the coincidence between art and life, and identifying all human discourse as insubstantial artifice, is that we come to perceive much of "life" (specifically, knowledge, history, and therefore historiography) as an infinite series of imitations imitating imitations. In addition, the insubstantiality of discourse in both the historical and poetic modes paves the way for an infinite number of imitations within imitations. For it seems clear that in historical discourse and, indeed, in "histories," reportedly factual accounts may derive from what someone said about what someone said about what someone said, ad infinitum. And it seems clear, as well, that the fictional "I" or "we" within an actual author's poetic utterance *can be said* to produce a poetic utterance containing a (more) fictional speaking subject, who in turn can be said to do likewise, and so on. More simply, the insubstantiality of discourse allows us to insert an utterance within an utterance and to generate a potentially endless series of

either fictional or non-fictional stories, or a potentially infinite number of stories
within stories within stories.

Thus in *Don Quixote*, the author's dramatization of the time-honored paradox of life in art and art in life repeatedly leads us to confront a literary variation
on the equally classical paradoxes of infinite series and infinite regress. Whether,
in a manner of speaking, we move laterally or horizontally within the text,
instances of imitation in *Don Quixote* leave us with the impression that with each
succeeding or receding imitation, we find ourselves at a farther remove from the
original source, the original utterance, and the original model, and thus from
"truth," "life," and "nature." In particular, the author of the fiction exploits the
insubstantiality of discourse through such related narrative techniques as the
frame story, embedding, the effect of Chinese boxes, *mise en abîme*, and levels of
narration, in order to enhance the appearance of the knight's and the squire's
"reality," as well as the "history's" "veracity." As Riley asserts, such feats of poetic
legerdemain "give the novel an appearance of receding depths, by comparison
with which most other prose fiction is two-dimensional" (1962, 42). Indeed, it
seems clear that Cervantes draws on such techniques in order to test the limits of
and dramatize the overlap between literary "verisimilitude" and historical "truth"
(Riley 1962, 43). Additionally, however, it also seems clear that the author of *Don
Quixote* enlists such techniques in order to underscore their status as techniques
and to draw the interested reader's attention to the appearance of "more original
sources" and the "receding depths" of "reality" as illusions or discursive tricks.

In part, my aim in the following pages is to discuss how the fiction's artful
discourse of imitation flaunts the insubstantiality and trickery of discourse itself
as a form of artistic *imitatio* that calls for *inventio*. In this chapter I will pay special attention to how Cervantes conflates such apparent contraries as source and
copy, model and imitation, or container and contained. And I will examine how,
as a result of these conflations, Cervantes encourages and frustrates our efforts
to identify the "reliability" of competing voices and the "reality" of competing
versions that relate the same "events." Through an inventive use and demonstration of discursive trickery, *Don Quixote* represents an instance of discourse and
imitation acting against themselves. Yet the work also represents, for the very
same reasons, an effective use of discourse and imitation acting in their own
defense. Cervantes' text invites us to take part in a complex, literary game and to
do so both in jest and in earnest. For if the fiction reveals that both the process
and products of imitation and discourse involve the creation of "appearance," it
also reveals that only within that process and its products is "truth"—as learned
ignorance—able to occur.

Hence the present analysis centers on a use of imitation and discourse in *Don Quixote* that is inherently *festive*. The work presents both a parody and celebration, praise and censure, of imitation and discourse, whose insubstantiality guarantees, not only their fictiveness, but also their suppleness. As Cervantes' mock encomium of discourse reveals, our recognizing the fictiveness of our discourse and imitations allows us to fashion, refashion, and enlarge the categories by which we fashion or refashion ourselves and our experience. We can thus undertake such refashionings and enlargements more in dialogue than in conflict with the empirical world of matter and social intercourse, as well as the inner world of desire, illusion, and dreams.

Inside and Outside the Frame: A Story About Stories Within Stories

If, through its mad protagonist and his adventures, *Don Quixote* remains chiefly a parodic imitation of chivalric romances (*libros de caballerías*), it also contains imitations of virtually all genres of fictional and nonfictional discourse that prevailed in Cervantes' time. To begin with an obvious example, the nameless innkeeper of the first sally, the characters in his employ, Ginés de Pasamonte, and the other galley slaves are all drawn in parodic imitation of picaresque literature. The picaresque model that looms especially large is the work by Cervantes' chief rival in the domain of prose fiction and the most successful such work of the time: Mateo Alemán's *Guzmán de Alfarache*, also published in two parts (1599, 1602). This is so, notwithstanding Cervantes' causing his fiction's most accomplished trickster, Ginés de Pasamonte (Gi-nés-de-Pa-sa-mon-te), to make explicit reference only to *Lazarillo de Tormes* rather than to what sufficiently informed readers know to be this character's immediate model, Guzmán de Alfarache (Guz-mán-de-Al-fa-ra-che), of like-sounding name, who is likewise a galley slave engaged in writing his autobiography (Dunn 1982, 119). However, in a manner that parodies and transformatively imitates both the character and actions of his model, whom Alemán portrays as *having written* the tale of his own *religious conversion*, Ginés de Pasamonte is *in the process of writing* as well as "living" the story of his *impenitent*, criminal exploits.

Another example: the interweaving tales of Dorotea, Cardenio, Fernando, and Luscinda creatively imitate what was called the "sentimental novella" (*novela sentimental*) as well as the "comedy of intrigue" (*comedia de enredo*) before culminating in the crowded, multigeneric parody of *anagnorisis* and poetic justice at Juan Palomeque's inn.[1] Just as the tales of Zoraida, Ruy Pérez de Viedma ("the Captive"), and Ana Felix creatively imitate the "Moorish novel" (*novela morisca*), so the tales of Marcela, Grisóstomo, and the "feigned Arcadia" overtly parody and imitate the pastoral novel. One finds a striking parody of formal disputation in the debate between the protagonist and the canon of Toledo that, as already discussed in connection with the *Dialogues* by Pero Mexía, traces back to the Scholastic model of Disputed Questions and, ultimately, the Socratic Dialogues of Plato.[2] Don Quixote provides equally formal, mock "declamations" on the Golden Age, Liberty, and Arms and Letters. Moreover, Cervantes' fictional work not only offers a parody of other fictional forms, but also constitutes a putative "history" and biography that imitates and parodies historical narratives. Likewise, the Prologue of 1605 is chiefly, though not exclusively, a parodic imitation of prologues (including itself) and their process of creation (including its own).

To return to the main narrative, the most obvious examples of embedding imitations within imitations occur when the author has his characters tell stories or read them aloud. Probably the most conspicuous instance of a presumably "more imaginary" story being told within the "history" occurs when the priest reads aloud the exemplary "Tale of Impertinent Curiosity" (El curioso impertinente) at Juan Palomeque's inn (I, 33–35). Here the author introduces what appears to be a subordinate level not simply of *imitation*, but specifically of *narration*. In addition, however, this circumstance dramatizes equally well the potential for both an endless series and infinite levels of imitation.

Indeed, that *exemplary* tale remains a fiction (an imaginary tale) *within* the heterocosm of the characters. In short, that tale is doubly fictional: a fiction for fictional "persons." Yet unlike those imaginary "persons" or characters, the reader can also view that exemplary tale as *either* the author's transformative imitation or his transformed model of the tales involving Dorotea, Cardenio, Fernando, and Luscinda. For part of that tale's meaning depends on where it is situated— indeed, where the author elected to situate it—within the main narrative. In this regard, it is unnecessary for the reader to know that the historical author, Cervantes, wrote "The Tale of Impertinent Curiosity" before Part I of *Don Quixote*. Rather, it is necessary to recognize only that, even as represented within the fictional frame of the putative "history," the writing of the exemplary tale most likely predates those characters' recent adventures, and certainly predates

---

1. Anthony Close focuses on this scene of anagnorisis at Juan Palomeque's inn to argue against the possibility of subjecting Cervantes' fiction to deconstructive readings (1990a, 69–91).

2. Along similar lines, Alban Forcione discusses Don Quixote's response to the canon of Toledo as a "mock-*discorso*" (1970, 110–13).

their arrival at Juan Palomeque's inn. A fact unknown to the characters, and hitherto unknown to the reader, is that, after a fashion, "The Tale of Impertinent
Curiosity" was awaiting, or was made to await, those four characters' arrival. On
the one hand, then, from the reader's extrafictional locus, which remains invisible to the characters, it seems possible to understand that the characters listen
not only to a mirror of their recent past, but also to a "model" story after which
their own stories, or "lives," are inventively shaped. Their "reality" may then seem
to *derive* from, and to seem "less real" or "more imaginary" than, what they are
themselves shown to perceive as an "imaginary" tale. On the other hand, owing
to where the exemplary tale appears in the context of the narrative, the reader is
no less justified in thinking that the same exemplary tale now functions as an
imitation and variation of the "model" story provided by those characters' recent
exploits. In short, both tales act alternately as "model" and "imitation" for each
other, depending on the vantage from which the reader chooses to view them.

Tellingly, the ability to perceive how the tales function in that seemingly contradictory fashion, and how those tales frustrate and parody the reader's efforts
to establish a hierarchy of comparatively "real" or "imaginary" levels of imitation, requires one to assess the narrative as the product of artistic design, and as
the utterance of an implied author. For this reason, an important dimension of
meaning to be found in the author's use of imitative levels—deployed in testing
the limits between the "real" and the "imaginary"—strains, without necessarily
exceeding, the reach of a structuralist framework such as that of Gérard Genette
(1980). Predicated upon the assumption of an ideal narrative as a self-enclosed
system, such a critical framework would lead one to identify either "subordinate
levels of narration" or "transgressions" of those levels *solely in reference to* an
"extradiegetic" perspective—the *highest* level—assumed to belong to a principal
narrator (Genette 1980, 228–31). Although it generates a host of useful observations and queries, that extradiegetic *point of reference* represents a critical
choice that may obscure subtleties inhering within Cervantes' work.

In the specific example of the relation between the tales of the four characters
named above and the exemplary "Tale of Impertinent Curiosity," only an *extrafictional* perspective shared by both reader and author (i.e., "above" or beyond
the "extradiegetic" level) lets the reader reflect upon *the arrangement of the tales*
as a *message* conveyed from the implied author to the reader. Such a message
forms part of the author's self- and reader-conscious *narrative*. In other words,
the embedding of that exemplary tale not only serves the function of reinforcing
and imitating recent "events" *within* the fictional frame of the narrative. In the
self-conscious work of *Don Quixote*, that embedding also serves to deepen the
continuing dialogue between author and reader, on an extrafictional plane,

about aesthetic questions that are first dramatized in the Prologue. Indeed, that instance of embedding constitutes a *technique* that one may also *interpret* as a *sign*. The author communicates a paradoxical message to the reader by enlisting the text itself as a practical dramatization of the same open questions that are dramatized, from a different perspective or series of perspectives, within the fictional frame of the "history." Further, the author seems to invite the reader to ponder how the *meaning* behind a particular construct—the reading of an exemplary tale by a particular group of characters in a particular set of circumstances— will differ according to circumstances, and according to whether one judges or interprets that tale from inside or outside the fictional frame. From the extrafictional perspective of the reader, shared by the implied author, one can judge that exemplary tale "correctly" as *either* the imitation *or* model of those tales involving Dorotea, Cardenio, Fernando, and Luscinda. Moreover, one can judge those characters' "lives" either as imitating, or being imitated by, the exemplary tale. Such simultaneously contrary meanings remain inaccessible to all our characters' perspectives, including the "extradiegetic" perspective of the narrator.

A related variation of imitations both within and of imitations ensues from Dorotea's acting as the princess Micomicona from Micomiconia, or Princess Monkey-Monkey from Monkey-Monkeyland. The emphasis in both her name and actions is, of course, on imitation as "aping." Furthermore, her assumed name, Micomicona, also characterizes her as a hyperbolically comic figure of drama. She is, on the one hand, a "comic lady" (*cómica*). On the other hand, the Spanish augmentative "*-ona*" affixed to that name alludes to her habit of "overdoing it" or "hamming it up" in a *doubly fictional* role. The princess, who is "really" Dorotea, acts in what amounts to the curate's comic drama, staged in order to return Don Quixote to his home in La Mancha. Hence Cervantes has Dorotea, a character fashioned after the heroine of the sentimental novella, *willfully* imitate a distressed damsel of chivalric romance whom Don Quixote must avenge and restore to her rightful throne. In this way, the author increases the string of imitations, together with the degree of his work's self-conscious, multigeneric parody. Through her "life," already a parodic imitation of a literary form, Dorotea parodies, imitates, and parodies the imitation of yet another literary form.

Furthermore, as emblematized, hyperbolically, in this multiply imitative imitation that Dorotea enacts and is, Cervantes' entire fiction projects an inventive imitation, or mirror, of itself to a degree that defies comprehensive treatment. Thus, to illustrate this point, let me note the fiction's act of self-imitation only in general terms. First of all, Part II imitates and varies Part I in structure and content alike. The first seven chapters of Part I treat of our protagonist's fall into madness, his first sally, and his first return home. Phrased another way, the action in these seven opening chapters represents Don Quixote's preparations for his second sally, or his first sally with Sancho. In parallel fashion, the first seven chapters of Part II relate his preparations for his third and longest sally, which is only his second with Sancho.

Further, in mock variation of the classical, heroic plot structure of sortie-achievement-return, each of the knight's three sallies follows a threefold pattern: adventures on the road, broken by sojourns at some interior setting, and return to home and bed. In Part I, apart from the protagonist's own domicile, the interior settings are two inns, which Don Quixote takes to be castles. In Part II, apart from his domicile and more inns, which he no longer takes to be castles, Don Quixote stays at the mansion of Don Diego de Miranda (II, 18), the probably modest home of Basilio (I, 22), the real castle of the duke and duchess (II, 30–57), which our hero thinks "enchanted," and the residence of Antonio Moreno in Barcelona (II, 62). The exterior settings of Part I are the road, or Spain's *Camino Real*, and the wilds of Sierra Morena. In Part II, though he spends more time indoors, Don Quixote also encounters adventures on the road and descends into the subterranean Cave of Montesinos (II, 22–23). More generally, the setting for Part I is rural and most of its characters are peasants, excepting Fernando, Cardenio, Luscinda, and the hidalgo protagonist who fancies himself a knight. Without abandoning either the country or peasant characters, Part II culminates in the courtly ambience of the duke and duchess's palace and the bustling city of Barcelona.

E. C. Riley has pointed out that one may discern, grafted on to the main narratives of Parts I and II alike, an equal number of interpolated tales, or "extraneous episodes," defined thus: "A story of more than anecdotic length, with a certain coherence, and of which the origin and development, but not necessarily the conclusion, have nothing to do with Don Quixote or Sancho" (1986, 79). In Part I, the interpolated tales deal with the following: (1) Marcela and Grisóstomo (I, 11–14); (2) Dorotea, Cardenio, Fernando, and Luscinda (I, 23–24, 27–29, 36); (3) "The Tale of Impertinent Curiosity" (I, 33–35); (4) the Captive and Zoraida (I, 39–41); (5) Doña Clara and Don Luis (I, 42–43); and (6) Eugenio and Leandra (I, 51) (Riley 1986, 79–86). The corresponding tales in Part II, which are better integrated into the core narrative about Don Quixote and Sancho, relate the stories of (1) Camacho's wedding (II, 19–21); (2) The braying adventure (II, 25,27); (3) Doña Rodríguez (II, 48, 52, 56, 66); (4) the nocturnal escape of Don Diego de la Llana's daughter in Barataria (II, 49); (5) Claudia Jerónima (II, 60); and (6) Ana Félix and Gaspar Gregorio (II, 54, 63, 65) (Riley 1986, 97–103).

Besides the unmanageable number of its episodes' prefigurations and reconfigurations of other episodes and of other fictional and nonfictional texts, the design of Cervantes' paradoxical fiction leads these interpolated tales and their characters to act as a series of mirrors on the main narrative and its protagonists. This is so, I believe, especially at the level of *Don Quixote's* thematics. But, rather than the grand theme of the Ideal against the Real that Friedrich Schlegel perceived in Cervantes' masterpiece, I would suggest that, beginning with its principals, the action in *Don Quixote* dramatizes a summarizing idea that relates, in that period's aesthetic terminology, to the potential dialogue or conflict between Art and Nature. From what was earlier discussed in reference to Mexía's distinction between "empiricals" (empíricos) and "rationalists" (racionales) within his *Dialogue of the Physicians,* one may describe the prevalent, Renaissance understanding of "art" as man's *symbolic activity.* One result of such activity is *scientia,* or systematic "knowledge," which prevents what Mexía calls "confusion and forgetting." The summarizing idea of Cervantes' fiction concerning the potential dialogue or conflict between Art and Nature would thus entail that author's dramatizations of potential dialogue or conflict between Literature and Life, History and Poetry, or Historical and Poetic Discourse. Characters in the main narrative and the interpolated tales thus come to mirror one another according to how they negotiate or enact this summarizing idea and its derivatives.

In particular, as evinced primarily in Don Quixote, characters in both the main and interpolated tales seem guilty of folly and meet a sorry end to the extent that they strive to make the worlds of matter and social intercourse conform to chosen codes, models, or a rigid system of symbols. In the cases of Don Quixote, Marcela, Grisóstomo, Anselmo, Leandra, the braying aldermen, or Claudia Jerónima, conflict or tragedy seem to ensue from a failure to conform one's symbolic "art" to or place it in dialogue with the demands of empirical and social experience. In Cervantes' fiction, the type of folly we may label as *insanity,* again such as that of Don Quixote, would therefore involve a thoroughgoing conflict between art and nature, or one's collapsing the dialogue, or the distinction, between literature and life or poetry and history. The lesser folly of stupidity or simplicity, such that of Mexía's "empiricals" and, in part, such as Sancho's gullibility or his artless repetition of proverbs, would involve a lack of inventiveness or an incompetent use of symbols.

Thus, as illustrated in these examples, the very construction of the author's "imitation" (book) of imitations and of itself as imitation and the ethical/aesthetic questions that arise therefrom form an integral part of Cervantes' self-allusive text. The behavior of extrafictional readers in their capacity as a interpreters of "this narrative" both mirrors and transforms the behavior of all characters and voices within the heterocosm, from the "extradiegetic level" on down. And yet our sharing an implied author's perspective does not so much invest our interpretations with *authority*, as it adds an extrafictional dimension of multiple, paradoxical meaning to the author's fictional narrative itself. That narrative invites the reader to ask what the author means, or what that author aims to dramatize, not only *within* a passage, but also by the author's constructing a passage in a particular way. By asking such questions, the reader may come to perceive not only how Cervantes dramatizes his content in the form of his narrative, but also how he self-consciously dramatizes what Hayden White would call "the content of the [narrative] form" (1987).

Original Copies: Versions of a Manuscript and a Battle in I, 8–9

A particularly self-conscious, and dizzying, instance of Cervantes' playfully embedding imitations within imitations occurs in that passage of *Don Quixote*, at the close of I, 8 and the beginning of I, 9, where a character dubbed only "second author" (segundo autor) seeks, discovers, and purchases a manuscript attributed to the Arab historian Cide Hamete. At this early stage in the narrative, the author introduces levels of what we may call either "reality" or "imaginariness." But it is important to stress that these levels resist anything akin to hierarchical plotting along a vertical axis. Moreover, in this passage, it comes to light that those shadowy and shifting levels of imitation may have formed part of the "history" from the start.

At the close of the eighth chapter in Part I, Don Quixote engages a Basque from Biscay in mortal combat. Both men are astride their mounts—one a nag, the other a mule—swords raised for the attack. But just as the story of their fight reaches its climax, we read:

> But what mars the whole tale is that the author of this history leaves the battle in suspense at this very point and place, with the excuse that he found nothing more written besides what he has already set forth.

> (Pero está el daño de todo esto que en este punto y término deja pendiente el autor desta historia esta batalla, disculpándose que no halló más escrito, destas hazañas de don Quijote, de las que deja referidas.) (*DQ* I: 8, 137)

The so-called second author first emerges in the very next sentence of the narrative. Perhaps like ourselves, he is a frustrated reader of the truncated history. He refuses to believe that the people of La Mancha could be foolish enough to let such a compelling story, and such a pivotal part of their past, fall into oblivion. The following chapter (I, 9) places that "second author" in the marketplace of Toledo, where he happens across the Arab manuscript by Cide Hamete that contains, to his happy amazement, a history of Don Quixote. Knowing no Arabic, he commissions its translation to a Spanish-speaking Moor. In seemingly miraculous fashion, this Arab history begins with nothing other than a continuation and conclusion of the battle left in suspense at the close of I, 8. And, only slightly less miraculous, what seems to be the manuscript's frontispiece contains a drawing of the same battle scene.

Now, thanks to the fluency of Cervantes' tale, we may easily miss the degree of narrative complexity that the text introduces in these few pages, at the close of I, 8 and the start of I, 9. So let us identify the different voices and levels of narration for which we now have specific evidence. The enunciating subject, or the implicit, fictional "I," who tells us that the story of the battle is left in suspense, puts himself forward here as the writer, or editor, who is responsible for the final version of the "true history." For reasons to be discussed presently, I believe this voice to be the same voice, and the same character, as the narrator of the Prologue. And for the sake of clarity, I shall refer to him hereafter simply as the "narrator." In any event, our narrator leads us to believe that his chief source for events from I, 1 to I, 8 is a narrative by yet another "historian," strangely identified in the above quotation as "author of this history" (autor desta historia).

That designation proves especially baffling, since the history we are reading seems to differ from what the narrator calls "this history." So, too, the "voice" we are now "hearing" (the narrator's) differs from that of the "author of this history," referred to in the third person.[3] More baffling still, the document ascribed to that "author" comes to an untimely end, and ceases even to be a source—much less the chief source—of the "history" we shall read from the start of I, 9 to the very end of Part II. So, no sooner do we learn of his "existence" as a source than that "author" ceases to be relevant at all to "this," the "history" we are reading.

In any case, the so-called author of this history is himself but another compiler, compositor, or editor, working from an unnamed source or series of sources where "he found nothing more written" (no halló más escrito). We never learn whether any of his sources is an eyewitness account. Hence the likelihood of other compilers, sources, and voices for utterances we read in the first eight chapters of the "true history." Indeed, it seems that we must now confront the possibility of countless and nameless imitations or models embedded within, or

---

3. As Mauricio Molho observes, this use of the third person makes the identification between the voice of the narrator-editor and that of the "author of this history" "a grammatically dubious case" (un caso gramaticalmente dudoso) (1989, 278).

issuing from, other models or imitations. Likewise, we must confront the *impossibility* of pinpointing an original or reliable source for events that precede the manuscript's discovery.

From I, 9 onward, the "true history" about the exploits of the knight and his squire, and about the fashioning of the "true history" itself, chiefly relies on the account by the "second author," which is a *transcription* of the *translation* of Cide Hamete's manuscript. The Arab historian is put forth as an eyewitness to the events he narrates, and is nowhere said to rely on sources of any kind.

One may be tempted to hold that the chief sources for the entire "history" composed by the narrator consist of the narrative attributed to the "author of this history," the "second author's" account, the Moor's translation, and Cide Hamete's manuscript. But in the end, the narrator remains exceedingly vague about his sources for either the first eight chapters or the rest of what he proclaims to be his "true history." In the opening chapter of the narrative, for instance, in a passage relating to the possible surname of the crazed hidalgo, we read about an unspecified number of "authors who write on this subject" (autores que deste caso escriben) (*DQ* I: 1, 71). Further, we read about a discrepancy among various "authors" regarding the protagonist's first adventure—that is, about the very chronology of events in the "history": "There are some authors who say that the first adventure he met was that of Lápice Point. Others say it was that of the windmills" (Autores hay que dicen que la primera aventura que le avino fue la del Puerto Lápice; otros dicen que la de los molinos de viento" (*DQ* I: 1, 81–82). Immediately thereafter, we receive an archivist's nonsolution to that discrepancy:

> but what I have been able to find out in this matter, and what I have found written in the annals of La Mancha, is that he traveled that whole day and, when evening fell, his nag and he felt tired and nearly dead from hunger.

> (pero lo que yo he podido averiguar en este caso, y lo que he hallado escrito en los anales de la Mancha, es que él anduvo todo aquel día, y, al anochecer, su rocín y él se hallaron cansados y muertos de hambre.) (*DQ* I: 2, 82)

These passages may issue from the "voice" of the narrator himself. The reference to "the annals of La Mancha" clearly echoes the narrator's words in the Prologue concerning the "archives of La Mancha." But the implied author is hardly beyond confusing his readers about the narrative voice they are presumably now "hearing." Hence, those passages may also represent the voice of the "author of this history" or that of another narrator-historian in some unspecified source. In other words, that passage, like most others in the narrative, may represent or approximate the words of almost any "authorial" voice belonging to almost any level of narration.

What is more, besides written documents, the narrator relies on hearsay, as is evident from passages too numerous to name that begin with such phrases as "they say that" (dicen que), "opinion has it that" (hay opinión que), or even "they say that they say that" (dicen que dicen que) (Weiger 1988, 16–21), as anticipated in the following passage at the close of the Prologue to Part I: "*Opinion has it*, among all the inhabitants in the district of the Montiel Plains, that he was the most chaste lover and the most valiant knight" (*Hay opinión*, por todos los habitadores del distrito del campo de Montiel, que fue el más casto enamorado y el más valiente caballero) (*DQ* I: *Prologue*, 58).

Nonetheless, it seems that the final version of the "history" is the work of the narrator and that we ultimately rely on his point of view. Yet it remains unclear how much of the written or hearsay evidence for the "history" reaches that narrator through either the discovered manuscript or interviews he conducted among local inhabitants; or how much of that evidence derives from translations or one of his other sources, named or unnamed. It therefore remains unclear, as well, how much of the "history" is transcribed, revised, or made up, and just where passages deriving from documentary and hearsay evidence fall within that "history's" presumptive hierarchy of narrative levels and voices. We can never be certain which voice we hear, or whether we hear any voice unfiltered, in a particular passage of the "history." Each of the narrative voices and levels for which we have a label—"narrator," "author of this history," "second author," "translator," "Cide Hamete"—thus represents a polyphonous blend of other, equally polyphonous voices and levels. The final form of the "true history" thus encourages, frustrates, and parodies our efforts to distinguish the copy from its original, or its source. Indeed, regarding the "true history," one can employ such apparent contraries as "source" and "copy," or "model" and "imitation," as relative, often interchangeable, terms.

In this same section of the narrative, we find another self-conscious instance of artistic invention that is for, about, and against itself, and that illustrates why Cervantes stands, in the words of Robert Alter, "at the beginning of the Copernican revolution in the practice and theory of mimesis" (1975, 8). In particular, the "true history" provides no fewer than four versions of the scene depicting the battle between Don Quixote and the Basque from Biscay. In order of

appearance within the text, the first version of that battle between the protagonist and the Basque is the one left in suspense at the end of chapter 8, and seems
to be the work of the narrator (*DQ* I: 8, 137). The second version is told in
what seems to be the voice of the "second author" at the start of chapter 9,
reminding the reader where the previous chapter broke off (*DQ* I: 9, 139). A
third, pictorial version of the scene by an unnamed illustrator *is said* to appear
on the frontispiece of the manuscript (*DQ* I: 9, 144). Last, a fourth version
reportedly occurs at the very start of Cide Hamete's history (*DQ* I: 9, 145). In
brief, the four versions of that battle scene, as related in the "true history," may
be enumerated as follows:

1. the *narrator's* version (written)
2. the "*second author's*" version (written)
3. the *illustrator's* version (pictorial)
4. *Cide Hamete's* version (written)

One question that arises here is whether we can plausibly identify any of
these versions as an original or a model. If not, of what are these versions of the
battle scene imitations or copies? And is it tenable to claim that any of these versions contains or frames one or more of the others? With these questions in
mind, let us discuss each of the four versions and, therefore, join in Cervantes'
textual game involving the limits and overlap between "literary verisimilitude"
and "historical truth."

On the one hand, the model or models for the narrator's version of the battle
(1) may be found in one, two, or all three of the other versions—those of the
second author, the illustrator, and Cide Hamete. This is so because the narrator
may have possessed any of the following *sources* when he wrote his own version:
the discovered manuscript (including the illustration); the translation of that
manuscript; or the "second author's" account. On the other hand, the narrator's
imitative version may also derive from a "model" in the text of the so-called
author of this history. Indeed, the version of the narrator may derive from any
combination of "models" to be found in any combination of oral or written
sources, including such "new" sources as the "second author's" account, the translation, and the manuscript. A further difficulty arises in pinpointing the narrator's models, in that every unnamed source for the so-called author of this
history is likely to contain its own description of the battle. With respect to one
another, descriptions of the battle from sources both named and unnamed may
thus act as imitations, models, or parallel versions. The narrator's version is therefore just as original and "true," or just as derivative and possibly "imaginary," as

any other version, aside from an imitation or imitations that we can identify as its single or composite model. But any point of reference we use to identify either a sequential or hierarchical order amid the whirl of voices, perspectives, and "imitations" *within* the narrator's version would represent an arbitrary critical choice.

From a different perspective, one is led to similar conclusions about the untraceable genealogy of imitations, voices, and levels, in the version of the "second author" (2). Since the "second author" is unable to "speak" to us directly, both his version of the battle and his account of events from I, 9 onward occupy a level of narration beneath that of the narrator. So possible models for the "second author's" version of the battle would not include that of the narrator, but would include the version of the illustrator, or the version of Cide Hamete, or both. Regarding the second author's "old" sources, we never learn where he read about events that occur in the first eight chapters of the narrator's "true history." He may have read the work of the so-called "author of this history" or one of the latter's unnamed sources. Like the version of the narrator, then, that of the "second author" may simply parallel or imitate any combination of model descriptions that remain explicit or buried in that "second author's" old and new sources.

Adding to our confusion, the "second author's version may be viewed as both parallel and subordinate to the version of the narrator. For, if the narrator wrote his version before obtaining the account of the "second author," the versions of both those characters could derive from the same model or models. Hence, if the version of the "second author" is not a model for the version of the narrator, then both would occupy the same *level of imitation*, sharing an equal degree of reliability (or its opposite), though occupying different *levels of narration* within the "true history."

Let me violate sequential order to assess the last version of the battle to occur in a *verbal* medium (4), found at the beginning of the Arab manuscript. Because a popular prejudice in Cervantes' time held that Cide Hamete belonged to a race of liars, the manuscript itself can be seen as a contemporary variation on the paradox of the Liar from Crete, effectively telling us: "This history is false." Despite such popular bigotry, with which both the "second author" and Don Quixote agree, Cide Hamete's version is the only verbal "imitation" of the battle that can originate from direct observation of the "event." And yet, should we choose to believe in the originality of the manuscript, and so in the originality of Cide Hamete's version, we seem obliged to posit a missing fragment of that manuscript.

As hinted earlier, it seems nothing short of miraculous that Cide Hamete should begin both his narrative and his *observations* of Don Quixote at the climax of the battle between the protagonist and the Basque. But arguing in favor of the manuscript's integrity is the fact that it is said to include not only a picture of the battle, on what seems to be a frontispiece, but also a title page. How could such a missing fragment, which is missing that front matter, disappear from the rest of the manuscript without a trace? What might such a fragment contain? Is it the father and mother of all sources for the first eight chapters of the "true history?" Is the manuscript truly an eyewitness account, or is Cide Hamete concealing his sources? However we may choose to answer these questions will determine whether we consider the version by Cide Hamete a model, an imitation, or a parallel rendering of other versions of the same scene, to be found in sources both named and unnamed. As the text of the fiction reveals, once again, any such choice is arbitrary—grounded on our willingness to believe, or to suspend disbelief, in one or more of the narrative voices.

The pictorial version by an unnamed illustrator (3), we are told, portrays the combatants and Sancho. It is possible, though perhaps unlikely, that the picture imitates "events" that the artist observed firsthand. It is also possible, if perhaps unlikely, that the picture is modeled either wholly or in part after a description found in one of the sources for the "history's" first eight chapters, including the possibly missing fragment. What seems most plausible in the context of the "true history" is that the illustrator based his rendition on the beginning pages of Cide Hamete's narrative. It certainly accords with convention to believe that the illustration is intended to accompany the Moorish historian's narrative. But the union between the picture and the manuscript turns out to be more doubtful than appears at first blush.

Unlike the picture, the opening scene of the manuscript contains no reference to Sancho. More important, beneath each of the human figures in this picture, one finds an inscription in Spanish. One question that arises here is why an illustration, and its inscriptions, accompany a manuscript. But, more puzzling still, why should *Spanish inscriptions* appear on the frontispiece of an *Arab manuscript*? Though they seem to be part of the picture itself, and so the work of the illustrator, we never learn who wrote those inscriptions. No doubt they would be far more apt for a Spanish edition—indeed, a printed edition—of Cide Hamete's narrative. But if there were such an edition, it would mean that a translation of the manuscript, circulating in either published or unpublished form, appeared before the one commissioned by the "second author." Although there is no textual evidence for such a translation, it is important to note that the language in which those inscriptions appear (Spanish), as well as their content, suggest a host of possible models and sources for the picture on the frontispiece. If the illustrator's version is modeled directly after the version of Cide

Hamete, then this illustrator must have read the opening scene of the *Arab* manuscript. Otherwise his version derives only from hearsay. Yet in either case, we seem unable to explain why those inscriptions should aim at a different readership from that of the Arab history. Further, even allowing for artistic license, there are reasons to question whether the illustrator based his version on the manuscript at all.

Two of the inscriptions are at issue with the reported contents of Cide Hamete's narrative. A first inscription, beneath the figure of the protagonist, identifies him as "Don Quixote." No discrepancy here. But under the figure of the Basque appears an inscription that reads: "Don Sancho de Azpetia."[4] That name is never said, by any other voice, to occur in Cide Hamete's manuscript. Paying no mind to the apparent discrepancy between the picture and the translation before him, the "second author" blithely comments that there can be "no doubt" (sin duda) that "Don Sancho de Azpetia" is the Basque's true name (*DQ* I: 9, 144).

A third inscription, beneath the figure that the "second author" himself calls Sancho Panza (or Sancho Paunch), reads "Sancho Zancas" (or Sancho Bird-Legs). The "second author" finds the label entirely reasonable in view of Sancho's squat figure and thin shanks *as portrayed in the picture*, adding: "which must be what gave him the names Panza and Zancas, for he is called by both these names at different times in the history" (y por esto se le debió de poner nombre de Panza y de Zancas, que con estos dos sobrenombres le llama algunas veces la historia) (*DQ* I: 9, 144). But, in fact, this is the only time that Sancho is called Zancas in the so-called "true history" (Alter 1975, 9). Thus the "second author" may be mistaken. Or perhaps he is suppressing part of the translation. Or perhaps the "second author," so eager to point out that Cide Hamete belongs to a race of liars, is himself lying. Further compromising his reliability as a transcriber of the translation, the "second author" openly tells us that he has omitted certain "trifles" (menudencias), since "[they] have no concern with the truthful relation of the history; for no history is bad so long as it is true" (no hacen al caso a la ver-

---

4. Another subtlety in this passage that leads us to query the reliability of the "history" we are said to be reading arises from the curious name of the Basque. A certifiably Basque surname, coinciding with the name of a Spanish town, would be spelled with an extra *i*: Azpe*i*tia. The town bears the same name today as it did in Cervantes' time. Thus, the spelling in the inscription looks like a mistake rather than a plausible name for a Basque family or a Basque town. But whose mistake, if anyone's? Did some empirical person—author, printer—omit the *i* from the published fiction? Or is that curious spelling the empirical author's inventive simulation of a *possible* mistake by one of the fiction's "authors"? This is but one of many passages in the text that may be the result of either inventive genius or simple oversight. Here again, depending on one's mode of suspended disbelief, one will prefer to see either a careless or inventive author implicit in the text.

dadera relación de la historia, que ninguna es mala como sea verdadera) (*DQ* I: 9, 144). Likewise, the credibility of the *narrator* is compromised here since he nowhere intervenes either to correct the "second author" or to say that he, the narrator, has no evidence of Sancho's alternative surname. Outside of the unreliable versions of the narrator and the "second author," the illustrator's rendition of the battle may thus derive from any number of verbal and visual models, to be found in any number of verbal and visual sources.

Although all four versions appear related at first glance, their relation to one another or their possible models, within their possible sources, remains undecidable. Each one is an inventive imitation of an unknown model. In the end, the combined effect of those versions is an image of countless individuals imitating and transforming similar occurrences, or imitating and transforming snatches of one another's imitations—all within the fictional, textual equivalent of an echo chamber and a house of mirrors.

Hearing, and Believing, Voices

A similar confusion besets us if we attempt to establish a tidy hierarchy of narrators in *Don Quixote*, or a fixed hierarchy of narrative levels within which to situate the fiction's various imitations, models, sources, or copies.[5] Any analysis of narrators and narrative voices must first reckon, I believe, with the narrative voice of the Prologue, which cannot be divorced from the rest of the "book." With this proviso in mind, let us examine the narrating personae who, according to the "true history," "exist" within the heterocosm.

The narrator of the Prologue reportedly tells his friend that his, the narrator's, "historical" work is ready for publication. In essence, that narrator conveys the same information to us, claiming that he has "composed" both the "history" and the Prologue we are now reading. As the self-proclaimed "author" of the Prologue—that part of the "book" that was written last—he would have had to *compose* the *final version* of the "history." He is, therefore, the only "author" who has either direct or indirect access to all "sources" of the "history." As a result of

---

5. In the light of categories formulated by Genette (1980), James Parr has written the most recent attempt at providing a systematic hierarchization of narrative voices, and their varying degrees of reliability, within Cervantes' *Don Quixote* (1988, 3–20). For other important studies on narrative voices in the text, see George Haley, "The Narrator in *Don Quijote*: Maese Pedro's Puppet Show" (1964); the same author's "The Narrator in *Don Quijote*: A Discarded Voice" (1984); Colbert Nepaulsingh's "La aventura de los narradores del *Quijote*" (1980); Thomas Lathrop's "Who is the Narrator in *Don Quijote*?" (1988); and Mauricio Molho's "Instancias narradoras en *Don Quijote*" (1989).

his unique position, we may infer that the narrator of Prologue is also the narrator of the subsequent narrative, who intervenes in his own voice at the close of I, 8. His function, then, is less that of an "author" than an editor. Hence James Parr's apt designation of that character as an "editor persona" (1988, 10). Moreover, to borrow again from Parr, neither the narrator (Parr's "editor persona") nor any other compiler can be seen a genuine "author," unless one uses that term according to one acceptation prevalent in seventeenth-century Spain: namely, an "autor de comedias," which denoted either a "stage manager" or a "producer" of theatrical performances (1988, 12). In any case, all other narrative voices *within* the "history" occupy a level of narration somewhere *beneath* that of the narrator.

For the first eight chapters of Part I, the other narrative voices—about which we remain unenlightened until the intervention of the narrator—explicitly include those of the "author of this history" and the latter's unnamed source or sources. From I, 9 onward, the narrator's final version of the "history" is shown to encompass three other narrative voices and their corresponding texts: the "second author," whose account encompasses the translation by the bilingual Moor, in turn encompassing the discovered manuscript attributed to Cide Hamete. But, as already discussed, the narrator remains unhelpful about his sources for either the first eight chapters or the rest of the narrative. Furthermore, concerning that narrator's reliability, nothing in the Prologue inspires confidence in either his competence or his honesty as a historian.

Similarly, excepting the "author of this history," we have *specific* reasons to doubt the reliability of the "history's" other *known* mediators and narrators. Beginning with I, 9, the narrator *appears* to concede the role of principal narrative voice in the "history" to the "second author," who relays the contents of the translation from I, 9 to the very end of Part II. In a passage that parodies common opinion about the "truth" of historical narratives, the author has that "second author," presumably as quoted by the narrator, display subjective bias by *passionately* criticizing the lack of *dispassionate* objectivity in Cide Hamete's narrative:

> [W]hen [Cide Hamete] could and should let his pen flow in praise of such a good knight, it seems that he passes over such praise in silence: a bad thing to do and even a worse thing to intend, since historians are obliged and compelled to be accurate, truthful and *completely dispassionate*, and since no amount of self-interest, fear, resentment or sympathy should lead them to stray from the path of truth, whose mother is history, portrait of the times, repository of deeds, witness to the past, example and warning in the present, and portent of the future.

([C]uando [Cide Hamete] pudiera y debiera estender la pluma en las alabanzas de tan buen caballero, parece que de industria las pasa en silencio; cosa mal hecha y peor pensada, habiendo y debiendo ser los historiadores puntuales, verdaderos y no *nada apasionados*, y que ni el interés ni el miedo, el rancor ni la afición, no les hagan torcer del camino de la verdad, cuya madre es la historia, émula del tiempo, depósito de las acciones, testigo de lo pasado, ejemplo y aviso de lo presente, advertencia de lo por venir.) (*DQ* I: 9, 144–45; emphasis added)

Unaware of how the bombast of his own statement undercuts his criteria for historical credibility, the "second author" seems just as naive and unreliable as the narrator. Once again, the irony of the author is evident through the overstated naïveté of his character. More important, however, this passage of the narrative dramatizes and parodies the inseparable bond between "facts" and their interpretation, "events," and ideology—in anachronistic terms—or "events" and the fictive categories by which we "know" them. In the less anachronistic terms of Aristotle's *Poetics*, we may claim that here, as elsewhere in the narrative, Cervantes dramatizes the inseparable bond between "historical" and "poetic" *truth*. In other words, like other narrators and mediators, and like other characters, including the protagonist himself, the "second author" arranges, suppresses, or accommodates the presumed factuality of "events" about the "good knight" according to the categories that govern his discourse, or his opinion regarding their ultimate meaning and purpose.

The underlying ideology or *philosophia* of the "second author," like that of, say, the narrator or the protagonist himself, is shown to be an egregious case of naive and one-sided thinking. In particular, the "second author" fails to see the protagonist as a *paradoxical blend* of wisdom and folly, madness and sanity, or laudable and reproachable traits. Indeed, the "second author" seems to accept the protagonist on the latter's own, transparently lunatic terms. Even in less egregious cases, however, a character's "ideology" or "poetic truth" is shown eventually to bog down in antinomy and to lead him or her to suppress certain "facts," or to pass over multiple meanings inherent in those facts.

It is because almost every "ideology" or "poetic truth" presented in the narrative is shown to be wanting rather than complete that, in my view, it would require a naive form of critical bias to construe such passages in Cervantes' work as dramatized arguments in favor of moral or epistemological relativism. Each form of poetic truth is shown to be both futile and necessary, both revealing and concealing the meaning or "truth" of events. What is more, even such a lunatic form of poetic truth as that of the protagonist is shown to contain "truths" that remain either hidden or suppressed in other, "saner" ideologies or discursive systems. The "meaning" of events is thus shown to be infinite, unstable, and subject to enlargement or reformulation over time. To demonstrate, through the deft use of paradoxy, that fictive categories belonging to every *particular* form of poetic truth hamper one's ability to see many sides of a question is hardly the same as a dogmatic skepticism—a conspicuously limited form of poetic "truth" that asserts that all extreme positions are equally valid and, thus, equally meaningless.[6] If all forms of poetic truth are wanting, it does not follow that they are all wanting in the same way or to the same degree.

It is one thing to dramatize, as the author of *Don Quixote* does through his narrating voices, that fixed and finite categories will continually fail to shed light on the infinite, changing complexity of even the simplest human actions and events; that the mystery of even minuscule "truths" exceeds the categories and schemata of logic and language; that there can never be an utterly reliable or final version of historical events. It is quite another to hold, with apodictic certainty, that all categories are pointless, since there is nothing to shed light on and no such thing as shedding light. In other words, if Cervantes can enlist a playful rhetoric of paradoxy to send up the shortcomings of his characters' logical and linguistic categories, it is because those shortcomings can be recognized as such. He therefore avoids the absurd, "absolutist" posture of a skeptic zealot, or of a solipsist determined to proselytize.[7]

Although more a mediator than a narrator, the Moorish translator also seems to espouse a personal form of poetic truth whereby he judges the relevance or importance of certain facts relating to the "history" of Don Quixote and Sancho. That form of poetic truth, or the translator's unstated assumptions about the ultimate meaning and purpose of the protagonist's exploits, leads him to disregard the "second author's" charge neither to add to nor subtract from the contents of Cide Hamete's manuscript. In such cases, the author dramatizes that

6. On Cervantes' philosophical attitude of what one may call moderate skepticism, see Maureen Ihre's *Skepticism in Cervantes* (1982). For an excellent discussion concerning the influence on Renaissance authors of Cicero's popularization of skepticism in Academica, see Kinney 1989, 320–23.

7. The thesis of Cervantes as an epistemological relativist was first put forth, in its most *unequivocal* fashion, by Américo Castro in *El pensamiento de Cervantes* (1972). This view was already latent, however, in José Ortega y Gasset's *Meditaciones del Quijote* ([1914] 1984). Playing off Ortega's famous assessment of *Don Quixote* as an "equivocation" (equívoco), Angel del Río puts forth a similar view of Cervantes and his fiction in "El equívoco del *Quijote*" (1959). Early efforts to refute Castro's view include Alexander A. Parker's "El concepto de la verdad en el *Quijote*" (1948) and Richard Predmore's "El problema de la realidad en el *Quijote*" (1953). Most contemporary critics have adopted a more moderate, if similar, opinion of Cervantes' epistemological posture, deriving from the "perspectivism" of two important studies by Leo Spitzer (1955, 1962). For a rigorous, highly critical summary of this strain in Cervantes scholarship, see Anthony Close's *The Romantic Approach to "Don Quixote"* (1978, 212–42). Ciriaco Morón Arroyo links Cervantes' philosophical and theological opinions to those of his period (1976, 95–159).

not only the importance, but also the *intelligibility*, of "facts" that belong to the "history" depend on a vision of poetic truth that patterns them into a purposeful, meaningful whole. What emerges repeatedly from the text is that there is no such thing as a purely factual *account*, divorced from the context of a mediating voice, a particular perspective, or a personal form of poetic truth or ideological bias. Probably the most conspicuous example of how the translator's poetic truth leads him to tamper with the Arab manuscript occurs when that translator *is reported* (by either the narrator or the "second author" or both) voluntarily to omit Cide Hamete's description of Don Diego de Miranda's mansion:

> Here the author [Cide Hamete?] depicts all the details about Don Diego's house, including those details about what the house of a wealthy, rural hidalgo contains; but the translator of this history preferred to *pass over these and other similar trifles in silence*, because they ill accorded with the *main purpose of the history*, which finds greater strength in its *truth* than in its *cold digressions*.

> (Aquí pinta el autor [¿Cide Hamete?] todas las circunstancias de la casa de don Diego, pintándonos en ellas lo que contiene una casa de un caballero labrador y rico; pero al traductor desta historia le pareció *pasar estas y otras semejantes menudencias en silencio*, porque no venían bien con *el propósito principal de la historia*; la cual más tiene su fuerza en *la verdad* que en las *frías digresiones*.) (*DQ* II: 18, 169; emphasis added)

It would seem that "the truth," a phrase that recurs so frequently and variously throughout the "true history," here refers to "poetic" rather than factual or "historical" truth. It is poetic truth that determines the translator's understanding of the "history's" *main purpose*. Accordingly, "cold digressions" would amount to descriptions of factual details that the translator feels would only detract from the "history's" lofty "truth" and "purpose." Thus the reliability of the translator as one who "faithfully" renders the discovered manuscript into Spanish is, of course, open to reasonable doubt. We are led to believe that the translator omits the description in the manuscript because Don Diego's homestead is so generic that knowledge of its features would add nothing to our understanding about the *unique* meaning and purpose of Don Quixote's adventures. Interestingly, too, by stating the presumed reasons behind the translator's omission, the passage has a similar effect on the reader as a detailed description of the mansion.

Before casting judgment on the translator, however, we do well to bear in mind that we know about the translator's conception of poetic truth, and about his alleged reasons for suppressing the "trifles" in this segment of Cide Hamete's narrative—if that is what he did—only through the mediation of either one or two unreliable characters: the narrator and he "second author." Indeed, we have no way of discerning which of the words and judgments set forth in that passage belong to the translator or to some other voice. To whom and by what means did the translator convey his reasons for omitting Cide Hamete's description? Is it not possible that what we read in this passage is nothing but an unreliable narrator's conjecture, or biased paraphrase, about the translator's alleged reasons for allegedly omitting that segment?

If the translator passes over Cide Hamete's description "in silence," the character in whose "voice" this passage is relayed would need to have access to the manuscript. To verify the "silence," he would have to know enough Arabic to understand the relevant segment of the manuscript. The narrator seems more likely to meet both requirements than does the "second author," who hires the translator and appears to know no other language than Spanish. As a result, we may infer that the narrator enjoys direct access to archival documents, hearsay, the account of the "second author," *and* Cide Hamete's manuscript. Yet as far as I know, there is no passage in the "history" that specifically indicates whether he has access to the translation, except through the account of the "second author." Hence unless the narrator spoke with the translator, or read some unmentioned notes written by the translator in the account of the "second author"—suppositions for which there is no textual evidence—the narrator's representation of that translator's reasons for omitting a segment of the manuscript is at best the result of conjecture, here presented as yet another "truth." At all events, it is therefore likely that in this passage, we confront a narrator of dubious reliability, representing the dubious reliability of the translator, whose alleged omissions and ideological motivations are refracted through that narrator's own omissions and ideology.

Cide Hamete: Not a Liar but a "Lie"

Among all the "history's" other known mediators and narrators, Cide Hamete doubtless presents the most puzzling case. Notwithstanding the popular prejudice of Cervantes' day, the Arab historian's race is never put forth in the narrative as sufficient reason for doubting his veracity. The racist view that "all Arabs are liars" is first attributed to the "second author," who expresses that opinion shortly after he tells us about his hiring a "bilingual Moor" (morisco aljimiado) to translate the discovered manuscript (*DQ* I: 9, 142). Furthermore, the "second author's" complaint about the historian's race comes only as a result of Cide Hamete's failure to extol the protagonist's nobility. The same racist view is shared by Don Quixote. But the protagonist seems to become entrenched in that view only after the he learns that the Arab's "history" is not the epic that he, Don Quixote, had hoped for.[8] In both cases, then, the racist argument against Cide Hamete comes as an afterthought—an excuse, in fact—that follows from an ideological bias. Indeed, the reader who would disbelieve Cide Hamete strictly on racial grounds is thus shown to employ the same criteria for judgment as the simpleminded or perhaps even the insane.

By contrast, the best and most obvious reason for doubting Cide Hamete's veracity arises from his implicit claim to Godlike powers, especially that of omniscience. The most self-referential, and paradoxical, case in point of such alleged powers—and of one's reasons for calling those powers into question—occurs in what is supposed to be a private conversation between the knight and the squire, presumably recorded (and overheard?) by the Arab historian himself. That conversation not only concerns the first volume of Cide Hamete's "history," about which Sancho has just learned from Sansón Carrasco. It also concerns nothing other than Cide Hamete's supernatural knowledge. In the following passage, where that private conversation is presumably recorded by the Arab historian, and passed on to us through the threefold mediation of the translator, the "second author" and the narrator, both the protagonist and Sancho seem fully to accept Cide Hamete's magical, supernatural knowledge regarding their private exchanges:

[Sancho]: [And Sansón] says that they mention me in [the history] with my own name of Sancho Panza, and the Lady Dulcinea del Toboso, with other things which we did when we were alone, so that I signed myself with the cross, terrified to think how that historian could have known the things he wrote about.

[Don Quixote]: I assure you, Sancho, said Don Quixote, that the author of our history must be some *sage enchanter*; and to *those* [historians] nothing which they desire to write about remains concealed from them.

([Sancho]: [Y] dice [Sansón] que me mientan a mí en ella [la historia] con mi mesmo nombre de Sancho Panza [no mention of "Zancas"], y a la señora Dulcinea del Toboso, con otras cosas que pasamos nosotros a solas, que me hice cruces de espantado cómo las pudo saber el historiador que las escribió.

8. On "Don Quixote's alienation from his book," see the chapter by that name in Weiger 1988, 100–137.

[Don Quijote]: Yo te aseguro, Sancho—dijo don Quijote—, que debe de ser algún *sabio encantador* el autor de nuestra historia; que a *los tales* no se les encubre nada de lo que quieren escribir.) (*DQ* II: 2, 57; emphasis added)

Oddly, neither Don Quixote nor Sancho seems perturbed by the possibility that Cide Hamete may be listening to them at the very moment of this alleged conversation. Nor are they said to search for him anywhere during the course of the narrative. No doubt the Arab historian's uncanny ability to eavesdrop on private conversations is, of itself, no sign of omniscience. But nothing short of omniscience would allow him to know not only the content of private conversations, but also the content of private thoughts, frequently recorded in the "history." Yet it is worth noting that Cide Hamete seems to enjoy no monopoly on omniscience. For the private thoughts of the protagonist are also presented as empirical facts in the first eight chapters of the narrator's "history," said to derive from the work of the "author of this history," and thus falling outside the scope of Cide Hamete's discovered manuscript. One need only recall the scene in which Don Quixote, riding alone across the plains of Montiel, conjures up the image, in accord with his own idea of poetic truth, of none other than the sage author who will write his history (*DQ* I: 2, 80).

Nonetheless, a logical paradox emerges from the above quoted "conversation" between the protagonist and his squire. This passage calls our attention to the issue of Cide Hamete's fantastic status, not simply as an illusionist, but as a *magus*, wizard, or "sage enchanter." Such assessments move us to doubt the credibility of that Arab "historian's" narrative and, next, to doubt the "actuality" of the recorded "conversation" we are reading. To believe the content of that passage in the "history" leads us to disbelieve it. In the same vein, the passage also contains what we may regard as a slip of the pen on the part of Cide Hamete, as he allegedly records what we may regard as Don Quixote's slip of the tongue: "and *to those historians* nothing that they desire to write about remains concealed from them" (que a *los tales* no se les encubre nada de lo que quieren escribir). In other words, such "enchanted" authors, referred to in what may function as the pejorative terms "los *tales*," or "*those* historians," write or invent as they please. Hence this passage that presumably occurs in the discovered manuscript undermines, even as it affirms, the Arab historian's credibility and supernatural powers. Moreover, unless we accept Cide Hamete as an "enchanter" or a magus, *endowed* with superhuman powers—unless we forsake verisimilitude and accept the "truth" or "reality" of fantasy, in other words—we must acknowledge that much or all of his "historical" narrative is the result of his or some other character's "fiction."

If, bracketing the issue of Cide Hamete's omniscience, we focus solely on his ability to eavesdrop on private conversations, including the one just quoted, the Arab historian's account is credible only if we are prepared to grant him Godlike powers akin to ubiquity and invisibility. For instance, the conversation just quoted, in which Sancho informs his master about the recently published history of their adventures in Part I, occurs in our protagonist's private chamber. To overhear that conversation, Cide Hamete would not only have to escape the notice of the knight and his squire, but, what strikes this reader as even more unlikely, he would also have to get past the hidalgo's formidable housekeeper, who tried to deny entry to Sancho. That the Arab historian should remain undiscovered by all the characters appearing in his history, in this chapter and others, defies credibility. If he is ever discovered, there is no record of such an occurrence in his manuscript, which would amount to either a glaring omission or an instance of falsification in his "historical" narrative.

Concerning his possible ubiquity, Cide Hamete's purportedly eyewitness account often includes diverse events occurring simultaneously in different places. For instance, between II, 45 and II, 55, Cide Hamete observes what happens to Sancho as governor of Barataria and what happens to Don Quixote, at the same time, in the ducal palace. Furthermore, the Arab historian seems to join powers of omniscience, invisibility, and ubiquity in his narration of events (including private thoughts and conversations) that conclude with the fortuitous mock rescue by Don Quixote of Sancho from a pit into which the ex-governor had fallen and where he had wandered throughout the night (*DQ* II: 55).

Nonetheless, the veracity of Cide Hamete obviously becomes a moot point when we consider reasons that lead us to doubt his very "existence" within the heterocosm.[9] More specifically, if the foregoing reasons lead us to suspect that much of the history about Don Quixote and Sancho is the invention of Cide Hamete, we are finally led to suspect that the part of the "history" concerning Cide Hamete, the manuscript, the translation, and the translator may be part

---

9. To date, critics writing about the aesthetic purpose and function of Cide Hamete have generally considered him not only a character or voice within the heterocosm, but also the main narrator. The most recent study to hold such a position toward the Arab historian is Mancing 1981, 63–81. In his *Anatomy of Subversive Discourse* (1988), James Parr rhetorically asks: "Does anyone believe, really and truly, that there exists such a document [as Cide Hamete's manuscript], even within the world of the book?" (22). Yet Parr continues to view the Arab historian as a "character" and a "presence" in the story (1988, 30–31). These elegant and informative studies notwithstanding, I shall presently discuss my reasons for denying Cide Hamete's existence as a character and for considering his presence limited to that of a subordinate narrative voice attached to a Moorish *name*. For an influential analysis of Cide Hamete's role in reference to Cervantes' narrative technique, see Ruth El Saffar's "The Function of the Fictional Narrator in *Don Quixote*" (1968).

of an invention produced by a character who occupies a "higher" narrative level in the "history" than Cide Hamete: namely, either the "second author" or the narrator.

As is evident from the tales of Ricote and Ana Félix, the fictional Spain of Part II imitates the historical Spain of 1609 in that its Moriscos, too, suffer the cruelty of forced exile. In that light alone, there is nothing verisimilar about the character of an Arab chronicler, unless he truly "is" a sage enchanter, who would risk his life, traveling about the country, in order to write his history about a local madman. Furthermore, in his first conversation with both Don Quixote and Sancho, Sansón Carrasco reportedly tells them that Cide Hamete's history includes "the adventure of the windmills" (la aventura de los molinos de viento) (*DQ* II: 3, 60). But this adventure occurs before the protagonist's battle with the Basque from Biscay and, thus, before the opening episode of the discovered manuscript that we learn about from the "second author" and the narrator in I, 9. Adding to the obvious discrepancy, this conversation between Sansón, the knight, and the squire about Cide Hamete's history is presumably recorded by the Arab historian himself. Last, in Part I of the narrator's "true history," the manuscript is said to bear the title *History of Don Quixote of La Mancha, Written by Cide Hamete Benengeli, Arab Historian* (*Historia de don Quijote de la Mancha, esrita por Cide Hamete Benengeli, historiador arábigo*) (*DQ* I: 9, 143). Yet according to what Sancho is said to report to Don Quixote, Cide Hamete's history is titled *The Ingenious Hidalgo Don Quixote of La Mancha* (*El Ingenioso Hidalgo don Quijote de la Mancha*) (*DQ* II: 2, 57), thus echoing the truly duplicitous title that the book by the actual author, Miguel de Cervantes Saavedra, shares with the (imaginary) "book" by the narrator, in turn made to share the name of the actual author.

From the foregoing discussion, it seems that the fiction's twofold game of literary verisimilitude and historical truth invites us to find it plausible that, either wholly or in part, those sections of the "history" relating to the existence of Cide Hamete, the discovered manuscript, the translation, the translator, and even the "second author" represent the invention of the narrator. In the first place, it seems clear that accepting the account of the manuscript's discovery by the "second author" in I, 9 would entail rejecting the title that Sancho is said to communicate to his master after learning it from Sansón Carrasco. Indeed, accepting the account of the manuscript's discovery would lead us to the absurd inference that, particularly through the assertions ascribed to Sancho and Sansón, Cide Hamete misrepresents both the content and title of his own narrative. In the second place, should we reject all or part of the account regarding the manuscript's presumed discovery, we clearly would have little reason to accept subsequent accounts, attributed to the "second author" and the narrator, of what that manuscript contains. At the very least, discrepancies concerning the manuscript, its author, and its contents all point toward the possibility of tampering or misrepresentation on the part of either the "second author" or the narrator.

What leads me specifically to view the narrator as an "inventor" in this regard—either wholly or in part—is that the title belonging to the published version of his "history" coincides with the second title given for Cide Hamete's manuscript. It seems that, true to form, the narrator unwittingly alerts readers to his subterfuge by conferring the title of his own "history" upon the "manuscript" of the "nonexistent" Cide Hamete. No other "author" in the "history" could even know about that title, much less invent it, since it belongs to the narrator's *final version*. By inventing an "Arab" manuscript and its author, the narrator is, of course, employing a favorite device of both fraudulent historians and chivalric authors who wish bestow credibility and *authority* upon their narratives.[10] That the invention should here achieve the opposite effect is, surely, part of the author's *dual parody* of both chivalric romances and spurious "histories." In short, I would suggest that the "character" of Cide Hamete is meant to be seen as an *impossibility*, or wholly the invention of the narrator. Indeed, Cide Hamete is at once the lie and the fiction of the fictional narrator. Within the heterocosm, the material associated with the "manuscript" may derive from some other "source," or other "sources," used by the narrator. Or, what appears less likely—but who knows?—it may be *nothing but* his invention. Similarly, the "second author" may represent a character or a voice, whose words are either misrepresented or, what also seems unlikely or inverisimilar, wholly invented. In any case, what is important to stress is that the *two inseparable aspects* of the "history" about Don Quixote thus become *either total or partial inventions* of the narrator: the first aspect of the "history" being the adventures of Don Quixote and Sancho (presented as Cide Hamete's eyewitness account, in manuscript); the second, the accounts of the "true history's" compilation and "sources." More specifically, the second aspect of the narrator's "true history"—that is, its compilation—includes the story about the manuscript, its presumed translation, the translator, as well as the "second author" and the latter's accounts concerning the discovery and contents of the manuscript.

Any attempt to determine precisely how much of the "history" derives from "reliable" sources would doubtless amount to idle speculation, and solemnly miss the point of the author's elaborate, fictional parody of narrative and historical

---

10. Wardropper (1965) provides a fine discussion, with examples, of how some Renaissance and Baroque writers in Spain mendaciously claimed to base their fraudulent histories on manuscripts by Arab historians.

reliability. Again, it seems that Cervantes' text invites us to play rather than dismiss a game called literary verisimilitude and historical truth. But it does not therefore invite us to believe that we can discover what "really happens" to Don Quixote and other characters within the heterocosm or what "really happens" to the "true history" in the course of its compilation. In any case, despite their possibly varying degrees of "imaginariness," Cide Hamete, the "second author," and the translator each represents a perspective and a narrative voice that form an integral part of the narrator's "history." In a sense, of course, it is the charge of "discreet readers" to determine whatever validity pertains to each perspective and narrative voice, including those of the narrator, in reference to the "history's" meaning, purpose, or "truth." In favoring the reliability of one perspective or narrator over another; in thinking that they must definitively favor any perspective or narrator at all; in thinking that they have successfully isolated a particular perspective or narrative voice in a given passage; or, perhaps, in refusing or failing to do any of these things, such readers may reveal (chiefly to themselves) their own critical powers and their own form of "poetic truth." However they negotiate these riddles, they will inscribe themselves into the text as its unique readers, translators, compositors, or second authors.

Ultimately, however, Cervantes' parodic fiction about the fraudulent "history" of the narrator (also named Cervantes?) seems to contain a broader, more self-conscious aim than that of offering a variety of ironclad ideologies or versions of poetic truth from which the reader is invited to choose either one or none. Instead, the author causes those many versions of historical and poetic "truth" to interact and to engage in a continuing dialogue. In doing so, he seems to invite the discriminating reader to accept both all and none of the rival versions of the protagonist's adventures; both all and none of the possible stories concerning the "history's" compilation. In other words, the author reveals that readers must place at least some trust in the narrator's assertions and suspend disbelief about what they read in the "history" for there to be a tale at all. To continue reading or to accept anything as "true" or "verisimilar" within the "true history" about Don Quixote and Sancho hangs on our accepting the mendacious *fantasy* named Cide Hamete: *magus*, wizard, "sage enchanter." This assertion holds, in particular, for Part II, where the majority of characters are shown to act on what they read or know by hearsay, not about the narrator's "true history," but Part I of the verifiably *exact* (*puntual*) "history" by Cide Hamete, or Cervantes' Moorish analogue of the Liar from Crete. Yet readers are simultaneously invited truly to believe and trust in nothing of what they read.

Hence the fiction serves to dramatize how, in reading, critically, both stories and histories, the reader must suspend both belief and disbelief. But more self-consciously, it dramatizes how "this narrative" (and by extension every narrative) is in large part of the readers' own making: a product of what they are prepared to believe and so of what they are prepared to piece together, discover, and invent— or "compose" (componer)—from the stimulus of the text.

Through his fiction's continuing interplay (now conflictive, now harmonious) of myriad "sources," "imitations," "models," perspectives, voices, and versions of poetic truth, the author of the fiction obliges each perspective and ideology to reveal the "truth" of its own limitations. He therefore dramatizes and suggests "truths" that remain invisible to those who would adopt such perspectives or ideologies. *Don Quixote's* dialogic play on a multiplicity of perspectives, versions, and interpretations of "events"—relating especially to the protagonist and his presumed exploits—thus represents a practical demonstration of such venerable, ontological, and cosmological paradoxes as the one beneath the many and the dynamic mingling of nonexclusive contraries (*coincidentia oppositorum*) in a continuing state of harmonious tension (*discordia concors*).

In isolation, every definitive "version" of historical and poetic truth in *Don Quixote* seems to contain a limiting bias that prevents its revealing more than a *fragment* of "the whole story." Indeed, pretensions to conveying anything akin to a "whole story" become the chief object of the author's parody. Through its dialogic play of limited, varied perspectives, *Don Quixote* gives an unfolding, narrative intelligibility to the complexities, paradoxes, and antinomies involved in the fully *discursive process* of both discovering and adding to (i.e., "inventing" in the root sense of *invenire*, "to invent" and "to discover") the meaning, purpose, or "truth" of knowledge and history. For in light of a core paradox concerning the overlap between art and nature, as broached in the Prologue of 1605, one perceives related paradoxes concerning the mutual dependence of what received opinion holds to be contrary categories of literature and life, history and poetry, or historical and poetic truth. Cervantes bodies forth the latent paradox in Aristotle's definition of art as an imitation of nature in order to create an intricate parody of how human beings, in a manner analogous to that of narrators and other characters within the heterocosm, transform and *make sense* of their world. The narrative dramatizes how, through the "art" of their discourse, or their fictive categories of thought and expression, human beings order and frame their experience, investing it and themselves with intelligibility, meaning, purpose, or "truth."

By forcefully dramatizing an interaction between competing varieties of poetic truth, *Don Quixote* also represents a parody of how every variety of ideological entrenchment blinds its devotees to philosophical, aesthetic, and ethical mysteries. Such mysteries continue to unfold in changing forms over time and ultimately remain beyond the grasp of definitive formulations, or logical and linguistic categories. Thus, from the start of his Prologue to Don Quixote, Part I, Cervantes draws on a central paradox that he discovers at the heart of Aristotle's *Poetics*. From this he creates his own paradox of poetic "history" that is not only too illustrative of discourse and human action, but also too funny, not to be taken seriously.[11]

---

11. In a justly famous essay titled "*Don Quixote* as a Funny Book" (1969), Russell argues against the tendency of the German Romantics and their contemporary sympathizers to search for hidden profundities in Cervantes' best-known fiction, since its first readers rightly understood that text to offer a comical rather than serious work. Expanding considerably on Russell's thesis, though without excluding some seriousness of ethical purpose on the part of Cervantes, Close (1978) engages in a trenchant, scholarly polemic that traces the genealogy and later metamorphoses of the "Romantic" tendency in criticism on *Don Quixote*.

"I Know Who I Am"

Don Quixote de la Mancha, Don Diego de Miranda,
and the Paradox of Self-Knowledge

Know, Fashion, and Conquer Thyself

In Cervantes' *Don Quixote*, the question of self-knowledge is far from an incidental issue. Indeed, it is hardly surprising that a work that repeatedly takes the
measure of its own identity, artifice, and ontological status should include a cast
of characters who are wrestling, or failing to wrestle, with the challenge expressed
in the delphic and Socratic maxim Know thyself. But in keeping with the practical orientation of such predecessors as Petrarch and Guevara, who address the
same problem of psychological paradox, Cervantes' characters are wrestling with
the imperative not only to know themselves, but also to act on that knowledge:
to *create* and *fashion* a social, moral, or religious persona. Beginning with the protagonist and his squire, the problem of self-knowledge (or self-deception) and
self-fashioning assumes a prominent place in virtually all the fiction's characters.

These characters embody what contemporary criticism often calls a host of differing "perspectives," in that they shape their "lives," with varying degrees of *inventio*, after an array of literary or quasi-literary "codes," models, and versions of poetic truth.

Cervantes foregrounds the *process* of self-knowledge and self-fashioning in chapters 16–18 of Part II, in which he narrates Don Quixote's four-day encounter with Don Diego de Miranda, whom the protagonist *reportedly* calls the Knight of the Green Cloak (el Caballero del Verde Gabán).[1] In this chapter, I shall devote the bulk of my discussion to the encounter between the protagonist and Don Diego primarily because I believe that it encapsulates the governing, paradoxical logic of *action* in *Don Quixote*, especially in Part II. Indeed, Cervantes' characters *act* according to their knowledge or ignorance of who they are or how they appear to others and according to the relatively wise or foolish models and codes to which they give their allegiance. In illustrating this point, it will prove helpful to glance briefly at how the problem of self-knowledge develops in the fiction's two principal characters.

At first, it seems that Sancho offers the most straightforward example in *Don Quixote* of a character's achieving and acting on his self-knowledge. In II, 53, this peasant turned squire decides to abandon his governorship, which was hitherto the object of his fantasies or delusions of grandeur, as well as the primary reason that he joined and often believed in the veracity and legitimacy of his master's enterprise. No doubt one detects a certain humility and a considerable degree of self-acceptance in remarks like the following: "I was not born to be a governor, nor to defend isles or cities from enemies who choose to besiege them" (Yo no nací para ser gobernador, ni para defender ínsulas ni ciudades de los enemigos que quisieren acometerlas) (*DQ* II: 53, 444). But it is doubtful that Sancho represents anything so simple as an exemplum of the Socratic ideal. As

---

1. It is worth noting that Don Quixote is never quoted as using this sobriquet for Don Diego. Rather, it is the narrator who claims, without direct quotation, that Don Quixote accorded Don Diego such a knightly epithet. At the start of their encounter, the protagonist addresses the rural hidalgo as "Gallant sir" (Señor galán). A loaded term in this context, *galán* most often denotes a stock character in drama: a "gallant," young lover. Later, he addresses him as either "Don Diego" or, pejoratively, as "mister hidalgo" (señor hidalgo). Furthermore, there is no mention of when, and in what circumstances, Don Quixote purportedly used this title to refer to Don Diego. Indeed, the narrator (apparently "speaking" in the voice of Cide Hamete) seems wrongly to assume that Don Quixote must have incorporated Don Diego into his chivalric world and viewed that secondary character as a fellow "knight," whose home is called a "castle" (castillo o casa), again by the narrator, in the heading of chapter 18, Part II. As I shall discuss in this chapter, despite these false clues from the narrator, the passages about the encounter between the two hidalgos reveal that after scrutinizing Don Diego and listening attentively to his opening remarks, Don Quixote considers Don Diego to follow a very different "profession" from his own, one that the protagonist fails to specify—probably because the profession of a "more than moderately wealthy," rural hidalgo falls outside his chivalric schemata.

suggested even in the words just quoted, his chief motivation for leaving Barataria is that the diet, dangers, and material rewards of that position ran contrary to his dreams. Moreover, despite their seeming humility, his remarks sound a clear note of self-importance. So here, as elsewhere in the fiction, Sancho's self-awareness remains limited and involves something less than a radical transformation.[2]

Of course the problem of self-knowledge and self-delusion pervades the author's characterization of his protagonist. In Don Quixote, we confront the representation of an individual engaged in a desperate, paradoxical attempt both to forge and preserve his identity. The forging of that identity begins with a fit of lunatic self-delusion, at the start of Part I, when the "ingenious" hidalgo transmutes his social persona, his "nag" (rocín) and his memory of a local peasant woman, respectively, into the knight-errant Don Quixote, the steed Rocinante, and the princess Dulcinea, "lady of his thoughts" (señora de sus pensamientos) (DQ I: 1, 78). The protagonist does so in full accord with the code, or what Dunn calls the "semiotic system," of chivalric fiction, which our hero takes to be history (1982, 19–20). That forging continues beyond the knight's mock dubbing at the inn, and even beyond his defeat at the hands of the merchants from Toledo at the end of his first sally from home.

However, it is important to bear in mind that it is the reader alone, and not the protagonist, who can acknowledge that the identity of Don Quixote is *in the process of* being forged. In the protagonist's mythical conception of reality, and of himself, knightly heroes remain changeless, archetypal figures, with identities forged from time immemorial. Hence Don Quixote's irate response to his kindly neighbor Pedro Alonso: "I know who I am" (Yo sé quién soy) (DQ I: 5, 106).[3] These words echo nothing less grandiose than God's own tautological act of self-naming to Moses from the burning bush, expressing the deity's absolute subjectivity and eternal self-sufficiency: "I am who am" (Exod. 3:14). What the protagonist seeks, in Godlike fashion, is an immutable, self-conferred identity that emanates from an originary act of self-definition and self-naming. He expects that his quasi-divine act will translate, as from a divine *logos*, into a temporal

2. Likewise, I do not see the same degree of "quijotización" in Sancho as Madariaga (1978, 137–45).

3. The Spanish phrase "Soy quien soy" (I am who I am) provides the subject and title of an illuminating philological study by Leo Spitzer (1947) that does not concern, and does not cite, the above passage in *Don Quixote*. As Spitzer points out, Spaniards in the fifteenth through sixteenth centuries most commonly uttered this phrase to express their firm sense of identity—one might even say, despite the anachronism, their self-image—especially as regards their social station, their socioeconomic status, and their implicitly honorable family heritage (1947, 113). Spitzer holds that this phrase sometimes recalls but does not derive from the utterance that God speaks to Moses from the burning bush, in Exodus 3:14 (Spitzer 1947, 113–21). My contention here is only that Cervantes' use of a similar phrase in *Don Quixote* alludes to the famous quotation in Exodus.

unfolding of heroic deeds that are generative of lasting renown, or "eternal fame and glory." But the words that our protagonist speaks immediately thereafter, "and I know that I can be not only those I have just named, but also the Twelve Peers of France and even the Nine Worthies" (y sé que puedo ser no sólo los que he dicho, sino todos los doce Pares de Francia, y aun todos los nueve de la Fama) (*DQ* I: 5, 106) suggest that his identity is still *in potentia* and has yet to find its definitive shape. Though he is clearly unable to acknowledge it, Don Quixote has little more than a name and a vaguely defined profession. He is still very much involved in a *process* of forging a "timeless" identity that unfolds in the narrative, even more paradoxically, as the protagonist's frantic search for an exemplary model.

A crucial phase of Don Quixote's search for his identity occurs near the middle of Part I, in the wild uplands of Sierra Morena. There, he squanders an opportunity for self-knowledge, as against self-definition, when he encounters the figure of Cardenio. Indeed, rather than seeing any *mirror* of himself in that character's madness—a species of love malady that makes Cardenio suffer fits of violent anger amid lucid intervals—the protagonist looks upon Cardenio as a potential *model*. As already discussed, Cardenio turns out to be, if not a model, yet certainly an important source of inspiration for the amorous penance in which the *concept* of Don Quixote's knightly "self" is definitively fashioned and forged. For it is after contemplating and finally rejecting what for him are the equally "historical" models of Cardenio and Orlando that Don Quixote achieves "perfect imitation" by transforming his quest for a model into what Harry Levin calls an "*imitatio Amadís*" (1969, 38).

Yet despite the protagonist's apparent success, the narrative goes on to reveal that his undertaking this perfect *imitatio* of a literary model, and his choosing self-definition over self-knowledge, will exact a high price. It is pertinent to recall that Sancho asks his master to explain why the penance is necessary, since other knights who acted thus "had reason to perform such follies and penances" (tuvieron causa para hacer esas necedades y penitencias). By means of an ingenious rationalization, Don Quixote responds that he wants his "lady" to know that "if I do this in the dry, what will I do in the wet?" (si en seco hago esto, ¿qué haré en mojado?) (*DQ* I: 25, 305). At one level, the protagonist's brief reply represents his unwitting pun on his own humoral imbalance, which deprives his brain of moisture. He undertakes this penance "in the dry" as a choleric who is given to outbursts of wrath and who suffers from an excessively active imagination. Were he to become "wet," the physiological support for his penance, and for his existence as Don Quixote, would disappear. At another level of allusion, however, the protagonist's reply echoes the words that Christ speaks to the women of Jerusalem on his way to Golgotha: "For if these things happen when the wood is green [wet] what will happen when it is dry?" for which the common Spanish rendering is "Si esto lo hacen *en mojado*, ¿qué harán *en seco*?" (Luke 23:31). Hence, the protagonist's utterance represents an instance of dramatic irony that evokes the divine model whom he ignores in favor of Amadís. But they also augur what amounts to the *via dolorosa* that he will endure between this pivotal choice and the time when, in the final chapter of the "history," sleep restores water to his arid brain, thus allowing him to be shriven in a lucid state, to settle his affairs, and to speak with his friends before dying.

From the moment of his "penance" onward, Don Quixote's struggle in Part I consists largely of confirming and preserving his identity. He seeks no further models for imitation. Moreover, by the end of Part I, his efforts to forge and confirm his identity enjoy, from the knight's point of view, what Williamson calls "a qualified success" (1984, 99). But, in the course of Part II, the dissemination of Cide Hamete's history and Sancho's "enchantment" of Dulcinea cause the protagonist to lose authorial control over the *text* of his persona and his whole chivalric enterprise, which have thus become public domain (El Saffar 1975). Most characters judge him and do to him as they please—granting him his name, perhaps, but often investing that name with an identity of their own choosing and mocking the protagonist with a degree of cruelty that is absent in Part I. Indeed, Part II, which is Don Quixote's *via dolorosa*, will show the protagonist trying in vain to "disenchant" Dulcinea and to repair the damage caused by the Cide Hamete's history. Put another way, he tries and fails in Part II not simply to forge and confirm, but also to *recover* the identity he had managed to fashion in Part I. He likewise loses the power to act on that identity as the exemplary successor of Amadís and the knight-errant destined to restore the Golden Age.

A parallel to the "mirroring" adventure with Cardenio occurs in Part II, when Don Quixote confronts and "defeats" the university graduate, Sansón Carrasco, posing as the ominously named Knight of the Mirrors (Caballero de los Espejos). Once again, each character is a mirror, an obverse reflection, a blend of likeness-in-unlikeness with respect to the other; twin spirits, perhaps, but not fictional twins. As a direct consequence, the protagonist will later suffer defeat at the hands of the same "person," though the latter is then in the guise of the Knight of the White Moon (el Caballero de la Blanca Luna), a fitting emblem, it seems, for the complementary "lunacy" of both "knights."

It is therefore not as an exemplum of the know-thyself" ideal that Don Quixote is, in Sancho's words, "victor over himself" (vencedor de sí mismo) (*DQ* II: 72, 580).[4] In the knight's reply to this statement by his squire, one discerns

---

4. Sancho, who is shown throughout the narrative to derive much of his knowledge and language from the pulpit, presumably does the same here and thus echoes the title of a famous work of ascetical theology by the Dominican Melchor Cano (1509?–1560) titled *Treatise on the Victory over Self* (*Tratado de la victoria de sí mismo*) (1962).

self-defeat rather than self-awareness or self-acceptance, as well as the futile desire
to persist in a kindred form of madness and self-delusion:

> Leave off your foolishness, said Don Quixote; and let us put our best foot
> forward as we enter our village, where we shall give free play to our imagi-
> nations, and to our designs for the pastoral life we intend to undertake.

> (Déjate desas sandeces —dijo don Quijote—; y vamos con pie derecho a
> entrar en nuestro lugar, donde daremos vado a nuestras imaginaciones, y
> la traza que en la pastoral vida pensamos ejercitar.) (*DQ* II: 72, 580)

Strictly speaking, of course, it is impossible for the personality called Don
Quixote to attain self-knowledge, since that would entail his coming to realize
that his models for imitation are fiction rather than history and that "he" is but
the poetic construct of his crazed, hidalgo self. After a restorative sleep, it is therefore the hidalgo who achieves some degree of self-knowledge and conquers the
delusion of this chivalresque identity. As the dying hidalgo asserts: "I was mad,
and now I am sane; I was Don Quixote of La Mancha, and I am now, as I have
said, Alonso Quixano the Good" (Yo fui loco, y ya soy cuerdo; fui don Quijote
de la Mancha, y soy agora, como he dicho, Alonso Quijano el Bueno) (*DQ* II:
74, 590). And yet, without denying that the hidalgo attains a degree of self-
knowledge that remains impossible for Don Quixote, I would suggest that a
moral paradox informs the seemingly straightforward portrayal of our protagonist's two personalities.

If Don Quixote's *imitatio Amadís* makes him just the opposite of a Christ figure, what occurs during the course of his *via dolorosa*, particularly the mockery
he suffers in the ducal palace and the city of Barcelona, shows his moral superiority over those who deceive him and subject him to ridicule. Not that his
lunacy ceases to be lunacy or to provoke laughter for characters and readers alike.
But throughout Part II, Don Quixote remains far more sinned against than sin-
ning. Unlike his mockers, he deceives no one; and, unlike the Don Quixote of
Part I, attacks no one. Further, the association between him and Christ in the
penance of Sierra Morena alludes to Don Quixote as the author's innovative
Silenus—certainly mad, yet suffering unjustly and capable of showing "nobility"
and even wisdom in his madness.

The hidalgo, by contrast, seems to be a Silenus in reverse, thus making the
hidalgo–Don Quixote union a doubly paradoxical one of contrary Sileni within a
Silenus. What marks the hidalgo's presumptive "return to sanity" is his speaking
repeatedly, in the final chapter, about the "mercies" of God (misericordias) as well

as his speaking in the most socially sanctioned species of historical discourse—that of law—in order to complete his will. Yet the saintly epithet Alonso Quixano the Good, mentioned for the first time in this chapter, and by the hidalgo himself, leads us to suspect that he has retained his penchant for self-flattery and self-naming which he revealed at the start of the "history." What is more, in his explicit claim to have returned to sanity, and definitively *to be* "Alonso Quixano The Good," lies a tacit claim along the lines of "I know who I am." Indeed, Alonso Quixano the Good is an imaginary moral and religious self. Further, his speaking in the socially sanctioned language of law does not prevent his using that language to foist an impossible fiction on the world, specifically on his niece, who will forfeit her inheritance unless she marries a man who not only has never read chivalric romance, but who "does not know what books of chivalry are" (no sabe qué cosas sean libros de caballerías) (*DQ* II: 74, 590). Indeed, the niece's prospective husband must prove incapable of understanding this section of the will.

The hidalgo "dies" a Christian death and is saved, thanks to the represented mercy of God and the actual mercy of the author, Miguel de Cervantes: "father" and "stepfather" of both personalities. Saved but not altogether "cured." It seems to me that when confronted with the self-conferred epithet Alonso Quixano the Good, we sense an invitation from the author to question, though not necessarily to deny, the propriety of that title in relation to the protagonist, and even in relation to the analogous selves that we, too, are apt to "beget" in the domain of history. Is Alonso Quixano, or any idle reader, really "the Good"? Perhaps we may answer that complex question in language that resembles the seventeenth-century articulation of the hidalgo's presumed surname, Quixano (pronounced "qui-shá-no"): "Alonso 'quizá no' ('perhaps not') el Bueno (the Good)."

Exemplars at First Sight: Don Quixote Meets Don Diego de Miranda

Let us now turn to the encounter between Don Diego and Don Quixote. Respectively, the three chapters devoted to that encounter comprise (1) the dialogue between master and squire about the former's victory over the Knight of the Mirrors, followed by the first meeting between Don Quixote and Don Diego, which gives way to their mutual introductions; (2) the adventure with the lion, which results in the protagonist's adopting the name Knight of the Lions (Caballero de los Leones) and culminates in Don Diego's earnest invitation for the knight and squire to stay at his home; (3) Don Quixote's four-day visit at

Don Diego's estate, as well as his acquaintance with Don Diego's wife and son, Doña Cristina and Don Lorenzo.

The self-conscious narrative of these episodes involving the protagonist and the man in green leads both the reader and Don Diego to engage in an exercise of self-examination.[5] In a manner that seems to anticipate later critical reception of his work, but in fact adheres to the Silenic quality of both his fiction and his protagonist, the author startles the potentially "idle reader" (desocupado lector) into a critical response of self-reflection. In particular, Cervantes seems to cast those episodes in the form of a debate between two contrary readings: one hard, the other soft, on both the protagonist and his chivalric ethos.[6]

According to the first of those readings, Don Diego would seem to represent an "exemplary" Christian figure.[7] Moreover, in his introductory remarks to Don Quixote and Sancho, the man in green describes himself in a manner that broadly follows the same pattern as the description of the hidalgo, whose name is disputed among the "authors who write about this matter" (autores que deste caso escriben) (DQ I: 1, 171). Presented as the protagonist's polar opposite—or so it would seem—Don Diego gives his full name, his place of origin, and a description of his very different social status, which is "more than moderately wealthy" (más que medianamente rico). His favorite "pastimes" (ejercicios) (DQ II: 16, 153) include hunting and fishing, again echoing the description of the book's opening chapter. But Don Diego is careful to clarify: "I keep neither a falcon nor hounds, but rather a meek partridge or a daring ferret" (no mantengo ni halcón ni galgos, sino algún perdigón manso, o algún hurón atrevido).

More interesting, in a manner similar to that of the protagonist, Don Diego chooses *to define himself* according to his choice of reading matter, contained in his personal library. As against the protagonist, however, Don Diego has a collection, "up to six dozen books" (hasta seis docenas de libros) (DQ II: 16, 153), that is primarily composed of works of Christian devotion and honest entertain-

---

5. A study of Don Diego and Don Quixote that centers, not on the problem of self-knowledge, but on the *cuerdo loco* (mad/sane) paradox of these episodes, with important references to Erasmus, is Márquez Villanueva (1975, 147–227). As will become apparent, I owe a great debt to this essay, although my reading of these episodes differs in many respects from that of Márquez Villanueva.

6. Important critical studies that address the divisions between Cervantes scholars, largely along the lines of how they judge the protagonist, include those by Allen (1969–79) Predmore (1967), and Efron (1971).

7. Close states: "I have no doubt that Don Diego is meant to be seen as an exemplary figure" (1990b, 48). This does not mean that Close perceives the encounter between Don Quixote and Don Diego as a univocal instance of authorial moralizing: "However—and this is the point I wish to stress— the dialectical opposition of life-styles in the episode involving Don Diego is not explicitly resolved; it is simply presented and left to the discreet reader's judgement" (1990b, 52).

ment. Also in contrast to the protagonist, yet in perfect conformity with the teachings of both Christian humanists and Tridentine moralists, he says that "those [romances] of chivalry have yet to cross the threshold of my door" (los [libros] de caballerías aún no han entrado por los umbrales de mis puertas) (*DQ* II: 16, 153) (Forcione 1970, 11–48, and Riquer 1973, 279–84). He actively cultivates the virtue of religion by attending daily Mass and keeping his devotions to the Blessed Virgin. He strives to live the moral virtues by avoiding occasions of sin and idle gossip. He also exercises the theological virtues of faith, hope, and charity: "I always keep faith in the mercy of God, our Lord" (confío siempre en la misericordia de Dios nuestro Señor); and "I share of my goods with the poor" (reparto de mis bienes con los pobres). Nonetheless, he never boasts of his good works, "so as never to let hypocrisy and vanity into my heart" (por no dar entrada en mi corazón a la hipocresía y vanagloria). He lives the social virtue of hospitality by frequently dining with friends and entertaining them: "my guests are clean and well groomed, and by no means few" (son mis convites limpios y aseados, y no nada escasos) (*DQ* II: 16, 153).

Don Diego would also seem an archetype of both marital fidelity and parental love, spending most of his time at home, he says, "with my wife and with my children" (con mi mujer, y con mis hijos), and hoping that his son will pursue a career in either law or sacred theology, "the queen of all [the sciences]" (la reina de todas [las ciencias]). It seems, too, that his purity of heart leads him both to recognize and praise the Christian simplicity of Sancho, just as his humility leads him to confess: "I am not a saint, but a great sinner" (No soy santo, sino gran pecador) (*DQ* II: 16, 153). What is more, in these three chapters the temperate gentleman exemplifies the most important cardinal virtue of prudence or *discreción*—always and everywhere the quintessence of the golden mean.[8] It would seem that his chief concern is, and should be, to remain as he is:

---

8. Bates (1945) discusses the various, often ironic, uses of *discreción* in Cervantes' works. In particular, she addresses the precise distinction between "prudence" and *discreción* in the time of Cervantes that thus broke with the formerly synonymous meaning of the two terms in medieval works of moral theology (1945, 14–17). As virtues, rather than simply as qualities of mind (e.g., shrewdness), the two terms continued to be used interchangeably. Regarding the character of Don Diego, I think it important to bear in mind that Cervantes is playing on two related notions of the term *prudence*. The first, classical acceptation relates to the most cardinal (*cardo* in Latin means "hinge") of all the cardinal virtues (the others being justice, fortitude, and temperance), and denotes both the ability and the readiness to suit the proper means to a morally praiseworthy end. Thus prudence is the sine qua non of all the virtues. It orders and compels actions according to their proper ends. Classical prudence may often involve risk and necessitate decisive action. The second, "decadent" acceptation of prudence denotes a self-serving tendency to avoid risk and to decide only in favor of such actions as will benefit oneself. Both forms of prudence are grounded in a type of "foresight" (*pro-videre*): one suiting means and actions to objectively

orthodox, sane, sober. Paraphrasing Fray Luis de León, one may choose to dub him "the perfect husband" (el perfecto casado), a character who seems to emerge directly from either the philosophy of Christian Epicureanism, as described by Erasmus and his followers, or even from the catechism of the Council of Trent.[9]

By contrast, the identity of his counterpart is fully bound up with romances of chivalry, which makes Don Quixote a negative example of secular and pernicious reading. On numerous occasions, the protagonist claims to make a religious vocation of knight-errantry. His devotions to Dulcinea are a blasphemous parody of authentic Christian worship, and he never once attends Mass. Buoyed by his recent defeat of the Knight of the Mirrors, he boasts hyperbolically about his heroic deeds and his published history:

> [And] so, because of my brave, numerous and Christian deeds, I have proved deserving to appear in print in nearly all, or in most, nations of the world. Thirty thousand volumes of my history have been printed, and it is on the way to being printed a thousand times thirty thousand, unless heaven prevents it.

> ([Y] así, por mis valerosas, muchas y cristianas hazañas he merecido andar ya en estampa en casi todas o las más naciones del mundo. Treinta mil volúmenes se han impreso de mi historia, y lleva camino de imprimirse treinta mil veces de millares, si el cielo no lo remedia.) (*DQ* II: 16, 151)

---

good ends; the other suiting means and limiting actions to subjectively beneficial ends. Implicitly, Don Diego, a decadent, prebourgeois version of the *caballero*, claims to live the classical virtue of prudence while, in fact, adhering to the more self-serving type. I submit that this decadent form of prudence lies at the heart of what Márquez Villanueva ably describes as Cervantes' moral critique of Erasmus's Christian Epicureanism (1975, 173–74). For a thorough discussion of the classical understanding of prudence, in contradistinction to its more modern acceptation, see Pieper 1966, 3–40.

9. Márquez Villanueva convincingly argues that Don Diego's moral philosophy derives from Christian Epicureanism in "El Caballero del Verde Gabán" (1975, 168–75). Although I subscribe to this reading in the main, I also believe that Cervantes ironically adds such elements of Tridentine religiosity as daily attendance at Mass and Marian devotion to reinforce the impression in his readership of Don Diego's self-proclaimed sanctity. The typical portrait that Cervantes has Don Diego draw of himself, moreover, aims less at describing a particular philosophical posture than a clichéd, popular misunderstanding of what virtue and sanctity entail. That Don Diego is attempting to emulate his own understanding of Erasmus's Epicurean philosophy is true, as Márquez shows. But one ought to avoid implying that Don Diego is a careful student of Erasmus, or a careful reader generally. Helmut Hatzfeld sees Don Diego as a typical example of Tridentine piety and Ignatian spirituality in *El "Quijote" como obra de arte del lenguaje* (1966, 135–36; 184). A similar view is put forth by Joaquín Casalduero in *Sentido y forma del "Quijote"* (1970, 259–65). In an important, recent reading, Anthony Close (1990b, 47–52) judges Don Diego as an "exemplary figure" and Don Quixote as an example of rashness and temerity, but without denying the ambiguity of the episodes, and without stressing the obvious religious features of Don Diego's self-portrait.

He will thus continue to seek vainglory and pride as a *summum bonum*, directing all his energies toward the acquisition of lasting fame and renown. Indeed, in his final advice to Don Diego's son, Lorenzo, Don Quixote implies that the vainglorious desire for fame is properly the chief motivation behind the actions of both poets and knights-errant:

> [T]o reach the inacesible summit of Fame, you need only quit the somewhat narrow path of poetry, and to pursue the narrowest of all, which is knight-errantry.
>
> ([P]ara llegar a la inaccessible cumbre de la Fama, no tiene que hacer otra cosa sino dejar a una parte la senda de la poesía, algo estrecha, y tomar la estrechísima de la andante caballería.) (*DQ* II: 19, 176)

He lives on the margins of established law and society. He shows nothing but insolence toward sacred theology, deeming both his own profession and poetry to be superior to the true queen of sciences (*DQ* II: 18, 171). He pursues everything but the golden mean, as confirmed in his adventure with the lions. In that case, by excess, his rashness vitiates the cardinal virtue of courage or fortitude; and, in virtually all his actions, Don Quixote is shown to be extravagant, choleric, and unrestrained: "I delivered myself into the arms of Fortune" (entreguéme en los brazos de la Fortuna). Far from exercising the virtue of hospitality, he fosters no desire for a settled, familial life. Moreover, he proudly tells Don Diego that he has "pawned" his entire "estate" (empeñé mi hacienda) (*DQ* II: 16, 151). Lacking both a home and a wife, he is enamored of a poetic commonplace, remotely inspired by the person of a local peasant woman, Aldonza Lorenzo. So, confirmed in both his heresy and his lunacy, he seems to represent what one may call, again in paraphrase of Fray Luis de León, "the world's most imperfect celibate."

Even their physical appearance underscores the opposition of the two characters. Don Diego's young and frisky "dapple gray mare" (yegua tordilla) is a clear opposite to the haggard Rocinante. Don Diego is handsome, ruddy, clean, and impeccably dressed, in contrast to an unkempt Don Quixote, whose exceedingly gaunt body and dried flesh are quite probably filthy and foul smelling. Their similarities seem purely accidental. For example, both men have thin faces, though Don Diego is said to be of "aquiline visage" (rostro aguileño) rather than of "gaunt visage" (rostro enjuto), like his contrary. Both are called hidalgos, though Don Diego is a wealthy enough to bear the title "don," whereas the "ingenioso hidalgo" is not. Both men hail from La Mancha; and both are either in or near their fifties.

Extravagant Virtue, Prudent Vice: A Lesson in Heroic Sanctity by the Knight of the Lions

Yet, such a hardheaded assessment of the two characters seems based on a reading that focuses solely on first impressions. It is for this reason, I believe, that the author has the embodiment of the *doxa* fall on its knees in the character of Sancho Panza, who begins to worship and kiss the feet of Don Diego as though that fiftyish hidalgo were truly "a saint in short stirrups" (un santo a la jineta) (*DQ* II: 16, 154)—a view that corresponds to Don Diego's self-definition, and which the squire probably shared, in essence, with many of Cervantes' contemporary readers.

There is indeed another side to the question of Don Diego's exemplary virtue. In these chapters, one observes the progressive undoing of Sancho's, and perhaps the reader's, first impressions as well as Don Diego's original self-definition. For if we scrutinize Don Diego's stated principles in light of his actions, we find him wanting from both a religious and a moral point of view.

Despite his praise of theology and discriminating reading, he parenthetically asserts that he *skims* profane books more frequently than devotional works, and does so chiefly in search of "arresting" and "startling" inventiveness: "I skim my profane books more often than my devotional ones, provided they give me honest entertainment, delight me with their language, and arrest and startle me with their inventions" (Hojeo más los que son profanos que los devotos, como sean de honesto entretenimiento, que deleiten con el lenguaje y admiren y suspendan con la invención) (*DQ* II: 16, 153) (Johnson 1990, 97–98). Hence Don Diego's failure to provide a single citation from any of the works; and hence his commonplace generalizations about those works' presumably edifying content and their graceful form. The opening proclamation about his litany of virtues and ideals amounts to his pharisaically thanking God that he is unlike the rest of men, thereby making him as guilty as Folly herself of *philautia* and pride. Moreover, he stresses only the negative side of virtue: avoid idle gossip; shun hypocrisy (Márquez Villanueva 1975, 169). He makes only token gestures of compassion, giving occasional alms, rather than displaying the prescriptive "predilection for the poor" of traditional Catholic doctrine. He does not say "I share my goods" but rather, "I share *of* my goods with the poor" (reparto *de* mis bienes con los pobres) (*DQ* II: 16, 153). His usual guests are, like Don Diego himself, "clean and well groomed" (limpios y aseados) (*DQ* II: 16, 153)—living emblems of genteel cleanliness and politeness. Though Don Diego claims to spend his days with his wife and children (in the plural), the protagonist's specific question about the number of children in the wealthy hidalgo's family forces the latter to admit: "I, Don Quixote, have one son" (Yo, señor don Quijote, tengo un hijo) (*DQ* II: 16, 154).[10] Furthermore, in what is easily his greatest breach of charity, he says that he would probably consider himself more fortunate never to have been a father at all, since his only son, Lorenzo, has chosen to pursue a career in the frivolous pseudoscience of poetry. Don Diego seems disappointed, at bottom, that Lorenzo has failed to emulate his father's social conformism: "not because he is bad, but rather because he is not as good as I should like" (no porque él sea malo, sino porque no es tan bueno como yo quisiera) (*DQ* II: 16, 154).

As to the moral virtues, if Don Quixote is culpable of an excess of fortitude known as rashness, Don Diego is shown to suffer from the defect of cowardice.[11] For it is ultimately out of cowardice, rather than rightful caution or sanity, that he fails to keep Don Quixote from what appears to be certain death in the latter's adventure with the lion. To be sure, Don Diego tries to dissuade the protagonist from the rash confrontation; yet he does so, again, in a politely conformist manner that not only misrepresents Don Quixote's profession of knight-errantry, but also appeals to a calculating, self-serving notion of prudence, leaving no room for decisiveness or heroism:

> Sir Knight, knights-errant ought to pursue adventures that offer hope of success, and not those that rule out such hope from the start; for bravery that crosses over into the region of temerity is more a case of lunacy that fortitude. What is more, these lions are not coming after you, nor do they even dream of doing so. They are to be presented to his Majesty, and it would be ill advised to stop them or to hinder their journey.

> (Señor caballero, los caballeros andantes han de acometer las aventuras que prometen esperanza de salir bien dellas, y no aquellas que de en todo la quitan; porque la valentía que se entra en la juridición de la temeridad,

10. As one may infer from the religiously orthodox, Epicurean lexicon of the following question that Don Quixote puts to Don Diego, the protagonist knows very well the kind of archetypal self-portrait that Don Diego seeks to convey: "Don Quixote asked him how many children he had, and told him that one thing held to be a supreme good by ancient philosophers, who lacked true knowledge of God, was found in the goods of nature, in those of fortune, in having many friends and in having many good children" (Preguntóle don Quijote que cuántos hijos tenía, y díjole que una de las cosas en que ponían el sumo bien los antiguos filósofos, que carecieron del verdadero conocimiento de Dios, fue en los bienes de la naturaleza, en los de la fortuna, en tener muchos amigos y en tener muchos y buenos hijos) (*DQ* II: 16, 172).

11. He shares this defective trait with Cardenio. For a classical, Aristotelian and Thomistic summary of the virtue of fortitude, see Pieper 1966, 114–41.

más tiene de locura que de fortaleza. Cuanto más que estos leones no vienen contra vuesa merced; ni lo sueñan: van presentados a su Majestad, y no será bien detenerlos ni impedirles su viaje.) (*DQ* II: 17, 161)

Don Diego's idea of virtue commands no authority and he is woefully ignorant of his audience. Thus his rhetoric fails from a lack of both ethos and pathos. Further, both his rhetorical failure and his meager efforts contrast ironically with his boastful promise to Sancho: "I will see to it that he does not [attack the lions]" (Yo haré que no lo sea) (*DQ* II: 17, 160). Apparently saving his most "powerful" rhetoric for last, Don Diego is paraphrased as providing a final bit of advice to Don Quixote, yet seeming to adopt a tone more suitable to a gentlemanly debate than to an admonition against imminent suicide:

> Once more the hidalgo entreated Don Quixote not to do anything so mad, since to pursue such a folly was to tempt God. To which Don Quixote responded that he knew what he was about. The hidalgo responded, in turn, that Don Quixote examine the matter carefully, since he [the hidalgo] was of the opinion that Don Quixote was mistaken.

> (Otra vez le persuadió el hidalgo que no hiciese locura semejante que era tentar a Dios acometer tan disparate. A lo que respondió don Quijote que él sabía lo que hacía. Respondióle el hidalgo que lo mirase bien; que él entendía que se engañaba.) (*DQ* II: 17, 162)

The reader also learns how Don Diego faintly realizes, but finally shies away from, his duty to intervene—once again, for reasons of calculating, self-serving "prudence" (cordura):

> The man in the green coat was inclined to thwart him; but he thought himself unequal in arms, and he did not think it prudent to confront a madman, as he now judged Don Quixote to be utterly mad.

> (Quisiera el del verde gabán oponérsele; pero viose desigual en las armas, y no le pareció cordura tomarse con un loco, que ya se lo había parecido de todo punto don Quijote.) (*DQ* II: 17, 162)

In other words, the hidalgo calculates, not the means necessary to bring about a morally sound end—namely, the extreme case of saving a man's life, which requires extreme measures—but only the risk to his own person. What is more, he is the one, mounted on his light-footed mare, to lead both Sancho and the wagon driver in frantic flight:

> Don Quixote once again hurried the lion keeper and repeated his threats, which gave the hidalgo a chance to spur his mare, Sancho his ass, and the wagon driver his mules, all of them attempting to get as far as they could from the wagon before the lions sprang loose.

> ([E]l cual [don Quijote], volviendo a dar priesa al leonero, y a reiterar las amenazas, dio ocasión al hidalgo a que picase la yegua, y Sancho al rucio, y el carretero a sus mulas, procurando todos apartarse del carro lo más que pudiesen, antes que los leones se desembanastasen.) (*DQ* II: 17, 162)

Earlier in the narrative, it was also his cowardice that led Don Diego, sporting a scimitar, to flee from Don Quixote and Sancho on the road, and to offer a lame excuse (complete with dramatic irony) for doing so: "Truly, I would not have passed you by, were it not for my *fear* that my mare's company would unsettle your horse" (De verdad, que no me pasara de largo si no fuera *por temor* que con la compañía de mi yegua no se alborotara ese caballo) (*DQ* II: 16, 150; emphasis added).

In sum, without the theological virtue of charity, there can be no sanctity. And our self-proclaimed Christian exemplar is lacking in the cardinal virtues of justice (in particular, toward his own son) as well as fortitude. Don Diego's practice fails to match the bluster of his preaching.

Regarding his physical appearance, I believe that a simultaneously conflicted and unifying semiology is at work in the portrayal of Don Diego's attire, which, unlike the hidalgo's conventional house, is described in notable detail:

> an overcoat of fine green cloth, with strips of tawny [literally: lion-colored] velvet, and a hunting cap of the same velvet; his mare's trappings were for riding in the country, in short stirrups, and likewise purple and green. He wore a Moorish scimitar, hanging from a wide sword belt of green and gold, and his leggings were of the same make as the belt; his stirrups were not gilt but lacquered with green, so shiny and burnished that, because they matched his whole outfit, looked better than if they had been of pure gold.

> (un gabán de paño fino verde, jironado de terciopelo leonado, con una montera del mismo terciopelo; el aderezo de la yegua era de campo, y de

la jineta, asimismo de morado y verde. Traía un alfanje morisco pendi-
ente de un ancho tahalí de verde y oro, y los borceguíes eran de la labor
del tahalí; las espuelas no eran doradas, sino dadas con un barniz verde;
tan tersas y bruñidas, que, por hacer labor con todo el vestido, parecían
mejor que si fuera de oro puro.) (*DQ* II: 16, 149–50)

In his very specific interpretation of Don Diego's appearance, Márquez
Villanueva claims that the "motley," the "tropical" glossiness, and the generally
"loud tone" (tono chillón) of the character's outfit derive from the northern
European model of dress for jesters and buffoons (1975, 219–23). That critic
goes so far as to say that "Don Diego de Miranda dresses to look like a parrot"
(don Diego de Miranda viste como un papagayo) (Márquez Villanueva 1975,
220). In response to Márquez Villanueva and others, Gerald Gingras argues that
Don Diego's choice of material ("fine cloth" [paño fino]), his color coordination
(green with patches of tawny velvet) and even his choice of spurs (gold bur-
nished with green) were typical of the rural Spanish hidalgo, thus revealing Don
Diego's conservative tastes (1985, 129–40). In my view, there is no reason to
deny that the underlying theses of both contrary readings, and those of other
readings, remain plausible, up to a point, though applicable at different stages of
the unfolding narrative. In view of Cervantes' perplexing description, it seems
unnecessary to decide conclusively whether his attire marks Don Diego as either
perfectly sane and wise or perfectly mad and foolish.[12] As his garments paradoxically reflect, Don Diego can just as rightly be seen as both sane and mad to some
degree. In other words, the author's description, presumably transmitted to the
reader through the fictional and, perhaps, doubly fictional filters of Cide Hamete,
the translator, the "second author," and the narrator, is "clear" only in its perplexity and conflictedness.

Another disputed point is whether the time-honored association in Spanish
between the color green and lechery, as in the expression *viejo verde* (dirty old
man), is at all relevant in the case of Don Diego, self-appointed archetype of marital fidelity (Chamberlain and Weiner 1969, 1–6, qtd. in Márquez Villanueva
1975, 150–51 n. 4). Arguing, not just from the colors of the outfit, but from
imagery that relates to emblematic symbolism, Percas de Ponseti asserts that he is

12. As Márquez Villanueva argues (1975, 224–26), Don Diego embodies Cervantes' version of an
Erasmian mad/sane paradox. For this reason, I find it perplexing that he should insist on a univocal interpretation (favoring folly and madness) of the character's clothing. The same scholar again takes up the
subject of Don Diego's attire (1980, 92–96), insisting on the same unproblematic, univocal interpretation of the character's appearance. In this article, Márquez Villanueva states more than once that the
"green" of the character's "overcoat," and not just the general tone of his appearance, is "loud" (chillón),
an assertion for which there is no textual evidence. Presumably this scholar means to imply that green, as
such, is intended to be seen as a loud color.

ultimately meant to be seen as a shifty philanderer—on the prowl, and with much to hide—whose clothing and mount symbolize his deceitfulness through the imagery of chameleon-like disguise and camouflage (1988, 36–53).[13] Again, no univocal answer seems possible in this regard, since there is no textual evidence of Don Diego's alleged sexual dalliance. The reader remains uninformed about Don Diego's recent whereabouts, although the character has clearly not been hunting, since he is lacking both his "meek partridge" and his "daring ferret." Further, the reader remains uninformed about whether Don Diego's reference to his "children" (hijos) is, perhaps, a Freudian slip. Arguing along these lines, one may also choose to recall the excuse he improvised for riding past Don Quixote and Sancho on the road—namely, that his mare would probably arouse even Rocinante. It could thus appear that he is not only cowardly, but also somewhat preoccupied with sex. Indeed, despite this remark's expressing a plausible and typical concern of persons in the country, familiar with the behavior of horses, the author seems to draw our attention to the sexual innuendo by having Sancho (a peasant who is undoubtedly familiar with animal behavior) insist that Rocinante is incapable of any such "vileness" (vileza) (DQ II: 16, 150). So if the emblematic symbolism is "clear," its function in the text is ambiguous.

Less debatable, perhaps, is the immediate consequence of the author's lavishly detailed description of Don Diego as a type of sixteenth-century fashion plate. By any estimation, the striking hidalgo's impeccable, matching attire betokens at least a trace of vanity, which is one of the vices he claims to scorn as unchristian. Only a noteworthy degree of elegance and dash in Don Diego's appearance could justify the repeated emphasis of Don Quixote's addressing him as "Gallant sir" at the start of their encounter, together with the protagonist's reported assessment of Don Diego as "a man of formal bearing" (un hombre de chapa) and "cut from fine [noble] cloth" (de buenas prendas) (DQ II: 16, 150).[14] Furthermore, it is before the characters exchange any words that the protagonist shows obvious surprise at the physical appearance of Don Diego, identified by

13. Percas de Ponseti makes the compelling distinction between the superficially "impressionistic," favorable portrait of Don Diego, for which she holds Cide Hamete responsible, and the subtly "expressionistic," critical portrait, for which she holds Cervantes responsible (1988, 36–53). Indeed, as this scholar suggests, the two portraits overlap. Percas de Ponseti also wrote an earlier study on Don Diego (1975, 332–82). And, as she argues in both studies, Cervantes' duplicitous portrait aims at contradicting first impressions. As I shall argue presently, his complex portrait also undoes second impressions, suggesting the open form of a continuing dialectic.

14. Although this statement conflicts with the thesis of Gingras (1985, 129–40) concerning the "conservatism" of Don Diego's tastes, it does not conflict with the rationale behind the pertinent legal "decrees"(pragmáticas) that Gingras cites in support of his arguments. Indeed, as Gingras implies, these decrees were aimed at curbing the ostentatious, extravagant habits of the hidalgo class. Don Diego's "conservatism" is, therefore, relative to a decadent norm. Again, his attire signals his conformism as well as the noticeable, if less than glaring, vanity of his display.

his favorite color: "and if the man in green looked closely at Don Quixote, much more closely did Don Quixote look at the man in green" (y si mucho miraba el de lo verde a don Quijote, mucho más miraba don Quijote al de lo verde) (*DQ* II: 16, 150).

To continue our contrary reading, we not only notice Don Quixote's quoting from Ovid on the nobility of poetry, "*est Deus in nobis*" (*DQ* II: 16, 156), but we also observe that he is thus putting a decidedly Christian spin, *a lo divino*, on a pagan text. So just as Don Diego's "reading" habits tended to profane the sacred, Don Quixote's tend, in this instance, to sanctify the profane. Furthermore, one can hardly accuse Don Quixote of failing to assimilate his sources. Again, without vague generalization, but quoting directly from a ballad, he first defines himself to Don Diego as a knight "like those of whom the people say, / they go seeking their adventures" (destos que dicen las gentes / que a sus aventuras van) (*DQ* II: 16, 151).[15] To the degree he is quixotic, and he is not always so, Don Quixote appears throughout the text as a paradigm of the irascible activist. Yet it is he, rather than the sober champion of ascetic devotions, who is said to admire the wondrous, contemplative silence of Don Diego's quasi-monastic mansion: "[W]hat pleased Don Quixote most was the marvelous silence that was present throughout the house, which resembled a Carthusian monastery" ([D]e lo que más se contentó don Quijote fue del maravilloso silencio que en toda la casa había, que semejaba un monasterio de cartujos) (*DQ* II: 16, 173).[16] In his opening remarks, the ardent seeker of lasting fame and honor regrets having to describe himself at all, and closes, not with a grandiloquent "I always keep faith in the mercy of God, Our Lord," but with a self-deprecating reference to his unkempt and weary appearance: "the sallowness of my complexion and my weary leanness" (la amarillez de mi rostro y mi atenuada flaqueza) (*DQ* II: 16, 152).

It strikes me as no accident that in Cervantes' text, a childless, lifelong bachelor, in love with an imaginary damsel, should utter the work's most apposite words about parental love: "Children, sir, are parts of their parents' very entrails,

15. About these verses, Luis Andrés Murillo notes in his edition of *Don Quixote* (*DQ* I, 140 n. 7): "They come from either an ancient ballad (now lost) or from the pen of Alvar Gómez of Ciudad Real who used them in his rendering of Petrarch's *Trionfi* (*T.C.*, III, vv. 79–84), though nothing resembling those verses appears in the original work" (Son o de un romance antiguo [perdido] o de la pluma de Alvar Gómez de Ciudad Real que los empleó en su traslación de los *Trionfi* de Petrarca [*Triumphus Cupidinis*, III, vss. 79–84], sin que haya en la obra original nada que se parezca a ellos). The same verses appear twice in Part I of Cervantes' fiction: I, 9; and I, 49.

16. On the predominantly mystical sources and the significance of "marvelous silence" (maravilloso silencio) in this passage, see Márquez Villanueva (1975, 155–59). Trueblood also discusses silence and silences in *Don Quixote* (1958, 160–80). A more recent study on silences in several of Cervantes' works, with ample bibliography on the *Quixote*, is Egido 1991, 21–46.

and so we should love them, whether they are good or bad, as we love the souls that give us life" (Los hijos, señor, son pedazos de las entrañas de sus padres, y así se han de querer, o buenos o malos que sean, como se quieren las almas que nos dan vida). No less sagely, Don Quixote urges against the tendency of some parents to force their son's choice of career. He suggests, instead, that they let their son "follow the subject to which he seems most inclined" (seguir aquella ciencia a que más le vieren inclinado). Never losing sight of his audience, and arguing with the utmost reasonableness—showing both ethos and pathos—Don Quixote also proffers considered and balanced praise of poetry and its virtues, beginning with the assertion that "although [the science] of poetry is less practical than delightful, it is not one of those [sciences] which dishonor the persons who possess them" (aunque la [ciencia] de la poesía es menos útil que deleitable, no es de aquellas que suelen deshonrar a quien las posee) (*DQ* II: 16, 155).

The protagonist is also far less crazy and rash than one is first led to assume by his adventure/nonadventure with the lion. With flawless moral and *pedagogical* reasoning, Don Quixote states that he was right in attacking the lions, though he *knew* it to be a rash act: "which I *knew* to be a reckless temerity" (que *conocí* ser temeridad esorbitante) (*DQ* II: 17, 167; emphasis added). Following a perfect description of the classical virtue of fortitude, he goes on to give the *reason* behind his intentional madness: "[F]or just as it is easier for the spendthrift to become generous than it is for the miser, so it is easier for the man who is rash to become truly brave than it is for the coward to reach true bravery" ([Q]ue así como es más fácil venir el pródigo a ser liberal que al avaro, así es más fácil dar el temerario en verdadero valiente que no el cobarde subir a la verdadera valentía) (*DQ* II: 17, 167). The knight finishes his lesson with a rather pointed reference to Don Diego's natural weakness: "[M]ark my words, Don Diego, sir, . . . for it sounds better when persons hear 'such and such knight is reckless' than when they hear 'such and such knight is fainthearted and cowardly'" (créame vuesa merced, señor don Diego, . . . porque mejor suena en las orejas de los que lo oyen "el tal caballero es temerario y atrevido" que no "el tal caballero es tímido y cobarde") (*DQ* II: 17, 167–68). Neither truly a *don* nor a *caballero*, the protagonist demonstrates the most salient virtue of knighthood to the *caballero* Don Diego de Miranda. What is more, he does so by proposing the classical, Aristotelian remedy for defective vice, which consists of compensating by way of excess.[17] He corrects Don Diego's reductive view of knight-errantry, a profession that the latter seems to confuse with that of a courtly knight:

17. As Aristotle writes in *Nichomachean Ethics*: "We must also examine what we ourselves drift into easily. For different people have different natural tendencies towards different goals, and we shall come to

But the knight-errant searches out the corners of the earth; enters the most intricate mazes; pursues the impossible at every step; endures, at the height of summer, the sun's burning rays in the deserted plains, and in winter the harsh inclemency of winds and ice. No lions shall daunt him, nor monsters make him shudder nor dragons bring him fear. For to seek them, confront them and overcome them all are his foremost and rightful exercises.

(Pero el andante caballero busque los rincones del mundo; éntrese en los más intricados laberintos; acometa a cada paso lo imposible; resista en los páramos despoblados los ardientes rayos del sol en la mitad del verano, y en el invierno la dura inclemencia de los vientos y de los yelos; no le asombren leones, ni le espanten vestiglos, ni atemoricen endriagos; que buscar éstos, acometer aquéllos y vencerlos a todos son sus principales y verdaderos ejercicios.) (*DQ* II: 17, 167)

Such "exercises" belong to an entirely different order from that of Don Diego's pastimes (which he called his "exercises") of fishing and hunting for small game. More important, the ethos of Don Quixote, erstwhile promoter of lunacy and heresy, stresses the positive and heroic side of all the virtues, whereas Don Diego's ethos stresses only the negative, Epicurean admonition: "nothing in excess" (Márquez Villanueva 1975, 177).[18] Indeed, as the Church had firmly established by Cervantes' time—and as every informed Catholic knew since the

---

know our own tendencies from the pleasure or pain that arises in us. We must drag ourselves off in the contrary direction; for if we pull far away from error, as they do in straightening bent wood, we shall reach the intermediate condition" *Nichomachean Ethics* (1985, 52–53; 2.9.1109b). Aristotle closes this second book of his *Ethics* with the following assertion: "All this makes it clear, then, that in every case the intermediate state is praised, but we must sometimes incline towards the excess, sometimes towards the deficiency; for that is the easiest way to succeed in hitting the intermediate condition and [doing] well" (1985, 53; 2.9.1109b). An earlier remark in Aristotle's *Nichomachean Ethics*, book 2, supports the opinion that Don Quixote previously expressed to Don Diego: "In some cases the deficiency, in others the excess, is more opposed to the intermediate condition; e.g., it is cowardice, the deficiency, not rashness, the excess, that is more opposed to bravery" (1985, 50; 2.9.1109a). Also, on the remedy for either excessive or defective vice, see Aquinas's *Commentary on the "Nichomachean Ethics"* (1964, 164–68). In paragraph 381 of that work, Aquinas writes: "However, sometimes we must incline toward excess and sometimes toward defect either on account of the nature of the virtue or on account of our inclination. . . . Thus the mean according to which a thing is done well [i.e., virtuously] will be easily discovered (168).

18. Speaking of the ideal knight errant's heroic virtue to Don Lorenzo, Don Quixote states that "he must be arrayed with all the theological and cardinal virtues, . . . and to speak again of lofty matters, he must keep faith in God and in his lady; he must be chaste in thought, honest in word, generous in works, brave in deeds, long suffering in trials, charitable toward the needy, and, last, champion of the truth, though its defense cost him his life" (ha de estar adornado de todas las virtudes teologales y cardinales, . . .

time of Saint Isidore of Seville (530?–636)—virtue lived to a *heroic* degree was, and still is, the very definition of sanctity and the standard for canonization.[19] The seemingly obvious *doxa* of Sancho's popular wisdom and of Don Diego's first attempt at self-figuration and self-knowledge thus seems to collapse upon critical examination.

Open Synthesis: The Silenic Unfolding of Character, Setting, and Action

Nonetheless, we would be mistaken, I believe, to think that Cervantes' narrative undermines one set of hypotheses only to leave another intact. The text both elicits and frustrates the reader's attempt to decide, once and for all, which of the two characters is morally superior. It argues for and against both sides of the same question with equal conviction and doubt, in the manner of Plato's Parmenides and of Cicero's Academic Skeptic and, so, in the manner of Erasmus's *Praise of Folly*. Like every element and image in the chapters devoted to narrating their encounter, both characters—at the level of word, deed, and physical appearance—are rife with paradox. The two fiftyish hidalgos, their interaction, their appearance, their mounts, the physical objects of their surroundings, all represent a blend of alternately conflicting and converging contraries. In conceptual terms, they represent what Cusanus would call a *coincidentia oppositorum*. In terms of auditory or musical imagery, they represent a *discordia concors*; and in visual imagery, a Silenus. Likewise, the two contrary readings that I have summarized here "stand" as contradictory and complementary, the object of praise and censure, parody and exaltation, both preserved and undone in the text. Thesis and antithesis "resolve" into the open synthesis of mystery and progressively learned ignorance.

As suggested earlier, both characters try to define themselves according to a belief system derived from their favorite type of *exemplary* literature. Let me now add that, in the author's text, characters are shown to be mad, and impervious to

---

y volviendo a lo de arriba, ha de guardar la fe a Dios y a su dama; ha de ser casto en los pensamientos, honesto en las palabras, liberal en las obras, valiente en los hechos, sufrido en los trabajos, caritativo con los menesterosos, y, finalmente, mantenedor de la verdad, aunque le cueste la vida el defenderla.) (*DQ* II: 18, 171–72).

19. Saint Isidore's formula in the *Etymologies* (1.39.9) is "For hero is the name given to men who by their wisdom and *courage* are worthy of heaven" (qtd. in Curtius 1973, 175). On the history of the canonization process and the centrality of "heroic virtue," see *The New Catholic Encyclopedia* (1967), s.v. "Canonization of Saints (History and Procedure)."

the paradoxical nature of truth, to the extent that they insist on remaining what one may call, paraphrasing Dunn, a stable sign within a closed semiotic system. In other words, characters are mad in the measure that they futilely attempt to collapse, in their own persons, the distinction between life and discourse, contingency and code, and in particular, experience and fiction.[20] For Don Quixote, the semiotic system is chivalric romance, which for him remains closed and univocal in meaning. Don Diego finds an analogous system in secular and devotional literature of the Christian Epicurean and Tridentine varieties.

The case of Don Diego is, of course, far less extreme than that of Don Quixote. Yet it is significant that we should observe Don Diego at a stage of his life which resembles that of Don Quixote in the first chapter of Part I. There, the protagonist named himself, his horse, and his lady in accord with the semiotic system of chivalric romance, which he invested with the status of exemplary history and the authority of Holy Writ. Like Don Quixote's initial self-fashioning—indeed, a form of self-creation—Don Diego's original self-definition finds expression in an atemporal or habitual *present*, in perfect accord with his own semiotic system of exemplarity: "*I am* an hidalgo"; "*I spend* my time with my wife"; "*I have* some six dozen books"; "at times *I dine* with my friends (*Soy* un hidalgo; *paso* la vida con mi mujer; *tengo* hasta seis docenas de libros; alguna vez *como* con mis amigos) (*DQ* II: 16, 153; emphasis added). Indeed, Don Diego presents himself as a man virtually exempt from history and contingency and as little less than an archetype: whole, changeless, complete.

In addition, the reader receives the distinct impression that before his encounter with Don Quixote, Don Diego de Miranda has failed to perceive his life as a narrative or *history*.[21] Up to this moment, it seems that nothing in his experience has posed an effective challenge to his self-definition. All previous events in his life have managed to fit neatly within the pattern of his exemplary plan, derived from a conformist understanding of his "readings." Indeed, Don Diego perceives himself as incarnating the socially approved abstraction of a Christian hidalgo in search of conformist anonymity. Despite their contrary ideologies, then, both characters base their actions on the assumption that "life" will conform, in a predictable fashion, to their poetic code or semiotic system. Thus, they suffer from contrary species of folly, which nonetheless belong to the same genus.

20. Dunn makes a point similar to mine, but without suggesting that this attitude is the measure of a character's madness or folly, in a comparison between Ginés de Pasamonte's self-naming and Don Quixote's naming of himself, Dulcinea, and Rocinante (1982, 119–20). As Dunn astutely observes, Ginés de Pasamonte, like Don Quixote, "aspires to make his life total discourse, to abolish the difference between story and diegesis, between the teller, the telling, and the told" (Dunn 1982, 119).

21. I am grateful to Carroll Johnson, whose insightful questions led me to clarify my observations on this aspect of Don Diego's self-portrait.

Unlike the self-styled knight, however, Don Diego is shown to be capable of reassessing his original position in the face of "startling," "arresting" occurrences. The hidalgo, who is certainly more a Gentleman than a Knight of the Green Coat, reveals his fundamental sanity in that he ultimately acknowledges the sound reasoning of Don Quixote on such matters as the nobility of poetry and religious and moral virtue, judging the protagonist to be "a madman veering toward sanity" (un loco que tiraba a cuerdo) (*DQ* II: 17, 166), or in the opinion of Lorenzo, a "loco entreverado" (*DQ* II: 18, 173): a significantly "mixed breed of lunatic," given to lucid intervals. So to speak, Don Diego stands as one of the fiction's mixed breed of nonlunatics, or *cuerdos entreverados*: a fundamentally sane man, given to momentary, sometimes severe lapses of moral folly. More important, however, Don Diego shows a capacity for reflective *admiratio* and awe, when confronted with actions at the level of *usus et experientia* that challenge his formerly untested assumptions (*doxa*)—that is, when brought to a state of aporetic crisis concerning the very precepts after which he first attempted to shape his identity.

Along these lines, we encounter a spate of terms in II, 16–18, beginning with Don Diego's surname, which relate both conceptually and etymologically to *admiratio*, the Latin verb forms *miror* and *mirari* (to look or gaze) and to the ideas of surprise, wonder, and mystery that figured prominently, as we have seen, in Covarrubias's definition of *paradox*. Such terms include *arrest, astonish* [or *startle*], *gaze, marvel, miracle* (*suspender, admirar, mirar, maravilla, milagro*).[22] It is of particular interest to observe this chain of signifiers in reference to the itinerary of Don Diego's scrutinizing gazes, his growing sense of surprise, shock, and reflective wonder. At first, Don Diego is understandably stunned by the protagonist's *physical appearance*: "The traveler pulled in his rein, with growing *astonishment* at the figure and face of Don Quixote" (Detuvo la rienda el caminante, *admirándose* de la apostura y rostro de don Quijote) (*DQ* II: 16, 150; emphasis added). Fittingly, however, it is only at the level of physical appearance that the man in green makes his *first* judgment, filled with *admiratio*, about the protagonist:

> The judgment that the man in green reached about Don Quixote was that he had never before seen any man of such bearing and mien. He was *astonished* at the lankiness of the man's horse, the length of his body, the leanness and sallowness of his face, his weapons, his gestures and demeanor.

22. For words and concepts related to the verb *mirar*, including the surname Miranda, I have found especially useful the entry mirar in Joan Corominas's *Diccionario crítico etimológico de la lengua castellana* (1954, 3:382–84).

(Lo que juzgó de don Quijote de la Mancha el de lo verde fue que semejante manera ni parecer de hombre no le había visto jamás: *Admiróle* la
longura de su caballo, la grandeza de su cuerpo, la flaqueza y amarillez de
su rostro, sus armas, su ademán y compostura.) (*DQ* II: 16, 150–51;
emphasis added)

His sense of wonder increases after the protagonist gives an accounting of himself—in *words*. Following a "long pause" (buen espacio), during which he ponders
both the appearance and words of Don Quixote, Don Diego asserts: "[B]ut you
have not succeeded in relieving my *amazement* at the sight of you . . . , rather,
now that I know [who you are], I am even more *astonished* and *amazed* ([P]ero no
habéis acertado a quitarme la *maravilla* que en mí causa el haberos visto . . . ,
antes, agora que lo sé [quien sois], quedo más *suspenso y maravillado*) (*DQ* II: 16,
152; emphasis added).

Likewise, Sancho's choosing to kiss the man's feet, because the squire thinks
him capable of working "miracles" (milagros [from the Latin *miracula*]) (*DQ* II:
16, 153), provokes "further amazement in Don Diego" (nueva admiración a
don Diego) (*DQ* II: 16, 154). Next, our wealthy hidalgo is notably impressed
with the logical quality of the madman's discourse: "The man in green stood
amazed at Don Quixote's *arguments*" (*Admirado* quedó el del verde gabán del
razonamiento de don Quijote) (*DQ* II: 16, 157; emphasis added). At the close
of II, 16, Don Diego has again reached an important judgment about the protagonist, "pleased in the extreme with Don Quixote's discretion and eloquence"
(satisfecho en estremo de la discreción y buen discurso de don Quijote), which
reflects his ability to alter his opinions according to the demands of experience:
"[*H*]*e was beginning to change his opinion* that the man was a nitwit" ([*F*]*ue per-
diendo de la opinión* que con él tenía, de ser mentecato") (*DQ* II: 16, 157;
emphasis added).

If II, 16, the first of these three chapters, centers on appearances and *words*
(*palabras*), the next chapter centers on *deeds* (*hechos, obras*), shown to be the final
manifestation of discourse and the criterion by which Don Diego ultimately
assesses the protagonist. In the wake of Don Quixote's confrontation with the
lion, together with the protagonist's account of that pivotal, name-changing
event, Don Diego (who is identified here by his significant surname, Miranda,
rather than by either his cloak or his characteristic color) responds with reflective, contemplative silence: "All this time *Don Diego de Miranda had not spoken a
word*, devoting all his attention to watching and noting the *deeds and words* of
Don Quixote (En todo este tiempo *no había hablado palabra don Diego de*

Miranda, todo atento a *mirar y notar* los *hechos y palabras* de don Quijote) (*DQ* II: 17, 166; emphasis added).

Although he is probably overstating his views out of courtesy to his listener, Don Diego tells Don Quixote, at the end of the chapter that "all that you have *said and done* is balanced on the scale of reason itself" (todo lo que vuesa merced ha *dicho y hecho* va nivelado con el fiel de la misma razón) (*DQ* II: 17, 168; emphasis added). It seems, in other words, that Don Diego disagrees with those readers who would dismiss the protagonist's actions as *simply* rash. Although Don Diego never formulates his judgment in such terms, he clearly realizes that in Don Quixote, he is pondering a moral and rational enigma, or an axiological and logical paradox. Furthermore, Don Diego's continuing meditation on both the words and deeds of the newly dubbed Knight of the Lions leads to a conversation of respectful intimacy with Don Lorenzo:

> I don't know what to tell you, son, said Don Diego. I can only say that I have seen him *do* things that make him the maddest man in the world and [heard him] *speak* words so shrewd [literally: discreet] that they *efface and undo* his deeds. Speak to him yourself, and take the pulse of what he knows, and, since you are of sound judgment, assess what part of his shrewdness or his folly approaches right reason; though, truth to tell, I think him more mad than sane.
>
> (No sé lo que te diga, hijo—respondió don Diego—; sólo te sabré decir que le he visto *hacer* cosas del mayor loco del mundo, y *decir* razones tan discretas, que *borran y deshacen* sus hechos; háblale tú, y toma el pulso a lo que sabe, y, pues eres discreto, juzga de su discreción o tontería lo que más puesto en razón estuviere; aunque, para decir verdad, antes le tengo por loco que por cuerdo.) (*DQ* II: 18, 170; emphasis added)

It is appropriate that Don Diego should be the one to observe that the knight's words "undo" the apparent lunacy of his deeds. For, in a compelling instance of paradoxical reversal, it is through this "deed" of respectful conversation with Lorenzo that Don Diego manages, if only in part, to "efface" and "undo" the folly of his formerly harsh "words" about his son. Here, as elsewhere, Don Diego shows himself to be the convex image—the complementary and nonexclusive opposite—of Don Quixote.

At the level of "life" and experience, and perhaps owing in part to the advice of Don Quixote, Don Diego *begins* to overcome the unjust and uncharitable rigidities of a discursive, semiotic system that has thus far governed his thought, expression and action. In a descriptive scene containing paradox at the level of both statement and structure, the protagonist and his squire depart from the home of the Mirandas. Both Don Diego and his son stand together in a shared state of reflective amazement over the paradox of Don Quixote's words and deeds:

> Once again father and son were *astonished* at Don Quixote's *mongrel discourse*, now shrewd, now outlandish; and at the firmness and fixity he showed in pursuing at all cost the quest of his *adventurous misadventures*, to which he held as the aim and target of his longings.

> (De nuevo se *admiraron* padre y hijo de las *entremetidas razones* de don Quijote, ya discretas y ya disparatadas, y del tema y tesón que llevaba de acudir de todo en todo a la busca de sus *desventuradas aventuras*, que las tenía por fin y blanco de sus deseos.) (*DQ* II: 18, 177; emphasis added)

Paradoxically, then, despite his many shortcomings, our notorious skimmer of books is portrayed outside his library as a mirror, albeit an imperfect mirror, of the judicious reader. And his experience within the fictional frame is remarkably analogous to our own outside it. If Don Diego's assessments deserve the modifiers "reflective" and "judicious" which they are given here, it is because he manages to entertain the possibility of "truth" contained in the radically opposed ethos of Don Quixote, in accord with a dialectical method that traces back to Plato's *Parmenides* and includes the dialogical writings of Cicero, Augustine, Lucian, Erasmus, and the Christian humanists. But, in Cervantes' text, such dialogue is never confined to an exchange of abstract ideas or words (without deeds) between characterological types. Rather, in these chapters, what one may call Cervantes' Silenic imagery and his overarching spirit of dialogism extend to the deeds, physical surroundings, and unfolding process of verbal and nonverbal interaction between two individualized and paradoxical characters—characters who are progressively rendered in their individuality, despite their own "attempts" to remain as timeless archetypes.

Furthermore, as individual readers, our contrary readings, one favoring the ethos of Don Diego, the other favoring the ethos of Don Quixote, as that of the model Christian "hero," may lead us to understand the same "truths" about Don Diego that he comes to understand about himself. Increased knowledge for the reader is textually represented as self-knowledge for Don Diego. For readers of the fictional text, arguing two sides of a question takes the form of contrary readings. For Don Diego, it takes the form of an encounter with a contrary character: his mirror in age, appearance, folly, regional origin, and social status. Don Quixote's passing through "the threshold of his door" was the "startling," experiential equivalent of Don Diego's reading the romances of chivalry.

Significantly, this experiential "reading" translates into Don Diego's starting to alter his social conformism. He shows a truly charitable and respectful "predilection" for Don Quixote and Sancho. He shares his home, his goods, his friendship, and his familial life with guests who are nothing if not "poor," unable to return the favor, and far from "clean and well groomed." That the protagonist's presence in Don Diego's home marks a startling disruption of their domestic routine seems plain from the reaction of both Don Lorenzo and Doña Cristina: "Mother and son were *stunned* by the sight of Don Quixote's strange appearance" (Madre y hijo quedaron *suspensos* de ver la estraña figura de don Quijote) (*DQ* II: 18, 169; emphasis added). And although it ranks among the many things left unwritten, one may find it tempting to ponder how Don Diego's neighbors might have responded to his entertaining such unusual guests. Thanks in no small measure to Don Quixote's appearance, words and deeds, but also thanks to Don Diego's attitude of openness and generosity, the protagonist's visit with the Mirandas represents nothing less than the paradox, or the apparent *impossibility*, of a chivalric-Epicurean, "domestic" adventure.

If, in another instance of dramatic irony, Sancho overstates the case of Don Diego's virtue in thinking that the latter "must be able to perform miracles," it is nonetheless true that these chapters contain a series of marvels (*mirabilia*) bearing on the incipient transformation of the man in green. Thus his surname, Miranda, signals the appearance of such extraordinary marvels in the most ordinary circumstances, inviting one to "gaze" and "wonder," to "gaze" intently and "wonder" reflectively, and to become increasingly aware and self-aware. But, even more reflectively, the gerundive inflection of Don Diego's surname also draws the reader's attention to the "things *continually* to be wondered at" (*miranda*) when he adopts this character's perspective, or when he recognizes the specularity of the text and Miranda as a mirror of himself. For Don Diego represents a fellow "reader" (judge) of Don Quixote. Ultimately grounded either inside or outside the fictional frame of the author's text, Don Diego and the reader are involved in an analogous adventure, an analogous internal debate, an analogous dialogue, an analogous process of self-examination and self-reflection.

Revealing truths beyond the two extremes, the unfolding story of Don Diego's momentary crisis paradoxically upholds, undoes, conflates, and enlarges such formerly rigid contraries as sacred and profane, sanity and lunacy, poetry and history, action and contemplation, vice and virtue, and especially self and other. For, if they so choose, one paradox that Don Diego and the reader come specifically to understand in these chapters is that self-knowledge takes the form of an unfolding, social, and dialogic enterprise. The self-fashioning that follows from that knowledge constitutes both an individual and collective work of art—a voluntary act of inventive *imitatio* that is in dialogue or in conflict with the world of empirical experience. To be sure, the process of Don Diego's reflective wonder about the appearance, words, and deeds of the protagonist, as well as his subsequent judgments and actions, jointly mark at least his temporary willingness to relinquish the fixity of his semiotic system, which resulted in his *sancta mediocritas* and his static, archetypal understanding of self.[23] But to paraphrase Close, the character of Don Diego is far from resolved (1990b, 52). There is no guarantee, and no explicit indication, that he will continue to act on what he learns about himself from his encounter with Don Quixote.

In what concerns the self-satisfied mediocrity and physical cowardice latent in his ethos, it is worth pointing out that the character's *first name*, Diego, is a diminutive of *Santiago* or Saint James. This name therefore contrasts Don Diego ironically with "Saint James the Moorkiller" (Santiago Matamoros), Spain's national exemplar of the Christian hero, or the quintessential "saint in short stirrups." It is hardly accidental that the "tawny velvet" of his cap and cloak should be described as "terciopelo *leonado*" [literally: lion-colored velvet]—another, more cryptic, reference by the author in these chapters to the idea of "lion" turned pussycat. But, if the name Diego suggests ironic censure of folly (cowardice), that name may also contain a hidden note of praise. One must bear in mind the clear affinity between Spain's semiofficial, chivalric understanding of "heroic virtue" and Don Quixote's derivative ethos of knight-errantry. It is because of the affinity between those two conceptions of "sanctity"—those two conceptions of the Christian knight—that the protagonist laughs at Sancho's assessment of Don Diego as a "saint." For that laughter amounts to Don Quixote's scornfully dismissing Don Diego as a "knight."

Yet in the chapter devoted to Don Quixote's examination of the icons, our hero proves unsuccessful in his efforts to maintain any equation between sainthood and knighthood. His failure in this regard becomes especially evident in his contrived description of Saint Paul: "knight-errant in life, tenderfoot saint in death" (caballero andante por la vida, y santo a pie quedo por la muerte) (*DQ* II:

23. On Neoepicurean *aurea mediocritas*, see Márquez Villanueva 1975, 161. Lurking beneath this doctrine, of course, is lukewarmness, one of the chief enemies of the spiritual life, associated with worldly riches, first denounced in the Book of Revelation, in John's letter to the seventh church at Laodicea: "I know all about you: how you are neither cold nor hot. I wish you were one or the other, but since you are neither, but only lukewarm, I will spit you out of my mouth. You say to yourself, 'I am rich, I have made a fortune, and have everything I want,' never realizing that you are wretchedly and pitiably poor, and blind and naked too" (Rev. 3:15–18).

58, 473). Indeed, Paul's sainthood effectively resists the Procrustean bed of Don Quixote's code, or semiotic system. So, the protagonist's ethos of heroism may be an effective mirror for Don Diego, but is hardly superior, or free of defects.[24] Don Quixote, like Don Diego, represents at once a paradoxical character and the object of Cervantes' parody or unstable irony. In this light, one may come to understand that besides satirizing cowardice, the name "Diego" also satirizes a facile, quixotic equation between heroic virtue and manliness, on the one hand, and military prowess and vain temerity, on the other. In short, the doubly satirical name also alludes to the spiritual strength of *character* (an interior and enlarged form of Santiago-like fortitude) that this Diego reveals, in inchoate form, after pondering the cogent lunacy of the Knight of the Lions—a lunacy that posed a bracing challenge to the cowardice first intimated in his habit of pious skimming.

Equally important, both the character and the reader have come to observe that one's self-knowledge and identity are neither devoid of all structure nor perfectly completed forms, but an aesthetic project that, like the text, remains perennially "under construction" and dialectically in the making. Indeed, with respect to the self, and with respect to discourse about the self, Cervantes' text dramatizes the paradoxical need for sameness in change and stability in instability. If they are to understand the action within Cervantes' narrative, both characters and readers must rely on the *momentary stability* of logical and semantic categories that govern two contrary codes, and that govern two contrary readings of the episodes involving Don Diego and Don Quixote. This is so whether that "action" takes shape as a fictional narrative (reader) or as a "historical" experience (Don Diego). On the other hand, the chief defect of each code is shown to derive from its static, archetypal, and atemporal pretensions.[25] Such rigidity of thought and discourse is shown to obviate understanding, foreclose (by trying to "resolve") mystery, and prevent dialogue.

Don Diego's novel openness to apparent contradiction—to a dialogic process revealing virtue in apparent vice, sanity in apparent madness, or self in other—enables him to invest his discourse, for a time, with a humanizing flexibility. Thus, he begins to enlarge, through an ultimately mysterious act of freedom, his logical and semantic categories of both judgment and action. His attitude of

24. Castro (1974, 141) gives his famous assessment of how Cervantes viewed "saints in short stirrups"—an assessment that, I believe, unduly glorifies the purportedly liberating (because individualistic) ethos of Don Quixote. In a similar vein, Márquez Villanueva seems to overstate the same issue, dismissively claiming that Cervantes views "saints in short stirrups" *simply* as "objects of laughter" (cosa de risa) (1975, 168).

25. On Cervantes' language of travel and motion, see Hutchinson 1992.

reflective wonder (*admiratio*) and respect toward Don Quixote reveals the likelihood of his openness to further novelty, mystery and paradox.

Reinforcing the idea of stability in instability, and the need for openness to novelty and paradox, the symbolism in these chapters appears more dynamic than "emblematic." What is more, it seems more tenable to perceive the author's symbolism, throughout the narrative, as shifting and kaleidoscopic in its significance, thus predicated upon a narrative logic of developing intelligibility and cumulative effect.

Likewise, as set forth in these chapters, it is important to stress that the life narrative of Don Diego, together with its "meaning," remain unfinished. What is more, at the *close* of II, 18, his story and its meaning have begun anew. It is a story that "ends" with a fresh beginning, with intimations of a forthcoming conversion or its opposite. The character seems to recognize, and through him the reader may choose to recognize, their shared moral place in the middest: somewhere between vice and virtue, or madness and sanity. Within the larger narrative that centers on Don Quixote, the tale of Don Diego's moral, logical, and semantic impasse does not constitute a full story about his life, but rather a life story *in potentia*.

As already discussed, Don Diego's original self-definition shows him at a stage of his life analogous to that of the mad hidalgo in the first chapter of Part I, when the latter set the terms of a semiotic system that would govern the rest of his personal history. Respectively, those two pregnant moments of the narrative reveal one hidalgo relying on an archetypal, literary understanding of self to embark on a career of choleric extravagance, and thus avert historic oblivion; the other relying on an equally archetypal, literary understanding of self to sink into sanguine conformism, and thus embrace historic oblivion.

By the time he meets Don Diego on the road, the knight seems to possess a "history" in every sense of that term. For this reason, he casts his self-definition chiefly in the preterite tense: "I *departed* my native land, *pawned* my estate, *left* my luxury behind, and *delivered* myself into the arms of Fortune" (*Salí* de mi patria, *empeñé* mi hacienda, *dejé* mi regalo, y *entreguéme* en los brazos de la Fortuna). Nonetheless, the protagonist strives to make his life narrative flow with an inexorable logic from the archetypal self-definition that begins his historical summary: "*I am* a knight 'of those whom the people say, / they go forth, seeking their adventures'" ([*S*]*oy* caballero "destos que dicen las gentes / que a sus aventuras van") (*DQ* II: 16, 151; emphasis added). In fact, Don Quixote seems to believe that by uttering this archetypal definition of his ethos (coterminous with his madness) he will do away with Don Diego's sense of wonder: "but you will cease to do so [to wonder] when I tell you, as I am telling you, that I am a knight" (pero dejará vuesa merced de estarlo [maravillado] cuando le diga, como le digo, que soy caballero) (*DQ* II: 16, 152). He is, of course, mistaken in this prediction.

More significant, however, what Don Quixote says about his historic self is erroneous, if not mendacious. Intentionally or no, he is "telling lies." The reader will remember that the protagonist, while still an hidalgo, pawned only part of his estate, and that he did so not to pursue his career in knight errantry, but to purchase more romances of chivalry. Furthermore, the knight left no life of "luxury" (regalo), but a marginal hidalgo's life of idleness, ennui, and addle-brained fantasy. In addition, Don Quixote grossly misrepresents both the content and success of his written "history."

Fittingly, then, II, 16 begins with the knight's continued delusions of grandeur rather than with the meeting between him and Don Diego. In that moment of the narrative, Don Quixote refuses to acknowledge that he has not defeated a fellow knight, but his neighbor, the university graduate Sansón Carrasco. Furthermore, our hero attributes the likeness obtaining between his "enemy's" visage and that of Sansón to the ubiquitous enchanters. His story and his self-ignorance have therefore proceeded apace with his semiotic system and his original self-definition, both of which remain not only fixed and closed but also in a state of continuing conflict with the physical objects, events, and persons of his surroundings. If Don Quixote continues to stand as a moral paradox, it is because his lunacy remains integral to his "heroism"—the reforming ideals warped by his madness, his real virtues such as courage, honesty, and fidelity, and his depth of conviction. None of this, however, makes him either sane or self-aware. And the text nowhere presents the knight's depth of conviction, or fanaticism, as a measure of morality. But to compromise the knight's lunacy would mean compromising his ability to act as an effective mirror on Don Diego and on other characters and codes within the heterocosm. In other words, it would compromise the wisdom contained in his particular enterprise and his particular form of madness.

What we observe in Don Diego, by contrast, is but the beginning of a life narrative that is potentially different in kind. But the chapters devoted to the beginning of a potential story seem to deny their readers the false solace of closure. We are left to conjecture about the potentially heroic, felicitous, tragic, or pathetic outcome of Don Diego's life narrative, and about whether he will continue to grow in self-knowledge once his "adventure" with Don Quixote comes to an end. Even when we reach the close of the chapters concerning the encounter between Don Quixote and Don Diego, I believe it would be rash to judge Don Diego an exemplary figure. His ability to undertake a *pursuit* of "virtue" will depend on his willingness not only to continue pondering, but also to continue assimilating features of the knight's heroic/lunatic ethos. Indeed, as Don Diego himself seems to recognize, the remedy for his own folly lies precisely in those features of Don Quixote's ethos that our man in green and tawny velvet once found most insane and imprudent.

It is true that Don Diego begins to reform his behavior toward his son. Moreover, his behavior toward Don Quixote and Sancho evinces a willingness to overcome his habits of timidity, lukewarmness, and conformism. But a potential for self-absorption continues to linger in Don Diego, as suggested in his vain sartorial habits. In addition, one negative element of his portrait remains unaddressed: namely, if he is not a philanderer—and, despite the emblematic symbolism noted by Percas de Ponseti, there is no textual evidence to suggest that he is—Don Diego shows a rather alarming disregard for his wife.[26] The contrast between the emblematic symbolism and the evidence—together with Don Diego's confusing remark about how many children he has—may point to a life that is as deficient in erotics and marital love as it is in heroics.

Don Diego, then, remains a moral paradox as well—worthy by turns of praise and blame—an exemplum, as it were, of virtually every reader's moral place in the middest. As we accompany Don Quixote and Sancho at the close of II, 18, we leave Don Diego in his embryonic stage of self-awareness, marked by his capacity for self-scrutiny, reflective wonder, and incipient moral reform. Hence, without denying the relevance of other, earlier meanings (folly and sane conservatism, vanity and conformism), I would suggest that at this stage of the narrative, we also regard Don Diego's identifying color, repeated thirteen times over the course of three chapters, in an equally traditional fashion: as a *latent* symbol, beneath the tawny velvet (an image of comfort) and gold (a paradoxical image of riches, maturity, spring, and harvest), of surprising rebirth and *hope*. But that hope and rebirth, for character and "involved reader" alike, remain an open question.

In addition, it is worth noting how, in these chapters, Cervantes structures his temporal and spatial settings to underscore his thematics of moral and social exemplarity and, so, to underscore his axiological paradoxy. Don Quixote and Don Diego meet, examine each other and introduce themselves *while traveling* on horseback. Their common status as "knights" and "horsemen" (caballeros) also provides the first, most evident source of their opposition. Furthermore, Don Quixote has been traveling *away from home* in search of *adventure*, whereas Don Diego is *on his way home* after what is clearly a short *trip*, or perhaps only a

---

26. Márquez Villanueva views Doña Cristina as "a piece of furniture that Don Diego acquires in order to bring maximum order and comfort to his home" (una especie de mueble adquirido por don Diego para traer a su casa el máximo de orden y comodidad) (1975, 177 n. 46).

stroll. In the following chapter, while Don Quixote *dismounts* in order to await his confrontation with a caged lion in an open field, Don Diego *flees*, remaining safely astride his mare, at a considerable distance from potential danger. Don Quixote's "victorious" return and triumphant remarks provoke neither action or reaction, but only humble reflection and more judicious words from Don Diego, for whom a chivalric "adventure" has just become a historical reality.

On the one hand, however, it is important to realize that at the literal level of action, Don Quixote's adventure with the lion is more apparent than real. His "heroic deeds" take the absurd form of his "confronting" a lion's hind quarters. On the other hand, his challenge proves ironically heroic and startling in its anticlimax because of what it reveals about the *inner* qualities of our Silenic hero. The significance, "reality," and "heroism" of this "adventure" are not lost on Don Diego, as shown in his generous invitation, itself revelatory of his Christian, Epicurean ethos:

> And let us make haste, since it is getting late; and let us go to my village and my home, where you can rest from your recent labors, which, if not of the body, are of the soul, and which are likely to weary the body.

> (Y démonos priesa, que se hace tarde, y lleguemos a mi aldea y casa, donde descansará vuestra merced del pasado trabajo, que *si no ha sido del cuerpo, ha sido del espíritu,* que suele tal vez redundar en cansancio del cuerpo (*DQ* II: 17, 168; emphasis added)

Don Diego's laudatory "deeds" are likewise hidden and spiritual; and they occur in the setting of his home. Furthermore, they are no less "real" than those of Don Quixote. At the level of action alone, such deeds consist of his playing host to Don Quixote and Sancho for four days and his undertaking a respectful conversation with his son. Yet at another level, they reveal a potentially heroic self-transformation. Oddly enough, the potential for such courage and self-reform is shown to be present in his Neoepicurean ethos, but emerges only thanks to his ability to transform and enlarge that ethos according to the demands of experience.[27] Thus the paradoxical *admiratio* of Cervantes' text

---

27. It is indeed paradoxical that Cervantes should so portray the compatibility between a radical Christianity, based on heroic virtue, and an Epicurean philosophy, popularly—and wrongly—thought to border on a moral philosophy of hedonism. As Márquez Villanueva rightly points out, such Christian humanists as the martyr Saint Thomas More found Epicureanism to be the most compatible of all pagan philosophies with Christianity (1975, 171). Thus, the Christian ethics of Cervantes diverges radically from the abstemious hauteur of Neostoicism, as propounded by writers such as Francisco de Quevedo.

arises from his investing the ambience of Don Quixote's lunacy and nonadventures, as well as the domestic ordinariness of Don Diego's conduct, with *hidden* wonders or "marvels."

It is therefore especially fitting that *the enclosed mansion* where Don Diego's deeds unfold should remain undescribed, except where its most salient feature of "marvelous," monastic silence is noted. In this regard, the image of the mansion as a monastery appears in a positive light—a symbol *in bono*. Thus, regarding his "travels" and the manner in which he makes use of both his time and his property, Don Diego represents Don Quixote's obverse reflection, both his opposite and likeness in appearance, word, and deed. More specifically, as reflected in both his person and his home, Don Diego de Miranda displays his laudable capacity for contemplation and wonderment—again appearing strangely like and unlike Don Quixote. But before his encounter with the knight, Don Diego seems to embody the defective traits of personal and social inaction, as well as timid, sedentary conformism. With regard to Don Diego's defects, then, the paradoxical image of the "monastic" mansion betokens the owner's social insularity— a symbol *in malo*. Don Quixote's wisely foolish words and deeds, expressed and enacted before the two men arrive at the mansion, eventually call forth Don Diego's strengths, obliging him to probe his conscience, face his weaknesses, and take his first steps toward self-reform.

The third chapter (II, 18) summarizes the events of four days in Don Diego's home. It therefore signals a dramatic shift in narrative setting and greatly reduces the proportion between textual space and the story's presumptive duration. The reader receives no explicit information about how Don Diego reacts to the behavior of Don Quixote during this visit. Yet it seems plausible to claim that the wealthy hidalgo is probably less than pleased about the protagonist's encouraging Lorenzo's literary endeavors, praising the boy as though he deserved to be poet laureate of Spain, and finally urging the youth to forsake his poetry and university studies in order to pursue a career in knight errantry.[28] One may easily speculate

---

28. As even the doubly fictional "voice" of Cide Hamete (a creation of the narrator) "realizes," such adulation may prove an impediment to the self-knowledge of Don Lorenzo: "Is it not fitting that they say that Don Lorenzo took delight in hearing Don Quixote praise him, even though he judged him to be mad? Oh, power of adulation, how far you extend, and how vast the frontiers of your pleasurable dominion!" (¿No es bueno que dicen que se holgó don Lorenzo de verse alabar de don Quijote, aunque le tenía por loco? ¡Oh fuerza de la adulación, a cuánto te estiendes, y cuán dilatados límites son los de tu juridición agradable!) (*DQ* II: 18, 175). Just before he departs, Don Quixote gives the youth some sound advice in this regard, echoing the prologuist of Part I: "for there is no father or mother for whom their children are ugly, and regarding offspring of the mind we are even more prone to such beguilement" (porque no hay padre ni madre a quien sus hijos le parezcan feos, y en los que lo son del entendimiento corre más este engaño) (*DQ* I: 18, 177). There is a double irony here, together with a twofold parody of both the protagonist and the narrator, speaking in the "voice" of the Arab historian. First, it is extremely

that in other ways as well, the protagonist's behavior would have made the master of the household uneasy. Even so, the narrative reports no explicit conflict or disagreement between these two characters. Tellingly, however, Don Quixote is eager *to leave* the mansion, claiming that idleness and luxury are unfit for a man of his profession. But another clear, if implicit, source of Don Quixote's discomfiture is that he not only starts to enjoy the Epicurean life, but also perceives in Don Diego a disquieting mirror reflection of himself and his own failings.[29] Here, as elsewhere, Don Quixote resists being either startled or lulled into self-examination—into rethinking his *imitatio Amadís*. It is from just such a contemplative and domestic "adventure" that Don Quixote chooses *to flee*.

In sum, the temporal and spatial structure of these episodes about a knight-errant and a "knight" complacent—about an encounter between two contrary and complementary characters, their analogous adventures, and their analogous acceptance and rejection of adventure—reinforces the textual interplay between contemplation and action, poetry and history, being and becoming, and self and other. Moreover, the structured openness of the chapters merges the chrono-topical, or temporal/spatial, image of Don Quixote's *quest on the road* with that of Don Diego de Miranda's *days spent* leisurely (or was it idly?) *at home*. The incomplete and unfolding tale concerning Don Diego's aporetic crisis of self-knowledge thus holds together opposing images of fixity and flux, harmony and discord, quest and flight, in a paradoxical state of cooperative tension.

Reading the Mirror: The Unexemplary Quest for Heroism, Truth, and Self

In the character of Don Diego, Cervantes puts forth his parodic exemplum of a particular kind of moral agent and "idle" or "leisurely" reader. Like the reading

---

odd that the narrator should draw our attention to the problem of self-knowledge only in this most obvious (and probably least perilous) instance, while failing to suggest that this is one of the chief issues affecting the protagonist and pervading the entire chapter. Of course, this reference is also one of the means whereby Cervantes underscores the ethical and aesthetic problem for the reader. Second, as a type of reader and judge akin to the narrator, here assuming the mask of Cide Hamete, Don Quixote fails to realize that his advice applies most tellingly to his own case; for, as Don Quixote, he is the "ugly" lunatic "son" of his own poetic understanding. As two embodiments of a literalist *doxa*, both the narrator and Don Quixote are portrayed as rather insufferable preachers, adept at seeing the mote in another person's eye.

29. In his elegant article, Randolph Pope (1979, 207–18) argues that, while visiting the Mirandas, Don Quixote feels tempted by wealth and comfort to forsake his heroic quest. Yet it seems to me that the "temptation" arising here is less to wealth and comfort than to the "deadly sin" of envy toward Don Diego.

and writing of Cervantes' narrative, Don Diego's *ethical* progress in self-knowledge will continue to depend on his *aesthetic* refashioning of historical and literary models, including the historicopoetic model of Don Quixote. In other words, it will depend on Don Diego's commitment to enlarging, through *inventio* and critical reflection, the logical and semantic categories that govern the rhetoric of those models, or those "texts." In particular, Don Diego's potential for growth in virtue, which he has yet to live to an "heroic degree," would depend on whether he chose to pursue a *quest* for self-knowledge. Such a quest would entail a laudably social form of self-love and learned ignorance, because purged of self-referential pride, self-preference, conformism, and pseudomonastic isolation from the "other," or the opposite, within himself.

As a paradoxical exemplum of readers and moral agents, and of readers as moral agents, Don Diego discovers the limited power of our codes, of fictions, or of the artifice of discourse to make sense of experience or define our individual and collective lives. His scrutinizing the paradox that Don Quixote offers in appearance, word, and deed incites Don Diego to reflective wonder and "alienates" or detaches him, in an example of logical paradox, from the terms that define his semiotic system or ethos. In a practical fashion, he learns from Don Quixote's *example* that those systems deriving from the poetic imagination can achieve only a partial stay against our confusion and perplexity. And the "alienating" effect which the character called Don Quixote produces in Don Diego provides an analogue of the effect, or the *admiratio*, that the fiction called *Don Quixote* seems designed to produce in its readers.

Nonetheless, as Don Diego discovers from his reflecting on the paradox of Don Quixote, and as the reader discovers from his or her negotiating the paradoxes of Cervantes' textual maze, codes of limited yet real power, and partial stays against the confusion of experience remain infinitely superior to the darkness, discord, and chaos that would result from an absence of logical and semantic codes. In Mexía's phrase, our lacking the *art* of our codes, fictions, or semiotic systems would lead all human activity and knowledge to end in "confusion and forgetting." Consequently, the narrative links Don Diego's paradoxical "exemplarity" to his remaining unfinished, both ethically and aesthetically, and his continually beckoning toward ethical and aesthetic completion. Don Diego becomes laudable and exemplary to the degree that he recognizes his insufficiency and rejects the status of finished exemplar. Within Cervantes' innovative rhetoric of moral and poetic exemplarity, which makes virtue or "heroism" inseparable from deficiency, Don Diego comes to exemplify an innovative form of prudence and fortitude. For he would rather observe and listen, in reflective silence, to an opposing view than suppress, or *silence*, such a challenge to his formerly untested assumptions.

On the one hand, then, Don Diego's attitude compares favorably with the unreflective *complacency* and *spiritual* cowardice expressed in the un-Socratic adage "I know who I am" and in the quest-as-flight that doom the knight to *self*-defeat. As Cervantes' narrative progressively reveals, the fixity and antinomy—the wholly internal reference and self-contained quality—of Don Quixote's self-figuration come to deprive him of semantic and social space. His unswerving commitment to a rigid code and to an ethos of life-as-discourse ensnares him in a vicious circle of contradictions, misadventures and rebuffs. His archetypal pretensions render him a victim of his own *art*, a fool fooled, or a variation of "the trickster tricked" (*burlador burlado*). In contrast to Don Diego's attitude of self-examination, Don Quixote's increasing failure to reconcile experience with the fixities of his code provides little occasion for reflective wonder or reassessment, but serves only to increase his chronic melancholy. In part, Don Quixote represents the *reductio ad absurdum* of readers, authors and texts that equate "truth," not with a quest, but with aprioristic certainty or formulaic closure.

On the other hand, Don Diego's habit of playing it safe, in a spirit of "prudent" conformism, compares unfavorably with the heroic *excess* that leads Don Quixote to confront the literal and symbolic lion, and likewise to persevere, with unbroken fidelity, in his mission and his service to Dulcinea. In the face of danger and contradiction, our hero courageously pursues his absurd project to its absurd end, thus letting the "knight's" defeat yield to the hidalgo's triumph and self-conquest. Thanks to his historicopoetic personalities, our fully Silenic protagonist finds success and, indeed, "salvation" in apparent failure. His mad enterprise provides the medium for his attainment of "heroic virtue," since the personality called Don Quixote constitutes the only "heroic" part of the moribund Alonso Quixano, at the end of the tale, and the only part of our formerly homebound protagonist that allows him to *perform* and *share* his real "virtues." Thanks to the transformative "mercies of God," our hero's insane, chivalric career comes to mark his path to "eternal glory" in a manner that *infinitely* exceeds the fantasies that motivated our crazed hidalgo at the start of Part I. As an inventive *imitatio* of the "holy fool," the specifically Pauline or Franciscan "fool for Christ" and Folly's children who attain *divinitas* in Erasmus' paradoxical encomium, our hero comes to represent, in his moment of death, the seeming oxymoron of lunacy beatified, or an extreme, Cervantine refashioning of folly praised.

In short, both Don Diego and Don Quixote emerge from the narrative as Silenic figures and each of them acts as a mirror for the other. They shape their "lives" after contrary yet complementary codes. In the realm of action, they reveal complementary forms of cowardice and heroism, just as they reveal complementary forms of wisdom and folly in the realm of thought and expression, or knowledge, self-knowledge, and discourse. Neither of them cuts a straightforward, "exemplary figure." And neither ultimately proves deserving, without qualification, of an epithet such as "the Good."

More self-consciously, however, the dialectical encounter in these chapters between Don Diego de Miranda and Don Quixote encapsulates the reader's encounter with Cervantes' Silenic fiction-as-history, ingeniously crafted to resist closure and mirror its potentially idle or active readers. As shown rather than preached in Cervantes' narrative, an openness to paradox engenders a sense of communion between self and other in a common quest for truth. But that quest pursues a necessarily elusive and unfolding truth—about an evolving yet "real" self, other, society, or world. *Don Quixote* dramatizes the degree to which that "truth," or the Truth-as-One, lies forever in the future, *infinitely* approachable or knowable in itself, yet surpassing the *limits* of time and history and the *terms* of our consoling fictions. Particularly in these chapters, Cervantes' work depicts seemingly ordinary encounters between self and other, or between reader, text, and life, as potential encounters with the marvelous: *est Deus in nobis.* Hence, such encounters provide no occasion for final certainty. Instead, they call for reflection in the face of unfolding mystery, and for the *continuing action* of *mutual* self-fashioning, dialogue, and self-renewal.

Concluding Remarks

It is now a commonplace of literary studies to cite *Don Quixote* as the forerunner of the modern and contemporary novel. And in my view, among the most perceptive observations on that subject is the following assertion by Robert Alter: "The novel begins out of an erosion of belief in the authority of the written word and it begins with Cervantes" (1975, 3).[1] Nonetheless, a possible inference of the preceding study is that in *Don Quixote*, Cervantes effects an "erosion of belief" that hardly seems confined to "the *written* word." As both a synthesis and refashioning of Western paradoxy, the text invites readers to question the "authority" of all human discourse (historical, poetic, oral, or written) that shapes those constructs we call knowledge and history.

---

1. Parr's elegant and witty *Anatomy of Subversive Discourse* (1988) argues that Cervantes' satire of the written word in Don Quixote goes to the extreme of subverting and desacralizing Holy Writ.

Even if one may justifiably balk at defining its "purpose," an unsettling *effect* of paradoxy in *Don Quixote* arises from the drama it creates of discourse undoing its own "authority," or exposing its own fictiveness, and thus revealing through countless examples how deceptively art masquerades as nature, literature as life, or "telling" as "being." Such is the effect of Cervantes' "story" transparently masquerading as "history" and, perhaps less transparently, of the mutual masquerade involving historical and poetic discourse in both the Prologue and title page to Part I. Such also is the effect in the main narrative of such parodic characters as the protagonist, Cardenio, Ginés de Pasamonte and the youths of the "Feigned Arcadia" who openly shape their "historical" actions after poetic models. But categories of thought and expression likewise exemplify their own fictiveness in *Don Quixote* through less parodic characters such as the Captive and Zoraida, whose "lives" seem unwittingly to imitate fictional discourse in the form of a Moorish novel.

Moreover, through the verbal medium of Cervantes' text, human discourse exposes its inherent deceitfulness or lack of *moral* authority through such characters as the "noble" duke and duchess, their subjects, and Sansón Carrasco in Part II. In the first place, as readers of Cide Hamete's history, in Part I, and as the protagonist's true enemy "enchanters," these individuals both lie and *enact* their lies in an effort to gain authorial control over the knight's elaborate fiction, the better to use him as their character or plaything and thus entertain themselves at that knight's, or their "fool's," expense. Further, these characters' words and deeds alike expose the inability of discursive categories in thought or language—the most careful plans or authoritative pronouncements—to accommodate the ultimately unfathomable variety of "nature" or "life." As ingenious variations on the topos of the trickster tricked (*burlador burlado*), these fictional persons unwittingly *imitate* the protagonist by becoming ensnared as *characters* within his and their own fictions, trapped by his and their own language, or victims of his and their own art.[2] And from yet another perspective, exposing the unfounded "authority" of discourse is also the effect of how Cervantes characterizes the seemingly exemplary Don Diego de Miranda, content to model his life after commonplaces deriving from works of moral philosophy or Christian piety.

Yet, finally, I would contend that undermining the "authority" and exposing the masquerade of discourse remains integral to the purpose of an author, implied by the text, whose self-undermining discourse creates the illusion of receding depths and of more or less original sources, imitations or models for the "true history" we

---

2. Ruth El Saffar, in her groundbreaking study titled *Distance and Control* (1975), was the first to analyze in detail how characters in *Don Quixote* lose authorial control over, and distance from, their own fictions.

are "now reading." For it is the same, textually implied author who "speaks" primarily through the voice of his narrator, a fictional "author," in turn represented as using discourse to beget the "lie" of an Arab source that will lend "authority" to his "history." Cervantes thus extends Guevara's use of historical "spoof," or what I have termed icastic fantasy, in order to create the Aristotelian contradiction of historical *poesis*. So what Alter rightly calls the "self-conscious genre" of the novel would seem to begin with Cervantes' purposeful conflation of historical and poetic discourse. Or put another way, it would seem to begin with his conflation of "stories" and "histories" engaging in mutual parody and self-parody, and his thus provoking an erosion of belief in the authority of the word.

However, to view the paradoxy of *Don Quixote* as a discursive act of "subversion" that begins and ends in an "erosion" seems to be, in every sense, only part of the story. Indeed, I would contend that both the purpose and effect of Cervantes' paradoxical discourse in *Don Quixote* consist of creating a feast of discourse through an act of narrative rhypography that celebrates and extols humanity's place in the middest. In view of this study's preceding discussion, Cervantes' fiction emerges as a dramatized mock encomium of "the word" (*razones, logoi*), or a mixed, cornucopian satire within the multigeneric, Menippean tradition aiming at *homo significans*, or "man" the symbolic, signifying animal. And the symbolic quality and animality of that paradoxical creature remain, in Cervantes' text, of equal importance. For the spirit animating Cervantes' paradoxy, or his parody of discourse, differs sharply from the urge of his protagonist to decry and seek liberation from the contingencies of social intercourse, time and matter, including the matter of one's own body.

Just as parody in *Don Quixote* achieves more than what the friend of the Prologue calls an "invective" against the "authority and sway" of its historical and poetic models, so that fiction's paradoxy achieves more than an invective against the authority of the word. For if both *Don Quixote* and Don Quixote jointly come forth as nothing less than a mock encomium of poetic and historical discourse, that "encomium" provokes an equal measure of praise, censure, *admiratio*, and laughter. The effect, and most likely the purpose, of Cervantes' self-conscious mock encomium is at once metafictional, metahistorical, and metadiscursive. Its purpose and effect consist, in other words, of provoking "alienation" or critical reflection on the logical and linguistic categories of received opinion (*doxa*). Beginning with a Prologue and title page in which historical and poetic discourse exchange their "masks," Cervantes creates a fiction that absorbs and transforms the "facts" of its own history as an empirical text. He creates a fiction that tirelessly exposes, varies, and celebrates the masquerade of art as nature, literature as life, and of "telling" as "being" and "truth." It is also beginning with the Prologue that Cervantes dramatizes and thematizes not only the "common" paradoxes of art in nature, or literature in life, but also the more startling paradox that "nature," "life," "being," and "truth" must pass through the fictive categories of discursive imitation in order "to appear," or in order to be continually discovered, refashioned, and, in that way, rediscovered.

Moreover, because it assumes the viciously circular structure of a dramatized mock encomium aiming at human discourse, the author's fiction manages to exploit simultaneously all the types and topical strains of Renaissance paradoxy that I sought to classify in the opening pages of Chapter 3. Against the most common assumptions (*para-doxa*) about language, thought, truth, the "cosmos," and the self, both the form and content of *Don Quixote* serve to dramatize the "startling truth" that every utterance in either the historical or poetic mode is an act of imitation. Hence, the text exemplifies that one may *truthfully* recast every such utterance in the baffling rather than simply negative terms of a prototypical "antinomy": "This statement is false." That possible recasting holds for any statement that one may choose to utter about the "truth" of history, which reaches us only by means of *fragments* riven with error, bias, and mendacity, as dramatized explicitly in the narration relating the "discovery" of Cide Hametes's manuscript. The fiction self-consciously uses historical and poetic discourse both for and against themselves (logical paradoxy). It thus invites us to reevaluate rather than simply negate the discursive categories and semiotic systems whereby we judge matters such as sanity, madness, fact, fiction, the laudable, or the base (axiological paradoxy). Further, *Don Quixote* dramatizes that, by means of the same, fictive categories, we attempt "to know" and utter "true" propositions about what are shown to be a protean world and a protean self that unfold in time as a continuing dialectic between act and potency, being and nonbeing, likeness and unlikeness, or self and other (cosmological and psychological paradoxy). And as a mock encomium of discourse, *Don Quixote* offers a poetic imitation which contains and fails to contain imitations of imitations within imitations, all deriving from rival semiotic systems or *doxa*. As a fictional analogue of the imitations constituting "life," the fiction's discourse creates a finite emblem of the incomprehensible and the infinite. For that discourse simulates how in life and literature alike, the countless imitations deriving from discursive categories unfold as a *via negativa*, or an endless, negative assertion of the unfathomable "Truth-as-One." But Cervantes' mock encomium of discourse also presents a Ciceronian paradox, or what we may call a committed rhetoric, with ethical as well as aesthetic implications.

Cervantes' fiction about a protagonist who strives to imitate a particular type of poetic discourse represents the particular *imitatio* that we know as "discourse" less as a series of "words" (*dichos*) than of deeds (*hechos*). To be sure, the madness of the protagonist places his deeds outside the realm of moral culpability. Not so, however, with the narrative voices and other characters in the fiction who are likewise defined by their discourse and often by the *deceitful* fictions that they choose to create. Although, to paraphrase the narrator's words in the Prologue to Part I, we are known to possess "free will" or our "souls in our bodies," the fiction represents that it finally lies beyond our power to choose whether "life" will entail imitations derived from models and our discursive categories. Rather, from the opening words of its fictional Prologue, the text dramatizes how our power of choice first seems to consist of whether we shall undertake our life-as-*imitatio* (as we undertake our "inventive" reading of the text itself) in a manner that is "leisured" yet self-aware or uncritical and "idle." In addition, our power of choice is shown to consist of how we respond, fail to respond, or refuse to respond to the aporia created by the protagonist and the "history," which move many of the fiction's characters to *admiratio* or, in the narrator's phrase, "great silence" (*silencio grande*).

The aping method of "perfect imitation," as espoused and counseled by the narrator's "comical" friend in the Prologue of 1605, seems accurately to describe the ethos of most characters in the fiction who, like the protagonist and the narrator himself, act "without questioning the words" (*sin ponerlas [razones] en disputa*) that configure their verbal and nonverbal deeds. An altogether different species of *imitatio* seems to inform the author's poetic "deed" of aesthetic refashioning and enlargement through discourse. It seems hardly accidental that such an author should represent uncritical imitation of a "code" or "poetic truth" in a particular *form* as the measure of folly, and insanity, in his fiction. For, on the one hand, such intellectually "idle" folly is shown to blind one to the generally unyielding constraints of time, space, matter, and even (in the case of Don Quixote) such bodily needs as eating and sleeping. On the other hand, that "idle" folly is also shown to blind one to the less unyielding, though no less "real," constraints of prevailing systems in discourse and to the social and cultural arrangements that those systems bring about. The author's fiction seems to invite our reflection on the possibilities for personal and collective inventiveness that lie hidden within "nature," ourselves, and existing "models." It is hardly incidental to Cervantes' fiction, I believe, that the discourse, rhetoric, and poetics of *Don Quixote* should praise the "folly" of how we use our discourse to fashion a life that is specifically human. And it hardly seems incidental to Cervantes' self-conscious paradoxy that *Don Quixote* should encourage a continuing sense of wonder in the face of ethical and aesthetic projects (knowledge, truth, history, or oneself) that promise to remain both possible and unfinished.

WORKS CITED

Albrecht, James, ed. 1975. *A Treasury of Prayers*. New Rochelle, N.Y.: Scepter Press.
Alemán, Mateo. 1983. *Guzmán de Alfarache*. Edited by Francisco Rico. 1599, 1602. Barcelona: Planeta.
Allen, John J. 1969–79. *Don Quixote: Hero or Fool?* 2 vols. Gainesville: University Press of Florida.
Alter, Robert. 1975. *Partial Magic: The Novel as Self-Conscious Genre*. Berkeley and Los Angeles: University of California Press.
Aristotle. 1982. *Poetics*. Translated by James Hutton. New York: Norton.
———. 1985. *Nichomachean Ethics*. Translated by Terrence Irwin. New York: Hackett.
Auerbach, Erich. 1957. *Mimesis: The Representation of Reality in Western Literature*. Translated by Willard Trask. New York: Doubleday.
Avalle-Arce, Juan Bautista. 1976. *"Don Quijote" como forma de vida*. Valencia: Editorial Castalia.
Avalle-Arce, Juan Bautista, and Edward C. Riley, eds. 1973. *Suma cervantina*. London: Tamesis.
Azar, Inés. 1988. "The Archeology of Fiction in *Don Quijote*." *Cervantes*, special issue (Winter): 117–26.
Bakhtin, Mikhail. 1968. *Rabelais and His World*. Translated by Helen Iswolsky. Cambridge: MIT Press.
———. 1984. *Problems of Dostoevsky's Poetics*. Edited and translated by Caryl Emerson. Minneapolis: University of Minnesota Press.
Báñez, Domingo. 1966. *The Primacy of Existence in Thomas Aquinas*. Translated by Benjamin S. Llanzon. 1584. Chicago: Henry Regnery.
Barilli, Renato. 1989. *Rhetoric*. Translated by Giuliana Menozzi. Minneapolis: University of Minnesota Press.
Barthes, Roland. 1986. *S/Z*. New York: Hill and Wang.
———. 1989. "The Discourse of History." In *The Rustle of Language*. Translated by Richard Howard, 127–40. Berkeley and Los Angeles: University of California Press.
Barwise, John, and John Etchemendy. 1987. *The Liar: An Essay on Truth and Circularity*. New York: Oxford University Press.
Bataillon, Marcel. 1961. *"La Célestine" selon Fernando de Rojas*. Paris: Didier.
———. 1966. *Erasmo y España*. Translated by A. Alatorre. Mexico: Colegio de Mexico.
———. 1971. "Un problème d'influence d'Erasme en Espagne: L'*Eloge de la Folie*." In *Actes du Congrès Erasme, 1969*, 136–47. Amsterdam: Acadèmie Royale Néerlandis.
Bates, Margaret. 1945. *"Discreción" in the Works of Cervantes*. Washington, D.C.: Catholic University of America Press.

Buceta, Erasmo. 1935. "Introducción." In *Paradoxas racionales*, by Antonio López de Vega, edited by Erasmo Buceta, vi–xliii. Madrid: Centro de Estudios Históricos, Revista de Filología Hispánica.

Burckhardt, Jakob. 1950. *The Civilization of the Renaissance in Italy.* 1860. New York: Phaidon.

Burgess, Thedore C. 1902. *Epideictic Literature.* Chicago: University of Chicago Press.

Campbell, Richmond, and Lanning Sowden, eds. 1985. *Paradoxes of Rationality and Cooperation: Prisoner's Dilemma and Mewcomb's Problem.* Vancouver: University of British Columbia Press.

Canavaggio, Jean. 1958. "Alonso López Pinciano y la estética literaria de Cervantes en el *Quijote.*" *Anales Cervantinos* 7:13–107.

———. 1977. "Cervantes en primera persona." *Journal of Hispanic Philology* 2:35–44.

Cano, Melchor. 1962. "Tratado de la victoria de sí mismo." In *Tratados espirituales.* Edited by Vicente Beltrán de Heredia. 1547. Madrid: Editorial Católica.

Cargile, James. 1979. *Paradoxes: A Study in Form and Predication.* Cambridge: Cambridge University Press.

Caro Baroja, Julio. 1965. *El carnaval: análisis histórico-cultural.* Madrid: Taurus.

Casa, Frank. 1968. "Pleberio's Lament for Melibea." *Zeitschrift für Romanische Philologie* 84:19–29.

Casalduero, Joaquín. 1970. *Sentido y forma del "Quijote."* Madrid: Insula.

Cassirer, Ernst. 1963 The Individual and the Cosmos in Renaissance Philosophy. Translated by Mario Domandi. New York: Harper & Row.

Casirrer, Ernst, Paul Oskar Kristeller, and John Herman Randall. 1950. T*he Renaissance Philosophy of Man.* Chicago: University of Chicago Press.

Castillo, Carlos. 1945. "Cervantes y Pero Mexía." *Modern Philology* 43:94–106.

Castro, Américo. 1965. *"La Celestina" como contienda literaria.* Madrid: Revista de Occidente.

———. 1967. *Hacia Cervantes.* Madrid: Taurus.

———. 1972. *El pensamiento de Cervantes.* 1925. Barcelona: Editorial Noguer.

———. 1974. *Cervantes y los casticismos españoles.* Madrid: Alianza Editorial.

Castro, Antonio. 1989. "Introducción." In *Silva de varia lección*, by Pero Mexía, edited by Antonio Castro. 2 vols., 1.1–137. Madrid: Cátedra.

Cave, Terence. 1979. *The Cornucopian Text: Problems of Writing in the French Renaissance.* Oxford: Clarendon Press.

Cervantes Saavedra, Miguel de. 1973. *Viaje del Parnaso.* Edited by Vicente Gaos. Madrid: Castalia.

———. 1978. *El ingenioso hidalgo don Quijote de la Mancha.* 2 vols. Edited by Luis Andrés Murillo. Madrid: Castalia.

———. 1985. *Novelas ejemplares.* 2 vols. Edited by Harry Sieber. 1613. Madrid: Cátedra.

Chamberlain, V. A., and Jack Weiner. 1969. "Color Symbolism: A Key to a Possible Interpretation of Cervantes' 'Caballero del Verde Gabán.'" *Romance Notes* 10:1–6.

Chambers, Leland. 1981. "*Harmonia est Discordia Concors:* The Coincidence of Opposites and Unity in Diversity in the *Quijote.*" In *Cervantes, su obra y su mundo: Actas del I Congreso Internacional sobre Cervantes*, edited by Manuel Criado del Val, 605–15. Madrid: EDI-6.

Champlin, T. S. 1988. *Reflexive Paradoxes.* New York: Routledge.

Chesterton, Gilbert Keith. 1931. *St. Francis of Assisi.* Garden City, N.Y.: Doubleday.

Cicero. 1953. *Paradoxa Stoicorum.* Edited by A. G. Lee. London: Macmillan.

Clarke, Dorothy C. 1968. *Allegory, Decalogue, and Deadly Sins in "La Celestina."* Berkeley and Los Angeles: University of California Press.

Close, Anthony. 1978. *The Romantic Approach to "Don Quixote."* Cambridge: Cambridge University Press.

————. 1990a. "Constructive Testimony: Patronage and Recognition in *Don Quixote*." In *Conflicts of Discourse*, edited by Peter W. Evans. Manchester: Manchester University Press.

————. 1990b. *Don Quixote*. Cambridge: Cambridge University Press.

————. 1993. "A Poet's Vanity." *Cervantes* 13:31–63.

Colie, Rosalie. 1966. *Paradoxia Epidemica*. Princeton: Princeton University Press.

Concejo, Pilar. 1985. *Antonio de Guevara: un ensayista del siglo XVI*. Madrid: Ediciones Cultura Hispánica.

Copleston, Frederick. 1972. *History of Medieval Philosophy*. Notre Dame: University of Notre Dame Press.

————. 1985. *A History of Philosophy*. 9 vols. 1946–74. New York: Doubleday.

Corominas, Joan. 1954. *Diccionario crítico etimológico de la lengua castellana*. Bern: Editorial Francke.

Covarrubias, Sebastián de. 1984. *Tesoro de la lengua Castellana o Española*. 1611. Madrid: Ediciones Turner.

Curtius, Ernst Robert. 1973. *European Literature and the Latin Middle Ages*. Translated by Willard Trask. Princeton: Princeton University Press.

————. 1990. *European Literature and the Latin Middle Ages*. Translated by Willard R. Trask. Princeton: Princeton University Press.

Dawson, Christopher. 1938. *Progress and Religion: An Historical Inquiry*. New York: Sheed and Ward.

————. 1965. *The Dividing of Christendom*. New York: Sheed and Ward.

————. 1985. *Christianity and the New Age*. Manchester, N.H.: Sophia Institute.

del Río, Angel. 1959. "El equívoco del *Quijote*." *Hispanic Review* 27:201–21.

Derrida, Jaques. 1981. *Dissemination*. Translated by Barbara Johnson. Chicago: University of Chicago Press.

Deyermond, A. D. 1961. *The Petrarchan Sources of "La Celestina."* Oxford: Oxford University Press.

————. 1971. *A Literary History of Spain: The Middle Ages*. New York: Barnes & Noble.

Dijk, Theun van. 1974. "Action, Action Description, and Narrative." *Poetics* 5:287–338.

Donne, John. 1980 *Paradoxes and Problems*. Edited by Helen Peters. Oxford: Clarendon Press.

Dunn, Peter. 1975. *Fernando de Rojas*. Boston: Twayne.

————. 1976. "Pleberio's World." *PMLA* 91:406–19.

————. 1982. "Cervantes De/Re-Constructs the Picaresque." *Cervantes* 2:109–31.

Durán, Manuel. 1960. *La ambigüedad en el "Quijote."* Xalapa: Universidad Veracruzana.

Eco, Umberto. 1986. *Art and Beauty in the Middle Ages*. Translated by Hugh Bredin. New Haven: Yale University Press.

————. 1994. *The Limits of Interpretation*. Bloomington: University of Indiana Press.

————. 1995. *Six Walks in the Fictional Woods*. Cambridge: Harvard University Press.

Efron, Arthur. 1971. *"Don Quixote" and the Dulcineated World*. Austin: University of Texas Press.

Egido, Aurora. 1991. "Los silencios del *Persiles*." In *On Cervantes: Essays for L. A. Murillo*, edited by James Parr. Newark, Del.: Juan de la Cuesta.

Eisenberg, Daniel. 1982. *Romances of Chivalry in the Spanish Golden Age*. Newark, Del.: Juan de la Cuesta.

————. 1983. "El 'Bernardo' de Cervantes fue su libro de caballerías." *Anales Cervantinos* 21:103–17.

————. 1987. *A Study of "Don Quixote."* Newark, Del.: Juan de la Cuesta.

El Saffar, Ruth. 1968. "The Function of the Fictional Narrator in *Don Quijote*." *MLN* 83:164–77.

————. 1975. *Distance and Control in "Don Quixote."* Chapel Hill, N.C.: North Carolina Institute.

Elliott, J. H. 1990. *Imperial Spain*. London: Penguin.

Erasmus, Desiderius. 1964. *The "Adages" of Erasmus*. Translated by Margaret Mann Phillips. Cambridge: Cambridge University Press.

————. 1974. *The Praise of Folly*. Edited and translated by Hoyt Hopewell Hudson. Princeton: Princeton University Press.

————. 1979. *The Praise of Folly*. Edited and translated by Clarence H. Miller. New Haven: Yale University Press.

Fajardo, Salvador. 1994. "The Prologue to *Don Quixote I*." *Journal of Interdisciplinary Literary Studies* 6:1–17.

Flew, Anthony. 1979. *A Dictionary of Philosophy*. New York: St. Martin's Press.

Forcione, Alban K. 1970. *Cervantes, Aristotle, and the "Persiles."* Princeton: Princeton University Press.

————. 1982. *Cervantes and the Humanist Vision*. Princeton: Princeton University Press.

————. 1984. *Cervantes and the Mystery of Lawlessness*. Princeton: Princeton University Press.

Francis of Assisi, Saint. 1972. *Writings and Early Biographies*. Edited by Alphonse Habig. Chicago: Franciscan Herald Press.

Frye, Northrop. 1973. *Anatomy of Criticism*. Princeton: Princeton University Press.

Gallardo, Bartolomé José. 1863–69. *Ensayo de una biblioteca de libros raros y curiosos*. Madrid.

Gaylord, Mary. 1982. "The Language of Limits and the Limits of Language: The Crisis of Poetry in *La Galatea*." *MLN* 97:254–71.

————. 1986. "Cervantes' Portraits and Literary Theory in the Text of Fiction." *Cervantes* 6:57–80.

————. 1991. "Fair of the World, Fair of the Word: The Commerce of Language in *La Celestina*." *Revista de Estudios Hispánicos* 25:43–58.

Genette, Gèrard. 1980. *Narrative Discourse*. Translated by Jane E. Lewin. Ithaca: Cornell University Press.

————. 1993. *Fiction and Diction*. Translated by Janet E. Lewin. Ithaca: Cornell University Press.

Gibbs, J. 1960. *Vida de Antonio de Guevara*. Valladolid: Editorial Miñón.

Gilman, Stephen. 1953. "Diálogo y estilo en *La Celestina*." *Nueva Revista de Filología Hispánica* 7:461–69.

————. 1956. *The Art of "La Celestina."* Madison: University of Wisconsin Press.

————. 1972. *The Spain of Fernando de Rojas*. Princeton: Princeton University Press.

Gingras, Gerald. 1985. "Diego de Miranda, 'Bufón' or Spanish Gentleman? The Social Background of His Attire." *Cervantes* 5:129–40.

Gómez, Jesús. 1988. *El diálogo en el renacimiento español*. Madrid: Cátedra.

Grant, Helen F. 1972. "El mundo al revés." In *Hispanic Studies in Honour of Joseph Manson*, edited by D. M. Atkinson and A. H. Clarke, 119–37. Oxford: Oxford University Press.

————. 1973. "The World Upside-Down." In *Studies in Spanish Literature of the Golden Age*, edited by R. O. Jones, 103–6. London: Tamesis.

Grassi, Ernesto, and Lorch, Maristella. 1986. *Folly and Insanity in Renaissance Literature*. Binghamton, N.Y.: Medieval and Renaissance Studies.

Green, Otis H. 1957. "El ingenioso hidalgo." *Hispanic Review* 25:175–93.

————. 1960–63. *Spain and the Western Tradition*. 4 vols. Madison: University of Wisconsin Press.

Greenblatt, Stephen. 1980. *Renaissance Self-Fashioning*. Chicago: University of Chicago Press.

Greene, Thomas M. 1982. *The Light in Troy: Imitation and Discovery in Renaissance Poetry*. New Haven: Yale University Press.

Grey, Ernest. 1973. *Guevara, A Forgotten Renaissance Author.* The Hague: Martinus Nijhoff.

Guevara, Antonio de. 1984. *Menosprecio de corte y alabanza de aldea.* Edited by Asunción Rallo. Madrid: Cátedra.

Guillén, Claudio. 1988. *El primer siglo de oro: Estudios sobre géneros y modelos.* Barcelona: Editorial Crítica.

Gutiérrez, Constancio. 1951. *Españoles en Trento.* Simancas: Consejo Superior de Investigaciones Científicas.

Habig, Marion Alphonse, ed. 1972. *Francis of Assisi: Writings and Early Biographies.* Chicago: Franciscan Herald Press.

Haley, George. 1965. "The Narrator in *Don Quijote*: Maese Pedro's Puppet Show." *MLN* 80:146–65.

———. 1984. "The Narrator in *Don Quijote*: A Discarded Voice," In *Estudios en honor a Ricardo Gullón,* edited by L. González del Valle and D. Villanueva, 173–85. Lincoln, Neb.: Society of Spanish and Spanish American Studies.

Hamburger, Käte. 1973. *The Logic of Literature.* Translated by Marilyn Rose. Bloomington: Indiana University Press.

Hampton, Timothy. 1990. *Writing from History.* Ithaca: Cornell University Press.

Hankins, James. 1991. *Plato in the Italian Renaissance.* New York: E. J. Brill.

Hatzfeld, Helmut. 1966. *El "Quijote" como obra de arte del lenguaje.* Madrid: Imprenta Aguirre.

Huizinga, Johan. 1950. *The Waning of the Middle Ages.* London: Edward Arnold.

———. 1957. *Erasmus and the Age of Reformation.* New York: Harper & Row.

———. 1970. *Homo Ludens: A Study of the Play Element in Culture.* Boston: Beacon Press.

Hutcheon, Linda. 1980. *Narcissistic Narrative: The Metafictional Paradox.* Waterloo, Ontario, Canada: Wilfrid Laurier University Press.

Hutchinson, Steven. 1992. *Cervantine Journeys.* Madison: University of Wisconsin Press.

Ihre, Maureen. 1982. *Skepticism in Cervantes.* London: Tamesis Books.

Iser, Wolfgang. 1987. *The Act of Reading.* Baltimore: Johns Hopkins University Press.

Johnson, Carroll B. 1983. *Madness and Lust: A Psychoanalytic Approach to Don Quixote.* Berkeley and Los Angeles: University of California Press.

———. 1990. *"Don Quijote": The Quest for Modern Fiction.* Boston: Twayne.

Jones, Joseph R. 1975. *Antonio de Guevara.* Boston: Twayne.

———. 1986. "The Liar Paradox in *Don Quixote* II, 51." *Hispanic Review* 54:183–93.

Kahn, Victoria. 1985. *Rhetoric, Prudence, and Skepticism in the Renaissance.* Ithaca: Cornell University Press.

Kaiser, Walter. 1963. *Praisers of Folly.* Cambridge: Harvard University Press.

Kamen, Henry. 1983. *Spain: 1467–1714.* New York: Longman.

Keen, Maurice. 1968. *Medieval Europe.* Middlesex, England: Penguin.

Kelley, Donald R. 1991. *Renaissance Humanism.* Boston: Twayne.

Kerrigan, William, and Gordon Braden. 1991. *The Idea of the Renaissance.* Baltimore: Johns Hopkins University Press.

Kermode, Frank. 1967. *The Sense of an Ending.* New York: Oxford University Press.

Kinney, Arthur F. 1989. *Continental Humanist Poetics.* Amherst: University of Massachusetts.

Klibansky, Raymond. 1939. *The Continuity of the Platonic Tradition.* London: Warburg Institute.

———. 1943. "Plato's *Parmenides* in the Middle Ages and the Renaissance." *Medieval and Renaissance Studies* 1:281–330.

Klubertanz, George P. 1960. *St. Thomas Aquinas on Analogy.* Chicago: Loyola University Press.

Knowles, David. 1962. *The Evolution of Medieval Thought.* New York: Random House.

Koons, Richard C. 1991. *Paradoxes of Belief and Strategic Rationality.* Cambridge: Cambridge University Press.

Kristeller, Paul Oskar. 1961. *Renaissance Thought: The Classic, Scholastic, and Humanist Strains.* New York: Harper & Row.

Kristeller, Paul Oskar, and Ernst Cassirer, eds. 1967. *The Renaissance Philosophy of Man.* Chicago: University of Chicago Press.

Lathrop, Thomas A. 1988. "Who Is the Narrator in *Don Quijote?*" In *Hispanic Studies in Honor of Joseph H. Silverman,* edited by Joseph Ricapito, 297–304. Newark, Del.: Juan de la Cuesta.

Lausberg, Heinrich. 1975. *Elementos de retórica literaria: introducción al estudio de la filología clásica, románica, inglesa.* Madrid: Gredos.

Levao, Ronald. 1985. *Renaissance Minds and Their Fictions.* Berkeley and Los Angeles: University of California Press.

Levin, Harry. 1969. "The Example of Cervantes." In *Cervantes: A Collection of Critical Essays,* edited by Lowry Nelson, 38–48. Englewood Cliffs, N.J.: Prentice Hall.

Lida de Malkiel, María Rosa. 1945. "Fray Antonio de Guevara: Edad media y siglo de oro española." *Revista de Filología Hispánica* 7:346–88.

———. 1962. *La originalidad artística de "La Celestina."* Buenos Aires: Eudeba.

———. 1970. *Dos obras maestras españolas: "El libro de Buen Amor" y "La Celestina."* Buenos Aires: Eudeba.

López de Vega, Antonio. 1935. *Paradoxas racionales.* Edited by Erasmo Buceta. 1643. Madrid: Centro de Estudios Históricos, Revista de Filología Española.

López Pinciano, Alonso. 1969. *Philosophía antigua poética.* Edited by Alfredo Carballo Picazo. 1596. Madrid: CSIC.

Lyons, John D., and Stephen D. Nichols, eds. 1982. *Mimesis: Mirror to Method.* Hanover: University Press of New England.

McGaha, Michael, ed. 1980. *Cervantes and the Renaissance.* Newark, Del.: Juan de la Cuesta.

McInerny, Ralph. 1996. *Aquinas and Analogy.* Washington, D.C.: Catholic University of America Press.

McPheeters, D. W. 1954. "The Element of Fatality in the *Tragicomedia de Calisto y Melibea.*" *Symposium* 8:331–35.

Madariaga, Salvador de. 1978. *Guía del lector del "Quijote."* 1947. Madrid: Espasa-Calpe.

Maiorino, Giancarlo. 1990. *The Cornucopian Mind.* University Park: Pennsylvania State University Press.

Mancing, Howard. 1981. "Cide Hamete Benengeli vs. Miguel de Cervantes: The Metafictional Dialectic of *Don Quijote.*" *Cervantes* 1:63–81.

———. 1982. *The Chivalric World of "Don Quijote": Style, Structure, and Narrative Technique.* Columbia: University of Missouri Press.

Marichal, Juan. 1984. *Teoría e historia del ensayismo español.* Madrid: Alianza Editorial.

Mariscal, George. 1991. *Contradictory Subjects: Quevedo, Cervantes, and Seventeenth-Century Spanish Culture.* Ithaca: Cornell University Press.

Martín, Adrienne Laskier. 1991. *Cervantes and the Burlesque Sonnet.* Berkeley and Los Angeles: University of California Press.

Martín, Francisco J. 1993. "Los prólogos del *Quijote:* la consagración de un género." *Cervantes* 13:77–87.

Martínez Bonati, Félix. 1992. *"Don Quixote" and the Poetics of the Novel.* Translated by Dian Fox. Ithaca: Cornell University Press.

Márquez Villanueva, Francisco. 1968. *Espiritualidad y literatura en el siglo XVI.* Madrid: Alfaguara.

———. 1973. *Fuentes literarias cervantinas.* Madrid: Gredos.

———. 1975. *Temas y personajes del "Quijote."* Madrid: Gredos.

———. 1980. "La locura emblemática en la segunda parte del *Quijote*." In *Cervantes and the Renaissance,* edited by Michael McGaha, 87–112. Newark, Del.: Juan de la Cuesta.

Martin, Robert L. 1970. *The Paradox of the Liar.* New Haven: Yale University Press.

———. 1984. *Recent Essays on Truth and the Liar Paradox.* Oxford: Clarendon Press.

Mexía, Pero. n.d. *Diálogos del ilustre cavallero Pero Mexía.* 1547. Madrid: Compañía Ibero-Americana de Publicaciones.

———. 1989. *Silva de varia lección.* 2 vols. Edited by Antonio Castro. 1540. Madrid: Cátedra.

Miller, Clarence. 1979. Introduction to *The Praise of Folly,* by Erasmus. ix–xxv. New Haven: Yale University Press.

Miller, Henry Knight. 1956. "The Paradoxical Encomium." *Modern Philology* 53:145–78.

Molho, Mauricio. 1989. "Instancias narradoras en *Don Quijote." MLN* 105:273–85.

Morón Arroyo, Ciriaco. 1973. "Sobre el diálogo y sus funciones literarias." *Hispanic Review* 41:275–84.

———. 1976. *Nuevas meditaciones del "Quijote."* Madrid: Gredos.

Murillo, Luis. 1959. "Diálogo y dialéctica en el siglo XVI español." *Revista de la Universidad de Buenos Aires* 4:55–66.

———. 1980. "*Don Quixote* as Renaissance Epic." McGaha 51–70.

———. 1988. *A Critical Introduction to "Don Quixote."* New York: Peter Lang.

Murphy, James J., ed. 1983. *A Synoptic History of Classical Rhetoric.* Davis: University of California Press.

Nauert, Charles. 1995. *Humanism and the Culture of Renaissance Europe.* Cambridge: Cambridge University Press.

Nepaulsingh, Colbert. 1980. "La aventura de los narradores del *Quijote*." In *Actas del Sexto Congreso Internacional de Hispanistas,* edited by Alan M. Gordon and Evelyn Rugg, 515–18. Toronto: University of Toronto Press.

Nicholas Cusanus. 1986. *Of Learned Ignorance.* Translated by Germain Heron. 1440. New Haven: Yale University Press.

Olin, John C. 1979. *Six Essays on Erasmus.* New York: Fordham University Press.

Orozco Díaz, Emilio. 1970. *Manierismo y barroco.* Salamanca: Ediciones Anaya.

———. 1988. *Introducción al barroco.* 2 vols. Ed. José Lara Garrido. Granada: Universidad de Granada.

Ortega y Gasset, José. 1984. *Meditaciones del "Quijote."* Edited by Julián Marías. Madrid: Cátedra.

Parker, Alexander A. 1948. "El concepto de la verdad en el *Quijote*." *Revista de Filología Española* 32:287–305.

———. 1985. *The Philosophy of Love in Spanish Literature: 1480–1680.* Edited by Terence O'Reilly. Edinburgh: Edinburgh University Press.

Parr, James. 1984. "Extrafictional Point of View in *Don Quixote*." In *Studies on "Don Quixote" and Other Cervantine Works,* edited by Donald R. Bleznick. York, S.C.: Spanish Literature Publications.

———. 1988. *Anatomy of Subversive Discourse.* Newark, Del.: Juan de la Cuesta.

Parsons, Charles. 1974. "The Liar Paradox." *Journal of Philosophical Logic* 3:381–412.

Pease, Arthur S. 1926. "Things Without Honor." *Classical Philology* 21:27–42.

Pelikan, Jaroslav. 1987. *Jesus Through the Centuries: His Place in History and Culture.* New York: Harper & Row.

Percas de Ponseti, Helena. 1975. *Cervantes y su concepto del arte.* 2 vols. Madrid: Gredos.

———. 1988. *Cervantes the Writer and Painter of "Don Quijote."* Columbia: University of Missouri Press.

Peters, Helen. 1980. "General Introduction." In *Paradoxes and Problems*, by John Donne, edited by Helen Peters, xvi–xlix. Oxford: Clarendon Press.

Pieper, Josef. 1963. *Leisure as the Basis of Culture*. New York: Random House.

———. 1966. *The Cardinal Virtues*. Notre Dame: University of Notre Dame Press.

Plato. 1973. *The Republic and Other Works*. Translated by B. Jowett. New York: Doubleday.

Porqueras Mayo, Alberto. 1957. *El prólogo como género literario: Su estudio en el siglo de oro español*. Madrid: CSIC.

———. 1968. *El prólogo en el manierismo y barroco españoles*. Madrid: CSIC.

———. 1981. "En torno a los prólogos de Cervantes." In *Cervantes, su obra y su mundo: Actos del I congreso sobre Cervantes*, edited by Manuel Criado del Val. Madrid: EDI-6.

Pope, Randolph. 1979. "El Caballero del Verde Gabán y su encuentro con Don Quijote." *Hispanic Review* 47:207–18.

Predmore, Richard L. 1953. "El problema de la realidad en el *Quijote*." *Nueva Revista de Filología Hispánica* 7:489–98.

———. 1967. *The World of "Don Quixote."* Cambridge: Harvard University Press.

Quine, Willard V. 1966. *The Ways of Paradox and Other Essays*. New York: Random House.

Quinones, Ricardo. 1972. *The Renaissance Discovery of Time*. Cambridge: Harvard University Press.

Quint, David. 1983. *Origin and Originality in Renaissance Literature*. New Haven: Yale University Press.

Rajan, Balachandra. 1985. *The Form of the Unfinished*. Princeton: Princeton University Press.

Rallo, Asunción. 1987. *La prosa didáctica en el siglo XVI*. Madrid: Taurus.

Riffaterre, Michael. 1990. *Fictional Truth*. Baltimore: Johns Hopkins University Press.

Riley, E. C. 1962. *Cervantes's Theory of the Novel*. Oxford: Clarendon Press.

———. 1963. "Aspectos del concepto de *admiratio* en la teoría literaria del Siglo de Oro." *Studia Philologica: Homenaje a Dámaso Alonso*. Vol. 3, 173–83. Madrid: Gredos.

———. 1981. "Cervantes: A Question of Genre." *Medieval and Renaissance Studies on Spain and Portugal in Honour of P. E. Russell*, 69–85. Oxford: Society for the Study of Medieval Languages and Literature.

———. 1986. *Don Quixote*. London: Allen & Unwin.

Riquer, Martín de. "Cervantes y la caballeresca." 1973. In *Suma Cervantina*, edited by Juan Bautista Avalle-Arce and Edward C. Riley, 273–92. London: Tamesis.

Rivers, Elias. 1960. "On the Prefatory Pages of Don Quixote, Part II." *MLN* 75:214–21.

———. 1974. "Cervantes' Art of the Prologue." In *Estudios literarios de hispanistas norteamericanos dedicados a Helmut Hatzfeld con motivo de su 80 aniversario*, edited by J. M. Sola-Solè, A. Crisafulli, and Bruno Damiani, 167–71. Barcelona: Hispam.

Rojas, Fernando de. 1974. *La Celestina*. Edited by Dorothy Severin. Madrid: Alianza Editorial.

Russell, P. E. 1969. "*Don Quixote* as a Funny Book." *Modern Language Review* 64:312–26.

Saintsbury, Richard Mark. 1988. *Paradoxes*. Cambridge: Cambridge University Press.

Saldívar, Ramón. 1980. "Don Quixote's Metaphors and the Grammar of Proper Language." *MLN* 95:252–78.

Savoye, Jaqueline. 1985. *Les Dialogues espagnols du XVIe siecle ou l'expression littéraire d'une nouvelle conscience*. Paris: Didier.

Searle, John. 1979. "The Logical Status of Fictional Discourse." In *Expression and Meaning*. Cambridge: Cambridge University Press.

Smith, Barbara Herrnstein. 1978. *On the Margins of Discourse*. Chicago: University of Chicago Press.

Socrate, Mario. 1974. *Prologhi al "Don Chisciotte."* Venezia: Marsilio Editori.

Spitzer, Leo. 1947. "Soy quien soy." *Nueva Revista de Filología Hispánica* 1:113-27.

———. 1955. *Lingüística e historia literaria*. Trans. J. P. Riesco. Madrid: Gredos.

———. 1962. "On the Significance of *Don Quijote.*" *MLN* 77:113–29.

Suleiman, Susan, and Inge Crosman. 1980. *The Reader in the Text.* Princeton: Princeton University Press.

Sullivan, Henry. 1996. *Grotesque Purgatory: A Study of Cervantes's "Don Quixote," Part II.* University Park: Pennsylvania State University Press.

Swearingen, Jan C. 1991. *Rhetoric and Irony: Western Literacy and Western Lies.* New York: Oxford University Press.

Tertullian, Quintus Septimus Florens. 1954. *De Carne Christi. In Corpus Christianorum, Series Latina.* 2 vols, 2.873–917. Turnhoutt: Typographi Brepols.

Thomas Aquinas. 1964. *Commentary on the "Nichomachean Ethics."* 2 vols. Translated by C. I. Litzinger, O. P. Chicago: Henry Regnery.

Todorov, Tzvetan. 1990. *Genres in Discourse.* Translated by Catherine Porter. Cambridge: Cambridge University Press.

Tompkins, Jane. 1980. *Reader-Response Criticism.* Baltimore: Johns Hopkins University Press.

Tracy, James. 1996. *Erasmus of the Low Countries.* Berkeley and Los Angeles: University of California Press.

Trueblood, Alan. 1958. "El silencio en el *Quijote.*" *Nueva Revista de Filología Hispánica* 12:160–80.

Urbina, Eduardo. 1990. *Principios y fines del "Quijote."* Potomac, Md.: Scripta Humanistica.

Vilanova, Antonio. 1949. *Erasmo y Cervantes.* Barcelona: CSIC.

———. 1965. "La *Moria* de Erasmo y el prólogo del *Quijote,*" In *Collected Studies in Honor of Américo Castro's Eightieth Year,* 423–33. Oxford: Lincombe Lodge Research Library.

———. 1989. *Erasmo y Cervantes.* Barcelona: Lumen.

Wardropper, Bruce. 1964. "Pleberio's Lament for Melibea and the Medieval Elegiac Tradition." *MLN* 79:140–52.

———. 1965. "*Don Quixote:* Story or History?" *Modern Philology* 63: 1–11.

———. 1986. "*Don Quixote:* Story or History?" *Critical Essays on Cervantes.* Boston: G. K. Hall.

Weiger, John. 1988. *In the Margins of Cervantes.* Hanover: University Press of New England.

White, Hayden. 1987. *The Content of the Form.* Baltimore: Johns Hopkins University Press.

Whitrow, G. J. 1988. *Time in History.* Oxford: Oxford University Press.

Willeford, W. 1969. *The Fool and His Scepter.* Chicago: Northwestern University Press.

Williamson, Edwin. 1984. *The Half-Way House of Fiction.* Oxford: Clarendon Press.

Wolgast, Elizabeth Hankins. 1977. *Paradoxes of Knowledge.* Ithaca: Cornell University Press.

INDEX

Alemán, Mateo, 165
Alter, Robert, 174
analogy, doctrine of, 24–25, 25 n. 16
antinomy, 39–41
Apuleius, 16
Aristotle, 106–7, 107 n. 20
art
    conflict with nature, 170
    as imitation, 106–7
    naturalness of, 103
artifice, knowledge and, 110
artists, and their creations, 112–17
audience, Cervantes' treatment of, 137–39
Auerbach, Erich, 18, 19
Augustine, Saint, 18
Avalle-Arce, Juan Bautista, 116–17
axiological strain, of paradox, 78, 98

Bakhtin, Mikhail, 16, 19
Brethren of Common Life, 28

carnival, medieval, 19–20
Castro, Américo, 4, 28, 81–82
Cave, Terence, 32
Censure of the Court and Praise of the Village
    (Guevara), 48–55
Cervantes Saavedra, Miguel de
    influence of Erasmus on, 28–29, 28 n. 21
    on parental love, 210–11
    philosophical attitude of, 182 n. 6
    rhetoric of paradox and, 134
    self-parody of, 135–37
    structuring of settings by, 224–27
    use of paradox by, 33, 80–81

    use of satire by, 142–43, 146
    worldview of, 15–16
Cetina, Gutierre de, 68
character, 95 n. 12
Chesterton, G. K., 45
chivalry, 154–56. *See also* knighthood
Chrestomathy of Assort Reading (Mexía), 55,
    56
Christianity
    extremes in consciousness of medieval, 21
    medieval paradoxy and, 18–20
    paradoxy and, 17–18
Cicero, 16
Ciceronian paradoxy, 38
    in Spain, 68
Cide Hamete
    description of Don Diego's mansion by, 183
    narrative of, 175–78
    veracity of, 184–92
Ciruelo, Pedro, 68
Colie, Rosalie, 11, 38
    classifications for paradox, 75–76
    defense of the indefensible, 2
contradiction, paradox and, 38–39
Corpus Christi plays, 20
Cortés, Hernán, 68
cosmological strain, of paradox, 76–77
Covarrubias Orozco, Juan de, 69
critical reading, 100–103, 159–60
Curtius, Ernst Robert, 19
Cusanus, Nicolaus, 11, 23 nn. 14, 15, 28, 76,
    78–79, 213
    central doctrine of, 22–23, 23–24
    chief interests of, 24–25

Cusanus, Nicolaus (*continued*)
  paradoxy and, 24–25
  use of paradoxy, 25–26

Dawson, Christopher, 33–34
defense of the indefensible, 2
dialectical reasoning, 17
discourse, 94 n. 9
  defined, 94
  historical, 94
  modes of, in Prologue, 93–97, 156–57
  poetic, 94–95
The Divine Names (Pseudo-Dionysius), 15
Don Diego de Miranda, 183
  character of, 214–24
  encounter with Don Quixote, 199
  as parodic exemplum, 227–30
  physical appearance of, 207–10
  virtue of, 204–7
Donne, John, 68
Don Quixote. See also Prologue of 1605
  battle of Don Quixote and Basque from Biscay,
    174–75
  central issues in, 103–5
  characters' adventures in, 4–5
  conflict between Art and Nature in, 170
  embedding imitations within imitations,
    166–69, 171–74
  encounter of Don Diego and Don Quixote,
    199–203
  folly in, 170–71
  hierarchy of narrators in, 179–84
  as imitation, 105–6
  imitation in, 164
  as imitation of nature, 105–6
  important studies of, 81 n. 2
  knighthood and, 211–13
  as literary discourse, 3
  models in, 157–58
  Neoplatonist view of, 14–15
  paradoxy in, 232–33
  parallels of characters and reader in, 4–6
  prologue of. *See* Prologue of 1605
  self-knowledge and, 193–99
  as seriocomic book, 5–6
  title page of, 88–91, 96
  use of mad protagonist in, 165

Eckhart, Meister, 17
Eisenberg, Daniel, 152 n. 33

Erasmus of Rotterdam, 11, 27–30, 28 n. 20, 102,
  117–18, 121
  sources for satirical writings for, 16
  Spanish followers of, 69–70

Folly, 28–32
Francis of Assisi, Saint, 21–22
Frye, Northop, 16

Gaylord, Mary, 96
Grassi, Ernesto, 64
Guevara, Antonio de, 46, 48–55

historical discourse, 94
history, relating of, in Prologue, 143–44
Hudson, Hopewell, 29
Huizinga, Johan, 33

imitation, 26–27, 235
  Don Quixote as, 105–6
  embedding imitation within, 166–69,
    171–74
  knowledge and, 110
  linguistic from of, 110–11
infinity, problem of, 3

Kaiser, Walter, 29, 34
Kempis, Thomas à, 28
knighthood, 211–13. *See also* chivalry
knowledge, 110
Kristeller, Paul Oskar, 33

La Celestina (Rojas), 41–46
Lando, Ortensio, 68
laughter, Renaissance, 157 n. 36
Lemos, Luis de, 68
liar's paradox, 39–40, 78
linguistic imitation, 110–11
literary discourse, *Don Quixote* and, 3
literary paradoxy, 11
logic, terministic, 17
logical strain, of paradox, 78–79
Lopez Pinciano, Alonso, 102–3, 107, 158
Lorch, Maristella, 64
Lucian, 16

McInerny, Ralph, 25
Malkiel, María Rosa Lida de, 47
Mancing, Howard, 85
Marichal, Juan, 47, 47 n. 12

Márquez Villanueva, Francisco, 47, 47 n. 11, 208
    on paradox in *Don Quixote*, 1–2
medieval carnival, 19–20
Mendoza, Diego Hurtado de, 68
Menippean satire, 16
Mexía, Pero, 46–47, 55–68
Mirandola, Pico della, 34
Molho, Mauricio, 89, 172 n. 3
Murillo, Luis, 158
mysticism, 14

narrator(s)
    Cervantes as, 88–93
    deficiencies of, 140–42
    determining, 84–88
    hierarchy of, 179–84
Nature, conflict with Art, 170
negative assertions, 3, 3 n. 4
Neoplatonism, 14–15

Of Learned Ignorance (Cusanus), 11, 22–23
ontological strain, of paradoxy, 76–77

paradox
    in ancient Rome, 16
    as antinomy, 39–41
    axiological strain of, 78
    Christianity and, 17–18
    Christ's cross and, 18
    Ciceronian method of, 26–27, 38
    contradiction and, 38–39
    cosmological strain of, 76–77
    Cusanus and, 23–25
    definition of, 37–40
    generative quality of, 3
    goals of, 79–80
    logical strain of, 78–79
    in Middle Ages, 19–20
    ontological strain of, 76–77
    psychological strain of, 77–78
    Renaissance "epidemic" of, 25–26
    Renaissance types of, 75–79
    Saint Francis and, 21–22
    in Spain, 41
    in terministic logic, 17
    tradition of, 2
    as trope of thought, 70–71
    in works after Erasmus, 32–33
paradoxical encomia, 2 n. 3, 38
Paradox stoicorum (Cicero), 16

parental love, 210–11
Parmenides (Plato), 11, 76
    as abstract exercise, 12
    as example of paradoxical discourse, 13–14
    paradoxy in, 12
    ultimate truth in, 12–13
    Western mysticism and, 14
Paul, Saint, 18
Pelikan, Jaroslav, 18
Peters, Helen, 70 n. 26
Petrarch, 16
Petronius, 16
Plato, 11–14, 76
poetic discourse, 94–96
poetics, 106–11
Poetics (Aristotle), 106–7
Praise of Folly (Erasmus), 11, 27–30, 29 n. 23,
        102, 117–18, 121
Prologue of 1605. *See also Don Quixote*
    author's self parody in, 134
    axiological paradox in, 98
    central issues of *Don Quixote* in, 103–4
    Cervantes as narrator in, 88–93
    Cervantes' paternity of characters in, 112–22
    Cervantes' treatment of the audience and,
        122–30, 137–39
    critical reading and, 159–60
    determining narrator of, 84–88
    imitation in, 148–51, 156
    issue of artists and their creations in, 112–17
    as key to *Don Quixote*, 82, 82 n. 5
    list of narrators deficiencies in, 140–42
    modes of discourse in, 93–97, 156–57
    overview of, 81–84
    reading of, 100–103
    relating of history in, 143–44
    structure of, 84
    textual revisions and, 144–47
    theoretical issues about poetics and poetic
        creation in, 106–11
Pseudo-Dionysius, 15, 15 n. 5, 76
psychological strain, of paradoxy, 77–78

Quinones, Ricardo, 34

Rabelais, François, 19
Rallo, Asunción, 48 n. 13
Reader-Response Theory, 161 n. 38
Renaissance laughter, 157 n. 36
Renaissance paradoxy, types of, 75–79

Renaissance writers, 33–35, 61 n. 22
rhetorical paradoxes, 38
Riley, E. C., 169
Rojas, Fernando de, 41–46

Sánchez, Francisco, 69
Sancho Panza, 177, 178–79, 185, 204
satire, Cervantes' use of, 142–43, 146
Schlegel, Friedrich, 170
self-knowledge, in *Don Quixote*, 193–94
Silenus, 31, 31 n. 27
Smith, Barbara Herrnstein, 93–94, 94 n. 10, 95
    n. 11
Spain
    Ciceronian paradoxy in, 68
    paradoxy in, 41

terministic logic, in paradoxy, 17
title page, of *Don Quixote*, 88–91, 96
Torquemada, Antonio de, 69

Valdés, Alfonso de, 69
Valtanás Mexía, Father Domingo, 68–69
Varro, 16
Vega, Antonio López, 69
Vega, Lope de, 142, 146
Vilanova, Antonio, 117, 117 n. 23
Vives, Juan Luis, 34

Wardropper, Bruce, 94
Weiger, John, 86
Western mysticism, 14
White, Hayden, 171